The Causes of the Second World War

History of the Contemporary World

Consultant Editors: Dr Peter Catterall &
Professor Lawrence Freedman

This series aims to provide students of contemporary history, politics and international relations with concise, critical overviews of the major themes and the development of key geographical regions that have dominated discussion of world events in the twentieth century. The emphasis in the regional histories will be on the period since the Second World War, but coverage will extend to the earlier twentieth century wherever necessary. The books will assume little or no prior knowledge of the subject, and are intended to be used by students as their first point of entry into a wide range of topics in contemporary international history.

Published

The Causes of the Second World War
Andrew J. Crozier

Forthcoming

South Africa in the Twentieth Century: From Empire to Nation
James Barber

The West and the Third World
D. K. Fieldhouse

Decolonization and its Impact
Martin Shipway

The Communist Movement since 1945
Willie Thompson

The Causes of the Second World War

Andrew J. Crozier

First published 1997
Reprinted 1998

Blackwell Publishers Ltd
108 Cowley Road
Oxford OX4 1JF
UK

Blackwell Publishers Inc.
350 Main Street
Malden, Massachusetts 02148
USA

British Library Cataloguing in Publication Data

A CIP catalogue record for this book is available from the British Library.

Library of Congress Cataloging-in-Publication Data
Crozier, Andrew J.
    The causes of the Second World War/Andrew J. Crozier
    Including bibliographical references and index.
    ISBN 0–631–17128–2 (alk. paper).—ISBN 0–631–18601–8 (pbk.: alk.
    paper)
    1.   World War, 1939–1945—Causes. I. Title
    D741.C77 1997
    940.53'11—dc20   96–39011
                                                                                CIP

Typeset in 10 on 11.5pt Bembo
at The Spartan Press Ltd,
Lymington, Hants
Printed in Great Britain by MPG Books Ltd, Bodmin, Cornwall

This book is printed on acid-free paper

Contents

Consultant Editor's Preface

The Second World War was the greatest conflict in history. Total casualties will never be known, but an estimate of some 50 million, over ten million in the Soviet Union alone, would not be unreasonable. It was a war which unleashed unprecedented atrocities. its effect on thrones may have been less marked and direct than that of 1914–18, though a number of monarchies were extinguished in the communist dominance of Eastern Europe that swiftly followed. Nor did it drastically reshape the map of the world, although much redrawing has come in its wake; two long-term effects were the gradual integration of Western Europe and the process of decolonization. To some extent this demonstrated a reworking of mental maps in its aftermath; the Federal Republic that emerged in West Germany, for instance, no longer saw itself as the dominant factor in a now divided *Mitteleuropa*, but as part of Western Europe.

The emergence of a united Germany in 1870–71 had earlier undermined the delicate power equilibrium in Europe. Both World Wars were, as Andrew Crozier shows, at bottom Anglo-German wars to either maintain or challenge that equilibrium; wars which ended, in 1945, with its replacement by an entirely new balance of power for the ensuing fifty years, that between the USA and the Soviet Union. This was arguably the main effect of the Second World War, though it was not the object envisaged by any of the protagonists, still less by Roosevelt or Stalin, in September 1939.

The European conflict that then began was, however, only one of several that eventually became intertwined in the phenomenon known to history as the Second World War. One of the principal achievements of this book is the successful interweaving of these tensions and conflicts. It is the first book of its kind to try and fully integrate events in the Far East and in Europe. In the process Andrew Crozier shows how events elsewhere impacted upon policymaking in particular theatres, particularly for Britain with its global interests. Indeed, it is one of the principal theses of the book that it was because of the global interests that Britain was seeking to defend, that the European war that began against Germany in 1939 became a global war by the end of 1941. The very real and sometimes underestimated problems of

British policymakers in the era of appeasement thus play an important part in his story.

But they are by no means the whole story. The canvas painted on here is broad, involving detailed analysis of the policymaking processes in their domestic contexts of all the main combatant powers. In doing so, Andrew Crozier provides a clear and in-depth assessment of the causes that led to the series of conflagrations that became the Second World War.

This book marks the first in a new series examining the **History of the Contemporary World**. The aim of this series is, using the latest published research, to provide new, detailed and comprehensive guides to major events in recent history. The result is a key new textbook analysis which offers fresh new insights into perennial problems; such as the weaknesses of the Versailles system, the nature of Hitler's foreign policy, the character of appeasement, the extent of American isolationism or the drive behind Japanese expansionism.

Peter Catterall
Institute of Contemporary British History

Preface and Acknowledgements

The events relating to the outbreak of the several wars in Europe and Asia that culminated in 1941 in a war of truly global dimensions are not easily narrated and analysed within a single volume. Quite apart from the complex nature of the subject, the limitations of space in a book intended for both undergraduate and sixth form audiences make the author's task even more awesome. One very clear problem that presents itself at the outset relates to the structure that should be imposed on a book of this nature: should the author attempt an integrated, chronological narrative in which the events in both Europe and Asia are treated side by side, as, arguably, they would have appeared to contemporary foreign ministers and diplomats; or should the author adopt a geographical framework in which the deep origins of the European and Far Eastern Wars are treated as distinct series of events until they merged between September 1940 and December 1941? There is no easy answer to this dilemma. The writer has, however, after considerable thought, and despite what some may argue is the essential conventionality of the approach, elected to employ the geographical method.

There are a number of reasons for this. First, this book is intended as a simple introduction to the subject and not as a major work of scholarly exegesis. In this connection, it is the simplicity of the geographical approach that proves attractive. To blend the events that occurred in Europe and the Far East too intimately in too limited a space might make an already complex story even more convoluted, resulting in a situation in which the beginner in the subject might well easily become confused. Secondly, there are practical considerations to be borne in mind. As this book is certainly aimed in part at a sixth form audience, it should be constructed in such a way as to make it relevant to what will be the overriding concern of such a readership, namely, the A Level Examination. The author has had considerable examining experience with three A Level Boards and has some idea of the range and capabilities of the average candidate and the sort of question with which he or she will be confronted. Because A Level candidates still sit papers on variants of British and European History, questions relating to the origins of the Second World War will inevitably focus on Europe and candidates will respond appropriately. This book should cater for that. In view, however, of Japan's rise to prominence in the twentieth century, sixth formers and undergraduates should undoubtedly learn more about her past and that of the Far East in general. It is also unquestionable that there is a pressing need for British youth and the public at large to understand more about the interaction between Europe and Asia in the twentieth century. I would hope, therefore, that this volume will contribute to such an understanding and that in due course A Level syllabi and examinations will reflect the need for it.

There are, though, other considerations. It has never been established that extensive reference to Far Eastern factors is a categorical imperative in respect of an accurate analysis of the origins of the Second World War in Europe. On the contrary, one of the most distinguished modern international historians, Professor Akira Iriye, has unequivocally stated that 'it is quite possible to discuss the origins of the European war without paying much attention to Asian factors . . .'[1]. It would, however, be wrong to ignore Far Eastern events altogether with regard to the origins of the European war and they will be referred to as necessary in the sections of the book principally devoted to the breakdown of the *Versailles System*. They will, of course, be considered at greater length in the sections dealing with the origins of the War in the Far East and Pacific.

While objection to a geographical structure might be made on the grounds that it lends an artificial quality to the history of the period, in that events will not be presented in the integrated way they were to contemporary policy-makers, it can equally be contended that too rigorous a chronological approach might give rise to the impression that the dangers in the Far East represented from the point of view of European powers a menace equal to those arising in the continent of Europe itself. This too would represent a misleading and artificial version of history. As one eminent student of British foreign policy in the twentieth century has pointed out:

> . . . there is no need to strain too much to view the European and Asian crises in their precise relation to each other. Almost certainly the British Government's policies towards Europe would have been what they were even if the Japanese had got on with their silk-worming, instead of building aircraft-carriers. Nothing exemplifies this more strikingly than the fact that Alexander Cadogan, as Permanent Head of the Foreign Office, was only dimly *aware* of the Tientsin crisis of June 1939 – certainly the relevant papers were not put on his desk for attention.[2]

Finally, the geographical structure is better suited to the main thrust of the argument that will be deployed in this book. It will be argued that the collapse of the Versailles System in Europe became inevitable once Germany was dominated by a government whose foreign policy was a phased programme of almost limitless expansion. This certainly meant that war would at least break out in Europe at some point; that such a war would become a truly global conflict was implicit in the decision of the British government to resist Germany's further advance in 1939. Britain at this time was still the major world power with interests in the Mediterranean, Near East, Africa and Asia; her ally, France, had a similar, if lesser range of world interests. The involvement of both powers in yet another potentially costly and debilitating war with Germany, which was bound to restrict their ability to defend their interests outside Europe, inevitably presented other expansionist powers with a series of options for the realization of their own long-cherished aims. To use the imagery of the Japanese Emperor, Hirohito, both Japan and Italy could now assume the roles of thieves at a fire.[3] From the point of view of British chiefs of staff this eventuality was very much in their minds in their planning throughout the 1930s. Therefore, when Britain went to war in 1939 it was with the foreknowledge that a world war was probably on the cards. It was, of course, impossible in 1939 to predict with clairvoyant precision how a world war would develop; yet the historical reality is that by December 1941 Britain was enmeshed in one and as an ally of the United States and the Soviet Union.

This book is essentially a diplomatic history. This does not mean that there is a deliberate intention on the part of the author to avoid the impact of ideological and economic factors. Wars, however, are usually the result of the failure of governments to reconcile differences between themselves in a 'friendly' manner. Such failure is inevitably diplomatic failure, for diplomacy is the means by which relations between governments are mediated. Moreover, where diplomacy fails it is usually the consequence of misperception and miscalculation between the parties. In both Europe and the Far East/Pacific the principal parties all miscalculated badly. The German government's policy, based upon Hitler's programme, was predicated on the assumption that the British government would eventually throw in its lot with the Reich and accept German hegemony on the continent; it was also based upon a gross underestimation of the strength of the Soviet Union. But Hitler's anticipation of British acquiescence in his aims was a colossal blunder, for no British government could countenance the type of hegemony he was contemplating, particularly if achieved by force. For their part, the British government believed that *appeasement*, by which they meant the renegotiation of the *Versailles System*, would divert Germany from her expansionist modes and convert her into a *normal* power. This was, however, rooted in a very fundamental misunderstanding of the nature of Hitler's foreign policy; Germany could not be assuaged by the kind of political and economic changes and concessions that the British government was prepared to broker. Both governments miscalculated and diplomacy failed. In the Far East/Pacific there were similar miscalculations. The American combined policy of non-recognition of Japanese expansion in China and South-East Asia and economic sanctions did not have the effect of moderating Japanese policy. Similarly, the Japanese never seem to have apprehended how central to United States policy was the American requirement that they evacuate China entirely. From 1932 onwards it is arguable that Japan and the United States were on a collision course that diplomacy could not avert.

Eventually, the Japanese sought to break the impasse by force. True, the United States Pacific Fleet at Pearl Harbor was the main focus of attack, but more or less simultaneously (in fact, two hours earlier) Japanese forces opened fire on Kota Bharu on the Malayan coast. Malaya was a British possession and so the first link in the Pacific and European wars had been forged. Four days later Germany and Italy declared war on the United States and the linkage between the two theatres of war was complete.

My thanks are due to my colleague Dr. Peter Catterall who has diligently supervised the preparation of this text. I am most obliged to him for his constructive advice and unfailing help at all times. His meticulous reading of this work in its various drafts has saved me from many an error grammatical and historical. I am grateful too to Mr Peter Rose for his many perceptive comments and for supplying me with information that would otherwise be unobtainable. Thanks are also due to another colleague, Dr. Jon Smele, whose encyclopedic and prodigious knowledge of the Siberian aspects of the Russian Civil War and Allied Intervention was placed at my disposal. It inevitably behoves me to express my gratitude to Professor X, whom I cannot name for professional reasons, but who is undoubtedly the greatest living British authority on the international history of inter-war Europe. His comments on an earlier draft of this book have undoubtedly contributed to what I would hope are many of its innovatory features and to the publishers' agreement to the necessary expansion of the text in order to incorporate them. In addition I should not fail to mention the help given to me by the Library Staff of Queen Mary and Westfield College and, in particular, that of Ms. Susan Richards, to whom I am most obliged. In the preparation of the text Brian Place, Jay Hammond and François Crompton-Roberts of the Arts Computing Unit at QMW were always ready to place at my disposal their time and their expertise and eased me through many a crisis. I am grateful indeed to them all. Mr. Manabu Morimoto, financial counsellor of the Japanese embassy in London, was of great assistance in the preparation of the list of principal Japanese office holders during the inter-war years to be found in Appendix II. I am much beholden to him. I thank Tessa Harvey and Simon Prosser of Blackwell for their patience and their prodding and my head of department, Dr. Sarah Palmer, for her insistence on my having a brief period of study leave in order to complete this project. Finally, I thank my wife, Andrea, and my sons, Ian and David, for just putting up with me.

Andrew J. Crozier
Queen Mary and Westfield College

Maps

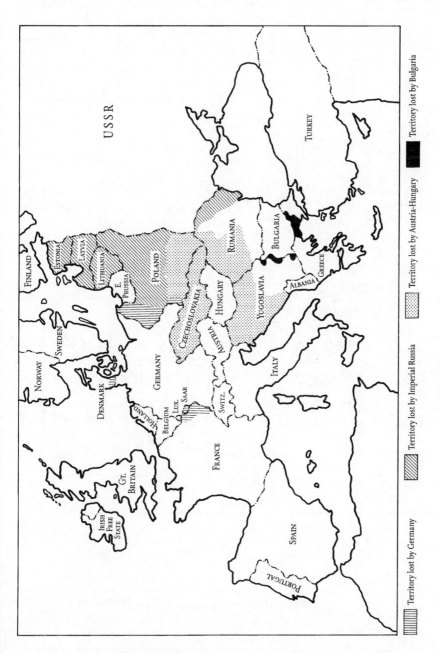

Map 1 Europe After 1919.

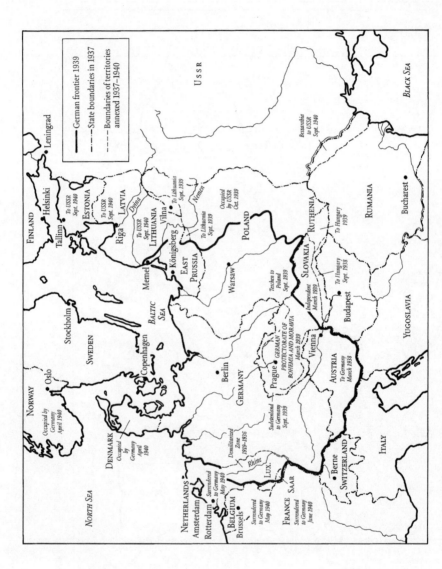

Map 2 Europe on the Eve of Germany's Attack on the USSR, June 1941.

Map 3 The Expansion of Japan, 1890-1939.

Map 4 North-east Asia showing locations of Nomonhan, Changkufeng and the extra-territorial interests of the powers at Kiaochow, Weihaiwei, Tientsin and Kwantung.

Introduction

Fifty years since the Second World War's end, its causes continue to fascinate scholars and the general reader alike; there is no end in sight to the various controversies that surround the events of the 1930s. Although interpreted much more sympathetically than once was the case, the British policy of *appeasement* still provokes and excites debate.[1] Similarly, the nature of Hitler's foreign policy remains a febrile point of discussion among academics and commentators.[2] One of the most sterile debates, however, and academic in the worst sense of the word, is surely that relating to the date at which the Second World War became a world war. Obviously, the Second World War in the form it assumed from 1941 until its endings[3] in 1945 was an amalgam of a number of disputes.[4] To argue, however, that a world war only existed from the time that all these disputes became 'hot' in 1941 would seem to rest upon the dubious premise that every dispute that lapsed into violence between 1939 and 1941 carried equal weight in provoking a world war, or, put another way, was capable of creating the conditions in which a world war was almost bound to ensue. If this was the case, it seems legitimate to ask, why it was that the Sino-Japanese War, which rumbled on from 1931 to 1945, with one brief and uneasy intermission, had not produced a world war earlier than 1941 or even than 1939? Here was a war that affected all the great powers who were signatories of the Nine Power Treaty of 1922 (the United States, Britain, Japan, France, China, Italy, Belgium, Holland and Portugal), which guaranteed the territorial integrity of China and the principle of equal economic opportunity (the 'Open Door') for the commerce and industry of all nations in that country. Nevertheless, Japan's aggression in China, her infraction of Chinese sovereignty and blatant effort to include China in a closed economic system dominated by her, although seriously disruptive of the international system, were not sufficiently critical in the nexus of interlocking, international relationships in themselves to drag the rest of the world into a global conflict.

This writer has no problem with 1939 as the *terminus a quo* of the Second World War. It is, of course, true, as A.J.P. Taylor pointed out over thirty years ago, that the war that broke out in 1939 was a European war, involving

Germany, Britain, France and Poland as principals; but the reality is that it was precisely the European continent, during the inter-war years, that contained the type of combustible material that could ignite the rest of the world. Three of its largest states, in terms of geography, demography and economic power, had substantial extra-European interests. The integrated territory of the Soviet Union extended beyond the Ural mountains to the borders of Manchuria and the Japanese, Okhotsk and Bering Seas in the Far East. For her part, France had significant colonial interests in South-East Asia and even more extensive interests in the African continent. Finally, Britain, more than any other European state, had imperial concerns and commitments which extended into every continent. Clearly, a war, wherever it started, involving one or all these powers could have very widespread implications. The principal challenge to these powers, however, did not come from outside Europe, but from Germany; from within the heart of Europe. And it was the decision of Britain to resist that challenge in 1939 which created the circumstances in which a global war would probably ensue. That one did justifies accepting September 1939 as the beginning of the Second World War.

It also justifies the structure of this book. Without the collapse of Europe into war for the second time in twenty-five years, it is not certain that the East Asian–Pacific war would have taken the form it did, or indeed have broken out. The background to the European war of 1939, moreover, was one in which arguably 'extra-European factors, in particular Asian issues, had been of little relevance'. The Sino-Japanese War had very little impact, for example, on the development of the Munich crisis in 1938, or on the Polish question in 1939, the issue that finally determined British resistance to German aggression. As one writer has commented:

> The system of European politics defined by the Versailles peace treaty . . . had little or nothing to do with Asia and so, to the extent that the crisis of 1939 could be said to have been inherent in Versailles, it was purely a European story with little input from the outside.[5]

This is evidently a rather narrow view, for naturally European powers, such as Britain, that also had interests in East Asia were bound to take account of developments in that region as the structure of peace in Europe established in 1919, and now fashionably referred to as the *Versailles System*, disintegrated. On the other hand, there is also a very substantial element of truth in it. Therefore, chapters 3 to 7 will deal fundamentally with the origins of the European war of 1939, or the breakdown of the *Versailles System*, with reference to the East Asian theatre as necessary.

The *Versailles System* was the framework of peace imposed upon Europe after the First World War and takes its name from the principal treaty of the peace settlement that ended it, the Treaty of Versailles of 1919 concluded between Germany and the Allied and Associated powers. After 1919, however, the international system had to take account also of changes in the structure of power in East Asia and the Pacific occasioned by the rise of Japan in the nineteenth century, the growing importance of the United States as an actor in the area, and the impact of the First World War. The equivalent of the

Paris Peace Conference for East Asia and the Pacific was the Washington Conference of 1921–2 and the treaties concluded at that conference collectively imposed upon East Asia and the Pacific a framework of peace referred to usually as the *Washington System*. As the *Versailles System* was challenged by Germany, so the *Washington System* was unable to satisfy the ambitions of Japan, which country increasingly attempted to break free of its provisions, particularly as they related to China. The breakdown of the *Washington System* took place more or less contemporaneously with that of Versailles, 'but the two were not intimately related, except in so far as both occurred at about the same time and had the effect of pitting revisionist powers (Germany, Italy and Japan) against status-quo powers'[6]. The breakdown of the *Washington System* will, therefore, be analyzed in chapters eight and nine with references to European developments where appropriate.

It was only with the outbreak of war in Europe that events in Europe and the Far East could become closely linked. The enormous strains this placed upon the principal imperial power in the Far East, Britain, and the conquest of France and the Netherlands in 1940, opened up Japan's options in the area considerably in the estimation of the more belligerent elements of her leadership. European and Asian politics, however, might be said to have become closely entwined with one another only with Japan's conclusion of the Tripartite Pact with Germany and Italy in September 1940.[7] This gave the Japanese more confidence in their ability to oppose American resistance to their view of the future of East Asia. The showdown at Pearl Harbor was from that time onwards not a certainty, but it became increasingly likely. These developments are covered in the concluding sections of chapter nine.

The Rise of Germany and Japan and the Decline of Britain

The causes of the Second World War at bottom relate to the rise to prominence of two powers and the relative decline of another. Those that rose to prominence were Germany and Japan; that which declined was Britain. This is not to suggest that the United States, the Soviet Union, France, Italy and China should merely be assigned *walk-on* parts in the events of the 1920s and 1930s. It was, however, Germany twice and Japan once that were ultimately prepared, in their ascendancy, to alter the power structures in their respective areas by force. It is also a fact that the declining power, Britain, critically intervened against Germany on both occasions and that the second of these interventions also exposed her interests in East Asia to the ambitions of Japanese expansionists. In other words, Britain's role in the international system as a world power was fairly critical in determining whether or not a war in which she was involved would be localized or become intercontinental.

The rise of German and Japanese power began almost simultaneously in the nineteenth century. The years 1866 to 1871 witnessed two revolutions, one in Europe and the other in Asia, which not only transformed the countries in which they took place, but were also to revolutionize the international system. Until the defeat of Austria by Prussia in 1866 and the subsequent creation in 1867 of the North German Confederation under Prussian leadership, the entity which acted 'as a national bond of the German nation' and linked together all the states descended from the Old [Holy Roman] Empire' was the German Confederation, established in June 1815.[8] For contemporaries it was the 'key-stone' of the European order: the guarantee of European stability and peace.[9] The subsequent absorption of the South German states of Baden, Bavaria and Württemberg in the sham federalism of the Second Reich, founded in 1871 in the wake of the Franco-Prussian War, arguably removed the remaining regional stabilizers in Central Europe, making peace and the European system less secure.

The unification of Germany, accomplished under the guidance of Bismarck, was accompanied by prodigious industrialization and economic growth. It was also accompanied by the development of a nationalism that, together with the military potential that Germany's industrialization un-leashed, fuelled expansionist designs which aimed at continental hegemony and more. The desire on the part of Germany's ruling elite to pursue a forward foreign policy of these dimensions was given further edge by the social changes in Germany attendant upon industrialization. The ruling landed classes perceived a threat to their ascendancy in the growth of the middle and working classes and it was hoped to divert this menace by a successful and prestigious foreign policy that also involved the construction of a substantial navy.[10] This led inevitably to antagonism in Anglo-German relations. Moreover, the general course of German policy ultimately resulted in war. In short, the consequences of German unification for the European system were to be devastating within fifty years.

The revolution that took place in Japan was a direct result of the encroachments of the western powers in East Asia during the nineteenth century. With the objective of opening China up to trade, missionaries and diplomatic representation, the west engaged in a number of wars with the Chinese, which resulted in the imposition on China of the *Unequal Treaties*. From the 1840s onwards a pressing concern of Japan's rulers was the avoidance of a similar fate; but while they avoided the wars, they could not avoid the *Unequal Treaties*.[11] Within five years of the arrival in Japan of the American sailor, Commodore Perry, the Japanese government had con-cluded the Harris Treaty of 1858 with the United States. Negotiated by the American Consul at Shimoda, Townsend Harris, this was the first of Japan's *Unequal Treaties* with the west. The major ports of Edo (Tokyo), Osaka and Kobe were to be opened to western commerce and rights of extraterritori-ality were conceded to all westerners in Japan. This meant that they would not be subject to Japanese law. Finally, from 1866 Western imports into Japan were to be subject to a very low *ad valorem* duty of 5 per cent.[12]

Patriotic elements in Japanese society, particularly the warrior class, the *samurai* of the provinces of Satsuma and Choshu, regarded the Harris Treaty as a disgrace to the nation and the emperor. Until this time, and for the preceding two hundred and fifty years, Japan had been governed by a system known to history as the Tokugawa Shogunate, under which the effective ruler of Japan was the *shogun*. This was an office hereditary in the Tokugawa family and, translated into English, meant 'barbarian-fighting general'.

Although the emperor was impotent in this system, his theoretical authority and prestige were, nevertheless, used by the *shoguns* to legitimate their rule. The discontented elements in Japan opposed this regime which had so failed and disgraced the nation and, ten years after the conclusion of the Harris Treaty, they succeeded in overthrowing the Shogun and, allegedly, *restored* the Meiji emperor[13] to his rightful powers. This, though, was a fiction, for under the *Meiji Restoration* real power remained in the hands of the men who made the revolution: the Meiji oligarchs such as Ito Hirabumi and Yamagata Aritomo. In authority, as in rebellion, the fundamental agenda of the Meiji oligarchs was a foreign policy one, namely, the return of Japan to full sovereignty and equality with the west. This meant, in practice, the annulment of the *Unequal Treaties*. The victors of Japan's civil war did this by fulfilling their slogan *fukoku-kyohei*: 'enrich the country, strengthen the army'. Under the imaginative resourcefulness of the Meiji oligarchs, Japan was to experience a rapid transformation in which the country was industrialized and provided with a modern system of defence. By 1911, she had an efficient army of over 300,000 men and the world's fourth largest navy of some 700,000 tons.

The internal reforms undertaken under the Meiji Restoration meant that it was impossible to maintain the *Unequal Treaties* indefinitely. The beginning of their demise was signalled in the Anglo-Japanese Treaty of Commerce and Navigation in 1894; by 1899 British nationals resident in Japan were to be subject to Japanese law.[14] During the 1890s Japan also served notice that she was a force with which to be reckoned in East Asia by her defeat of China in the Sino-Japanese War of 1894–5. Increasingly from this time onwards the Japanese saw in the decaying empire of the Manchus in China a legitimate field for expansion and penetration. This brought them into competitition with the Russians who had similar designs. Rivalry over influence in Korea had been the essential cause of the Sino-Japanese War; rivalry too over influence in Korea and Manchuria lay behind the Russo-Japanese War of 1904–5, the result of which was profoundly to shock the west. The defeat of Russia made Japan a front rank international actor; it also secured for Japan interests in Manchuria which were to provide her with a base from which she was able to expand further on the Asian mainland during the 1930s.

The unification of Germany and the Meiji Restoration in Japan were ultimately to have very important consequences for British power, but in the short term these two events differed in their effects upon Britain. Whereas Britain had by 1902 entered into an alliance with Japan, relations between Britain and Germany had tended to become antagonistic. It was indeed Germany's unification that first began to undermine that British global supremacy which had been so much a characteristic of the nineteenth century. By 1850 Britain was the world's foremost colonial, sea and industrial power; her influence and power were decisive, or seen to be decisive, throughout the world. It may well be that that influence and power rested upon an economic base that was exaggerated by contemporaries and, subsequently, by historians and upon the weakness of continental Europe in the period after 1815.[15] But influence and power do not merely reside in substance: image too is important.[16] Seen from the vantage point of Britain's potential rivals, the image of British power was very substantial indeed and British supremacy a reality in all continents. It is apparent, however, that the international structure on which that supremacy rested was materially altered by the unification of Germany and in such a way as to curb substantially Britain's international influence. Commenting at the time, the British Conservative leader, Disraeli, was of the opinion that the unification of Germany represented a revolution of even greater consequence than the French Revolution: the balance of power in Europe, he thought, had been destroyed, and to the substantial disadvantage of Britain.[17] Writing many years later, Professor Northedge argued that this was the point at which Britain's decline began, German unification having deprived Britain of the ability 'to act as a mediator in European politics, leaning always towards the weaker side in continental controversies'[18].

The menace that German power represented entered the popular mind in Britain. The image of Germany as reflected in contemporary literature underwent a gradual transformation, in which the likeness of Germany as a 'charming, picturesque . . . abode of enthusiastic thinkers, poets, musicians and scholars, who live in quaint, medieval-style cities or statelets' was replaced by 'the land of Prussian monocled officers and ruthlessly technological scientists . . . who have state loyalty instead of human morality'[19]. The fear that unified Germany's military and political potential aroused in Britain coincided with a recognition of her growing economic potential and the threat this represented to British manufacturing.

This at first manifested itself in an attempt to stigmatize German imports. In the early days of German industrialization there was a lack of self-confidence among German manufacturers who sought to penetrate the 'considerable, trend-setting British market' by exporting 'copy-cat products'. The response of the British government was to pass the Merchandise Marks Act of 1887 under which imported goods that might imitate British products had to bear an indication of their origin. The consequence was unexpected. Consumers now began to realize that many of the excellent products they had acquired were of German origin: *Made in Germany*, therefore, became a symbol of quality rather than of inferiority.[20] Within Britain the increasing sense of rivalry with Germany was intensified in the closing decade of the nineteenth century by a vociferous German colonial lobby whose ambitions if realized would have affected Britain's interests in South Africa and whose actions created very substantial mistrust between London and Berlin.[21]

By the first decade of the twentieth century the challenge to Britain within and without Europe represented by Germany was a major concern of the British government. This challenge took the form of clear German aspirations to continental hegemony and overseas expansion, which was underpinned by an increasingly powerful economy and an ambitious programme of naval construction. British anxieties were reflected in the palpable anti-Germanism of documents such as the foreign office Crowe Memorandum of 1907 and in the naval reforms of the British first sea lord, Sir John Fisher.[22] Fisher modernized the British fleet and concentrated it in the home waters of the Channel, the Atlantic and the Mediterranean. Ultimately, though,

British apprehensions regarding Germany were expressed in the decision to resist her in 1914, although neutrality in this war may not have been an option. As the foreign secretary, Sir Edward Grey, formulated it, if Germany and Austria won, what would be the position of an isolated Britain? Equally, if Russia and France won, what would the future hold in store for the British Empire?[23] It was, though, Germany and Austria against whom Britain went to war and it was Germany that represented the principal danger for Britain: the power that had to be reduced if Britain was to preserve her world position.

But the perceptible German challenge to British supremacy by the end of the nineteenth century should not be seen as a unique phenomenon. Other states were modernizing, industrializing and expanding; catching up with Britain. The Russian Empire now stretched to the Pacific and the Himalayas and was coming into conflict with British imperial interests in the Indian sub-continent and with the rising power in the Far East, Japan. And there was the essentially pacific challenge of the rapidly developing economic power of the United States. All this was represented in the very rapid relative decline of British naval supremacy at the end of the nineteenth century. As late as 1883 Britain possessed almost as many battleships as the rest of the world put together, but fourteen years later, despite having increased her battleship strength by sixty-three per cent, she was now outnumbered by all other states by approximately three to two.[24] It was this that made the Anglo-Japanese Alliance of 1902 so attractive in London: it redressed the naval balance and reduced the costs of naval construction. The proposers of this arrangement were the Japanese who were alarmed at the threat posed to their interests by the Russian Empire. The British, equally preoccupied with a Russian threat to their interests, produced the draft treaty. The alliance provided for mutual assistance if either party became involved in a war in East Asia with more than one power.

From the Japanese point of view, this alliance reduced the risk of having to fight Russia, and her ally, France, simultaneously. From the British point of view, the advantage of the alliance lay in the fact that, given the enlargement of her competitors' navies, those of the Franco-Russian alliance and Germany, it was imperative that she find allies to reduce the burden of naval spending, particularly in view of the costs of the Boer War. The alliance with Japan meant that Britain could now reduce her naval strength in Chinese waters and increase that in home waters at no extra cost. It was subsequently modified in 1905, so that it became operative against a single power, and was renewed in 1911. While, therefore, the emergence of Japan unquestionably transformed the global structure of power, it did so in the short term to Britain's advantage rather than disadvantage. Significantly, when war broke out in Europe in 1914 Japan entered it on Britain's side, declaring war on Germany, although not obliged to do so, on 23 August 1914. The Japanese did this partly out of loyalty, but also, and of great consequence for the future, for reasons of perceived advantage: that is to say, they anticipated that fighting on the side of the Allies would ultimately improve their position in East Asia. It is evident, though, that however advantageous the Anglo–Japanese Alliance may have been to the British, it did mark and is historically symbolic of, Britain's relative decline.

The Versailles System and the Powers

Britain's incipient decline was, however, brilliantly masked by her role in the defeat of Germany in the First World War. She fought the war to preserve her imperial and world role and by 1919 Britain would appear to have been spectacularly successful in eliminating Germany as an imperial and naval threat. The German Navy no longer existed. It was first surrendered and subsequently scuttled in Scapa Flow by its skeleton crews. Moreover, under the terms of the Treaty of Versailles, German naval reconstruction was severely circumscribed. Added to this, all Germany's overseas colonies and possessions had been captured during the course of the war and at its end were distributed by the Principal Allied and Associated Powers among themselves as mandates of the League of Nations.[25] The elimination of Germany as a naval and imperial power gave rise to great satisfaction throughout the British Empire. This mood was well illustrated at the Imperial Conference of 1921. The Australian prime minister, Hughes, described himself and his fellow heads of government as 'so many Alexanders' without any worlds left to conquer.[26] The South African prime minister and imperial statesman, Jan Smuts, thought that the British Empire had 'emerged from the war quite the greatest power in the world . . . only unwisdom or unsound policy . . . could rob her of that great position'[27]. Most of this kudos naturally centred upon Britain. While it is possible, as will be demonstrated,[28] to look back on this period and observe just how damaging the First World War had been for the long term maintenance of Britain's world role, it was not so apparent to public opinion at the time within and without Britain. All the major powers, including the United States and the Soviet Union, once it became established after 1922, regarded Britain as the one global power. This was a view that was to last well into the Second World War and after. Indeed, William T. Fox, the first to use the term *super power*, was in no doubt in 1944 that Britain ranked as one along with the United States and the Soviet Union.[29]

The consolidation of the peace, however, was to prove problematic. While Britain may have been regarded as the one global power, the reality was that it was a status that had been underpinned by the financial and economic strength of the United States. Access to the American capital market and the sale of securities in the United States had become critical by 1916 for the financing of Britain's war effort and that of her Allies. Without this advantage the continued prosecution of the war would have been inconceivable.[30] In military terms also the entry of the United States into the war had proved critical to the ultimate victory of the Allied and Associated Powers. Finally, it had been the American agenda for the post-war settlement, President Wilson's Fourteen Points, that had replaced the expansionist agenda of the secret treaties that had been concluded between the Entente powers.[31] However, having done so much to win the war and to shape the peace, the

American government proved unable to influence its development directly, for the Senate failed to ratify the Treaty of Versailles by the necessary two-thirds majority. This imposed upon Britain a position of international leadership for which she was not as well equipped as others thought. This was well articulated in a letter to *The Times* by Andrew Bonar Law, the Conservative leader, in October 1922, in which he stated: 'We cannot act alone as the Policeman of the World'[32].

There were further difficulties. While British statesmen and their imperial colleagues might evince satisfaction with the results of the First World War, the French were fearful for their *security* against a revival of German power. For the French the Treaty of Versailles was 'a Boche peace, a Wilsonian peace – anything but a French peace'. In the view of Professor Adamthwaite, Versailles was for the French 'a defeat'[33]. During the Paris Peace Conference, the French had argued the case for the dismemberment of Germany by the creation of an independent Rhineland state, which 'would bar the natural invasion route, giving allied forces time to come to the rescue'[34]. Failing that, or the Anglo-American guarantee of French territorial integrity, which had been offered in place of dismemberment and which lapsed once the American Senate proved unable to ratify the Versailles Treaty, the French relied upon the literal fulfilment of the Treaty of Versailles as a means of containing Germany: a policy which led to the occupation of the Ruhr and the simultaneous effort to promote Rhineland separatism.

The French inclination to maintain the Treaty of Versailles rigorously in force conflicted with British aims. Britain had wanted a democratized Germany contained within Europe. That had now been achieved and the British could see no reason why the *Versailles System* should not be modified and adjusted particularly in its financial aspects. The British were a trading nation, interested in an economically fully restored Europe of which a rehabilitated Germany would be a necessary and critical part. Hence the inclination to see a reduction in the reparation payments Germany was obliged to make to the victors under the terms of the Versailles treaty, which it was felt might also lead to an easing of international payments problems through a lightening of the war debt burden. The perceived constant obstructionism of the French in respect of treaty revision caused the British to blame them for the failure to bring tranquillity and stability to the peace.[35]

Worst of all, the German nation refused to acquiesce in the *Versailles System*. Revision of the Versailles Treaty was demanded throughout the political spectrum in Germany and to achieve this the German government could take advantage of the situation created by the American failure to ratify the peace. In addition, the open dissension between Britain and France over the implementation of Versailles provided opportunities for revisionism and the sidestepping of treaty obligations. Thus the military and financial provisions of the Versailles Treaty were constantly evaded.[36] Furthermore, Germany's economic potential could always be exploited: there was an acute perception in this respect among German politicians and businessmen that Germany's neighbours were far more dependent upon her than she on them.[37] Finally, although the *Versailles System* imposed constraints upon Germany in the short term, the post-1919 situation in Europe was one that in the long term was arguably favourable to her. The disappearance of the Austro-Hungarian Empire and the internal turmoil in the former Russian Empire, following the Bolshevik Revolution, opened up the whole of Central and Eastern Europe to German political and commercial penetration.[38] Here was a great prize if Germany could throw off the shackles of Versailles.

Neither was German society as a whole very happy with the post-1919 constitutional arrangements in Germany, those of the Weimar Republic, which were easily associated with a shameful peace. The problems confronting Germany and popular disaffection with the system were such that, as one historian has suggested: 'Perhaps the remarkable thing about the Weimar Republic is not that it collapsed but that it lasted as long as it did'[39]. During the 1920s the Weimar regime survived a number of crises, but it could not survive the effects of the world economic recession and its electorate succumbed to the blandishments of Hitler and the National Socialists in 1933.

Hitler's Foreign Policy

All German governments since 1919 had been revisionist in respect of the *Versailles System*; Hitler's government was no less so. The first three points of the Nazi Party's *Official Programme* made it clear that their fundamental objective was nothing less than the complete dismantlement of the *Versailles System*. But there was an expansionist dynamic about Hitler's foreign policy and the Nazi regime that went far beyond the revision of the Treaty of Versailles. This is clear from an examination of Hitler's writings during the 1920s, which reveals that Hitler had more or less finalized his foreign policy programme by the time he completed his *Second Book*, in 1928.[40] Once in office he rigorously adhered to this programme, with opportunistic deviations, into the war years, maintaining even the correctness of it until his suicide in the bunker in 1945.[41]

This book, therefore, will incline towards the view of the Third Reich as presented by the so-called *Intentionalist School* of historians, such as Klaus Hildebrand, Andreas Hillgruber and Eberhard Jäckel. According to this school, the course of the history of the Third Reich was largely determined by the will of Hitler. This is of particular relevance to German foreign policy of the period, which closely conforms with Hitler's statements and utterances.[42] Taken together they constitute a foreign policy programme which, in essence, aimed not merely at the overthrow of Versailles, but also at total hegemony in Europe. This was to be realized through the subjugation of France first and then, the destruction of the Soviet Union, which at one stroke would destroy the communist world menace and secure for Germany the *Lebensraum*, or *living-space*, Hitler deemed essential for Germany's surplus population. It was assumed, moreover, that this could be achieved, if not in alliance with Britain, with at least her benevolent neutrality. Once *Fortress Europa* had been completed, or hegemony in Europe established, Hitler looked forward ultimately to a titanic struggle with the United States for the domination of the globe, which Hitler assumed Germany would win because of the preservation of her racial purity.

The opposing *Functionalist*, or *Structuralist School*, dismisses the notion of a planned and structured foreign policy and argues the case that war was very much the consequence of the needs generated by the economic and social conditions created by the Nazi regime. While the picture that the *Structuralists* paint of economic conditions in the Third Reich is probably accurate,[43] it has by no means been established that those conditions had any impact on Hitler's thinking or motivation. In fact, there is not a shred of evidence to support such a contention. Correspondingly, this view will not feature in the analysis of events leading to the outbreak of war in 1939. Quite to the contrary, such evidence as there is emphasizes that policy was driven by long established political priorities. On one occasion, for example, it was suggested to Hitler by Robert Boothby, a Conservative politician, that national socialism and the National Socialist Movement were driven by economic imperatives, to which Hitler replied quite bluntly that national socialism was a purely political movement.[44] The views of the *Functionalists/ Structuralists* will, however, be examined in Chapter 10.

Appeasement

Assuming Hitler did indeed have a plan, was the British government ever aware of it? There was, of course, from 1933 onwards a distinct feeling in London that Germany had once more under the Nazis given way to her expansionist inclinations. This was a perception that steadily increased throughout the 1930s until in 1939 it was decided to resist because of the palpable threat to Britain and her empire to which continued and uninterrupted German expansion on the continent would give rise. It does not appear, however, that Hitler's foreign policy either in the extent of its aims, or the steps by which those aims were to be achieved was ever properly understood in London. Nevertheless, what was quite evident was that the arrival in office of Hitler and the Nazi takeover in Germany boded ill for the future of peace and stability in Europe. As has already been suggested, the policy of the British government towards the *Versailles System* was to revise those parts of it that hindered the economic revival of Europe. That had been so since the beginning of the 1920s. By the beginning the following decade, however, the British foreign office was beginning to reconsider the entire edifice. Hitler's advent did not give pause to this process, but rather accelerated it. The failure to revise the Treaty of Versailles had given rise to Hitler and the excesses of his regime; the revision of the treaty might make Hitler a conventional statesman and Germany a stable element in a stable Europe. What was contemplated, therefore, was the revision, or reconstruction, of the entire *Versailles System* in such a way as to bring Germany into satisfactory treaty relations with all her neighbours. Fundamentally, this was the policy of *appeasement*. What was meant by *appeasement* was the *appeasement of the European situation*, or, put another way, the pacification of Europe. What was not implied was the *appeasement of Germany* in the way that the word would be understood today, in the sense of acceding to the demands of a potentially hostile nation in the hope of maintaining peace.[45] Undoubtedly, there was a mood in Britain which favoured concession to Germany and resistance to French policy which found expression in the daily and weekly press and in some of Britain's most respected institutions.[46] But appeasement was more than a mood: it was a practical policy designed to deal with a practical situation and was pursued by all British governments from 1919 onwards. It most emphatically was not the personal property of Neville Chamberlain, although he most certainly shared in its development from 1933 onwards as chancellor of the exchequer.

The Far Eastern Crisis

What also gave impetus to appeasement in Europe was the deterioration after 1931 of the situation in the Far East, where Britain had considerable interests. Although Japan emerged from the First World War as a victor power, her relationship with the western powers was one that was to become increasingly uneasy as a result of both the Paris Peace Conference and the Washington Conference of 1921–2. Before and after 1914 Japan's efforts to penetrate and consolidate her position in China, mainly in Manchuria, had met with western resistance. Moreover, the sense of being denied equal treatment by the international community was further intensified by the passage of immigration legislation in the United States before and after the First World War, which clearly discriminated against Japanese immigrants. Neither did the Paris Peace Conference afford the Japanese much satisfaction in this respect, for the powers would not admit the principle of racial equality. In addition, Japan had to face strong resistance from the British Pacific dominions regarding their acquisition as League mandates of Germany's island possessions north of the equator in the Pacific Ocean; and China by no means regarded the Japanese inheritance of Germany's rights in the Shantung peninsula as settled following Germany's defeat in the war.

At the Washington Conference further indignities, from the point of view of a growing and important segment of Japanese opinion, were to follow. Although it would be true to say that the naval disarmament treaty of 1922 was not completely unfavourable to Japan, for it conceded to Japan naval predominance in the Western Pacific and control of the approaches to the China coast, it did not seem quite so straightforward to Japan's increasingly vociferous nationalists. To them Japan had accepted inferior naval status. Furthermore, the Washington Conference saw Japan effectively relinquish the full inheritance of the rights previously exercised by Germany in Shantung, although this had been conceded during the course of the war. Finally, the Washington Conference confirmed that, as a consequence of American pressure, Britain would not be renewing her alliance with Japan in 1923. All this left Japan isolated and sharpened the feeling that she was to be excluded from the western world. This was not necessarily the perception of the *westernized* elites, who continued to be prominent in the government and the foreign ministry and for whom the *Washington System* reflected not only their realism in coming to terms with the combined superior strength of Britain and the United States, but also Japan's growing status. It was, however, most decidedly the perception of the emerging and chaotic nationalist organizations in Japan, which expected Japan to gain nothing from international cooperation. The Japanese Army served as a focus for this discontent, as it did also for expansionist pressures and demands.

All this frustration and the distress occasioned by the effects of the world economic recession at the end of the 1920s erupted in the Japanese conquest of Manchuria in 1931–2 and its conversion, in fact, if not in law, into a Japanese colony. This caused alarm bells to ring in Whitehall. True, Britain had no interests in Manchuria, but she did in China as a whole and the extension of the fighting to Shanghai in January 1932 was an indication of the threat that Japan might represent to them. In 1919 the British armed services had been made subject to the Ten Year Rule, under which their estimates were to be prepared on the basis that no major war was to be expected during the course of the next ten years. This was now revoked. Progressively, however, the international climate of the 1930s worsened. Refusing to accept the delicately phrased criticism contained in the report of the League Enquiry into the Manchurian Incident, Japan left the League of Nations in March 1933. By this time Hitler had assumed power in Germany and in a dispute over disarmament Germany left the League of Nations the following October. Finally, Italy, always an unstable element in the Allied camp since the fascist takeover, began to move into Germany's orbit, following the conquest of Abyssinia in 1936. In Europe, in the Mediterranean and in the Far East, Britain's post–1919 commitments began to look very burdensome.

Britain's International Commitments during the Inter-War Years and their Implications for World War

Britain's international commitments were summarized in a foreign office memorandum of April 1926. They were very extensive and were naturally the concomitant of her position as a global power. As a member of the Council of the League of Nations, Britain, with her worldwide obligations, was liable to be called upon to uphold the League Covenant in any part of the globe. Under the Treaty of Versailles and the Locarno treaties, Britain was obliged to resist a 'flagrant' breach of the demilitarized Rhineland zone. There were also commitments in the Pacific under the various Washington treaties. In addition there were commitments to Egypt; to Abyssinia, under the Tripartite Treaty of 1906; in the Hedjaz, Iraq, Transjordan and Arabia; to Portugal, under the various treaties concluded since 1373; and to the entirety of the commonwealth and empire, which included, of course, the defence of Australia and New Zealand. Britain's commitments were naturally not made any easier by the termination of the Anglo–Japanese alliance which deprived Britain of the means of controlling the actions of Japan.[47]

A serious problem, therefore, confronted Britain's military planners by the middle of the 1930s. They suspected, if Britain were to become involved in, or embarrassed by, a European conflict, that that would be a signal for Italy or

Japan to take advantage of Britain's predicament. As the chiefs of staff of the armed forces warned in a memorandum of 1937, Britain had commitments in Europe, the Mediterranean, and the Far East. It would, they thought, be possible to cope with an emergency in one of these areas; but, they continued:

> . . . the outstanding feature of the present situation is the increasing probability that a war started in any one of these three areas may extend to one or both of the other two.[48]

In other words, if war broke out in Central Europe it was unlikely to be contained there, for if Britain were to become involved it would rapidly escalate into a World War.

This was the fundamental premise to which Neville Chamberlain, prime minister 1937–40, was referring in his statement made to the House of Commons on 24 March 1938 in the wake of the annexation of Austria by Germany (the *Anschluß*) thirteen days earlier. Implicit in the *Anschluß* was a threat to Czechoslovakia, which, unlike Austria was not German–speaking, although it contained a substantial German minority, the majority of whom wished to be incorporated in the German Reich. As an international effort to save Czechoslovakia from an act of German aggression was not likely to be successful, because of the logistical problems involved in rendering immediate and effective support to the Czech defences, the British cabinet decided that it would be better to try to solve the problem presented by the German minority by peaceful means. Accordingly it was agreed by the government that Britain could not guarantee Czechoslovakia or come automatically to the assistance of France should she become involved in a war with Germany as a consequence of her alliance obligations towards Czechoslovakia. This view was made public in Chamberlain's Commons statement of 24 March. In the course, however, of cabinet discussions leading to this statement, Chamberlain had himself commented that the entry of France into a war with Germany over a Central European issue would place Britain in a difficult and dangerous situation; for Britain 'could not afford to see France destroyed'. Chamberlain, therefore, also informed the Commons:

> But while plainly stating this decision [not to guarantee Czechoslovakia, or come automatically to the assistance of France] I would add this. Where peace and war are concerned, legal obligations are not alone involved, and if war broke out, it would be unlikely to be confined to those who have assumed such obligations. It would be quite impossible to say where it would end and what Governments might become involved. The inexorable pressure of facts might well prove more powerful than formal pronouncements and in that event it would be well within the bounds of probability that other countries, besides those which were parties to the original dispute, would almost immediately become involved.[49]

Here was an admission that it would be almost impossible for Britain to stay out of such a war and that its logical end might be a world war. This was both a forecast and a warning that was intended as a deterrent.[50] If Britain had to go to war, she could not do so with the expectation of limiting the fighting to Europe. Germany would be dragged into the vortex of a global conflict for which she might not be very well equipped.

In 1938 there was no war over Czechoslovakia. The problem presented by the minority German community in that state was solved brutally, but peacefully. Yet within twelve months of the Munich Conference of September 1938, which 'solved' the Czech question, Europe was at war, as a result of the unprovoked aggression of Germany against Poland, with Britain as one of the principals. As British politicians and service chiefs had anticipated, the war that began in Europe in 1939 had by the end of 1941 become a world war. The German attack on Poland, which precipitated initially a European war, was in a very real sense the start of the Second World War for it was out of the conditions created by that conflict that a struggle of truly global dimensions developed.

1

The Powers in 1919 and After

The First World War destroyed the old European order and confirmed the changing power structure in the Far East. In Europe the collapse of the Austro-Hungarian Empire into its component parts and the long period of introversion in Russia following the Bolshevik Revolution turned Central and Eastern Europe into a political and economic power vacuum. Although defeated, Germany emerged from the conflict with her industrial and territorial resources remarkably intact; once she recovered freedom of manoeuvre in foreign policy she would be able to penetrate the power vacuum to her east and south. In the long term, Germany's potential to become the dominating power in Europe remained unaffected. In France there was a recognition of this situation which resulted in a preoccupation with *security*, all the more pressing now that she could no longer rely upon her traditional ally in the East, Russia, and now that the wartime alliance with Britain had come to an end.

In some respects, though, there were familiar features from the pre-1914 world. Britain remained the most formidable global power in the eyes of her friends and enemies alike. It may well be that the First World War weakened Britain economically to a considerable degree, but during the inter-war years that reality was not always perceived, even in the United States, which by 1919 was the world's leading industrial and financial power. American power, however, was not for the time being to be converted fully into political and military strength, although the United States did demonstrate an ability to impose its will particularly in the Far East and Pacific as was to be demonstrated in the Washington Conference of 1921–2. The purpose of this conference was, among other things, to regulate the growing power of Japan, the intentions of which country were regarded with growing suspicion in Washington by the end of the First World War. For her part, Japan had by 1919 further consolidated her position in China and Manchuria, although not to the degree she would have desired.

The Bolshevik Revolution, which the pressures of war had made virtually inevitable, was to have very important consequences for the functioning of the international system during the inter-war years. Russia, or the Soviet Union as she was to become, was transformed into a pariah state, with which the capitalist west would only have the most minimal contacts. Inevitably this had an important impact on the power structure in Europe. There thus now existed an ideological divide in Europe and the world which was to characterize significantly the conduct of diplomacy during the 1920s and 1930s.

What, however, had been the impact of the First World War on the victors and vanquished?

The Victors

Of the victors Britain appeared, at least on the surface, the most impressive. With further territorial gains in Africa and the Middle East, her empire was now at its greatest territorial extent. The large areas of red on the map of the world concealed, however, the increasing incapacity of the British economy to sustain such worldwide commitments effectively when confronted with growing demands for independence in India and continuous trouble in the Middle East. Britain's war effort had been financed by borrowing with government expenditure standing in 1918 at £2,579 million against a revenue of £889 million; in five years the national debt had risen tenfold to £7.5 billion.[1] Subsequently, in the post-war years it was deemed necessary to reduce drastically expenditure on the armed forces in order to balance the budget.

The reduction of expenditure on the armed forces was, however, prompted by more than a perceived need for retrenchment. As in other countries, social expenditure on the part of government rose after 1918 in comparison with the pre-war years. Given the growth of the Labour Party and the Labour movement as a whole in Britain, it was deemed more dangerous to risk a conflict with Labour, in the broad sense, at home than to take a chance with defence abroad[2]; this inevitably reduced the taxable capacity for armaments and war expenditure. Speaking about this prioritization in the House of Commons in March 1934, the prime minister, Stanley Baldwin, was quite blunt. After 1918, he stated, government had faced a choice between disarmament, social policy and financial rehabilitation, or heavy expenditure on armaments. He continued: 'Under a powerful impulse for development every government of every party elected for the former'[3]. So severe were the cuts in military expenditure that, as they applied to the new service, the Royal Air Force, they were tantamount to dismemberment. Retrenchment of this magnitude clearly imposed limitations on defence policy and promoted Britain's interest in the maintenance of peace. The objective of military retrenchment, however, was not merely to adapt to reduced circumstances, or to divert the funds to social expenditure, but rather to create the conditions in which Britain's pre-war economic, and thereby military strength, could be restored. In other words, the aim was a return to *pre-war normalcy*, which implied the maintenance of Britain's global and imperial role.[4]

The interest of the British government in the maintenance of peace was further encouraged by the realization that without the goodwill of the United States and access to her capital market, Britain could not face another war with Germany with any prospect of success: on her own she could not compete with the productive capacity of German heavy industry. Britain had borrowed to finance not merely her own war costs, but also those of her allies and for her borrowing and the procurement of war supplies she had been very dependent on the United States. Just how dependent was revealed in the autumn of 1916 when the British foreign office convened an interdepart-mental committee of government departments to assess precisely that. The views of the various departments were printed for circulation to the cabinet on 6 November 1916. These revealed that a high percentage of guns, shells, explosives, machine tools and preserved meat were procured in America and, according to the board of trade, the United States was 'an absolutely irreplaceable source of supply' for industrial raw materials, foodstuffs and cotton. Finally, of the £5 million that it cost daily to run the war, £2 million had to be found in America.[5] These were sobering facts.

The return to *pre-war normalcy* proved difficult to accomplish. Although national income rose by almost 40 per cent between 1913 and 1937, the record of economic performance was marred by persistent high unemployment and poor performance in exports, particularly in the staple industries. The fall in the export capacity of these industries caused the unemployment of between 7–800,000 'or virtually the whole of the intractable core of the unemployed in the 1920s'[6]. Throughout the inter-war years unemployment tended to hover at around one and a half million (see table 1).

Table 1 British unemployment 1922–1939

1922	1,543,000
1929	1.216.000
1932	2,745,000
1937	1,484,000
1938	1,791,000
1939	1,514,000[7]

During the 1920s and 1930s the number of people employed in the cotton industry declined from 568,000 in 1923 to 378,000 in 1939[8] and British cotton's proportion of the world's mill consumption of cotton declined from 20 per cent in 1910–13 to 9 per cent in 1936–8. Correspondingly, Britain's share of the world's cotton exports decreased from 58 to 28 per cent.[9] Employment figures in the coal industry told the same story. An industry that was employing 1,133,700 in 1914 was employing in 1936, 767,100,[10] while exports in the industry in 1937–8 were down to approximately 50 million tons, compared with almost 100 million tons in 1913.[11] Moreover, during the inter-war years the tonnage of British shipping on the high seas diminished by over 8 per cent, while British shipyards were producing in 1937 less than half the tonnage for 1913.[12] In 1933 launchings from British yards fell to 7 per cent of the pre-war figure.[13] For a nation whose wealth was fundamentally based on international trade these latter figures were very critical; they reflected the fact that Britain's 'share of the world export trade in manufactured goods fell from 27.5 per cent in 1911–13 to 23.8 per cent in 1921–5 and to 18.5 per cent in 1931–8 . . .'[14]. All this had implications for Britain's long-term ability to sustain the extended imperial commitments assumed in 1919 and foretokened a policy of peace and moderation not least because it was believed that it was only through peace that trade, prosperity and British power could be revived.

It would, however, be wrong to see the inter-war years in Britain as a period of total decline and stagnation. There were, of course, the sunrise industries of electronics, car manufacture, aviation, chemicals and the manufacture of synthetic fibres. In these Britain was very much in the forefront of world developments. In addition, their contribution to the economy was of increasing importance. The contribution of electronics to gross output, for example, rose from 1.9 per cent in 1924 to 3 per cent in 1935. Car manufacture was responsible for an increase in employment in the industry from 220,000 insured workers in 1924 to 380,000 in 1939.[15] Moreover, Britain, through her empire, controlled a considerable portion of the world's resources of oil, tin, copper and rubber and by 1937 her overseas investments were sound. Finally, and most important, all this evidence of economic stability and advance reinforced the perception of all the major powers during the inter-war years, including the United States and Soviet Union, that Britain was the one global power.

The economic determinism of some writers,[16] which emphasizes the decline of Britain, has tended to obscure the important point that: 'If reality governs the course of war, reputation determines that of peace. A weak state which others regard as strong and do not challenge will be strong. A strong state which others regard as weak may, as a direct result, decline in power'[17]. During the 1920s British prestige was higher than it had been since the 1850s and the 'reputation shielded the reality until the mid-1930s, when Great Britain clashed directly with the central aims of Germany, Italy, and Japan while failing to live up to her name'[18]. Writing in 1919, Colonel House, President Wilson's emissary and adviser, commented:

> The war has left but two great powers in the world, where before there were seven. While Russia has collapsed internally, and Germany and Austria have fallen through defeat, France and Japan have gone from first to second rate powers because the United States and Great Britain have become so powerful. While the British Empire vastly exceeds the United States in area and population and while the aggregate wealth is perhaps greater than ours, yet our position is much more favourable.[19]

The image of British power was so compelling that in both the United States and the Soviet Union conspiracy theories explaining the apparent failure of the British to resist earlier than they did in the 1930s were readily accepted. In America the myth of the Cliveden Set and a conspiracy between British capitalism and nazism, disseminated by the communist writer, Claud Cockburn, was credible because in the United States it was assumed that moral degeneracy and lack of will explained appeasement rather than lack of economic and financial strength. But that was for the future. In 1919 the view of British opinion outside the restricted elite responsible for running the nation's affairs was one of satisfaction and over-confidence bordering upon euphoria. The gradual apprehension of decline was yet to come.

In France the sense of victory was tempered by the appalling cost that had been required to achieve it. In financial terms the war had been a disaster. France was now on the verge of bankruptcy: she had accumulated massive debts to pay for the war and liquidated a very substantial portion of her foreign investments. The French portfolio of pre-war overseas investments, which stood at $8,600 million in 1914, had by 1929 diminished to under $4,000 million.[20] Part of this loss was, of course, the result of the Bolshevik repudiation of debts incurred by the imperial Russian authorities. Some 98 per cent, however, of the French war effort had been funded by loans[21], which meant that by the end of the war France owed Britain just over $3 billion and the United States almost $4 billion. Moreover, inflation was a serious problem with the franc having lost some 50 per cent of its value during the course of the war. In 1914 it had stood at 25 to the pound sterling; by July 1926 it had fallen to 243.

The material cost had been prodigious. Roughly 10 per cent of French territory had been devastated by the war; the areas affected containing some of France's most valuable industrial resources. The cost in flesh and blood had also been profligate. Some 16 per cent of those mobilized had been killed, amounting to a total of one million three hundred and twenty-two thousand individuals. This was the highest proportionate loss of all the major belligerent states. In addition some one million men were rendered permanently disabled. In terms of pensions for widows, disability and the care of orphans, these figures represented a further charge on the already shattered finances of the French state. They also indicated severe demographic and economic consequences. By 1916 the birth-rate was only half what it had been in 1912. This meant that by 1938 the number of persons achieving the age of twenty was about 50 per cent of what had come to be regarded as the annual norm. In 1939, therefore, France would not be able to mobilize the same number of men as in 1914. While, however, the French manpower shortage might well have been becoming acute at this time, it must be remembered that from the beginning of the 1920s the manpower deficit in France was believed to be about three million.

The picture, though, was not one of total gloom. During the early 1920s new wealth was created in France by the rapid recovery of her economy. There was a slump in 1920–1, but in 1921 the economy began to expand at the rate of 9.5 per cent per annum so that by 1924 industrial production had recovered to the level of 1913. Inflation, by making French exports competitive, was a critical factor in this phenomenon. By 1923 France had, therefore, recovered the potential to pursue an independent foreign policy. There was no need for her to borrow, reducing the leverage that could be exerted by her creditors, mainly the United States and Britain, but also, and rather humiliatingly, Argentina, Uruguay and Spain.

That France proved unable to exercise such independence reflected partly the caution of her government. During the war France had been very dependent on imports, particularly of coal. Half her requirements of this commodity were supplied by imports, 70 per cent of which were British. This encouraged an inclination not to act alone. There was also the problem of currency instability, which was not solved until the late 1920s and which was exacerbated by the failure fully to employ modern methods of direct taxation and to restructure and modernize accounting procedures. The lack of urgency displayed here owed much to the convictions that Germany should pay the costs, through reparation payments, of French reconstruction and that interallied war debts should be cancelled or linked to reparations. In other words, external solutions to French fiscal and financial problems proved more attractive than internal reform. External solutions, though, implied dependency.

Internal French problems also gave rise to caution in foreign policy. The war had resulted in the mobilization of the economy, giving rise to accelerated migration from the country to the towns with attendant social distress. Given the reluctance of the upper classes and middle classes to accept direct taxation, this distress was exacerbated by indirect taxation, which hit the poorest sectors of society particularly hard. None of this was offset by adequate social security policy. Inevitably, trade union membership increased as did worker militancy. In December 1920 the French Communist Party was formed.

French military strength was also much less formidable than it appeared on paper. Some 170,000 men had to be stationed permanently in Morocco and Syria and risings in these territories in the mid-1920s gave rise to the posting of further reinforcements to them. Inevitably, this weakened the resources available for home defence. The reduction in the period of compulsory enlistment from three years to one during the 1920s and the unattractiveness of long term enlistment promoted by the general climate of pacifism, poor conditions and low pay naturally restricted the manpower available which was not redressed by the resources theoretically available in Africa. As General Lyautey observed, it was possible to press black conscripts, but this had the effect of producing large numbers of enlisted men and not soldiers. Finally, the very real differences that emerged in the early 1920s between Britain and France over the application of the peace was a handicap. Germany could exploit these differences and frustrate French policy. The fact of the matter was that the construction of alliances with the small states of Eastern Europe was no compensation for the now defunct alliance with Britain,[22] nor, for the defunct alliance with Russia.

All these factors and the recognition of Germany's fundamentally superior strength and *potentiel de guerre*, ensured that concern about French security would soon replace the elation of triumph. As one French politician put it in 1924: 'The dangerous years are not principally those of the present; they are those which will come after'[23]. In the years following 1919 *security* became the national obsession of the French. It was to result in attitudes towards the application of the peace settlement that were apparently severe and clearly designed in the opinion of contemporaries and subsequent historians to maintain Germany in an artificial state of weakness.

Italy emerged from the First World War as divided as she had entered it. Although an ally of the Central Powers, Germany and Austria–Hungary, she had not entered the war in 1914 on the ground that, as her alliance partners were the aggressors, she was not bound to render assistance to them under the terms of the existing treaty arrangements. When, however, in 1915 Italy entered the war on the side of the Allies, in accordance with the Treaty of London she concluded with them in the spring of that year, she did so against the wishes of the mass of public and parliamentary opinion. Socialists, Catholics and parliamentarians, led by Giolitti, the most prominent and respected of Italian liberals, opposed Italian intervention which had been contrived in secret. But public demonstrations for intervention, encouraged by the government and condoned by the police, and a pro-intervention Italian press, largely funded by French money, gave some credence to the spurious popularity of intervention. One of the reasons for Italian entry into the war on the side of the Entente powers was undoubtedly the desire to incorporate into the Italian state as many Italian-speaking areas still ruled by the Habsburgs as possible: in effect, the revival of irredentism. On the other hand, as Professor Procacci has argued, in a country in which one of the major issues was whether it should be ruled in a liberal or authoritarian manner:

> . . . the deciding factor was probably the conviction that a short victorious war would, by imposing stricter discipline on the country, make it easier for the state to move towards a more authoritarian . . . position, would give new life to the forces of conservation and the established order and remove the threat of subversion.[24]

The war did indeed strengthen the government in relation to parliament, but did little to solve Italy's long-standing problems.

By 1919 Italy was in a state of acute political and social crisis. During the war trade union membership had soared and the country was convulsed with strikes and demonstrations. In the elections of 1919 the socialists emerged as clear winners with almost twice as many votes as the next largest party, the *Popolari*, or the Popular Party. Discontent with the existing Italian state and the political establishment stemmed from economic hardship and revulsion against a war that, from Italy's point of view, now seemed to have been pointless. This latter issue was emphasized by the withdrawal of the Italian prime minister and the foreign minister, Orlando and Sonnino, from the Paris Peace Conference in April 1919 because they considered that Italy's claims were being disregarded. Subsequently the government they led fell. All this gave rise to the fantasy of the *mutilated victory* and encouraged a nationalism of an adventurous nature typified by D'Annunzio and his invasion and conquest of the Dalmatian port Fiume in order to bring its Italian residents within the Italian national state. For a time there was talk of co-operation between the nationalist, socialist and anarchist movements, but eventually nationalism in Italy was to become associated exclusively with the forces of the right, which, after the defeat of the Turin metal workers' strike in April 1920, were in the ascendant. Although one of the victors, internal politics, and frustration at the fact that the rewards of war did not seem commensurate with the effort, combined to give Italy the character of a defeated power. The crisis of Italian politics eventually brought Mussolini to office as prime minister. The problem, however, for Italy's nationalists was that their fantasies were based upon inadequate industrial and capital resources and a national society that was fragmented. Had Mussolini known of and been able to exploit the oil resources of Italy's colony Libya,[25] there is no telling how different the course of twentieth century history might have been.

Potentially the most powerful of the victors was the United States of America. She had not entered the war in 1914 and when she did, in 1917, it was as an *Associated* rather than as an *Allied* power: having previously attempted to mediate in the war, the character of the *mediator* was maintained. Nonetheless, America's growing economic power, stimulated massively by war orders, which increased America's productive capacity by approximately 15 per cent, meant that she would have a substantial impact on the peace settlement when it was negotiated. Already by 1914 a naval power of considerable substance, in 1918 America's army also came of age on the Western Front in the removal of the St. Mihiel *fang*. To economic and military power were added financial power; by 1918 the United States had become the world's foremost creditor nation being owed $12,000 million, of which $10,350 were allied war debts.

Traditional accounts of the inter-war years tend to argue that, despite this financial, economic and military power, the United States lapsed into a mood of *isolationism* at the end of the First World War. It would be misleading, however, simply to describe the mood of America in 1918 as *isolationist* and stress a discontinuity in American foreign policy at this juncture.[26] On the contrary, Republicans as well as Democrats displayed an internationalism, qualified by a certain degree of nationalism, which expressed itself in a determination to thwart or minimize anything that might compromise the sovereignty, power and freedom of action of the United States. This was as characteristic of the Democratic administration of President Wilson as it was of its Republican successor. It found expression in opposition to Britain over matters relating to access to oil in the Near East, in resistance to British attempts to restore their pre-1914 trading position in Latin America, and challenges to the Anglo-Japanese Alliance and British naval dominance. Even the most Anglophile members of the American foreign policy-making-elite illustrated an ambivalence on this last point. Elihu Root, for example, considered the Five Power naval proposals prepared for the Washington Conference of 1921–2 desirable precisely because 'they made British action impossible without American support'[27]. The major difference between the American political parties was a reluctance on the part of the Republican leadership to bind the United States to what they considered to be the coercive elements of the proposed League of Nations.[28] This was crucial following the Republicans' victory in the mid-term Congressional elections of 1918, which overturned the Democratic majority in the Senate, and the succeeding victory of the Republican, Warren Harding, in the presidential election of 1920. The real difficulty, therefore, in America's foreign policy in the post-1919 period was that 'neither Congress not the American electorate understood or would support permanent institutionalized American involvement in world politics'[29]. This was to make American membership of the League of Nations, the organization that the American president, Wilson, did so much to create and which he thought essential for rectifying the flaws in the *Versailles System*, problematic. There was, nevertheless, between the two American parties a broad consensus on the aims of American foreign policy, namely, disarmament and the extension of the 'Open Door' principle in respect of trade, which would provide American business with ever more unrestricted access to world markets. It was in these two areas primarily that American opinion was to exhibit its internationalism.

It has never, in fact, been justified historically to imply that the United States could seal itself off from the rest of the world at this time. America now had extensive overseas investments which had to be protected. By 1929, for example, American direct investments in Europe amounted to $1,352 million and indirect investments $3,030 million.[30] She also had an interest, as has already been noted, in the expansion of her share of world trade through the promotion of the 'Open Door' concept. These concerns conspired to give the United States government an active interest in the maintenance of peace which meant in practice continuing involvement in international affairs, albeit often indirectly through essentially private economic diplomacy. Yet it remains true that the United States, in failing to ratify the Treaty of Versailles, declined the leadership of the world political and economic system and this duty, therefore, once more devolved upon Britain by default and to a lesser extent upon France.[31]

Whatever might be said about American foreign policy after 1919, the United States by the end of the First World War certainly could not disregard the growing power of another of the victor powers, Japan, whose ambitions were already beginning to conflict with American aims and whose naval strength was growing in the Pacific. Japan's status as a victor was compromised by the retention of a number of grievances from the pre-war period. When Japan defeated the Chinese in 1895, in a war that had its origins in rivalry over influence in Korea, the Treaty of Shimonoseki, besides obliging China to recognize the independence of Korea, provided for the cession to Japan of Taiwan and the Liaotung Peninsula in Manchuria. The Triple Intervention of Russia, France and Germany, however, forced the Japanese to return the Liaotung Peninsula to China, only for the Russians later to acquire the leasehold to the Kwantung Territory, in the Liaotung Peninsula, which included Port Arthur and Dairen. Nevertheless, following the defeat of Russia in 1905, Japan acquired Russia's property and interests in Port Arthur and the Kwantung leasehold under the terms of the Peace of Portsmouth. Chinese sovereignty in Manchuria as a whole was recognized, but Japan did obtain the right to protect the South Manchurian Railway zone with her own troops. The formation of the force, known as the Kwantung Army, that was stationed in this zone was to have fateful consequences for the future. However, the peace, which had been brokered by the United States, made no provision for the payment of an indemnity by Russia, which caused profound irritation in Japan. It seemed to the Japanese that there was one law for the Europeans and another for non-Europeans. Riots ensued in Tokyo culminating in the resignation of the prime minister, Katsura. Paradoxically, therefore, Japan's victory in her first major war with a European power did not have the effect 'of reassuring Japan that she was now a major power able to compete effectively with the others as at least an equal . . .'. On the contrary, she remained convinced 'of her continued vulnerability and the need to strengthen further her military capability'[32]. Her sense of social unacceptability and of being treated disparagingly and as inferior by westerners was heightened by the immigration legislation enacted in the United States and Australia before 1914, intended to put a brake on Japanese entry. This led to great embitterment in Japanese–American relations, although Japan's voluntary restrictions on emigration settled the matter for the time being.

Japan's experiences in the First World War and later at the Paris Peace Conference of 1919 seemed to confirm her difficulties in being accepted as an equal partner by the other powers. The war was seen by the Japanese as an opportunity to consolidate and further expand their interests on mainland Asia which by 1914 comprised the Kwantung leasehold and Korea, which had been annexed in 1910. After declaring war on Germany, the Japanese, therefore, decided to wrest from the Germans their privileges in China, namely the leasehold over the port of Kiaochow, obtained by Germany in 1898, and extensive economic rights in Shantung province. To effect this the Japanese occupied the whole of Shantung province and not merely Kiaochow. From the Japanese vantage point, the situation in 1914 must have appeared very auspicious for further penetration of China.

Although a nationalist reaction to European domination had set in in China by the turn of the century, which, following a rising in Wuhan in 1911, resulted in the overthrow of the Manchu dynasty, this revolution had the effect of further weakening the country rather than strengthening it. From 1912 until the later 1920s, China was to have no experience of a viable government capable of impressing unity on the entire country. Rather China fell under the control of warlords and local political regimes that tended to coexist with the continuation of the mortifying system of the *Unequal Treaties*, which conferred upon American, European and Japanese trading companies economic and legal privileges. In Peking a feeble Chinese government was recognized by the western powers as the nominal government of China, but it was incapable of resisting the encroachments of the west, or of establishing its authority over the local military leaders. Only in the south, in Canton, did a potentially viable government emerge in 1917 in the form of Dr. Sun Yat-sen's nationalist *Kuomintang*, originally founded in 1912. This was to lead to the anomaly of Chinese dual representation at the Paris Peace Conference in 1919.

Nationalism, however, was a potent force throughout China and the Japanese occupation of Shantung led to Chinese protests, which in turn resulted in the Japanese presentation to the Chinese government in Peking in January 1915 of the Twenty–One Demands. These consisted of four sets of 'demands' proper and a final set of 'desires'. The first set asked the Chinese to confirm Japan's succession to German rights in Shantung, but the package if accepted in its entirety, especially the final set of 'desires', would have had the effect of turning China into a Japanese protectorate. Western hostility to the 'desires', caused them to be dropped. The Americans ultimately informed the Japanese government that they would not recognize any Sino-Japanese settlement that infringed American rights or the 'Open Door' (equality of commercial access) in China, or violated China's territorial integrity. The British advised their ally that the 'desires' were not compatible with the terms of the Anglo-Japanese Alliance.[33] The Japanese decided not to press the 'desires', but under duress the Chinese government in May 1915 agreed to a modified version of the four sets of 'demands'.

From the Japanese perspective relations with the United States were becoming a particular problem, in the aftermath of the crisis created by the Twenty-One Demands. This was why former foreign minister, Ishii Kujiro, was sent to Washington in 1917 in an effort to put them on a more friendly basis. Ishii argued with the American secretary of state, Robert Lansing, that the United States should recognize Japan's special rights in China as the other Allies had done. Lansing was less than totally receptive to these suggestions. For the time being he was not inclined actively to contest Japan's interests, but he was of the opinion that they violated the 'Open Door' principle and were, therefore, likely in the long term to be prejudicial to the stability and integrity of China. President Wilson was himself veering towards a much more radical solution in which all the powers' rights in China should be terminated, but wanted no confrontation with Japan for the duration of the war. In the end an agreement of sorts was reached in the so-called Lansing–Ishii Notes of November 1917. The United States accepted that 'territorial propinquity' conferred upon Japan 'special interests' in China, while Japan agreed to respect the 'Open Door' in China and her territorial integrity. The weakness of this agreement was that it could be interpreted to the satisfaction of diametrically opposed viewpoints and 'did more harm than good to American–Japanese relations, since it raised expectations on both sides that could scarcely be fulfilled'[34]. The Paris Peace Conference and the ensuing Washington Conference were to demonstrate to the Japanese just how difficult it was to secure international recognition and acceptance of their objectives.[35]

But economically Japan had benefited greatly from the war. Just how greatly is demonstrated by the fact that between 1913 and 1921 her output of manufactured goods doubled and she was beginning to penetrate Britain's cotton and woollen goods markets in Asia. Another indicator of the boost that had been given to Japan's economy is to be found in the fact that Japan increased the value of her exports more than any other power in the period 1913 to 1929. During these years the total value of global exports increased by 66 per cent. Naturally this was reflected in the figures for individual countries. But while the value of Britain's exports rose by 15 per cent, those of Germany by 33 per cent, and those of France by 50 per cent, American exports rose in value by 200 per cent and those of Japan by 300 per cent! Japan's ambitions were being increasingly underpinned by a vibrant and efficient economy.

The Vanquished

The major defeated power in 1919 was unquestionably Germany. The war had imposed very severe hardships on both the military and civilian populations. Over two million had lost their lives in active service and disease and starvation had brought death to many at home. German industry, which had spectacularly increased its productive capacity prior to the war, had been disrupted as a result of Germany's war-time insulation from the world market and the German economy drifted towards collapse. Inflation during the course of the war had increased dramatically, and together with prodigious increases in indirect taxation, this had a most oppressive effect on the ordinary citizen. Inflationary influences had, in fact, been built into the economy by the decision to finance the war by massive borrowing rather than direct taxation.[36]

For a nation whose prospects had appeared so bright before 1914 the trauma of military defeat in these circumstances conspired to produce a revolutionary situation which became open rebellion when the sailors aboard the cruisers *Thuringen* and *Helgoland* mutinied on 29 October 1918. The mood of revolution spread rapidly throughout Germany and by 6 November workers' and soldiers' councils had been established in all Germany's principal cities. On 9 November the emperor was compelled to abdicate. Simultaneously Max von Baden resigned as chancellor quite deliberately in favour of the Majority Socialist leader Ebert in anticipation that he would curb the excesses of the revolution and might ultimately even restore the monarchy. The latter Ebert did not achieve, but he and his colleagues certainly ensured that the Weimar Republic which came into existence in 1919, was a state in which there was no institutionalization of revolution.

The Majority Socialists had been content with the parliamentary democracy conceded by the imperial authorities in October 1918.[37] The November revolution they considered to be extravagant and dangerous, for it complicated all the problems connected with the cessation of hostilities and making peace. The withdrawal of the armed forces from occupied territory, demobilization, the change from a war to peace-time economy, the discharge of Germany's obligations under the armistice and preparations for the peace negotiations had now to be carried out in a revolutionary atmosphere. In order that the government of the country could carry out these tasks efficiently and in circumstances of minimal disruption to social order and the economy, it was considered by the Majority Socialists essential to enlist the support of the ruling classes of the imperial regime – the bureaucracy, the officer corps and the leaders of business.[38]

One of the most famous examples of this process is the celebrated Ebert–Groener Pact of 10 November 1918. General Groener, who had succeeded General Ludendorff as quartermaster-general of the army and emerged as the dominant personality in the army leadership during the revolutionary months, agreed with Ebert on the necessity of resisting any further leftward developments in Germany and on the restoration of law and order by means of the convening of a National Assembly as soon as possible, which would decide Germany's constitutional future. Groener, therefore, pledged the army's support for the government in exchange for the government's support for the maintenance of discipline in the army and the authority of the officer corps. This was supplemented on 15 November by the so-called Central Working Association agreement between the employers and the trade unions. What was involved here was a concept of 'social partnership': the employers recognized the trade unions, conceded the eight-hour day and accepted workers' committees in organizations employing fifty or more. For the employers the importance of the agreement lay in the fact that it guaranteed to some extent the continuation of the free market economy during the uncertain period ahead when it might not have been possible to rely upon the resources of the state. From the point of view of the Majority Socialist leadership, this agreement was regarded as helpful in reducing the sources of social unrest.

During the ensuing months revolutionary outbursts, such as the *Spartacus Rising* of January 1919, were put down with a firmness that caused the Independent Socialists to leave the government and gave rise to controversy that has continued ever since. The use of *Freikorps*, which were anti-communist volunteer units composed of ex-soldiers, was, and still is, a particular point of contention. The Weimar Constitution was also elaborated and put into force following the National Assembly elections of 1919. The major achievement of the National Assembly was the preservation of the parliamentary democracy, which, in essence, had been introduced in the last weeks of the imperial regime. It did little, however, to change the balance of political and social power in Germany. German social structure was hardly affected and an imperial and monarchistic attitude continued to pervade the bureaucracy, judiciary and officers' corps. Industry and capital by and large maintained their power intact. All this gave rise to a belief prominent among German emigré historians in the 1930s that the German revolution had been subverted from within. According, for example, to Sebastian Haffner: 'The German Revolution of 1918 was a Social Democratic Revolution which was destroyed by the Social Democratic leaders: a precedent which scarcely has its equal in World History'[39]. This, however, begs the question of whether or not the kind of social and political transformation they envisaged could have been achieved without a civil war, which it is by no means certain that the left would have won, or that if it had, democracy would have been the consequence. It is, on the contrary, perfectly possible to argue that the Ebert–Groener Pact preserved Germany from an authoritarian military dictatorship and in this connection it is certainly a point worth making that General Groener until his death was an emphatic supporter of the Weimar Republic. Nevertheless, the fact remains that Weimar Germany was a state which at bottom was conservative and monarchist, although monarchism, following the election of Field Marshal Hindenburg as president in 1925, collapsed as a serious political movement once the monarchists had a surrogate monarch in the person of the president. The Weimar Republic was, however, indeed an 'unloved Republic'. Not even the Ebert–Groener Pact was to preserve Germany from nascent civil war, attempted coups and political assassinations in the five years following the end of hostilities.

The Weimar Republic was all the more disliked because of its association with the Treaty of Versailles by which Germany concluded peace with most of her former enemies except the United States. When Ludendorff at the end of September 1918 recognized that Germany was defeated and had proposed to the kaiser that Germany be turned into a parliamentary democracy it had not been solely in order to please President Wilson and American opinion and thereby secure better peace terms. It had also been proposed in order that the army would be dissociated from the conclusion of peace. On the other hand, the formation of a government representative of the Reichstag majority would mean that socialists and liberals would be associated with the defeat and subsequent peace. In the words of Ludendorff: 'They shall now have to drink the soup that they have landed us in'. (*Sie sollen die Suppe jetzt essen, die sie uns eingebrockt haben!*)[40] In this way was born the *Dolchstoßlegende*, the myth of the undefeated army stabbed in the back by treacherous socialists and parliamentarians. Germany in 1919 was very much a nation at odds with itself and the world. Despite, however, the internal instability of the Weimar Republic, there was a consciousness of the fundamental strength and superiority of power of the German Reich clearly articulated in a report by General Groener in May 1919 in which he stated:

> One must really face up to the result of the past war. It is the defeat, the, elimination of Germany as a European Great Power after the failure from the outset of its unconscious attempt . . . to compete with England for world rule . . . We unconsciously strove after world rule . . . before we had consolidated our position on the Continent.[41]

For the more aggressive elements amongst the German ruling classes, who shared Groener's assessment and were confident of Germany's underlying strength, there was a temptation to reverse the verdict of 1918. This implied that whatever peace Germany concluded with her former enemies she would attempt to undo it.

For Germany's former principal ally, the Austro–Hungarian Empire, there was to be no opportunity to undo any peace for, by 1918 that entity no longer existed. In a very real sense the First World War had been fought to preserve the integrity of the Habsburg Empire against the disintegrating forces of nationalism. The defeat of the central powers, therefore, ensured that Austria–Hungary would collapse into its component parts. Austria and Hungary became separate states, the latter losing much of its historic territory to the successor states of Czechoslovakia and Yugoslavia. From Austrian, German and Russian territory the state of Poland was recreated. This reorganization of the map of Eastern Europe took place to a large degree before the peace settlement which largely endorsed the actions of the governments of the successor states. Nevertheless, the situation in Eastern Europe in 1919 was pregnant with problems for the future. Many of these states contained minorities, of which the most important were the *Reichsdeutsch* German minorities.[42] These before 1914 had been members of a German state and particularly between 1918 and 1922 and after 1932 agitated for union with the Reich. Secondly, there were disputes between the successor states themselves over territory, such as those between Poland and

Czechoslovakia over Teschen and Javorina. It was into this unstable area that Germany was to expand in the later 1930s.

The Ideological Divide

Instability in Eastern Europe was also the consequence of the collapse of the Russian Empire in 1917. Russia, although having contributed to the ultimate victory of the Allies, was herself a vanquished power; one, moreover, convulsed by civil war. Russia's defeat coincided with and was partly the consequence of political and social revolution at home which resulted in the apparent triumph of socialism in Russia in its most extreme form. The advent of a communist government in a major European state was a most unwelcome development for the ruling classes and elites of the Allied powers and also for those in Germany. Paradoxically, however, it had been the German government that had assisted the revolution in Russia by transporting Lenin from Switzerland in a sealed train, to use Winston Churchill's lurid description, 'like a plague bacillus', with the clear objective of weakening Russia's war effort by promising internal political subversion in the Russian Empire.

At a war cabinet meeting of 14 November 1918, the British prime minister, David Lloyd George, stated:

> . . . it was important that the public in England should realise more fully what Bolshevism meant in practice. France was more secure against Bolshevism, owing to the existence of a large population of peasant proprietors. Here we had a great, inflammable, industrial population, and it was very desirable that our industrial population should know how industrial workers had suffered equally with the rest of the population of Russia at the hands of the Bolsheviks.[43]

Still, Lloyd George was not in favour of anything resembling an anti-Bolshevik crusade, although other British ministers were, such as Winston Churchill, Milner and Curzon. British intervention in Russia, however, was initially directed at Germany and conceived, following the Soviet authorities' conclusion of an armistice with Germany, in December 1917, and then the Peace of Brest-Litovsk in March 1918, as a means of preventing the Germans gaining access to Allied supplies, previously delivered to the imperial Russian authorities, and of maintaining an Eastern front which could divert German troops from the West. During the winter of 1917–8 the Germans managed to transfer forty divisions from the Eastern to the Western Front, comprising almost two million men. Anything, therefore, that would have relieved this situation was considered and attempted. The idea of intervention was first mooted by Marshal Foch at an Inter-Allied Conference in Paris of November 1917 and would have involved Allied seizure of the Trans-Siberian Railway. The British and Americans, however, dissociated themselves from such a notion in the first instance. This reluctance changed in February 1918 when the Bolsheviks secured a majority in the Archangel Soviet. The presence there of substantial war stores, supplied by the Allies, which were now being appropriated by the Bolsheviks without payment provoked second thoughts. The Allied military planners at the Supreme War Council at Versailles now began to conceive a plan which would secure the North Russian ports of Archangel and Murmansk and create a diversion in the east that might tie down some German forces. There were, of course, few British and French soldiers available for such a venture, so the planning involved a combined Allied effort including an American–Japanese occupation of Siberia. As early as March 1918 British and French forces were present in Murmansk.

This scheme, however, met with the opposition of President Wilson who was loath to intervene in the internal affairs of Russia and the Japanese government was reluctant to act without the United States. This was not true of the Japanese Army within which it was felt that the Bolshevik Revolution should be used as an opportunity to extend Japan's interests beyond Manchuria and into Siberia. By 1917 planning was afoot to seize the Siberian railways. The caution of the Japanese government, as opposed to the army, was rooted in the perception by early 1918 that the Allies might ultimately be defeated. If indeed that eventuality was realized, Japan would require a new ally and the prime candidate was the United States. Yet in his Fourteen Points of January 1918 President Wilson had argued the case for self-determination and called upon Germany to evacuate territory occupied by them against the will of the inhabitants. This naturally had implications for Japan's position in Manchuria, the subject of the recent Lansing–Ishii Notes. The Japanese prime minister, Terauchi, therefore, determined that Japan should take no action in Siberia without American approval. This decision created great tension in Japan. Foreign minister Motono in particular was of the opinion that Japan should intervene in Siberia in order to establish a pro-Japanese regime there.

This situation was ultimately resolved by President Wilson's concern for the fate of the Czech Legion that was trying to leave Russia by way of the Trans-Siberian Railway. This was a body of some 50,000 men who had defected from the Austrian forces during the First World War in order to fight for the Allied cause alongside the Russians. They now wished to leave Russia and resume fighting on the western front, but the agreement between them and the Soviet authorities concerning their exodus broke down. Wilson thought the cause of the Czech Legion was something that the United States could honourably support and it was agreed that American troops would intervene jointly with the Japanese at Vladivostok and with the British and French at Archangel and Murmansk in North Russia. This agreement was reached in August 1918, by which time most of the Czechs had evacuated European Russia and the war was winding down in Europe. There was, therefore, no reason for the troops of the Allied and Associated Powers to be in Russian territory at all.[44]

The British, French and Japanese had, however, been conniving with and supplying the anti-Bolshevik White Forces for months, and the intervention now began openly to assume the character of an anti-Bolshevik campaign. Indeed the French had hoped from the beginning by intervention to assist in the creation of a united White government capable of overthrowing the Bolsheviks and resuming the war against Germany. As one British foreign office official commented in May 1919: '. . . our original intervention in Russia was alleged to be directed against Germany. Against whom is it directed now? If against the Bolsheviks, all talk of non-intervention is absurd.'[45] In October 1918 Clemenceau, the French prime minister, was very candid with Pichon, the French foreign minister. He stated:

> Bolshevism has become a force to be reckoned with. It threatens us through the Red Army, which is to be brought up to a million men in strength, and there are dreams of setting up Soviet regimes first throughout the old Russian territories and then in the rest of Europe. This new and monstrous form of imperialism will threaten Europe all the more fearsome as it comes precisely at the end of the war, which will eventually provoke, in all countries, a serious social and economic crisis . . . The Allies must therefore cause the Soviets to collapse. This will not be achieved by carrying the war to Russia but rather through economic encirclement of Bolshevism . . . occupation by Allied troops . . . of the Crimean and Ukrainian corn belts and the Donets coal-basin, which will be vital pledges for the payment of the 26,000,000,000 [francs] we have lent Russia and the Bolsheviks have repudiated . . . the armies of the Balkans, British armies in Turkey will, after the Turks have given in, furnish the few divisions needed to establish around Bolshevism, not only a *cordon sanitaire* to isolate it and kill it by starvation, but also the nuclei of friendly forces around which the healthy elements of Russia will be able to organize, and bring about the renovation of the country under the aegis of the Entente.[46]

Two months later he observed to an Inter-Allied Conference on 12 December 1919:

> He would suggest making, as it were, a barbed wire entanglement round Russia, in order to prevent her from creating trouble outside it, and in order to stop Germany from entering into relations with Russia, whether of a political or military character . . . The support of Poland was the best way to check Germany . . . It would be a great mistake if we did not maintain Poland in order to dam up the Russian flood and provide a check to Germany.[47]

Clemenceau, though, would not support the wilder demands of Marshal Foch, who in February 1918, for example, urged the imposition of a quick preliminary peace on Germany in order that the Allies might deploy their forces against the new enemy in the east.

The American–Japanese intervention in Siberia was supposed to be a quite modest affair. The Americans and the Japanese had agreed to send approximately 8,000 troops each, but the Japanese eventually had approximately 80,000 men in Siberia and by October 1918 had occupied the entire Trans-Siberian railway east of Lake Baikal. This was the work of the Japanese Army which acted in disregard of the government's wishes. It was not prepared to let the Americans or the more cautious politicians at home, such as the prime minister, Hara Kei, jeopardize Japan's gains in Manchuria or the opportunity of creating in Siberia a friendly and non-communist regime. The Bolsheviks, nevertheless, began to establish their authority in Siberia and the White Russian governments proved a liability rather than an asset. In January 1920 the Americans withdrew their forces and the British and French began to recall theirs, the British in fact commencing their evacuation as early as November 1919. The Japanese were the last to leave, even extending their occupation to North Sakhalin before departing in 1922. Sakhalin itself was not to be evacuated until 1925. These interventions left a bitter legacy in the relations between the Soviet Union and the rest of the world. They also left an impress on Japanese–American relations. The American intervention forces had been horrified by the behaviour of the Japanese and there was overt hostility between the two contingents. It was a portent of what was to come.[48]

There was one further interventionist episode before the former Russian Empire was finally reconstituted as the Union of Soviet Socialist Republics, for the Soviet authorities had to endure a war with Poland, newly recreated as a consequence of the defeat of Germany, Austria–Hungary and Russia. The war had its origins in the decision on the part of the Polish government to take advantage of Russia's temporary weakness in order to realise territorial ambitions in the Ukraine. The Polish attack in the spring of 1920 was reversed by the Red Army which by June seemed almost ready to take Warsaw. There followed, however, another change of fortune and the Soviet forces were just as hastily driven out of Poland. A compromise peace followed, the provisions of which were generally favourable to Poland. The 'miracle of Warsaw' is often attributed to the 'genius' of the chief of the Allied mission to Poland, the French General, Maxime Weygand. While, however, Weygand undoubtedly improved the administrative structure of the Polish Army, the defeat of the Red Army owed much to the strategy of Marshal Pilsudski and failure of co-ordination on the Soviet side which resulted in a lasting bitterness between General Tukhachevsky and Stalin.[49]

The withdrawal of the British intervention forces did not lead to direct British recognition of the Soviet government. Communism, marxism, bolshevism, however it was styled, was regarded in Britain as a continuing threat. Marxist theory asserted the universal application of its principles to all humanity and the ultimate success of Communism was considered to be contingent on its spread throughout the globe. From the beginning bolshevik foreign policy appeared to aim at world revolution. In 1919 Comintern, or the *Communist International*, was founded to assist in that process. It is, therefore, scarcely surprising that a government which had declared war on the rest of civil society, as it was then constituted throughout the world, should incur the suspicion and dislike of the threatened and be held in an opprobrium that at times bordered on hysteria. This has been luridly described by Ivan Maisky in his account of the early days of his embassy in London during the 1930s. Neville Chamberlain, then chancellor of the exchequer, in a conversation with Maisky referred to the Bolshevik authorities in the Soviet Union as '*our enemies*' and Mrs. Maisky had to endure, at the state opening of parliament in 1932, the apoplectic rage of an elderly duchess, who, on learning that Mrs. Maisky represented the Soviet Union, exploded: 'Do you know, I hate the Soviets!'[50] Although Britain recognized the USSR in 1924, a fundamental and thinly veiled hostility to its government persisted as the Campbell Case, the Zinoviev letter and the Arcos Raid illustrate.

This was not merely a matter of illogical prejudice, although it is evident that such prejudice existed. The anxieties of the British government regarding the international conduct of the Soviet authorities were, in fact, well founded. It is now quite clear that the British were able to listen to, intercept and read clandestine Soviet broadcasts and enciphered messages, which revealed that, while the Soviet government was overtly pursuing a policy of international contacts and economic reconstruction through trade, it was simultaneously controlling and bankrolling the subversion of British institutions at home and throughout the empire.[51]

For France the impact of the Russian revolution went beyond mere ideological revulsion. Russia could no longer be counted upon, given the political convulsions taking place there, to assist in future confrontations with Germany, at least in the short and medium terms. And, in any case, if the Bolsheviks secured power and established order could they ever be trusted? Essentially, what France was left with was the policy of the *cordon-sanitaire*, namely the creation of a French alliance system in Eastern Europe, which besides encircling Germany would also contain the Bolshevik menace.

This did nothing to improve relations between France and Russia which throughout the inter-war period were marked by wariness and suspicion. Except for the interlude of Louis Barthou as foreign minister, during 1934, it was the Soviet government which undertook all the initiatives in improving relations. Following the resumption of normal diplomatic relations in 1924, the Soviet government offered the French a Non-Aggression Pact in 1927. It was not, however, to be until 1935 that a Franco-Soviet Alliance was concluded. Even so the fundamental reluctance of the French to deal with the Soviets is revealed in the fact that it was never properly supplemented with staff talks. The extent of French mistrust of the USSR on the very eve of the Second World War is revealed by Georges Bonnet, who was then foreign minister, in his memoirs. He wrote:

> I had set myself against the project hatched by Stalin's genius, and pursued with implacable tenacity and diabolical cleverness, which consisted in pushing all the Soviet Union's adversaries – Germans and Allies alike – into one enormous free-for-all. From such a war of extermination Bolshevism would one day emerge triumphant.[52]

For Bonnet world domination was the fundamental aim of Soviet policy and this had to be resisted.

Allied intervention and the war with Poland undoubtedly contributed to the bolshevik perception of being in a constant state of war with the outside world. The subversive activities carried out by the Soviet regime and its agents in capitalist states were equally regarded by western international law as 'unfriendly,' or tantamount to the waging of war. The Soviet theory of international law, however, considered war, hot or cold, to be the natural condition of relations between socialist and capitalist states. This led to the introduction of a new device in international relations in the 1920s, namely, the *Non-Aggression Treaty*. A number of these treaties were concluded between the Soviet Union and its neighbouring states, starting with Turkey, Iran and Afghanistan in 1919–21. By specifically eliminating subversive activities and aggression, direct and indirect, between the parties to such instruments a basis for friendly relations was created and the possibility of further western intervention reduced. These treaties were, though, incompatible with membership of the League of Nations.

But while Soviet foreign policy was revolutionary it should also be borne in mind that it adopted traditional Russian foreign policy objectives even before Stalin became the dominant force in Soviet politics. Although a comparatively low-ranking figure in the Soviet hierarchy, this had something to do with the commissar for foreign affairs, G. V. Chicherin, and also the fact that the rise of bolshevism in Russia was associated with a groundswell of Russian nationalism. Thus it became an objective of policy to restore the frontiers of 1914, to reestablish Russia's position in Manchuria, to exercise control of the Dardanelles and to extend Russian influence into the Balkans, Iran and Afghanistan. These aims could, of course, be presented as nationalist; they could also be used to obscure genuine revolutionary ambitions by covering them with the cloak of nationalism.[53]

Throughout the inter-war years fear of the threat of bolshevism was widespread and found expression in bizarre ways. In 1924, for example, the *Boys Own Paper* carried a story about a public school which contained the following extract: 'Now, I'm all for rags that are cheery rags, but I bar dirty tricks and rebellion of the proletariat. So I mean to start a company of Fascisti to counteract the deplorable laxity of the present age.'[54] In a very crude way this represented a prevailing obsession in European society. In practical terms this mood predetermined that even when Soviet policy became pragmatic rather than ideological, particularly as the German threat grew, western governments found it impossible to have anything other than the most formal relations with the USSR, which country remained an outcast.

The Bolshevik revolution had immense consequences for European diplomacy in the inter-war years which cannot be properly understood without bearing in mind the way in which Russia's traditional role in Europe was affected by it and the almost hysterical anti-communist climate in which diplomacy was often conducted. Governments fearing internal subversion from socialist forces within their own countries were hardly likely to deal easily with a potentially powerful patron of their opponents. It is scarcely surprising that Bolshevik Russia was excluded from the Paris Peace Conference.

2

The Making of the Inter-War World, 1919–1923

If Russia played no part in the general peace arrangements of 1919, neither did the vanquished. The framework of the inter-war world was constructed by the victors of the First World War. It was they who created the *Versailles System* and the *Washington System*. The Versailles System was the product of the Paris Peace Conference and governed Europe. The Washington System was the product of the various treaties concluded at the Washington Conference of 1921–2 and governed relations between the powers in the Far East and the Pacific. The story of the causes of the Second World War is largely the story of the breakdown of these two systems.

The Versailles System

The Versailles System created during the Paris Peace Conference of 1919 has received much criticism in the past on the ground that its so-called imperfections led directly to war in 1939. Indeed, one contemporary wrote: '. . . if we made war to end war, we have certainly made peace to end peace'[1]. It may, however, be doubted whether the Versailles System was as bad as some contemporary critics suggested, or whether it could in itself have led directly to war. Still it was that settlement which set the framework for international politics in Europe during the inter-war years and it should, therefore, be examined in some detail. The Versailles System covered all the arrangements made by the Allied and Associated Powers with former enemy states. It should not be confused or equated with the Treaty of Versailles with Germany which was only one element of the peace settlement as a whole.[2]

At the beginning of the war the Allied or *Entente* powers had concluded a number of secret treaties which were annexationist in character, such as the Treaty of London by which Italy had been induced to enter the war. The revelation of these treaties by the bolshevik authorities at the end of 1917 had an immediate impact on the radical and Labour left in Britain. Lloyd George, the prime minister, consequently felt compelled, in an address to the TUC in January 1918, to call for a territorial settlement based on self-determination, 'government with the consent of the governed', and the creation of an international organization that would control armaments and lessen the prospects of war. In the United States President Wilson, who shared many of the beliefs of the British left with regard to the conduct of international affairs and who was determined to use the war to bring about change in the international system, elaborated his views on the future peace in the Fourteen Points of 8 January 1918. This and his subsequent pronouncements also called for a just peace based on national self-determination and a League of Nations which would preside over a regime of open diplomacy and thus diminish the risk of war. When, therefore, the Peace Conference began in January 1919 there was some conflict over the nature of the peace that was to be concluded. Britain, France, Italy and the British dominions still cherished annexationist ambitions that President Wilson was bound to oppose. It was out of the tension between these conflicting aims and views that the compromise developed that was the Versailles System.

When, at the end of September 1918, Ludendorff had proposed to seek a peace based upon the Fourteen Points, he had done so because, strictly interpreted, they would not have imposed a very great burden upon Germany. The first point required that the peace should be negotiated openly and that thereafter diplomacy should be conducted 'frankly and in the public view'. The second required complete freedom of navigation on the seas in peace and war. The third provided for an international regime of free trade and the fourth for general disarmament 'to the lowest point consistent with domestic safety'. Point five called for an 'impartial adjustment' of colonial claims that would also respond to the wishes of the governed. Points six to thirteen dealt with the future territorial settlement in Europe: Russian territory was to be evacuated and Russia was to be welcomed 'into the society of free nations under institutions of her own choosing'; Belgium was to be evacuated and restored; Alsace-Lorraine was to be returned to France; the frontiers of Italy were to be readjusted; the nations that comprised the Austro-Hungarian Empire were to be 'accorded the freest opportunity of autonomous development', Rumania, Serbia and Montenegro were to be evacuated and restored; the Turkish heartland (Anatolia) was to remain sovereign; and an independent Polish State was to be created. The fourteenth point called for the creation of an international association of nations.

Two of these points, however, were doubtful of realization from the start. Britain could never agree to the principle of freedom of the seas in war and peace, for this would have meant the abandonment of the weapon of naval blockade. Moreover, influential sectors of opinion in the United States were less than enthusiastic about free trade. The Republican party which won the mid-term Congressional elections in 1918 and had three candidates elected to the presidency in the 1920s, was a persistent supporter of protective tariffs, 'as a fundamental and essential principle of the economic life of the nation'. This mood culminated in the passage of the Hawley-Smoot legislation in 1930.[3] Equally, the Fourteen Points were qualified by the American Note to the German Government of 5 November 1918 and the terms of the armistice that was concluded six days later. The Note of 5 November while drawing attention to the Allies reservations about freedom of the seas, also made it clear that *restoration* of evacuated territories was understood by them to mean that Germany would be liable to pay 'compensation . . . for all damage done to the civilian population of the Allies and their property by the aggression of Germany by land, by sea, and from the air'. This was emphasized more abruptly in article nineteen of the armistice which mentioned that in the final peace there would be: 'Reparation for damage done.' The armistice also provided for the effective disarmament of Germany and the military occupation by the Allies of the left bank of the Rhine. There was, therefore, never any agreement that the peace with Germany would be founded purely and simply on the Fourteen Points.

The Treaty of Versailles between Germany and the Allied and Associated Powers, signed on 28 June 1919, confirmed much that had been contained in the armistice and pre-armistice negotiations. The first part of the Treaty formed the basic contract by which the powers were to form themselves into a League of Nations; this was the so-called Covenant of the League of Nations. Germany, however, was not to become a founder member of this organization. Neither was the League to have armed forces of its own, as the French would have wished. In general the Covenant reflected the Anglo-American view of what the League should be. Although Wilson had insisted on the notion of the 'collective guarantee', the League never became a system of collective security, for 'the Covenant was more concerned to safeguard the integrity of its members' rights to control their own destiny' than to organize international, collective action. As one writer has suggested: 'At its heart the League was a permanent international conference, more in aid of the "Old diplomacy" than the embodiment of the "new".'[4] Articles forty-two to forty-four of the Treaty provided for the demilitarization of the Rhineland, any breach of which was to be regarded as a serious threat to peace. The Rhineland was also to be subject to allied occupation for fifteen years, the occupying forces being progressively reduced after five year periods, provided Germany fulfilled the terms of the peace. The Saarland was placed under a League of Nations commission for fifteen years, during which time the French were to be allowed to exploit the coal of the Saar basin in compensation for the deliberate destruction of French mines by retreating German soldiers. Germany's western frontier was also altered by the return of Alsace-Lorraine to France, the transfer of Eupen and Malmédy to Belgium and, following a plebiscite, the return of the northern parts of Schleswig to Denmark.

In the east, the territorial provisions were more severe. Virtually all of Posen and West Prussia were transferred to the newly resurrected state of Poland; this meant that Poland had a corridor to the Baltic Sea and one-and-a-half million German inhabitants in these territories. It also meant that East Prussia was separated from the rest of the Reich. At the mouth of the river Vistula the German city of Danzig was made a Free City under the League of Nations, thereby providing Poland with port facilities on the Baltic. After various vicissitudes Upper Silesia, with its industrial resources, was acquired by Poland. Under article eighty, union between Germany and

Austria was forbidden, although this contravened the express wish of the Austrian constituent assembly for union, or *Anschluß*, with the Reich. In Lithuania the German city of Memel was, by 1923, under Lithuanian control, after initially having been placed under a French high commissioner. Finally, Germany surrendered all her overseas possessions to the Allied and Associated Powers.

These were the fundamental territorial provisions of the Treaty of Versailles; they were not unduly onerous. In terms of land, Germany lost 27,000 square miles and, in terms of human resources, between 6.5 and 7 million people, or between 10 and 13 per cent of her pre-war population. Her economic capacity was also reduced by 13.5 per cent.[5] Many of these losses, however, could have been reasonably anticipated in the event of a defeat and Germany, in comparison with her neighbours, was scarcely weakened in the long term. Her industrial base remained intact and Russia had been removed as a restraining element in Central Europe; South-Eastern Europe was exposed as a potential economic and political sphere of influence. Furthermore, however the terms imposed on Germany are construed, they were certainly very favourable in comparison with the terms of the Treaty of Brest–Litovsk that the Germans themselves had imposed on Bolshevik Russia in 1918.

For a nation, however, which prided itself upon its military tradition the disarmament clauses were drastic. The general staff was to be dissolved and the officer corps was not to exceed 4,000; the army was to be limited to 100,000 men. The functions of the army were to be the maintenance of civil order and the defence of the frontiers. The navy was limited to six battleships, with submarines prohibited. Neither the army nor the navy was to be allowed to maintain an air force. Equally unacceptable to German opinion were the reparations clauses. Although President Wilson was opposed to the notion of *indemnities*, he had agreed in the American Note of 5 November 1918 that Germany should be liable to pay compensation for civilian damages. Article 231 of the Treaty of Versailles provided the legal foundation for this by stating:

> The Allied and Associated Governments affirm, and Germany accepts, the responsibility of Germany and her Allies for causing all the loss and damage to which the Allied and Associated Governments and their nationals have been subjected as a consequence of a war imposed upon them by the aggression of Germany and her Allies.[6]

Given that the Germans had been told they were fighting a war of defence, this *War Guilt Clause* was an intolerable slur. Germany's total liability was not, however, established in the treaty, the task being delegated to a reparations commission. The issue of reparations was inevitably to become one of the most complex and misunderstood issues of the inter-war years.[7]

The Paris Peace Conference also dealt with Japan's claims to succeed to Germany's rights and possessions in China and the Pacific, although in a manner which inevitably gave offence to the Japanese. Japan's difficulties in dealing with the white and European world were well illustrated in her failure to have a declaration of racial equality written into the League covenant. In this matter the Japanese even had the support of the Chinese representatives, but there was also strong opposition from the British dominions, Australia and Canada and the United States. The opponents of the declaration of racial equality all feared that it would merely serve as a means by which further Asian, and principally Japanese, immigration into their territories would be expedited. When the Japanese suggested an amendment to the declaration so that the word 'race' would not appear in it, but rather 'nations', they were no more successful. Despite the fact that the League commission voted in favour of this amended proposal by eleven votes to five, President Wilson, the chairman of the commission and himself a supporter of the Japanese case, ruled that unanimity was essential on a matter of principle and so the amendment was lost.

This was undoubtedly a blow to the Japanese and the impression which it created was undoubtedly reinforced by the opposition of the British Pacific dominions, Australia and New Zealand, to Japan's continued occupation and possession of Germany's former insular possessions in the Pacific north of the equator. Under the terms of Article 119 of the Treaty of Versailles, however, Germany would transfer her sovereignty in these territories to the Principal Allied and Associated Powers, which included Japan; she, therefore, had an unassailable right to a say in their disposal. Already in occupation of them, the Peace Conference eventually agreed to Japan's continued possession as a mandatory of the League of Nations.

The ease with which this was ultimately accomplished owed something to Japan's conciliatory attitude in the matter of Shantung. By agreeing to the modified Twenty-One Demands in May 1915, China had recognized the right of Japan to succeed to Germany's rights there. It was, however, possible for China to argue that she had only done this under the threat of force. Although the Japanese were able at the Peace Conference to produce an incautious statement by a Chinese diplomat which suggested that China 'gladly' recognized Japan's right to succeed to Germany's rights in Shantung, this did not prevent the Chinese, backed up by public opinion in China, from resisting the Japanese claims with the support of President Wilson and the American secretary of state, Robert Lansing. The Japanese delegation countered by revealing that Britain, France, Italy and Russia had all recognized Japan's claims in 1917 in secret treaties. Moreover, they let it be known that, if China's objections to Japan's claims were upheld, Japan would leave the Peace Conference and refuse to participate in the League of Nations. This and a Japanese offer to surrender any German right that infringed Chinese sovereignty finally induced a spirit of compromise and it was agreed that the Treaty of Versailles would recognize the transfer of Germany's rights in Shantung to Japan, subject to such arrangements as she might make with China. The matter, though, could not end there. The news of this arrangement led to an eruption of national resentment in China in May 1919 and the Chinese representatives refused to sign the Treaty of Versailles. The Shantung question would not finally be settled until the Washington Conference.

On 28 June 1919 a reluctant German government signed the Treaty of Versailles. That, however, was not the end of the peace-making process. It was now necessary to conclude peace with the heirs of the Habsburg Empire, Austria and Hungary. It proved impossible to do this simultaneously as a communist revolution in Hungary meant that the powers were reluctant to deal with her until it had run its course. Thus peace was concluded with Austria first in the Treaty of Saint Germain-en-Laye of 10 September 1919. With due alterations the Versailles treaty provided the model for this and the subsequent treaty with Hungary. Austria was to preserve her independence, there being no question of a union with Germany. The Habsburg dynasty was renounced, together with all its external interests. Interestingly, there was also provision for the payment of reparations similar to that contained in the Treaty of Versailles. The territorial losses imposed on Austria included the lands that constituted the new state of Czechoslovakia and the cession of the Istrian peninsula, the Trentino and South Tyrol, which was predominantly German-speaking, to Italy. The resurrected Polish state acquired Galicia, while the new state of Yugoslavia received Bosnia–Herzegovina and the Dalmatian coast. The rump Austrian Republic was left as a mountain state with a large and prestigious capital city, Vienna, but scarcely the resources to sustain it and its population, which accounted for a third of the population of Austria. Fortunately, Austria was allowed to join the League of Nations and under the aegis of that organization, and with the aid of foreign loans, was able to survive into the 1930s by which time it had become economically viable despite the population imbalance. Interestingly, in 1938 Austria's gold reserves were four times those of Nazi Germany.

Eventually in Hungary the traditional ruling classes, the magnates and the gentry, reasserted their authority and the powers were able to conclude peace with the Magyar nation on 4 June 1920 in the Treaty of Trianon. Like Austria, Hungary renounced the Habsburgs and admitted her liability to pay reparations. She also lost vast tracts of her historic territory, the lands of the crown of Saint Stephen, to neighbouring states and successor states of the Habsburg Empire. Slovakia and Ruthenia were incorporated in Czechoslovakia; Croatia–Slavonia was ceded to Yugoslavia; and Transylvania was incorporated into Rumania. While many of these transfers involved populations that were non-Magyar, they, nonetheless, subjected some three million Magyars to alien rule, which was a substantial portion of the Magyar population of Europe. Also subjected to disarmament and reparations, Hungary was to become thoroughly revisionist.

In November 1919, peace was concluded with Bulgaria in the Treaty of Neuilly. This effectively reduced her position in the Balkans by forcing her to pay reparations, to disarm to a minimal level and to surrender rather modest amounts of territory to her neighbours. The most substantial territorial loss was Western Thrace which went to Greece. It was resented, but this peace was not unduly harsh.

The last treaty to be signed with a former enemy state was that with Turkey. Initially a treaty was signed with the Sultanic authorities in April 1920. This was the Treaty of Sèvres. It finally overturned the historic regime at the Straits, which connected the Aegean and Black Seas. They were to be controlled by an international commission, in which Turkey was to have only a minor role, and free passage through them of both war and merchant vessels was now permitted. (The Straits Commission was abolished in 1936 by the Montreaux Convention and Turkey was once again allowed to fortify the Bosphorus and Dardanelles.) The reparations penalties were modest, but the territorial losses vast. All the former rights of the Ottoman Empire in North Africa were renounced and the former Arabian provinces became League mandates or independent kingdoms. Most humiliating of all, Anatolia, the Turkish heartland, was to be divided into French and Italian spheres of influence under nominal Turkish sovereignty. This treaty, however, was never ratified because a nationalist revolution in Turkey led by Mustapha Kemal resulted in the overthrow of the Ottoman government and the ensuing war with Greece ended with the expulsion of all Greeks from Anatolia. Eventually the new, republican Turkish authorities concluded peace with the powers in the Treaty of Lausanne of 24 July 1923. This confirmed much of the earlier treaty, but Turkey regained some of the territory previously lost to Greece and reparations were waived. Perhaps most significantly, neither the French, nor the Italians were able to realize their imperialist ambitions under the new treaty arrangements.

The Peace Settlement that ended the First World War took some five years to complete. Undoubtedly there were many infelicities in it, but the task with which the peacemakers were confronted was not an easy one. The force of nationalism had meant that it was impossible to reconstruct the pre-war world and it was inevitable that there would be unsolved problems and continued uncertainties. This would not, however, have been so serious had the United States maintained her participation in the affairs of Europe and involved herself in the evolution of the peace that she had done so much to create and which her military, industrial and financial strength now compelled.[8] But American opinion was divided on the means by which the United States should assume the responsibilities that strength implies.

The mid-term congressional elections had resulted in a Republican majority in the Senate of 49 Republicans to 47 Democrats. Not only were the President's political opponents in control of the Senate, but one of his most hostile critics, Henry Cabot Lodge became the chairman of the Senate Foreign Relations Committee on which also sat six Republican 'irreconcilables'. These were Senators such as Hiram Johnson and William E. Borah who would have nothing to do with the Treaty of Versailles or the Covenant of the League of Nations on any grounds. They saw in the covenant a breach with the whole American past and a defiance of the maxims of George Washington as enunciated in his farewell address of 1796. They were of a mind that adherence to the League covenant would 'compromise America's independence and stain its purity'.[9] The opponents of the Treaty were not, however, an homogenous group and there were 'reservationists' who might have been persuaded to vote for the Treaty by a number of concessions. On the critical issue, though, Article 10 of the League covenant, Wilson would not budge.

In submitting the Treaty of Versailles to the Senate, President Wilson asked if the United States could refuse the 'moral leadership' that was being offered; and if it was possible for the United States to 'reject the confidence of the world?' The unwelcome answer was, 'Yes.' Wilson was unable to convince a sufficient number of senators of the virtues of the Versailles Treaty or the covenant of the League of Nations, which was an integral part of the Treaty, to secure the necessary two-thirds majority for its ratification. Article 10, it was felt, threatened the United States with numerous and unwelcome entanglements in the Old World and might be incompatible with the Monroe Doctrine. In November 1919 and March 1920 the United States Senate was unable to ratify the Treaty of Versailles, which meant in turn that the United States would not join the League of Nations.[10] In August 1921 separate peace treaties were concluded with former enemy states. In rejecting the Treaty of Versailles the United States Senate also rejected the Anglo-American Guarantee of French territorial integrity that had been agreed upon during the peace conference in place of the territorial safeguards that France had sought in the Rhineland, such as possession of the left bank of the Rhine or the indefinite occupation of the Rhineland. With the abandonment by America of her guarantee, the British guarantee also lapsed.

As has already been indicated, the failure of the United States to ratify the Treaty of Versailles should not be interpreted as a discontinuity in American foreign policy following the electoral success of the Republican Party. There was, in fact, 'a broad consensus about ends.' This consensus rested upon a belief in disarmament and the 'Open Door' as the twin pillars of a stable peace and the foundation of a world community. There was even agreement that it might be necessary for the United States to impose disarmament and the 'Open Door' upon other nations and a perception that once disarmament had been achieved, the power of the United States economy would be a formidable coercive weapon in the achievement of the 'Open Door'. For Wilson and his advisers, however, American leadership had to be exercised through the League of Nations and this was where the consensus collapsed. For the Republicans and some Democrats, quite apart from the reservations already mentioned, Article 10 of the League Covenant 'was too inflexible to achieve real disarmament or generate the pressure to widen successively the application of the open door to ever larger areas of the world'. They also felt that membership of the League might limit American freedom of action regarding the use of economic power.[11]

During the course of the 1920s the foreign policy of the United States was to prove internationalist politically and economically. In the political sphere this internationalism was supported by senatorial demands for the termination of the continued occupation of foreign countries, the recognition of the Soviet Union and the endorsement of the principle of self-determination for colonial peoples. It was also reinforced by calls for global disarmament led by 'isolationists' such as Senator Borah and a group of senators who came to be known as the *peace progressives*. What they particularly wanted was naval arms control. This was an appropriate area for governmental and political action and was ultimately to lead to the Washington Conference and the *Washington System*, in effect, the post-war settlement in the Far East and Pacific. In Europe, on the other hand, foreign policy was conducted through private and economic means and was concerned with issues such as reparations, war debts and the interest due on them. The United States government would not involve itself in these matters directly because the debts were private and it had not ratified the Treaty of Versailles. Nevertheless, American banks were keen to protect American investments in Europe and to ensure the repayment of loans. This required that the European economy should function efficiently for which American capital was essential and American capital was to become 'the main sustainer of the international economic system during the 1920s, particularly after 1924'[12].

There was, however, a fundamental weakness in America's economic relationship with the rest of the world after 1918, for her prosecution of export expansionism and the 'Open Door' was also combined with import protectionism and the 'Closed Door'. The protectionism of the United States business community and the Wilson administration as much as its successors was rooted in the expansion of foreign trade, which had accelerated during the war, and the desire to prevent the Allies and the Central Powers alike 'from regaining the commerce they had lost to the United States' as a result of the war. The tariff, in the opinion of government officials and private economic managers, was the means whereby the expansion and stabilization of the American economy could be achieved. Moreover, there was a fear, well expressed by Frank A. Vanderlip, the President of the National City Bank of New York, that in the years after 1918 the European powers would try to set up tariff or customs unions in order 'to benefit their position'. Thus Vanderlip anticipated that Britain and her colonies would establish a tariff union that could discriminate against the United States. An American tariff was, therefore, essential both for the purposes of retaliation and bargaining for better trading conditions.[13] It was also believed in the United States that the protection of business by a tariff would raise living standards in America, which in turn would stimulate a market for European luxury goods and foreign raw materials. In this way, it was held, the restrictive impact of the tariff would be offset and 'international economic equilibrium and European recovery' promoted in conjunction, of course, with continued lending to Europe by private investors.[14] Whatever was said, however, in defence of American protection, it cannot be said that it did anything other than infringe a very fundamental rule of international economics that trade should be reciprocal. American tariffs in making it difficult for Europeans to sell in the United States, made it in turn difficult for Europeans to buy American goods or to earn the dollars with which to repay the loans contracted during the war and thus contributed to the financial and economic problems of the 1920s.

Tariffs were a 'nationalist' qualification to the economic internationalism of the United States in the years after 1918. In the political field the failure of the United States Senate to endorse America's continued direct involvement in the affairs of Europe by refusing to accept the League Covenant marked a 'nationalist' qualification to the internationalism otherwise displayed, for example, in the field of disarmament. The essence of the Versailles System had been founded on the assumption of continuing American involvement in the affairs of Europe. The fact that this assumption was unfulfilled thus unhinged the peace from the beginning. Real power in the world had passed from Europe to Washington, but the refusal to exercise it effectively meant that the necessary unity of purpose among the Allies, essential for the safe progression of the peace, could not be imposed. Left to her own devices,

Europe began to disintegrate in disagreements and egocentric ambition. Had Britain and France been able to agree upon policy and co-ordinate their strategies towards Europe, it is possible that the *Versailles System*, or Peace Settlement of 1919, might have served as the basis of a lasting peace, but French preoccupation with security and British preoccupation with imperialism and extra-European commitments prevented this.[15]

The Washington System

The Versailles System, however, was only one aspect of the post-1918 world created by victors. The other was the Washington System, which was created as a consequence of the Washington Conference of 1921-2. The Washington Conference was convened primarily to inhibit a potential naval arms race that might easily have escalated to levels that would have been financially ruinous. Although President Wilson hoped that Germany's disarmament, provided for in the armistice terms and the Treaty of Versailles, would stimulate general disarmament, this did not materialize. Japan, for example, continued with the construction of a fleet of eight modern capital ships. In Britain, while naval spending declined from £356 million in 1918-9 to £80 million in 1921, fear of being outshipped navally by Japan and the United States prompted demands within the Admiralty for the construction of eight large battleships, supplemented by new or converted aircraft carriers, at a cost of £84 million. All this made a considerable impact on those powers with interests in the Far East and the Pacific. In Washington there was suspicion of Japan and Britain, which countries continued to be allies. Japan was, of course, already perceived as a possible enemy, but now some of America's naval planners began to regard Britain also as a potential enemy because of her loss of markets to the United States.[16] In 1919 President Wilson sanctioned a new naval construction bill which, if it had been completed, would have made the US Navy the largest in the world. This degree of naval competition was, however, likely to prove destabilizing to all concerned, particularly coming as it did after a very costly war. Within the United States voices were soon raised calling for an end to this arms race before it started in earnest, prominent among them that of Senator Borah. The main thrust for a disarmament conference came from the United States Congress, but it met ultimately with a sympathetic response in London and Tokyo where the opportunity to make economies in arms spending and a reluctance to offend the United States resulted in acceptance of the American initiative.

The Washington Naval Conference, the first international conference of its kind to be held in the United States, opened in November 1921 and resulted in the conclusion of the Five Power Naval Treaty, signed by the United States, Britain, Japan, France and Italy. The naval limitations referred to capital ships, that is to say, vessels displacing more than 100,000 tons and armed with eight-inch guns, and fixed the tonnage ratio between the United States, Britain and Japan at 5:5:3. Japan would, therefore, be permitted a capital fleet 60 per cent the size of the American and British fleets; or 30 per cent of the American and British fleets combined. France was allowed a tonnage ceiling of 1.75 in relation to the total tonnage of the United States and Britain. In theory this gave Britain a superiority of 150,000 tons over a hypothetical Franco-Japanese naval combination and preserved the two-power standard that the British naval planners required against potentially hostile powers. The powers also agreed not to construct further capital ships for a period of ten years. This left the Japanese Navy in a position of considerable disadvantage in respect of its two most formidable potential enemies, the United States and Britain, the decision having by now been taken by the British not to renew the Anglo-Japanese Alliance. This, though, was offset to an extent by the agreement among the other powers to refrain from constructing further naval bases and fortifications in the Western Pacific.

What in fact made agreement on naval disarmament easier was the termination of the Anglo-Japanese alliance. In London the foreign office favoured its renewal in 1923, but the United States was adamant in its opposition to it. The American secretary of state, Charles Evans Hughes 'viewed the renewal of the Anglo-Japanese Treaty in any form with disquietude . . .'[17]. He thought it would have a disastrous effect upon American opinion. There were two grounds for American objection. It was thought to conflict with the Wilsonian spirit of 'Open Diplomacy' and, secondly, its continued existence would mean that the United States would have to embark upon a naval construction programme that would enable the American fleet to match the strength of the British and Japanese Navies combined, which would only fuel a further cycle of the arms race.[18] The Americans now viewed Japan as their principal potential adversary. Opinion in London too was not blind to the evident expansionism of Japan. In the foreign office it was thought that Japan was aiming at hegemony in the Far East and there was concern over her increasing economic competition with and envy of Britain's empire. However, given that this was the case, Lord Curzon thought that there were advantages in renewing the alliance with Japan. He observed:

> There can be no doubt that while the Anglo-Japanese Alliance has lasted . . . it has enabled us to exercise a very powerful controlling influence on the sometimes dangerous ambitions of Japan.

Lord Balfour stressed its strategic value. A 'faithful friend' could very easily be turned into 'a formidable enemy'[19]. But these considerations were not sufficient to outweigh the implications for naval spending that the continuation of the alliance would entail and the simple fact that, in view of the adamantine American opposition to the renewal of the alliance, if it came down to a choice between the United States and Japan, the former must have priority.[20] In place of the alliance the Japanese had now to make do with the Four Power Treaty of 13 December 1921 in which the United States, Britain, Japan and France agreed 'as between themselves to respect their rights in relation to their insular dominions in the region of the Pacific Ocean' and to consult if those rights were threatened by any other power. These arrangements caused substantial disquiet in Japan where those who felt distrust of

Britain thought their anxieties confirmed. Britain's friends meanwhile felt discouraged.

The relations between the powers with interests in China and between them and China were in future to be governed by another treaty concluded during the Washington Conference, namely, the Nine Power Treaty. This bound the signatories (Japan, the United States, Britain, France, Italy, Belgium, the Netherlands, Portugal and China) to respect the territorial integrity and independence of China, to recognize the principle of the 'Open Door', or equal economic opportunity, and to assist in achieving in China stable political conditions. While this treaty inhibited further Japanese penetration of China, it did not challenge positions and rights previously acquired. In respect of Manchuria there was no specific guarantee of Japanese rights there, but both the United States and Britain assured Japan that they would not interpret the Nine Power Treaty in such a way as to infringe those rights.

Finally, it was at the Washington Conference that the question of Shantung was finally resolved. Japan agreed to restore the leased territory of Kiaochow to China and to withdraw her forces from the province. The Chinese for their part recognized the economic privileges of the Japanese in Shantung. It was also agreed at the Washington Conference that Japanese troops would finally be withdrawn from Siberia. In both these matters Japan had proved conciliatory and undoubtedly the objective of the Japanese government was to remove the tension that existed in Japanese–American relations concerning Japan's ambitions in mainland East Asia. But the impact of the Twenty-One Demands in America remained considerable. To some extent at least, therefore, the fundamental differences between the United States and Japan had been set by 1922; differences that were not to be resolved until the nuclear holocaust of 1945. For the United States, the Washington Conference was a very real diplomatic triumph. For many in Japan it signified isolation and an isolation on which her nationalists could feed.

Ultimately, neither the Versailles System nor the Washington System could last. In Europe, Germany regarded the Peace Settlement as having no legitimacy: it was a humiliating *Diktat* that had to be revised and broken so that Germany could resume her natural and rightful place in the European order. In the Far East, Japanese opinion increasingly felt that the Washington System too narrowly circumscribed Japan's freedom to prosecute her interests there and that it preserved too much Western influence in the region, particularly when Japan was increasingly discriminated against racially and economically by the western powers. The causes of the Second World War lie ultimately in the efforts of these two powers to break out of the systems which they felt constrained and confined them.

3

The Failed Peace, 1919–1933

Although, for the most part, peace was concluded in 1919 this in no sense implied that Europe was at peace. During the immediately following years the continent was the scene of a number of conflicts, some of which erupted into open warfare. On the coast of Dalmatia, Italian irregular forces led by the poet nationalist, Gabriele d'Annunzio, seized the port of Fiume; by 1924 Italian possession was officially recognized. In Anatolia the Turkish nationalist revolt resulted in confrontation between Turks and Greeks. In Eastern Europe, as has been noted, Poland sought to revive her medieval splendour by attacking Russia now under her new Bolshevik masters. And Hungary attempted to reverse the decisions of the war by irredentist incursions into Poland, Rumania and Czechoslovakia. These latter actions provoked the formation of the so-called Little Entente of Czechoslovakia, Yugoslavia and Rumania in 1921, which effectively brought about the failure of Magyar revisionism and, at least for the time being, settled the issue.[1]

German revisionism, however, was not so easily resisted. Germany was, of course, very much more powerful than Hungary and there was little unity among the powers regarding the policy that should be pursued towards her. Moreover, the one power that could have imposed some stability and unity on the European situation, namely, the United States, had washed its hands of European politics. The failure of the United States Senate to ratify the Treaty of Versailles and the implicit rejection of the Anglo-American Guarantee of France served to exacerbate British and French differences regarding the development of the peace. Conscious of the damaging impact of the treaty on the climate for international trade, Britain herself began increasingly to adopt a revisionist posture. The French, recognizing in the treaty perhaps their only means of ensuring their security, began to insist upon its literal fulfilment. In the light of recent research these images must to some extent be modified, but they retain sufficient substance to illustrate the divergencies of aim of which German policy was able to take full advantage.[2]

There was a widespread feeling in Britain by the 1930s that French policy had been largely responsible for the problems caused by the rise of national socialism. From foreign office officials to journalists, anti-Gallicanism was endemic among Britain's *foreign policy-making elite*. This mood was eloquently expressed shortly after the Munich Conference in 1938 in a comment made by Lord Astor, the Chairman of the Council of the *Royal Institute of International Affairs*, to the editor of the institute's prestigious annual *Survey*, Professor A. J. Toynbee. He told Toynbee that Hitler was the consequence of the French attempt to establish their hegemony in Europe after 1919.[3] It was also well illustrated in a letter sent to Neville Chamberlain by the former cabinet secretary, Lord Hankey, shortly after the abortive proposal for an 'indissoluble' Anglo-French union was made by Winston Churchill on the eve of the Fall of France in June 1940. Hankey stated:

> The more I reflect on the events of recent years the more clearly I realize that the French have been our evil genius from the Paris Peace Conference until today inclusive. Heaven forbid that we should tie ourselves up with them in an indissoluble union![4]

For those of this persuasion the apogee of French coercion of Germany was reached in the Franco-Belgian occupation of the Ruhr in 1923–4 when an effort was made to exact reparations from Germany by force. Reparations indeed served to poison the atmosphere in Europe throughout the 1920s and not merely between Germany and the Allies, but also between the Allies themselves. It was this issue that was to contribute so much to Anglo-French differences and make the long term maintenance of the Peace Settlement of 1919 so questionable.

Reparations

Anglo-French differences over reparations were, however, by no means very great in the beginning. Although President Wilson disliked the idea of indemnity payments by the vanquished to the victor powers, in the debate over reparations that took place in Britain and France following the armistice it was the principle of *indemnity* that triumphed over that of the *restoration of civilian damages*. The former implied much greater payment than the latter because Germany would be expected to indemnify the Allies against their *total war costs*. In the advocacy of the principle of indemnity it was the British who were clearly the front runners.

The reason for this is to be found in the fact that, as the Australian prime minister, William Hughes, pointed out, if civilian damages were to function as the basis of reparation payments, France and Belgium would gain considerably, Britain a little, but the dominions (Canada, Australia, New Zealand and South Africa) nothing at all, despite their considerable expenditure on the war. A war cabinet committee on indemnity, chaired by Hughes, was to recommend fabulous sums, such as £24,000 million, regarding Germany's liability in contrast to the treasury's estimate of Germany's capacity to pay at £3,000 million. Nevertheless, during the election campaign of 1918 Lloyd George and others excited the wildest expectations. The British electorate was led to believe that the whole cost of the war would be paid by Germany. In this way Lloyd George committed himself to a policy from which he would later find it difficult to dissociate himself.[5]

Why had the British political leadership acquiesced in such a programme? The answer to some extent lies in the budgetary indiscipline of the war years, during which insufficient revenue had been raised through taxation to fund the war effort. Budgetary preoccupations were also high on the agenda of the French finance minister, Louis-Lucien Klotz, in the autumn of 1918. During the war the gap between revenue and expenditure had risen by 187 billion francs. The French government was thus highly susceptible to a campaign demanding that the whole cost of the war be debited to Germany. Although he declined to make a demand for general war costs, Klotz gave rise to immoderate anticipations regarding the indemnity that could be claimed from Germany by stating in the Chamber of Deputies on 3 December 1918 that the issue of taxation with regard to the budget for 1919 would be deferred until Germany's reparation bill had been determined.[6]

Reparations do not, however, appear in the first instance to have been the primary objective of French policy with regard to post-war reconstruction. Under the inspiration of the minister of commerce, Etienne Clémentel, there was a pronounced effort during 1917 and 1918 to persuade the British and Americans of the virtues of continued inter-allied economic collaboration into the post-war period as a means of rehabilitating the devastated areas of France. The fundamental objective of French policy was to ensure the efficient restoration of the financial and industrial base of France through adequate access to raw materials. The schemes projected by the French also involved some discrimination against Germany in order that states that had suffered from German invasion and despoliation might have prior claims to supply and that Germany might not profit from the temporary disability of her erstwhile adversaries. This, though, was their undoing, for the restrictions envisaged offended free-trading sympathies in Britain and conflicted with the mantra of the 'Open Door' in the United States. In September 1918 Woodrow Wilson emphatically rejected any closed economic system among the victor states and effectively put an end to any discussion of such plans. This, however, was not the end of the French effort to bring the United States into a system of inter-allied economic collaboration. The means to this end would now be to demand from Germany levels of reparation that she would find it impossible to meet. In this way it was hoped that France's wartime partners would come to recognize the justice of French claims and the need for international collaboration.[7] But for practical purposes the French had come to regard the principle of indemnity as fundamental to their claim for reparation by the time the Peace Conference opened.

The consequence of all this was that the peace treaty ultimately imposed upon Germany a debt that was 'indefinite and unlimited'. The attempts by President Wilson to name a fixed sum in the treaty were frustrated by Lloyd George on the grounds that the Germans would find any sum excessive, thus risking throwing Germany into the arms of the Bolsheviks. Equally opinion in Allied countries was likely to consider any amount, however substantial, as insufficient. It was, therefore, decided to refer the assessment of Germany's liability to a Reparations Commission. Originally it had been proposed that there would be a time limit of thirty years on reparation payments, but even this was discarded in order to demonstrate that, whatever the cost, Germany would be compelled to discharge her entire obligation. It was also agreed to uphold the British proposal that civilian damage should be so construed as to include pensions and allowances paid to Allied servicemen and their dependants. Not only did this mean that the British dominions were now eligible to claim reparations, but that the sum to which Germany would be theoretically liable was effectively doubled. When the British delegation was finally confronted with the draft treaty the reality of what was proposed in the reparations chapter finally dawned on them. There was concern over the fact that the Germans were in effect being asked to sign a blank cheque and there was a perception that Germany was going to be required to pay far more than she possibly could. Nevertheless, Lloyd George remained reluctant to name a fixed sum in the treaty and with his French counterpart, Clemenceau, resisted a proposal by President Wilson that Germany's maximum liability should be fixed in the treaty at £6,000 million.[8]

The reparations chapter of the Treaty of Versailles, along with the other terms and conditions, was universally execrated in Germany. Article 231, which had been inserted to establish Germany's moral responsibility for the war and, therefore, her legal responsibility for all damage to property and persons, including pensions, was particularly disliked for the imputation of *War Guilt* it contained. The government of Philip Scheidemann resigned on the ground that it could not accept the terms offered by the Allies. In the *Reichstag* Scheidemann declared: 'What hand would not wither that binds itself and us in these fetters?' Eventually the social democratic chancellor, Gustav Bauer, formed a government based upon the SPD and the Centre Party that would sign the treaty, but he stated his position quite clearly in the Reichstag:

> The German Government undertakes to fulfil the peace conditions imposed on Germany. It wants, however, to declare at this solemn moment with frank clarity that it opposes from now onwards any reproach regarding bad faith to which Germany could be subjected now or later. The conditions imposed are far in excess of what Germany can actually achieve . . . We feel, therefore, bound to state that we make every reservation and reject all responsibility for the consequences, which could be inflicted on Germany, if the impracticality of the conditions, even given the most strenuous exertions of Germany's capacity, inevitably becomes clear.

On 20 June 1919, majorities of both the SPD and the Centre had voted to accept the treaty with two reservations; there was, though, a general rejection of the peace by the other parties. The spokesman for the German People's Party (DVP) declared that acceptance of the Treaty of Versailles would destroy the German state, for financial and military independence would be obliterated. Speaking for the German Nationalists (DNVP), Graf von Posadowsky-Wehner declared:

We are perfectly clear in our party of the serious consequences that a rejection of the peace treaty can bring about for our country and people . . . But the evil which could come of it can only be transitory . . . while, if we accept this treaty, we abandon countless generations of our entire people to misery.

Posadowsky-Wehner and his associates were, therefore, prepared to countenance the resumption of the war and the dismemberment of Germany rather than accept the Treaty of Versailles. Aversion to the proposed peace was widespread and deeply entrenched in German society.[9]

Moreover, there was a conviction that if Germany could prove historically that she was not responsible for the war then the treaty would lose all moral validity. This led to the publication of the German foreign office documents in the series, *Die Große Politik der europäischen Kabinette*, which had an impact on historical research, but politically scarcely paid the dividend for which the German government was looking. Revisionism, however, was to become the *leitmotif* of German foreign policy throughout the period of the Weimar Republic and it met with some success. With regard to the issue of reparations, German revisionism was greatly assisted by John Maynard Keynes' work, *The Economic Consequences of the Peace*, which, published in 1919, was a sustained denunciation of the economic sections of the treaty, and predicted the economic collapse of Germany and Europe.

Although British policy in respect of reparations must now be seen to be at least as culpable as that of France, there is considerable truth still in the view that British policy towards Germany was revisionist as soon as the ink on the Treaty of Versailles was dry, while French policy, in the absence of the Anglo-American guarantee, saw in the Treaty of Versailles the means through which the security of France was to be achieved. These Anglo-French differences in respect to the peace were first signalled in Lloyd George's *Fontainebleau Memorandum* and Clemenceau's reply. Lloyd George argued in favour of a just peace and urged moderation. If Germany were treated unfairly, he feared that she would turn Bolshevik or worse. He was opposed to placing Germans under foreign rule more than was minimally necessary; he wanted Germany to be able to join the League of Nations as soon as she was possessed of stable and democratic institutions; he felt it was futile to impose arms limitations on Germany unless the victors were prepared to impose such limitations on themselves; and he believed that reparation payments should only be paid by 'the generation that made the war'. The peace should be such as to commend itself to later generations as fair. In this way the causes of future wars would be eliminated. Lloyd George was, in effect, arguing for a restoration of Germany to something like her traditional position in Europe. Responding to this, the French prime minister made it clear that continental states were bound to view this suggestion from a different perspective and he sarcastically commented that: 'If it is necessary to appease her [Germany] she should be offered colonial satisfaction, naval satisfaction, or satisfaction with regard to her commercial expansion'[10]. Given, therefore, the nature of Anglo-French differences over the application of the treaty, it was always possible for the Germans to exploit them.

From the moment that the Treaty of Versailles came into force, it was met by German evasion and resistance. The disarmament clauses were never properly fulfilled and the interim reparation payments due before the Reparations Commission completed its labours were substantially evaded. Under the terms of the Treaty of Versailles Germany was to make payment of 20 billion gold marks in cash and kind, but the coal quotas were never met despite constant downward revisions.

On 27 April 1921 the Reparations Commission finally announced Germany's liability at 132 billion gold marks. At the London Conference of May 1921, however, the real burden was revealed as 50 billion gold marks including the balance of 12 billion unpaid on the interim payment. This portion of Germany's debt was divided into two categories of Bond, styled A and B. The other 82 billion gold marks of Germany's debt, however, were assigned to C Bonds, payment on which would commence when conditions, that can only be described as utopian, had been met.[11] On 8 May 1921 Keynes drew attention to the theoretical nature of the C Bonds when he stated in the *Manchester Guardian* that: 'It is probable that sooner or later, the C Bonds at any rate will be not only postponed but cancelled.' On 5 May 1921 the London Schedule of Payments was presented to the German government together with an ultimatum that the Ruhr would be occupied if these terms were not accepted. After the inevitable cabinet crisis in Berlin, the Wirth coalition, formed on 10 May, was able to gain Reichstag approval for the London Schedule, for sensible German opinion was cognisant of the reality with which they were being asked to comply. The C Bonds were a fiction.

The London Schedule marked the end of the fantasy claims of the period of the Peace Conference and represented an adjustment of reparations demands to realizable levels. What was proposed was a transfer of approximately 6 per cent of Germany's national income annually, a figure comparable to the burden imposed on western economies by the oil price explosion of the 1970s. For a government determined to restrict domestic consumption this was not an impossible levy.[12] Following, however, the payment of the first cash instalment in the summer of 1921, Germany made no further payments until after the invasion of the Ruhr and she steadily defaulted on payments in kind, despite constant adjustments. Increasingly the question arose as to whether or not to force Germany to pay.

The Genoa Conference and the Treaty of Rapallo

Before the occupation of the Ruhr, however, the British government under the leadership of Lloyd George attempted to involve Europe in an ambitious programme of European reconstruction. The British government had an interest in reconstructing as far as possible the pre-war economic order in Europe in order to resuscitate the flagging British economy. For this an efficiently functioning German economy was deemed essential and the key to this appeared to be the reintegration of Russia into the European economy. It was also anticipated that this would facilitate the payment of reparations. As Lloyd George told Aristide Briand, the French prime minister,

The only real way to get cash out of Germany . . . was to increase German exports; and the way to do that was to open up eastern and central Europe to German trade.[13]

As a result of a number of formal and informal Anglo-Franco-German contacts a scheme had been developed in London by the end of 1921 for an international consortium of British, French and German capitalists that would help restore and reconstruct Russia and Eastern Europe.[14]

Following discussions between Lloyd George and the French premier, Briand, held in London in December 1921, it was agreed that at the meeting of the Allied Supreme Council to be held at Cannes the following month three items – reconstruction, an economic conference and reparations – would be discussed. The long term prospects for an economic conference, however, had doubt cast over them from the second day of Briand's London conversations. Lloyd George explained that the primary anxiety for British opinion was the decline in trade; Briand responded that the main concern in Paris was Germany's willingness to fulfil her reparations obligations. Moreover, given that the prospect for a consortium was contingent upon the acceptance by the Soviet regime of Tsarist war debts and European control of Soviet railways and customs, its prospects for successful realization were minimal.

Briand was at this time under severe pressure. He was being attacked for being too subservient to British policy. It was argued that in exchange for participation in utopian schemes, the interests of the French taxpayer and the entire Treaty of Versailles were to be sacrificed. Briand tried to allay these fears by extracting from the British a security pact which would guarantee France against unprovoked attack by Germany. This, however, did not go far enough to mollify French opinion. During the Cannes Conference he was compelled to return to Paris to defend his policy, but in the circumstances in which he now found himself he resigned. Nevertheless, prior to his resignation it had been agreed that the economic conference should take place with Genoa as its venue. Moreover, Germany and Soviet Russia were to be invited to participate.

The attitude of Briand's replacement, Poincaré, virtually predetermined the outcome of the Genoa Conference. On assuming office he stated that his policy would be to uphold the treaties on which the peace was based. He doubted whether Lloyd George's scheme for the *Europeanization* of Russia through trade would work, although he accepted that the conference should go ahead following a meeting with Lloyd George at Boulogne in February 1922. There was not now, however, to be any discussion of the major matters affecting Europe such as the peace treaties, reparations or general disarmament. Poincaré was insistent too that in any arrangement with Soviet Russia she would have to agree to international undertakings regarding private property.

When the Genoa Conference finally convened in April 1922, its failure was soon assured by the conclusion by Germany and Soviet Russia of the Treaty of Rapallo. On discovering in February 1922 that the western powers were considering the imposition of burdensome conditions upon Russia, such as the recognition of Tsarist war debts, Lenin took the view that the conference itself could not be regarded as a serious enterprise. It became, thereafter, the object of Soviet policy to break the united front of the capitalist states by concluding an agreement with Germany. Such a development was aided by the behaviour of the British delegation, which, at the suggestion of Lloyd George, conducted informal talks with the Soviet representatives at Genoa, from which the Germans were excluded. Ago von Maltzan of the German Foreign Office, who was a strong advocate of a firm Russo-German relationship, used this opportunity to pre-empt a potential agreement between Soviet Russia and the Allies, and particularly one between France and Russia with all the old inferences of encirclement. He successfully played on the fears of his colleagues and thus prevailed upon Rathenau, the German foreign minister to agree to the conclusion of the Russo-German Treaty at Rapallo in 16 April 1922.

This instrument confirmed a clandestine military relationship already begun in 1921 between the two countries which now expanded and developed. Under its terms, Germany recognized the Soviet Union and full diplomatic relations were established between the two countries. Germany also renounced any financial claims against Soviet Russia, provided the latter did not satisfy similar claims from other states. This particular condition rendered any positive outcome of the Genoa Conference particularly difficult. It was also agreed that: 'The two Governments will meet the economic requirements of the two states in a reciprocally benevolent manner.'[15] Finally, the treaty provided for reciprocal most-favoured-nation treatment. The Treaty of Rapallo stunned the rest of the world and wrecked the Genoa Conference. The *Unholy Alliance* ushered in a period of close co-operation between Germany and Soviet Russia that was to last until 1933. Under the Rapallo relationship, the Germany Army, the *Reichswehr*, was able to experiment with prohibited arms inside Russia, while the Red Army derived the benefit of German military expertise. At a more general level, Russia could supply the raw materials required by Germany, while Russia was able to benefit from the supply of German manufactured goods and the technology they contained.

Some historians now see in the failure of the Genoa Conference the collapse of a significant revisionist effort, which can no longer simply be ascribed to the aberrant behaviour of the Germans and Russians. The conference itself, for all the good intentions that lay behind it, had not been very well planned. There had been too much secrecy and, simultaneously, too much press speculation. Finally, there had been a lack of vision, leadership and unity among the Allies and an equal lack of statesmanship among the German delegation which had 'exerted a disruptive influence on the efforts to advance European coopera-tion'[16]. Inevitably, the failure of Rapallo meant that the German problem throughout 1922 would move rapidly towards the point of major crisis.

The Occupation of the Ruhr

From the first the French had been doubtful of the utility of the Treaty of Versailles alone as a means of ensuring their security. These doubts had been intensified by the cancellation of the Anglo-American guarantee. As Germany began conspicuously to evade the terms of the peace, the French attempted to achieve security through a number of defensive arrangements, firstly, with Belgium in 1920 and then with Poland in 1921. Finally, France linked into the network of the Little Entente in 1924 when she concluded a treaty with Czechoslovakia. And it was security that lay at the bottom of the determination of the French to enforce Germany's compliance with the Treaty of Versailles by occupying the Ruhr.

In some respects the central problem with reparations was not so much French demands upon Germany, which following the London Schedule of Payments were no longer so excessive, but rather the attitude of the United States towards inter-allied indebtedness. Both Britain and France gauged reparations in relation to the amount they owed their creditors. In the tangle of international indebtedness the largest creditor by 1919 was the United States: she was owed substantial sums by Britain, who in turn functioned as a creditor to her continental allies. On international indebtedness, the British view, as signalled in the Balfour Note of 1 August 1922, was that a general or partial cancellation of debts would be the best solution; but the Americans expected to be paid and assumed that Britain would adopt the same attitude towards her debtors. It appears that the French also would have entertained considerably reduced reparations in exchange for substantial amelioration or cancellation of her war debts. In the circumstances, however, they were bound to insist upon reparations, partly to assist the servicing of the loans they had contracted and partly to facilitate the reconstruction of the devastated areas in France.[17]

After having made the first cash payment under the London Schedule of Payments, the German government requested in July 1922 a suspension of further payments due in 1922 and those due in 1923 and 1924. The British were sympathetic, but the French were hostile and the attitude of the United States made it difficult for them to adopt a flexible attitude. If the war debts had to be paid, then, from the French point of view, reparations were a convenient source for funding them. At this critical time, the British government was unfortunately preoccupied with an international crisis, the Chanak crisis, that almost involved a war with Turkey. This and by-election swings against the Coalition Government during 1922, which alarmed Conservative ministers and backbenchers alike, brought about the fall of Lloyd George and a general election. Lloyd George's successor, Andrew Bonar Law, was inevitably less well versed in dealing with matters such as reparations and failed to see the possibilities in the situation that could have avoided a crisis. The principal one was that Poincaré, himself was reluctant to undertake action such as the occupation of the Ruhr in order to guarantee the payment of reparations and would much rather have had a negotiated settlement. By December 1922, however, the Reparations Commission found Germany in considerable default in respect of timber deliveries. In addition, Germany was regularly defaulting on her monthly coal consignments. Finally, there had to be a new plan for cash payments by January 1923 and there was no sign of one. When the Allied and German delegates met on 2 January in Paris, the Germans attempted to divert discussion by suggesting a

Rhineland Pact that foreshadowed the Locarno arrangements of 1925. The British, for their part, advanced a scheme for a four year moratorium on cash and kind payments by Germany that would have meant essentially the cessation of reparations. Neither of these alternatives appealed to Poincaré. On 9 January 1923 the Reparations Commission found that Germany was in default on coal deliveries and voted by a margin of three to one for the occupation of the Ruhr.

This was a course of which the British government openly disapproved, but because of Britain's preoccupation with the Near East there was little that could be done to restrain France. On the other hand, Britain was reluctant to take her opposition to the extent of denying the French use of the railway facilities in the British Rhineland zone, essential for the efficient French occupation of the Ruhr. The German government responded with a policy of *passive resistance*. The object of this was to demonstrate the futility of French demands for *productive guarantees*. It was, however, hard to sustain this posture indefinitely and from the spring of 1923 attempts were made to end the crisis without admitting total defeat. The French, for their part, would not agree to negotiate until *passive resistance* was unconditionally abandoned: what was at issue for Poincaré was the survival of the Treaty of Versailles. The French won this struggle of wills when in August 1923 Gustav Stresemann became chancellor at the head of a *Grand Coalition* of Socialists, Democrats, Centrists and his own party, the German People's Party [DVP]. It was Stresemann who called off *passive resistance* on 26 September.

By this time a return to less confrontational methods was essential. The costs of *passive resistance* had been prodigious and had a most damaging impact on the German currency. Rather than impose taxes on the unoccupied part of Germany, it had been decided to support the population of the Ruhr by printing money with obvious inflationary consequences. The mark, already subject to inflationary pressure as a result of the German government's failure to finance the war adequately out of taxation, now collapsed. Standing at 8,000 to the dollar in 1922, the mark, was valued at one million to the dollar by the time Stresemann became chancellor. In effect, the German currency had ceased to exist. For this reason alone it became necessary to pursue a pragmatic foreign policy rather than an obdurate one. Stresemann's action in putting an end to passive resistance made this possible. In October 1923 the German government itself took the first step towards a realistic settlement of the reparations question when it asked the Reparations Commission to undertake an enquiry into the state of the German economy. The following month the introduction of the *Rentenmark* laid the foundations for the stabilization of the German currency.

The stabilization of the German currency was very much aided and abetted by London and Washington, whence the funding for it came, and its revival contributed partly to a fall in the value of the franc which, in turn, made the French government more amenable to a new international settlement of the reparations issue. The collapse of the franc was also prompted by the realization that reparations could never be an adequate substitute for appropriate French domestic taxation. It was, though, French speculators that brought about the beginning of the slide rather than the Anglo-Americans. In January 1923 the franc had stood at 15 to the $US, but by December 1923 it had fallen in value to 19.21 to the $US, which represented a thirty per cent depreciation. The steady improvement in Germany's currency and the weakness of the franc encouraged the Germans to resist French demands. The French were now at the mercy of Anglo-American creditors and it was only a $US 100 million loan from the American banks in March 1924 that facilitated a temporary stabilization of the franc.[18] There was, however, a condition, namely, that the French should now accept a reparations settlement that accorded more with Anglo-American requirements rather than theirs. This meant acceptance of the proposals of the Dawes Committee on the Payment of Reparations, which reported on 9 April 1924. Overall, the French occupation of the Ruhr was a defeat for France and for the French prime minister, Poincaré, in particular. In undertaking coercive measures against Germany he had undoubtedly wanted to pressurize the British and Americans into collaboration with France in solving the German problem in a manner that suited France, but he had failed as he had also failed in his encouragement of Rhineland separatism, which, had it succeeded would have provided France with a permanent gain. Furthermore, the actual occupation of the Ruhr changed the international perception of France, thus increasing her isolation. She was now regarded as militarist, aggressive and ruthless rather than as the victim of actual and potential aggression. Finally, in May 1924 Poincaré as a result of electoral defeat in May 1924, had to give way to a radical-socialist government headed by Edouard Herriot who was prepared to collaborate with the British in pursuit of a settlement with Germany.

Meanwhile, the American government, which, through the American banks, had at its disposal the necessary financial resources to provide not only the loan that the French desperately required to stabilize the franc, but also the loan to Germany that would be essential in a new reparations package, indicated in October 1923 that it had no objection to American citizens participating unofficially in a committee of experts that would investigate the issue of reparations. The United States government would not, of course, accept direct and official involvement because it was not a signatory of the Treaty of Versailles. This was, nevertheless, a clear indication that American government and financial circles, along with the British, had a profound interest in assisting in the settlement of Europe's economic problems and in rationalizing inter-governmental war debts. Although the French at first opposed the creation of such a committee, they were compelled to agree eventually, under pressure from the British and American governments, to its formation and ultimately its findings. Thus at the end of November 1923 the Reparations Commission appointed two independent committees of experts, one of them to investigate the methods by which the mark might be stabilized and the German budget balanced and the other to examine the payment of reparations. The committees were presided over by the American banker, Charles G. Dawes, and he was assisted by his fellow Americans, Henry M. Robinson and Owen D. Young.

The Dawes Report, or Plan as it is more commonly known, was published in April 1924. It did not make any suggestions as to Germany's total liability, although it clearly indicated a reduction in comparison with the London Schedule. Under the Dawes Plan, Germany's payments were fundamentally fixed at levels that were manageable and realistic with only very modest sums being transferred in the first few years. The regular annuities of 2,500 billion marks were not to begin until 1928–9. Meanwhile Germany was to receive an international loan of 800 million marks, mostly subscribed in America, to assist her in the discharge of her international financial obligations. Moreover, the Dawes Plan provided for the restructuring of Germany's finances and supervision of reparations payments. The American, Parker Gilbert, who was to be the agent general for reparations, was to ensure that reparations did not unduly disturb the stability of the mark and to report on the German economic and financial position. The Dawes Plan marked the return of New York banking to the European market and signified the interest of American financiers in a revitalized German economy that would in turn stimulate the European economy as a whole to the benefit, among other things, of American business.

On 14 April 1924 the German government agreed to negotiate on the basis of the Dawes Plan and at the ensuing London Conference of July and August 1924 it was endorsed by all the governments that had an interest in it. It was also agreed that the occupation of the Ruhr would be terminated by July 1925. By the time the London Conference took place some of the principal actors had changed. As already mentioned, Herriot had replaced Poincaré and since January 1924 Ramsay MacDonald had led a Labour government in which he took personal charge of foreign policy. While the underlying thrust of the foreign policies of Britain and France scarcely changed, both men were more inclined to reach agreement with Germany and to bring the existing tension to an end. This did not, however, mean the end of Anglo–French disagreements which Stresemann, now resigned as chancellor, but still in office as foreign minister, was able to manipulate to Germany's advantage.

The Dawes Plan, in reality, signalled the end of French paramountcy in inter-war Europe. It meant, in effect, that Rhineland separatism, of which France had sought to take advantage, was dead; that France could not again occupy the Ruhr; and that reparations could no longer be secured at the point of a bayonet. Germany had obtained considerable revision to her advantage and the disadvantage of France.[19] From the end of the war onwards French foreign policy had been confronted with a dilemma. Should France accept the limitations of collaboration with Britain, given the reluctance of the British to become too involved in Europe; or should France attempt an independent policy in the style of Poincaré? The failure of Rhineland separatism, the failure to obtain permanent bridgeheads across the Rhine in the Treaty of Versailles and the devastating effect of the occupation of the Ruhr on the French currency all indicated that Poincaré's policy was impossible for France.

In terms of military strategy, French thinking now inclined increasingly towards the defensive and the Maginot Line. From 1919 until 1926 French strategy in relation to Germany had been based upon the offensive, using the occupied Rhineland as a base, but the occupation of the Ruhr demonstrated the limitations of this thinking, in addition to which the occupation of the Rhineland as a whole could not last forever. Moreover, the unpopularity of conscription in France coupled with continuing instability of the franc from 1924 to 1927 dictated a smaller army in the future. In May 1924 the franc stood at 93 to the pound sterling, but had fallen to 164 in April 1925 and to 243 to the pound sterling in July 1926. This had a most deleterious effect upon the French government's finances and, therefore, prompted a need for cuts in defence spending. In these circumstances the ideas of Marshal Pétain, the hero of Verdun in the First World War, triumphed. He proposed a continuous line of fortifications along the Franco-German border to provide for French security after the termination of the Rhineland occupation. In this way security would be combined with economy. Detailed planning for the Maginot Line was authorized by the war minister, Painlevé, in December 1925, and his successor, Maginot, authorized the beginning of construction in 1928. Thus further interventions in the Rhineland were eliminated as an instrument of French policy, which meant also that France would not be able to assist her East European allies by direct incursions into German territory. The Maginot Line itself, by absorbing ten of France's twenty-five army divisions in the 1930s, limited the possibilities of any future offensive strategy. By the mid-1920s French foreign policy was being pushed decidedly in the direction of detente.[20]

If France emerged from the Ruhr occupation weakened, Germany's position was strengthened. The Germany economy almost collapsed as a result of the occupation, but the stabilization of the mark, the Dawes Plan and the associated American loan promoted a rapid recovery and the rationalization and modernization of German business.[21] It was not, however, the kind of recovery that those who devised the Dawes Plan envisaged. It was assumed that reparations would be discharged out of domestic tax surpluses and a favourable trade balance. That is to say, that Germany's exports would exceed her imports. But Germany's budget never showed during the later 1920s the surpluses that had been anticipated and there was a persistent tendency for imports to exceed exports. It was, therefore, American lending that was financing the discharge of Germany's reparation debt and the modernization of its industry. Nevertheless, even if Germany's prosperity during the so-called golden years of the Weimar Republic was based upon an unhealthy dependence on foreign loans and even if the German economy during this period has to be regarded as fundamentally 'sick'[22], the improvement in the economy seemed real enough. It was, therefore, possible for Stresemann to inform the executive of the German People's Party in November 1925: 'I believe the task of any foreign minister today is to take advantage of the world economic situation so as to conduct foreign policy by economic means, as this is the only respect in which we are still a great power.'[23] It was against this background of changed circumstances that Germany and France entered the Locarno era.

Locarno and the Illusion of Peace

If the Dawes Plan signalled the end of French predominance, the Locarno Pacts concluded the following year seemed to herald an era of peace. To contemporaries the Locarno Conference was an important event in international affairs. In its way its impact on British public opinion was almost as significant as that of the Munich Conference some thirteen years later.[24] It offered the prospect, however brief, of a further relaxation in international tension; it brought hope to a continent riven by conflict and despair; but its aftermath was a situation in Europe worse than that which it had sought to remedy. The ultimate failure of Locarno is historically very important in that the system it created was unable to withstand the first shocks administered to it by the world economic depression and then to prevent a further deterioration in relations between the European Powers resulting finally in world war.

The essential reason for the failure of the Locarno system is perhaps to be found in an optimistic belief, particularly in London, that diplomatic instruments could of themselves resolve international problems. Thus it was assumed that the irreconcilable differences between France and Germany which formed the basis of the problem of security in post-1919 Europe could be spirited away at the stroke of a pen in a security pact. This was, of course, to look at the issue from the wrong end of the chain of causation that terminated in a European security problem: an argument that favoured the cure of disease by the eradication of symptoms rather than the cause. Such assumptions during the euphoria of Locarno and the subsequent so-called Locarno Era effectively precluded an examination of the central problem in international relations throughout the 1920s, namely, the role that Germany should play in Europe. It was the failure of Britain, France and Germany collectively to address this issue that lay at the bottom of the collapse of the Locarno system. In practice, agreement on Germany's European role would have meant revision of the Peace Settlement of 1919 in the sense of Stresemann's objective of a 'negotiated rather than enforced application of the Treaty of Versailles'. It is, therefore, clear in retrospect that the Locarno system could only have functioned effectively had it been accompanied by certain concessions to Germany which would have convinced German society as a whole that genuine and friendly co-operation with other European powers would bring certain and swift redress of grievances.[25]

This proved impossible because of the lack of a vigorous and committed involvement on the part of a third party in the dispute between France and Germany over their future relationship with one another in Europe. The disinclination of American politicians to become involved politically in the affairs of Europe precluded the Washington government performing this function, which left Britain as the only power that theoretically could have become involved. But Britain was still mainly preoccupied with imperial and overseas affairs and reluctant to become too committed to Europe and her difficulties. It is also of importance that during the years 1924 to 1929 a foreign secretary held office in London who was temperamentally disinclined to pursue and encourage a deliberate policy of concessions to Germany. Undoubtedly the impact of Sir Austen Chamberlain's pro-French proclivities has been exaggerated, but it is obvious that his suspicions of German policy combined with his firmness and caution made it certain that any concessions obtained by the Germans would be strongly resisted and hard won.[26]

What led to the conclusion of the Locarno Pacts? In examining this issue it is impossible to ignore the personality of Gustav Stresemann and his political attitudes. On resigning as chancellor in November 1923 Stresemann did not leave government, but remained in office as foreign minister, a position he was to retain until his death in 1929. Prior to 1918 Stresemann's attitude in foreign affairs was that of an ardent nationalist. As a member of the Navy League and supporter of the colonial empire, it was natural that when he sought election to the Reichstag in 1907 he should stand as a National Liberal, which in essence was a conservative party. It was, however, his comportment during the First World War that branded him as an aggressive imperialist. He supported the incorporation of Belgium into the Reich; he advocated the expansion of colonial empire; he favoured unrestricted submarine warfare; and he endorsed the massive territorial losses suffered by Russia under the terms of the treaty of Brest-Litovsk, which identified him with Ludendorff. To focus, however, on Stresemann's nationalism in this period is to ignore elements in his political outlook that placed him firmly in the democratic camp. He distrusted the conservatives, whom he blamed for Germany's failure to take a more democratic course in the pre-war period and for the rise of socialism. Nevertheless, in 1918 it was Stresemann's identification with nationalist excesses that were most in the mind of his fellow Liberals and not his democratic credentials. Although he had become leader of the National Liberals in 1917, the majority of the party declined to work further with Stresemann when they formed the German Democratic Party (DDP) with the Progressives. Stresemann, therefore, founded his own German People's Party (DVP). At first this undoubtedly further condemned him in the eyes of the democratically and republican minded, for the DVP was both hostile to the revolution and the republic. Stresemann, though, did not press his claim to power following the 1920 elections when his party gained sixty-five seats in the Reichstag elections, by moving further to the right, but rather by moving to the left. In essence, he sought to strengthen the centre by keeping the DVP in the middle ground of politics. This was a difficult task as the DVP was very conservatively and nationalistically inclined. In addition, it implied a willingness to enter a coalition with republicans and socialists whom the DVP had previously opposed. As a man committed to parliamentary government, however, Stresemann had little alternative. It made of him a *Vernunftrepublikaner*, a republican by reason. Like it or not, as a parliamentarian, he had to accept the Weimar constitution as the basis of the political game.[27]

A realist in domestic politics, Stresemann proved himself also a realist in foreign affairs, the area in which he was to establish a reputation for statesmanship. Unlike many conservative Germans he accepted the reality of defeat. This, however, did not deter him from wanting substantial revision of the peace and he perceived in Germany's fundamental economic strength the means of achieving it peacefully. Undoubtedly Stresemann wanted Germany to assume her *rightful* place in the international order, but his methods of doing so seem sharply to differentiate him from the leaders of the Second and Third Reichs. Stresemann's methods of negotiation, co-operation and compromise might ultimately lead to German preeminence in Europe, but that was a position far removed from domination of the continent by force of arms.[28]

The major obstacle to Stresemann's programme of revision of the Treaty of Versailles was the French preoccupation with security. If further progress was to be achieved and if the French were to be precluded from settling that issue in a manner disadvantageous to Germany, they would have to be satisfied on that count. The French obsession with security was also obstructing efforts to achieve disarmament. In the winter of 1921–2 the Washington Conference had secured a measure of naval disarmament and limitation among the principal naval powers, the United States, Britain, Japan, France and Italy, but progress towards military disarmament remained difficult. The League of Nations with the Draft Treaty of Mutual Assistance of 1923 and the Geneva Protocol of the following year signally failed to bolster the peace by increasing security. Under the Draft Treaty victims of aggression were to be aided by League members, with the League Council specifying particular duties. The Draft Treaty also provided for regional security organizations under the supervision of the League and a disarmament plan. While, with some reservations, the French and other European governments approved this instrument, it was rejected by the British government in July 1924 largely because of imperial objections, particularly from the Canadians, who did not wish to be involved in a war with the United States on account of a third party.

The British prime minister, Ramsay MacDonald, in collaboration with his French counterpart, Edouard Herriot, however, produced a fresh plan known as the Geneva Protocol for the Pacific Settlement of International Disputes. This too attempted to link security and disarmament together with arbitration mechanisms that would determine an aggressor in the event of a violent dispute. Nevertheless, in March 1925 it went the way of the Draft Treaty when it was rejected by the British Conservative government that replaced MacDonald's, objections from the Empire again playing an important part in the decision. Thus the issue of French security remained as pressing as ever. Furthermore, with the election of a Conservative government in Britain at the end of 1924 and the appointment of Austen Chamberlain as foreign secretary, British foreign policy now began to take a decidedly francophile course. Chamberlain was prepared to solve the problem of French security by an Anglo-French alliance.

This, of course, would have been to the disadvantage of Germany. Moreover, such a possibility alarmed the British ambassador in Berlin, Lord D'Abernon. The behaviour of France during the occupation of the Ruhr had caused D'Abernon to develop a very unfavourable view of French policy, which he saw as a threat to the balance of power. France, he thought, was aiming at hegemony in Europe and in Poincaré he perceived the embodiment of the danger to peace. From 1923 onwards, therefore, D'Abernon was very active in promoting the idea of a reciprocal pact of guarantee that, in his view, would lay the basis of a firm peace by guaranteeing the security of all participating powers. To D'Abernon this seemed preferable to a policy aimed at achieving security through the permanent subjugation of Germany, which could only result in an atmosphere of permanent tension and drive Germany into the arms of Russia with war as the inevitable consequence. It was, therefore, substantially as the result of unofficial urging by D'Abernon that in January 1925 Stresemann approached the British government with a suggestion for a multilateral Rhineland pact of guarantee that would solve the French problem of security in a manner least disadvantageous to Germany. Stresemann was reasonably confident of success, for although D'Abernon had exceeded his instructions, the German foreign minister could not believe that an ambassador would act in this way without authority.[29]

At the prompting of Chamberlain, Stresemann also informed the French government of his proposal, but little was done about it until March 1925 when the Geneva Protocol was rejected. Chamberlain now decided to act upon the German proposals as a means of furthering peace and achieving French security. By the time the negotiations that were to result in the Locarno Pacts really began, Aristide Briand had become French foreign minister following the elections that had taken place in France. Briand, with one brief interruption, was to remain in that position until 1932. Thus the trio of individuals who were to dominate European politics in the latter half of the 1920s were all in office. Briand was the most *European* of these three and the most committed to the internationalization of European problems. He had to be, for following the Dawes Plan there was no prospect of France ever keeping Germany in a permanent state of subjugation. The best method, therefore, of ensuring that France would never be subjected again to German attack was to Europeanize the German problem by tying Germany into a European system that would not make it worth her while once again to resort to arms. There was scarcely an alternative to such a policy; if France now tried to enforce any part of the Versailles treaty she risked becoming totally isolated.

After much diplomatic work behind the scenes the statesmen assembled at the Swiss town of Locarno in October 1925. Here a number of treaties were concluded, the principal one being the Rhineland Pact, the Treaty of Mutual Guarantee between France, Belgium and Germany, which was guaranteed by Britain and Italy. Under the terms of this treaty, France, Belgium and Germany recognized their common frontiers as permanent, including the demilitarized Rhineland zone. Moreover, they undertook not to go to war with each other. Disputes would be settled by the League of Nations, which organization would also determine violations of the treaty, except those of a flagrant nature. By recognizing the permanency of the frontier settlement in the west, Stresemann hoped to assure the French of their security, but the German foreign minister would not recognize the same permanency in respect of Germany's frontiers with Poland and Czechoslovakia. Indeed he could not have done so without exposing himself to the most damaging attacks from the right in Germany. Arbitration treaties, therefore, were concluded by Germany with Poland and Czechoslovakia, and France concluded fresh mutual assistance treaties with these states. Nevertheless, the situation created in Eastern Europe by these treaties was not such as to enhance the perception of security among the governments of the region. Stresemann had stated that he did not intend to alter their frontiers by force, but he had also indicated that he could not regard the current territorial arrangements as permanent. Inevitably the provisional nature of the settlement in Eastern Europe suggested by the Locarno arrangements marred the sense of security that the French were now supposed to feel. Furthermore, should an armed conflict break out between one of the French Allies in Eastern Europe and Germany, it would be more difficult now for France to render assistance by counterattacking on the Rhine. Such an attack might be construed as a breach of the Treaty of Mutual Guarantee. Inevitably, therefore, the French system of security had been weakened.

Nevertheless, Locarno was generally greeted with enthusiasm. The signature of the Treaty of Mutual Guarantee was held to mark the end of war and the beginning of peace. Such euphoria was premature. Locarno meant different things to each of the principal powers involved: all of them incompatible with one another and the long term interests of peace. For Germany, Locarno was the beginning of revision, but for France it was the end of it. As far as the British were concerned, Locarno represented the limits of their commitment to Europe. Nevertheless, it was a commitment that was potentially formidable. Not only could the British not rely upon the United States to assist if she was compelled to fulfil her obligations; she could not even rely upon the empire. Under Article 9 of the Treaty of Mutual Guarantee the British dominions and India were not bound by the British obligation unless they specifically wrote themselves in. From the British point of view, a framework for the future of the continent had been established and it was now the task and duty of the continental powers to develop it while Britain reverted to her imperial interests. France and Germany were to work out their own salvation. Many Britons would have endorsed A. P. Herbert's comment that Locarno was *Locarny Blarney* and shared his opinion that:

> The foreigner's an alien,
> He does not rule the waves,
> Give me the good Australian,
> Who cleans his teeth and shaves.

For a time though it seemed that Locarno was working. Despite problems regarding the composition of the League council, occasioned by demands from Spain, Poland and Brazil for permanent seats, Germany finally entered the League in September 1926 with a permanent seat on the council alongside Britain, France, Italy and Japan. Briand, on behalf of the League, welcomed Germany in an effusive speech in which he affirmed the end of bloody Franco-German conflict. The following week such aspirations seemed confirmed when Stresemann and Briand met at Thoiry. What exactly passed between the two men will never be precisely known because the surviving records of their conversation are contradictory. It seems, however, that the two foreign ministers discussed a full and comprehensive settlement of all outstanding differences that would have involved the commercialization of part of the Dawes Plan reparation bonds, namely their sale to private investors with the proceeds mostly destined for France, in exchange for the evacuation of the Rhineland within a year, the return of the Saar, the withdrawal of the Inter-Allied Military Control Commission and the German re-acquisition of Eupen-Malmédy on the German–Belgian border by purchase. This opportunity to improve Franco-German relations was based upon the temporary collapse of the franc. Nothing would come of it. What was proposed was too much for French opinion to endorse and Poincaré, now prime minister, managed to restore the franc by conservative fiscal policies. The grand prospectus of Thoiry was reduced to piecemeal revision and caution returned to Franco-German relations.

On the German side it had never been absent. For the Germans, Locarno did not signify a swing to the west: the Rapallo relationship with the Soviet Union was continued and reinforced by the Treaty of Berlin of April 1926. This was a German–Soviet treaty of neutrality and non-aggression. It was not a sudden manoeuvre for the negotiations that led to it had proceeded simultaneously with those that culminated in Locarno. Its function from the German point of view was, apart from maintaining the Soviet relationship, to reassure the Soviet government in respect of Locarno. Stresemann also had an eye to gaining the approval of those in Germany who favoured the Russian connection.

For the Soviet Union the Treaty of Berlin was an integral part of its *cordon sanitaire* of non-aggression treaties against renewed western intervention.[30] During the 1920s Britain appeared to the Soviet leadership as 'the greatest of the world powers'. She was the 'ultimate enemy . . . the great proud bastion of world capitalism . . .'[31]. While, therefore, the Soviet Union pursued towards Britain an overt policy of obtaining diplomatic recognition and the promotion of trade as a means of constructing the Soviet economy, there was besides the covert policy of subversion both within Britain and throughout the Empire at large. British intelligence was, however, very well informed of this activity and, while Ramsay MacDonald's Labour government of 1924 recognized the Soviet Union, relations between Moscow and the succeeding Conservative government of Stanley Baldwin deteriorated. Incidents such as the Zinoviev Letter[32] and the Arcos Raid culminated in May 1927 in the severing of diplomatic relations between London and Moscow which were not to be resumed until 1930. In this period the last thing that Moscow wanted was the complete integration of Germany into the western or British system. This was why the Soviet Union objected with every means at its disposal to the negotiations that culminated in the Locarno Pacts. They tried to divert the Germans with an alliance directed at Poland. When that failed, they proposed a secret agreement, under which neither party would enter into political or economic alliances with third parties, and which would be accompanied by an understanding that was tantamount to a common policy in respect of the League of Nations. Only when these proposals failed did Moscow suggest a neutrality pact with Germany. Failure to agree to this, it was indicated, would result in the conclusion of an agreement with Poland that would guarantee Germany's frontier with Poland in exchange for Polish concessions regarding the Soviet–Polish border. The Germans, though, did not allow themselves to be deflected from their course. In order, however, to make the reality of Locarno less grievous for the Russians they concluded a commercial treaty with the USSR in October 1925. Moreover, as part of the Locarno package, it was agreed that if Germany joined the League she should be exempt from Article 16 of the League Covenant, under which she would be expected to contribute to sanctions against aggressors and to allow transit facilities through her territory for Armies discharging League obligations. As a formally disarmed state Germany could not, of course, be expected to endanger herself in this way. But the real reason for the concession on Article 16 was the need to reassure the Soviets regarding German policy. In any case, Stresemann certainly had no intention of allowing Germany to participate in League sanctions against the Soviet state. The German–Soviet relationship was crucial for the independence of German policy and the gaining of further concessions from the western powers. The value of the Soviet relationship for Germany was emphasized in April 1926 when Treaty of Berlin was signed.[33] Understandably this treaty caused considerable alarm to France and her Allies in Eastern Europe.[34]

France and European Union

It would be wrong to dismiss French policy in the later 1920s as obstructionist and unimaginative and lacking in any constructive thrust. On the contrary, it can be argued that Briand and the French government pursued a constructive policy that might have avoided war in the future had it found a more favourable response in Britain and Germany. In the autumn of 1918 Jules Cambon, former French Ambassador in Berlin, warned: 'France victorious must grow accustomed to being a lesser power than France vanquished.'[35] Here was an implicit recognition not only of the fundamental superior economic and military power of the German state, but also of the growing economic threat from across the Atlantic. In 1920, Professor Demangeon of the Sorbonne published Le Declin de l'Europe. This book indicated that one of the consequences of the First World War was a shift of the global centre of economic activity away from Europe and towards the United States. Indirectly, the book was a powerful statement of the need for collective European economic action. French politicians soon became keen enthusiasts for European union. In the purely political context, they were motivated to a considerable degree by the desire to solve the German problem in a manner most agreeable to France. If Germany could be brought into a European system from which she herself would derive economically considerable benefit, she would have little interest in resorting to war again and even perhaps in undoing the verdict of Versailles. The first French politician to proclaim the desirability of European federation was Edouard Herriot in October 1924. In January 1925 he declared in the French Chamber of Deputies: 'My greatest desire is to see one day appear the United States of Europe.' Subsequently, Briand was to become the French politician most associated with the European idea. For Briand and the French the European concept was essentially defensive and a strategy for peace. In many respects it was a continuation of the ideas associated with Clémentel at the end of the war.

In May 1930 Briand circulated the European powers with a scheme for a European Union. In order to allay American fears that it was designed to resist American economic power, which to a certain extent was part of the motivation, it was given a primarily political character. The Briand Plan, however, failed because the powers whose support might have led to its success were at bottom unenthusiastic. Britain was cautious of any European initiatives that might threaten her economic interests, compromise her imperial role or cut across her League obligations. For its part, opinion in Germany demanded substantial revision of the peace as a precondition of any moves towards integration. Indeed in Germany the right argued that acceptance of the Briand Plan would preserve the frontiers imposed upon Germany by the Treaty of Versailles in perpetuity. In all circumstances, the support of Britain would probably have been most critical for the success of the Briand Plan and in this respect it is significant that the British ambassador in Berlin, Sir Horace Rumbold, was of the opinion that acceptance of the Briand Plan by Britain might have compelled the German government to follow suit. It may, therefore, have been an opportunity lost; equally it may have been an idea ahead of its time. But judging from the reaction of Britain to the Schuman Plan in 1950 and the negotiations that led to the foundation of the Common Market in 1957, such ideas were always premature.[36]

The End of Reparations

By the time Briand submitted his scheme Stresemann was dead. Stresemann had himself not been overtly hostile to Briand's suggestions; but whether he could himself have continued to conduct a rational foreign policy against the increasing nationalist current in Germany must be open to doubt. On the eve of his death Stresemann had secured for Germany a further diplomatic success and revision of the peace, but not on terms which met with universal approval among German opinion. While in Paris in August 1928 for the signature of the Kellogg–Briand Pact, a treaty which owed its origins to one of Briand's initiatives and which outlawed war, but provided no means for enforcing its objective, Stresemann and the French prime minister, Poincaré, met for general discussions during which it was agreed in principle that early evacuation of the Rhineland could be accomplished in exchange for a fresh reparations settlement. During 1929 a committee of experts chaired by the American banker Owen D. Young produced a report which considerably reduced the annual payments Germany would pay under the Dawes Plan and fixed the date for final payment as 1988. The conditions, however, under which exemptions could be granted made it extremely unlikely that the full sum would ever be paid. In return for accepting the Young Plan, the Germans wanted both evacuation of the Rhineland and the return of the Saar. Neither Britain nor France could agree to this latter point, but neither could the newly elected minority Labour government in Britain endorse the conditions on evacuation of the Rhineland required by the French. Instead the British government urged unconditional evacuation. Moreover, the British chancellor of the exchequer, Philip Snowden, was adamant that Britain's share of the payments under the Young Plan should be revised in Britain's favour. Out of this unpromising scenario an agreement of sorts was hammered out at the Hague Conference of August 1929. Germany accepted the Young Plan, the Allies agreed that their occupation of the Rhineland would terminate by 30 June 1930 at the latest and the Young Plan was slightly modified in Britain's favour. German dissatisfaction was, however, registered in a referendum on the Young Plan which, while endorsing the new reparations arrangements, produced an opposition vote of almost six million. Significantly, the campaign against the Young Plan brought the Nazi Party to national attention for the first time. The following year the NSDAP was to achieve its decisive breakthrough in the election of 1930 when it increased its representation to 107 seats, becoming the second largest party in the Reichstag.[37]

Over the next three years both the Young Plan and the Briand Plan were engulfed by the reality of world economic depression and growing extremism in national and international politics. The Briand Plan was talked out of existence in a League Committee and at the Lausanne Conference in 1932 the Young Plan and reparations were effectively terminated. Meanwhile, the apprehension that the French and other nations felt with regard to German revisionism was revealed in 1931 when the Germans attempted to effect a Customs Union between themselves and Austria. While this technically did not amount to the *Anschluss* forbidden under the Treaties of Versailles and St. Germain, it was recognized as a major step in that direction. The Customs Union project, however, clearly violated the Geneva Protocol of 1922 which had determined the form of Austria's financial reconstruction and under which Austria's economic independence was not to be compromised.

During the period 1929 to 1931, France was in an unusually strong position. For various reasons the impact of the world economic and financial crisis was not immediate in France. Her economy was still experiencing a certain buoyancy from the era of post-war reconstruction and was in any case less dependent upon industrial exports than the economies of Britain, Germany and the United States. Even so industrial production by the end of 1929 had risen to a new high and the balance of trade was exceptionally favourable. Furthermore, in the wake of Poincaré's stabilization of the franc Paris had become a safe haven for capital. By 1930 the reserves of the Bank of France had risen to 80,000 million gold francs. All this gave France a considerable financial advantage over other powers – even Britain because of the weakness of sterling. In 1931 this position was made even more formidable as a result of the collapse of Austria's largest bank, the Credit-Anstalt, on 31 May. This enabled France to exercise her financial leverage and the Austro-German Customs Union Proposal was referred to the Permanent Court of International Justice at The Hague. By a majority of one the Permanent Court decided in September 1931 that

Austrian economic independence was compromised by the Customs Union project and it was abandoned.

The prime minister of France during 1931 was Pierre Laval and under his leadership France did attempt, in respect of Germany, an independent policy based upon her temporary financial advantage, although it was never pressed home. The weakness of the German mark during the summer of 1931 put future reparation payments in question even before 20 June when the American president, Hoover, unilaterally proposed a one year moratorium on intergovernmental debt payments. The French government, sensing that this would mean the end of reparation payments, delayed their acceptance of the Hoover proposal and in the interim attempted to reach an agreement with the Germans regarding future payments. But even though the Germans were in a hopeless financial position, they could not accept the French terms for a settlement and a loan of $500 million, namely, the suspension of all claims of a political nature for ten years. There were a number of reasons why the Laval government failed to capitalize on its advantage. Many of Laval's colleagues were cautious and felt that time would work to the advantage of France. In addition, there was a further consideration: 'Exercising financial diplomacy carried high risks because France as both creditor and debtor was in an ambiguous position. Insistence on securing reparations from a near-bankrupt Germany seemed avaricious; footdragging on interallied debts looked like a means of funding armaments.'[38]

Whatever the legalities, the decision of the Permanent Court in the matter of the Austro-German Customs Union scarcely rallied German opinion to the cause of international collaboration. Throughout 1932 Hitler's juggernaut gained momentum. He came second in the presidential elections that year on a second ballot and in the Reichstag elections of July and November 1932 the NSDAP secured 230 and 196 seats respectively. It was now the largest party in the Reichstag. Although it would be wrong and simplistic to ascribe the collapse of the Weimar Republic solely to the frustrated revisionism of the German people, there can be little doubt that the programme of the NSDAP, which demanded the dismantlement of the Treaty of Versailles, worked to Hitler's advantage.

Complications in the Far East

Meanwhile, a serious conflict had erupted in the Far East between China and Japan. For most of the 1920s under the direction of Shidehara Kujiro, Japan pursued an internationalist policy in China that claimed to respect China's right to determine her own future. Shidehara sought to preserve Japanese rights in Manchuria and China as a whole through a policy of conciliation and compromise, as was shown in his attitude towards the Chinese demonstrators responsible for the Thirtieth of May Incident in Shanghai during 1925, in which Chinese demonstrators were killed outside a police station in the foreign quarter of Shanghai. This occurrence and its aftermath illustrated profound xenophobia in China that was directed against the Japanese as much as other foreigners. Shidehara believed that a violent response to this would only increase the anarchy in China and expose the country to the attractions of Chinese Communism. Instead Shidehara agreed to a tariff conference that would return tariff autonomy to China. The Peking Tariff Conference did agree in principle to confer tariff autonomy on China in 1929 and even composed a graded tariff schedule, but the conference ultimately broke up without the conclusion of a general treaty. This was partly the result of the final collapse of the Peking government in 1926 and partly the result of a failure of the principal parties, Britain, the United States and Japan to reach a sufficient measure of agreement between themselves. According to one writer this signalled the beginning of the demise of the Washington System:

> For all practical purposes the Washington powers had ceased to function as a group by the fall of 1926. The vaguely defined 'spirit of the Washington Conference' had not been sufficient to ensure coordination of action among the principal powers. Their different interests in China were stronger than their interest in cooperation to found a basis of postwar international relations. They felt that their interests could better be safeguarded and promoted through bilateral arrangements with China rather than through multilateral agreements. They were thus unwittingly putting an end to one act of the Far Eastern drama and ushering in the next.[39]

The collapse of the Peking government meant that the southern based *Kuomintang*, in which Chiang Kai-shek was now the dominant personality, could attempt to control the whole of China. Shidehara did not attempt to oppose this. He held that it was for the Chinese themselves to determine their own system of government, although Sino-Japanese co-prosperity was to be based upon respect for Japan's economic rights in Manchuria and the safety of Japanese citizens and businesses in China as a whole. But Shidehara's conciliatory policy was now coming under sustained attack from the Japanese Army which resulted in the downfall of the government of prime minister Wakatsuki in April 1927 and its replacement by one headed by Tanaka Gi'ichi. Tanaka was his own foreign minister and he promised to reverse Shidehara's policy. Japanese nationals in China, he asserted, would be protected by Japanese soldiers and not by the rhetoric of Chiang Kai-shek. In practice, however, his policy differed little from that of Shidehara and he was prepared to recognize the authority of the *Kuomintang* in all China with the exception of Manchuria and Shantung. There was, however, a problem. The Manchurian warlord Chang Tso-lin, who enjoyed the support of the Japanese Army in Manchuria, the Kwantung Army, had aspirations to rule the whole of China and he was determined to establish himself in North China. This, though, cut across Tanaka's policy of compromise with Chiang Kai-shek. Tanaka thus put pressure upon Chang Tso-lin to withdraw from Peking into Manchuria and to recognize the authority of the *Kuomintang* in the rest of China. Tanaka at the same time agreed that, while *Kuomintang* forces would not be permitted to enter Manchuria, the Chinese flag should fly there in recognition of Chinese sovereignty.

This angered officers of the Kwantung Army, who did not want the Chinese flag flown. They feared also that Chang might now fall in with the *Kuomintang* and wanted his army disarmed before it re-entered Manchuria. Tanaka, however, would not agree to this, prompting an incident in which

Chang's train was blown up by officers of the Kwantung Army after it entered Manchuria resulting in his death. The officers of the Kwantung Army were of the opinion that this action would provoke disturbances among the Chinese leading to a situation in which Japanese forces could occupy the whole of Manchuria. This, however, did not occur, for Chang's son, Chang Hsüeh-liang, maintained order among his followers and completed his father's withdrawal. Moreover, he very soon learned the true story of his father's death and became an ally of the *Kuomintang*. Far from having secured Manchuria for Japan, the Kwantung Army had placed their domination of the territory under threat. Worse was to follow for the conciliatory Shidehara returned to office in 1929 as a result of Tanaka's fall from the premiership following his refusal to name the officer responsible for the assassination of Chang Tso-lin. At the London Naval Conference of 1930 the Japanese government accepted the extension of the 5:5:3 ratio, previously agreed for battleship tonnage at the Washington Conference, to cruisers. In fine detail the agreed package was more favourable to Japan than appeared on the surface, but not sufficiently so to satisfy the government's critics. For Japan's nationalists this perpetuation of Japan's naval inferiority was an unacceptable betrayal. In addition, it caused a major split in the Japanese Navy. Against the fiercest opposition the London Naval Treaty was eventually ratified, but at the cost of the life of the Prime Minister, Hamaguchi.

The militant nationalism that was now taking hold of Japan was reinforced by the impact of the world economic recession. Many workers in the urban areas lost their jobs. The fall in the price of silk and rice brought about grievous rural distress. The capitalist system itself attracted strong criticism . Among the military there was now a mood which favoured a military coup against a government which appeared weak and irresolute. The army wanted two things: internal political reform and the preservation and maintenance of Japan's position in Manchuria. The latter, though, assumed priority status. Fearing that the Japanese government, and particularly Shidehara with his aim of working with the Chinese, would obstruct this aim, it was decided to take pre-emptive action and on 15 September 1931 the Kwantung Army destroyed a section of the South Manchurian Railway at Mukden with explosives. Asserting that the Chinese were responsible for this, the Kwantung Army rapidly occupied the whole of Manchuria. In March 1932 the Japanese proclaimed the 'independent' state of Manchukuo. During January 1932 the fighting had extended to Shanghai. For Britain this was an ominous development since the bulk of Britain's Chinese investments were located there.[40] The Ten Year Rule was now rescinded. In Washington the United States government responded to the crisis with a policy of non-recognition which was to remain the sheet anchor of American policy towards Japan for the next decade.[41]

The prospects for the Disarmament Conference which opened on 2 February 1932 could not, therefore, have been more depressing. By the end of the year it had almost collapsed and was only saved by the Five-Power Declaration of 11 December that recognized Germany's claim to 'equality of rights in a system which would provide security for all nations'. The fact of the matter though was that by 1933 the hopes that had been engendered by Locarno seemed a distant dream. Furthermore, the Washington System in the Far East was now clearly disintegrating. Nevertheless, the search for peace and security in Europe would continue, albeit in increasingly disadvantageous circumstances.

4

The Challenge of Fascism and the Democratic Response

While the first major challenge to the international system during the 1930s occurred in the Far East, developments in Europe were to be most critical from the point of view of the maintenance or collapse of world peace. Increasingly the European political struggle in this period within states and between them assumed the nature of an ideological contest in which the alleged virtues of dictatorship were pitted against the virtues of parliamentary democracy. The states which tried to preserve peace in the 1930s were essentially those that remained committed to parliamentary democracy. Their task was not eased by what had been throughout Europe since 1919 a steady drift towards dictatorial forms of government all of which, with the exception of the Soviet Union, were fundamentally conservative and right-wing and frequently characterized by an intense nationalist and expansionist dynamic. This was particularly true of the states which adopted a form of government, increasingly popular in the inter-war years, which is usually described as *fascist*.

Fascism was not, however, universalist in the sense that communism was and was always characterized by national traits. It was, therefore, particular-ist and nationalist and not for export. This did not, of course, preclude alliances between fascist regimes, especially of an anti-communist/bolshevik nature. Neither did it rule out expansionism, particularly of a colonialist character where, as in the case of Italy, such expansionism formed part of the history of the country concerned. But, although fascism, given its obsession with national identity and self-assertion, was incompatible with the concept of international community, few fascist states indulged in the fantasies of their leaders' rhetoric. In practice fascist regimes tended to abide by the conventions of international law and society. Expansionism was usually restrained by the nationalist conceptions inherited from earlier regimes and the fear of defeat. The exception to this general rule was national socialism which was expansionist and anti-semitic to an extent that no other fascist regime was.

Italian Fascism

The first manifestation of this type of regime appeared in Italy during the 1920s. Mussolini and his Fascist Party were able by 1922 to seize power largely as a consequence of deep divisions within the Italian state that had been hastily, and in some respects artificially, contrived between 1860 and 1870. Italy was a country very clearly divided between the poverty-stricken, primitive, agrarian south and the industrialized and modernized north, characterized by the cities of Milan and Turin. There was also a bitter conflict between church and state: the Roman Catholic church, its seat in the Vatican, refused to recognize the Italian state, to which it had lost virtually all its sovereign territory during the unification process. Finally, the industrialization and urbanization process ensured that Italy was wracked by class conflict.

From 1870 onwards the ruling liberal groups had sought to provide Italy's parliamentary regime with some sort of stability through *trasformismo*, a sort of consensual government that incorporated the demands of opposition factions. In essence, Italian politics at this time were founded on interest groups and the most successful politicians were those who were able to construct broad coalitions by attaching opponents to their own factions through the promise of political favours. This system, however, proved ultimately to be immensely corrupt and ineffective in international affairs, with an attempted conquest of Abyssinia in 1896 ending in ignominious defeat at Adowa. At the turn of the century an effort was made by conservative politicians, led by General Pelloux, to strengthen the executive in an authoritarian direction so that it could more effectively suppress strikes and riot and pursue an active and successful foreign policy. The right, however, was not able to overcome the constitutional left, led by Zanardelli and Giolitti, which secured a notable election victory in 1900. Giolitti, speaking as minister of the interior, announced, in essence, the governmental programme for the rest of the pre-war period when, in referring to a strike in Genoa, he stated:

> The rising movement of the ordinary people increases daily; it is an invincible movement, because it is based on the principle of equality between men. No one can delude himself that he is capable of preventing the common people from winning their share of economic and political influence. Friends of institutions have one duty above all: to persuade these classes, and to persuade them with deeds, that they can hope for far more from existing institutions than from dreams of the future.[1]

Between 1900 and 1914 Giolitti was to be the dominant figure in a number of ministries. The period was characterized by a number of progressive measures and governmental neutrality in industrial disputes. In 1912 manhood suffrage was conceded with a view to reconciling the workers to the liberal parliamentary system.

Giolitti, though, was in reality perpetuating the old system, referred to as 'the government of evil' by Gaetano Salvemini.[2] However enlightened

Giolotti's policies, they could not ultimately prevent the regime being discredited in the eyes of the public. This process was assisted by the growth of nationalism in Italy before 1914 and the perceived failure of the system, in the eyes of the nationalists, to maintain Italy's national honour and interests. Even the acquisition of Libya as a result of war with the Ottoman Empire did little to assuage the demands of the nationalists who felt that Italy should have extended the war. Inevitably, criticism of the conduct of the Libyan war blended into criticism of the jobbing politicians and their system.

These criticisms were intensified during the First World War. Instead of assisting her Allies, Germany and Austria–Hungary, Italy at first remained neutral for which there was a majority in parliament and the country. The Italian parliament was, however, prevailed upon by nationalist demonstrations throughout Italy to surrender its neutralist inclinations and succumbed to the conviction that it was unfitting for a major European power to stand idly by. As one commentator has observed: 'Intervention betrayed a growing habit of mind in Italy to give priority to action at the expense of thought: under the fascists this was to be elevated into a dogma.'[3]

Intervention did little to save the reputation of the liberal, parliamentary regime, which was blamed for the mismanagement of the war and the misery that war inevitably brings. By 1918 the overwhelming majority of Italy's citizenry was alienated from it. The problems of government in post-war Italy were worsened by the superimposition of the electoral system of proportional representation on the manhood suffrage already conceded in 1912. The new parliamentary situation made the maintenance of stable government impossible by the traditional methods of *trasformismo*. Two mass parties had now emerged, the Socialists and the Roman Catholic Popolari, neither of which could function as the foundation of a government. The Socialists were divided amongst themselves and distrusted as revolutionaries; the Popolari, also divided, had to contend with the Vatican's suspicion of any dealings with the secular Italian state. In the circumstances, *trasformismo*, even operated by Giolitti, who returned to government after 1918, failed to produce a stable administration with any authority and legitimacy. To the instability of the government was added popular resentment of the peace as it affected Italy.[4] Mussolini and his fascist movement were able to exploit the shortcomings of this system and its perceived failures.

Italy was afflicted in the immediate aftermath of the war by severe unemployment and inflation. Between 1920 and 1921 there was a 500 per cent increase in unemployment and prices increased by 50 per cent. The inevitable consequence of this was social unrest which manifested itself in strikes, lockouts and peasant occupation of large estates. It seemed that property was being assailed by Bolshevism. At first it might have appeared that Mussolini's Fascist Movement, founded in Milan on 23 March 1919, was ill-suited to take anything other than the most conventional advantage of the situation, for the fascist programme had a radical character, as befitted a former socialist leader such as Mussolini, that declared opposition to the monarchy, church and capital. But this was deceptive in that from the first the Fascist Movement was essentially right-wing, allied as it was with nationalist groups such as the *arditi*, elite troops of the Italian Army who were known for their courage, brutality and patriotism. Mussolini, moreover, had broken from the Socialists initially over his desire for Italian intervention in the First World War and at the centre of fascism there was an ineluctable policy of national self-assertion in the form of demands for Fiume, Dalmatia and colonies. Finally, there could be no ambiguity about fascism's hostility towards socialism. This made fascism immediately attractive to the propert-ied classes who supplied the fascists with their expenses in the hope that their *squadre* would coerce the strikers and recalcitrant peasantry. For his part, Mussolini wanted money and he wanted power and he was prepared to adjust his views and aims to acquire both. Eventually the economic policy of fascism became *liberal*, republicanism was abandoned and following the election in 1922 of Pope Pius XI, with whom Mussolini already had good relations, the church withdrew its support from the Popolari on the grounds that socialism was more likely to be effectively resisted by the fascists.[5] Fascism, therefore, soon made its peace with the monarchy, the church and capital.

Although fascism was not at first very popular electorally, the action of the *squadre* in driving socialist governments out of cities and towns illegally prompted Giolitti to make an attempt to harness fascism to the cause of the government. In the elections of 1921 thirty-five fascist candidates, including Mussolini, were elected as part of the national list of government-backed candidates. Inevitably, the Italian establishment was conferring upon fascism an aura of respectability. This, however, made little difference to the tactics of Mussolini. In the Italian parliament the fascists sat with the nationalists, but they would not desist from the use of force. Although by 1922 the revolutionary threat had vanished in Italy, Mussolini was still able to play upon the fear of bolshevism. In August 1922 the socialist administration of Milan was expelled by the *squadre* and there were attacks upon the towns of Bolzano and Trent. Confronted with this situation the liberal politicians displayed an alarming paralysis. Skilfully, Mussolini held out the prospect that the fascists might participate in a government coalition, but what he really wanted was exclusive power. On 24 October 1922 in a speech in Naples, Mussolini declared: ' . . .either we are allowed to govern, or we will seize power by marching on Rome . . . [to] . . . take by the throat the miser-able political class that govern us'[6]. Five days later, after the somewhat myth-ical 'March on Rome' Mussolini was appointed prime minister by the king.

Mussolini was to remain in office for twenty-one years. Although his regime implied the maintenance of law and order at home, it was not immediately evident what it meant for the international community. Gradually though, Mussolini's writings and speeches made it clear that fascism was potentially disruptive of international order. Written in the 1930s, Mussolini's *Doctrine of Fascism* reveals that the regime was predicated on the notion of perpetual conflict. He wrote:

> As far as concerns the future development of mankind, quite apart from all present-day political considerations, Fascism does not on the whole believe in the possibility or utility of perpetual peace. Pacifism is therefore rejected as a cloak for cowardly supine renunciation as against self-sacrifice. War alone keys up all the energies of man to their greatest pitch and sets the mark of nobility on

those nations which have the bravery to face it . . . all doctrines which postulate peace at any price as their premise are incompatible with Fascism.[7]

Mussolini also starkly emphasized the ideological gulf that separated fascism from bourgeois democracy. Fascism rejected party politics: it was not itself 'a party, but anti-party and a movement'[8]. The ethos of democracy was totally rejected:

> Fascism points its guns at the whole block of democratic ideologies and rejects both their premises and their practical application and methods. Fascism denies that numbers as such may be the determining factors in human society; it denies the right of numbers to govern by means of periodic consultations; it asserts the incurable and fruitful and beneficent inequality of men, who cannot be levelled by any such mechanical and external device as universal suffrage. Democratic regimes may be described as those under which the people are deluded from time to time into the belief that they are exercizing sovereignty, while all the time real sovereignty belongs to and is exercised by other forces, sometimes irresponsible and secret.[9]

Fascism was anti-individualistic and recognized the 'individual only in so far as his interests coincide with those of the State, which stands for the consciousness and universality of man as an historic entity'. He continued:

> . . . Fascism stands for . . . the only liberty worth having, the liberty of the State and of the individual within the State. The Fascist conception of the State is all-embracing, outside of it no human or spiritual values may exist, much less have any value. Thus understood, Fascism is totalitarian and the Fascist State, as a synthesis and a unit which includes all values, interprets, develops and lends additional power to the whole life of a people.[10]

Such ideas were naturally alien to the bourgeois democracies of Western Europe and the Social Darwinism and confrontational language of Mussolini's writings suggested a conflict between fascism and democracy at some stage.

This did not happen immediately. During the early years of the regime a peaceful foreign policy was pursued that exploited fascism's success in having suppressed bolshevism at home and established public order. The fascist state was considered an important bastion against the spread of bolshevism in Europe and, therefore, to be esteemed. The high point of this early period was Italy's presence at Locarno in 1925 and her signature of the Locarno Pact as a guarantor. Nevertheless, Mussolini had already behaved in a reckless manner towards Greece over the murder of an Italian member of a boundary commission working in that country. The subsequent Italian bombardment and occupation of Corfu elicited an apology from Greece, but, owing to British insistence upon withdrawal, the objective of permanent occupation was not realized. Much more characteristic, however, of Mussolini's conduct of foreign policy in this early period was his attitude towards Yugoslavia. Like many Italian nationalists Mussolini loathed Yugoslavia because of her disputed possession of Dalmatia. But the inclination to destroy that state was mitigated for the time being by the knowledge that it was impossible to achieve and the desire to penetrate Yugoslavia economically, which was a particular aim of Italian industrialists. In 1924, therefore, Italy concluded a Treaty of Friendship with Yugoslavia.

Nevertheless, Italian diplomacy was becoming more bellicose by the end of the 1920s. Italian verbal aggression was directed principally against Turkey, Abyssinia, Yugoslavia and France. While in Western Europe relations with Britain remained cordial, there were numerous potential causes of conflict with France. The French protectorate of Tunis contained more Italian colonists than those of French origin and the frequent threat on the part of the French authorities to abolish Italian rights in the protectorate was an issue that could permanently be manipulated. In Central Europe Mussolini regarded the Little Entente as a means of French penetration of the Danube Basin and an obstacle to Italian ambitions in the area. He tried unsuccessfully to break it by bringing one of its members, Rumania, into an association with the defeated powers of Eastern Europe, namely, Hungary and Bulgaria. Even more irritating from Mussolini's point of view were the Italian anti-fascist exiles in Paris, whose political and propaganda activity he resented. Increasingly, Franco-Italian relations assumed the form of an ideological feud between democracy and fascism. In April 1926, for example, during a visit to Libya Mussolini referred to the Mediterranean as *mare nostrum* (our sea) which was a clear challenge to France and, to a lesser extent, Turkey.[11]

Mussolini, however, was careful not to be too belligerent and to adopt a reassuring posture when necessary. In 1928 Italy concluded a Treaty of Friendship with Abyssinia and in June of the same year he made a peaceful speech which contained a moderate programme of revision. But these manifestations of peaceful intent belied the reality of Italian foreign policy which essentially aimed at war and expansion. By 1925 Mussolini was clear that the objectives of Italian foreign policy were power and the foundation of an empire. Peace was folly; no stigma could be attached to strength. He declared his intention to construct an air force that would 'dominate the skies' and he wanted Italians to feel as though they were permanently engaged in war. Imperialism and revisionism, therefore, were the *leitmotifs* of Italian foreign policy in the 1920s as much as they were in the 1930s. Mussolini scorned the conventional methods of diplomacy and sought to make trouble where he could, not least by the internal subversion of states regarded as Italy's enemies. What restrained him in the 1920s was lack of economic and military power and 'the lack of any counterbalance to effective Anglo-French dominance in Europe'[12]. What he required was a solvent of the existing order that would allow him to embark on war with security. In the meantime, he maintained a degree of fluidity in international relations by pursuing a policy that alternated conciliation with bellicosity. The solvent of the international order was to be Nazi Germany.

National Socialism

Badly as the consequences of the First World War affected Italy, the trauma was much greater in Germany. At least Italy was a victor power. Germany, on the other hand, had been defeated and that defeat had come hard upon an expectation of victory which had been nourished over a period of four years. The reality of the German military position following the failure of the Schlieffen Plan to subjugate France rapidly in 1914 had been successfully concealed from the Reichstag and German public opinion. Some clearly understood that Germany's defeat was the consequence of German failure,[13] but much of Germany's citizenry easily absorbed the myth of the *Dolchstoß*, the stab in the back. How else could the collapse of an army, hitherto undefeated in the field, be explained except as the consequence of betrayal on the home front by liberal and socialist politicians? Given the wide acceptance of such an attitude, the terms of the Treaty of Versailles appeared all the more humiliating. It is evident that for German society as a whole and the National Socialists in particular the revision of the Treaty of Versailles was a pressing consideration.[14]

There were, however, in Germany, beneficiaries of defeat. Towards the end of the nineteenth century there had emerged in Germany a backward-looking attitude of mind which combined 'hostility to urban life and to Jews' with 'a romantic yearning for a mythical past, in which heroic and racially pure Germans lived together without class bitterness' in a *Volksgemeinschaft* or folk association. This *völkisch* ideology had emerged in a society made deeply anxious by the pace of change and modernization in Germany following unification in 1870. Industrialization and urbanization came to represent uncertainty and an all too abrupt break with tradition. *Völkisch* ideology was a compound of many things, of which naturism and Wotan worship were minority preoccupations, but it permeated broad swathes of the German middle-classes and its Darwinian concepts of the survival of the fittest and the associated belief in the racial and cultural superiority of the German people penetrated deeply. The excessive nationalism and anti-semitism of *völkisch* ideology was well-represented in the Pan German League of the Wilhelmine period.[15]

Nevertheless, prior to 1914 the popularity of *völkisch* ideology was on the wane. What gave it renewed life was the defeat of Germany and the nature of the peace. The worst fears of the *völkisch* right seemed to have been realized. Defeat had brought liberalism and a democratic constitution to the fore. Governments composed of parties that had formerly been in opposition were now in office. In addition, Germany was in a state of appalling international humiliation. Inevitably the forces of the left were linked with national shame and dishonour; the forces of the right with patriotism and tradition.

These conditions proved exactly the right environment for the growth and development of *völkisch* organizations all over Germany. They were particularly prevalent in Bavaria where the Munich-based *Thulegesellschaft* provided an umbrella organization for them. Among these *völkisch* groups was Anton Drexler's German Workers Party [DAP]. On 12 September 1919 Adolf Hitler, now an army informer, was sent to observe a meeting of this group; it was to change his life. Although attending the meeting as an observer and informer, Hitler made a speech 'in favour of a greater Germany' which 'thrilled' Drexler and all those who heard it.[16] Subsequently, Hitler was persuaded to join.

Born in the Austrian town of Braunau-am-Inn in 1889, Hitler's early life was a story of almost unremitting failure. In 1913 he left Vienna for Munich in order to escape military service. During the First World War, however, Hitler served with bravery in the German Army being decorated with the Iron Cross, both first and second class. A victim of a gas attack, he was convalescing in Germany when he learnt of Germany's defeat. This was for him a desolating experience; on his own testimony, it was the point at which he determined upon a political career. But there was little evidence at that time of what was to come. Even Hitler's commanding officer felt that he could not be recommended for promotion on account of his deficiencies as a leader.[17]

In both Vienna and Munich Hitler had absorbed the ideas of the *völkisch* movement. An avid reader of newspapers and pamphlets, he argued the issues which aroused him with his fellow inmates in the hostels in which he resided. In this way he honed the oratorical skills for which he was later to become renowned. Because of these skills Hitler became by the end of 1919 the propaganda chief of the DAP. Workshy of regular employment, Hitler could devote himself exclusively to politics and soon began to dominate the party. It was he, with Drexler, who wrote the twenty-five point party programme that was accepted in February 1920. In the same month the party changed its name to the National Socialist German Workers Party (NSDAP). The following year Hitler became leader of the party after a power struggle with Drexler over the fusion of the party with other *völkisch* organizations. There ensued the subordination of the entire movement to the dictates of the party's Munich headquarters.

The party continued to develop in Bavaria and South Germany and in 1923 became involved in a violent attempt to seize power. When the Stresemann government in September announced the ending of passive resistance regarding the Franco-Belgian occupation of the Ruhr, it seemed to Hitler as a portent of communism in Germany. In Saxony and Thuringia socialists and communists were co-operating in government and in October 1923 an abortive communist rising took place in Hamburg. The government acted quickly to end the threat of a rising in Saxony and Thuringia, but this had little impact on the insubordination of Bavaria regarding the central government. Following the cessation of passive resistance, pressure from the *Kampfbund*, an organization led by Hitler that comprised the NSDAP and other right-wing paramilitary groups, had compelled the Bavarian government to declare a state of emergency along with the appointment of Gustav von Kahr as state commissioner with dictatorial powers. The response of the Reich government was to declare a state of emergency throughout Germany. Although both the *Kampfbund* and the Bavarian authorities, led by Kahr, shared similar authoritarian objectives, namely, the overthrow of the Republic, the latter was more cautious, particularly after the firm action taken by Stresemann against the communists. As leader of the *Kampfbund*, however, Hitler was under pressure to fulfil the revolutionary expectations of his followers. Thus on the evening of 8 November 1923 he attempted to compel the Bavarian civil and military authorities to join him in 'the national revolution'. This was the beginning of the so-called Munich *Putsch*. From the start, however, the Reichswehr was opposed to this action; it was thus doomed to failure. On 9 November Hitler, in a last bid to rescue his venture, marched with his supporters into the centre of Munich where they were dispersed by the army and police.

The consequence of the failure of the *Putsch* was that Hitler and his fellow conspirators were tried for high treason before judges who were sympathetic to their motives. After a period of what is best perhaps regarded as involuntary leisure, Hitler was released from Landsberg Prison in December 1924. He then set about reorganizing the party which began to extend its organization throughout Germany. In 1926 Hitler successfully impressed his authority on the entire movement when at the Bamberg Conference he dissuaded a North German Working Group associated with the Strasser brothers and Joseph Goebbels, which wanted to stress the socialist aspect of the party, from altering the party programme. At the conference Hitler also stressed the need for legality in the NSDAP's bid for power: democracy was to be destroyed by its own mechanisms.

By the end of the 1920s the NSDAP was a truly national mass party. This development had been aided not least by the national exposure given to the NSDAP by its participation in the campaign against the Young Plan. The inspiration behind the campaign was Alfred Hugenberg, a newspaper magnate, who had profited from the electoral failure of the German Nationalist Party (DNVP) and its financial difficulties by moving it to the right and imposing upon it his anti-democratic and anti-republican views. In order to maximize his effort he enlisted the aid of Hitler and the NSDAP and thus brought the party to the attention of the entire nation through his newspapers. In 1930 the party succeeded in its first electoral breakthrough when its Reichstag representation increased from twelve to one hundred and seven in the elections of September that year.

During his imprisonment, Hitler began writing *Mein Kampf*, volume one of which was published in 1925 and two in 1927. The following year saw the completion of *Hitler's Secret Book*, which, however, was not to be published until the late 1950s with an English translation appearing in 1961. These items together with *Hitler's Table Talk*, *Hitler's Political Testament* and his speeches give a clear indication of what national socialism, once installed in power in Germany, meant in the field of foreign policy.[18] The first three articles of the Official Programme of National Socialism demonstrated that at the very least substantial territorial revision of the Treaty of Versailles would alone satisfy the NSDAP. These stated:

> 1. We demand the union of all Germans to form a Great Germany on the basis of the right of self-determination enjoyed by nations.
> 2. We demand equality of rights for the German people in its dealings with other nations and abolition of the Peace Treaties of Versailles and St. Germain.
> 3. We demand land and territory (colonies) for the nourishment of our people and for settling our superfluous population.[19]

Article one obviously implied severe modifications to the frontiers of Poland and Czechoslovakia which could only have been achieved by force. Article two was a demand for the union (*Anschluß*) of Germany and Austria, forbidden under the peace settlement.

The most disruptive article potentially was the third. What Hitler and the NSDAP meant by colonies was spelled out in *Mein Kampf* and in his later writings and utterances. He stated in *Mein Kampf*:

> We National Socialists consciously draw a line beneath the foreign policy of the pre-war period. We take up where we broke off six hundred years ago. We stop the endless German movement to the south and west and turn our gase towards the land in the east. At long last we break off the colonial and commercial policy of the pre-war period and shift to the soil policy of the future.

Hitler did not mean colonies in the conventional sense. *Soil policy* meant territorial acquisition and this land, for the German colonists of the future, was to be found in Russia. In Hitler's view, the Bolshevik revolution had destroyed the only creative element in Russian society, namely, the German and replaced it with 'the Jew'. The Russians themselves were not able to throw off the Jewish yoke, but this was not a task beyond the German nation. The Jew was a 'ferment of decomposition' and could not sustain the organization of a vast empire for any length of time. Russia, the Soviet Union, was ripe for dissolution. The German nation had been 'chosen by Fate as witness of a catastrophe which will be the mightiest confirmation of the soundness of the folkish theory'. Hitler continued:

> Our task, the mission of the National Socialist movement, is to bring our own people to such a political insight that they will not see their goal for the future in the breathtaking sensation of a new Alexander's conquest, but in the industrious work of the German plough to which the sword need only give soil.[20]

The central object of Hitler's foreign policy was, therefore, the acquisition of *Lebensraum*, or living space, principally in the Ukraine. (The German word *Lebensraum* is frequently mispronounced by English speakers as 'Leebensrowm'. This would indicate to a German *Liebensraum*, or a space in which to make love. The word should be pronounced 'Laybensrowm.') This policy of acquiring living space would also aim a mortal blow at bolshevism and world Jewry which through the Soviet Union was attempting to dominate the non-Jewish world. Thus the conquest of *Lebensraum* was designed also to eliminate two mortal enemies of the German nation.

Undoubtedly, malignant anti-semitism was a central feature of Hitler's programme. It was not, however, the only requirement in Hitler's mind for the long term health of Germany. He was convinced that the spiritual decay of Germany in the pre-1914 period was connected with industrialization and urbanization. Cities for Hitler were 'abscesses in the national body' in which 'all evil, vice and disease' were united. In his *Table Talk* he expanded upon the virtues of the rural life. The peasant was 'the solid backbone of the nation', for the uncertainties of making a living from the land taught 'energy, self-confidence and the readiness to make swift decisions', whereas the city-dweller had to have everything done for him.[21] The acquisition of

Lebensraum was essential, therefore, not only from the point of view of settling the surplus population, but also because of the need to redress the balance between the industrial and agricultural sectors in German society.

Lebensraum was also related to Hitler's concept of the process of world history, which he saw in terms of the rise and fall of states and empires. In a very real sense he attempted to impose upon contemporary Europe the processes of the *Völkerwanderung*, namely, the migration of the peoples of the first Christian millennium. Young, expanding nations, such as Germany, according to Hitler, could only secure their food supplies through the conquest of additional land. For some historians the ultimate objective of Hitler's policy was German domination of the globe. What, however, is beyond speculation is that the acquisition of *Lebensraum* in the Ukraine inevitably meant war, as did almost certainly its essential precondition, namely the achievement of implied German hegemony in non-Soviet Europe.

The one power that Hitler really feared was Britain. His racial-biological concepts, nevertheless, persuaded him that the 'Teutonic' British could perhaps be prevailed upon to acquiesce in these developments. Peace with Britain was in fact pivotal to Hitler's strategy for the conquest of *Lebensraum*. He hoped to achieve this by assuring the British that Germany would present no threat to Britain's imperial and overseas interests. Whether Hitler intended later to demand an overseas empire is still a matter of some conjecture, but it is clear that for the medium-term future he rejected *Lebensraum* in the Cameroons, or any other part of Africa, as secondary to its attainment in Europe. What is quite apparent from *Mein Kampf* and his other writings is that Hitler saw alliance with Britain, or at least the latter's benevolent neutrality, as essential to the isolation and destruction of France, the necessary preliminary to a march to the East.

What is suggested here is an outline of Hitler's foreign policy concepts as they had developed by 1928. If one accepts that he had a foreign policy programme and a plan for the expansion of Germany, it is evident that a national socialist regime in Germany meant war. But even for some of those historians who dispute that Hitler had a plan, war was integral to Hitler's purpose. He '. . . willed, wanted, craved war and the destruction wrought by war'[22].

The Democratic Response

The war that broke out in September 1939 was not exactly the war that Hitler had wanted. This was the consequence of the decision on the part of the democracies in the end to resist further alterations of the map of Europe as the result of violent action by Germany. What this meant was that France was not isolated and could not be eliminated at leisure as a prelude to the conquest of the Soviet Union. More importantly it meant that Britain had elected to oppose Germany, which it had been the object of Germany's policy to avoid. What led to this situation?

The French decision to oppose Germany was ultimately very contingent upon the attitude of Britain. For internal, structural reasons it was not possible for French governments to pursue a lone policy of outright confrontation towards Hitler and his demands. Moreover, it was not automatically assumed in Paris in 1933 that Hitler would embroil the world in a further war. The nazi regime did not, therefore, provoke in France an immediate attitude of belligerence. Indeed the attitude of France remained pacific and for a very practical reason. The huge losses of manpower sustained by France in the First World War meant quite simply that she could not afford the luxury of a further bout of warfare. Furthermore, there was amongst the French peasantry, who had borne the major cost in terms of blood and lives of the 1914–1918 war, a profound distaste for war and a disinclination to be led into it again. Pacifism was not confined to the ruralities of France. Both pacifism and anti-militarism were to be found among the French socialists and syndicalists who represented the interests of the French industrial workers. Pacifism found its clearest expression in the French Socialist Party where disarmament was widely regarded as the simple key to universal and perpetual peace. At the beginning of the 1930s Léon Blum, one of France's most notable socialist leaders, articulated, in a book entitled *Les Problèmes de la Paix* (1931), the virtues of disarmament through the League of Nations as a means of achieving not only security for France and revision of the Treaty of Versailles, but also economic recovery.

Reluctance to go to war, particularly with Germany, was not an exclusive phenomenon of the left. A number of extreme right-wing groups, many of them united in admiration of Mussolini and fascist Italy, were equally hostile to war. Organizations such as Charles Maurras' *Action Française*, the *Parti Populaire Français* of Jacques Doriot, and the *Croix de Feu* were particularly anxious not to embroil France in a war in which she would be an ally of the Soviet Union. As Pierre Taittinger the leader of the fascist *Jeunesses Patriotes* stated: 'I have been against anything that . . . could defend Bolshevism or check fascism . . .'. On the eve of war in 1939 the right indulged in a pro-German propaganda campaign which it was hoped would lead to the destruction of the bolshevik enemy both within and without France. Following the dismantlement of Czechoslovakia in 1939, the French right urged the British government to begin negotiations with Germany and to do nothing that would impair the cause of anti-communism. *Action Française* for its part warned of the dangers of a Jewish plot to involve France in a war with Germany that could only benefit the Jews.[23]

It would, however, be wrong to exaggerate the power of fascism and the fascist threat in France during the 1930s. The crisis caused by the Stavisky Scandal in 1934 clearly revealed its limitations. The suicide of the corrupt financier Serge Stavisky in January 1934, which had been brought about by police enquiries into allegations of fraud, caused a sensation, not least because of his apparent association with leading politicians; it also provided an opportunity for the extraparliamentary right in France openly to criticize and challenge the parliamentary regime of the republic, which they considered corrupt. On 6 February 1934 representatives of the far right demonstrated outside the Chamber of Deputies and the demonstration soon transformed itself into a riot in which there were fatalities as a result of police action. The situation was so serious that the prime minister, Edouard Daladier, who himself had only recently replaced his predecessor, Camille Chuatemps, in order to resolve the situation precipitated by Stavisky's suicide, resigned and was replaced by Gaston Doumergue. For long afterwards there was a conviction on the part of Republican politicians that there existed in France a co-ordinated conspiracy in the part of the far right to bring down the republic and institute in its place a fascist or national socialist regime, but the truth was rather less fantastic. The fascist or quasi-fascist right in France could perhaps force the resignation of a prime minister, but it was really too 'fragmented, incoherent and badly co-ordinated' to bring down the republic itself.[24]

Nevertheless, France was clearly a divided nation, not easily led into supporting a risky foreign policy. Furthermore, there was little in the international situation to encourage France to take up a policy of firmness. The British government refused to guarantee the peace settlement in Eastern Europe which had serious implications for the French alliance system. Inevitably France gradually lost the initiative and diplomatic leadership of Europe. Temporization gave way to inaction and inaction ended in appeasement. The French had failed to solve the German problem by coercion in the 1920s and latterly by persuasion in tying Germany into a European system with the Briand Plan. After 1933 Hitler finally presented the formulators of French policy with an intractable problem once he withdrew from the Disarmament Conference and the League of Nations. Disarmament could no longer provide security for France in the long term, but neither could a preventive war, had the will to carry one out existed and the means of successfully conducting it been available. An attack on Germany would have broken the entente with Britain and terminated the Locarno guarantee of French territorial integrity. It was simply not practical politics. In April 1934 the French government in recognition of the failure of the Disarmament Conference announced that France would in future ensure her own security. This was a declaration in effect that France would achieve security through rearmament; but, despite these brave words, in the end, the French government was constrained by the limitations imposed by British policy.

This is not, however, to claim that French policy lacked all independence, or to deny the existence of those in France who favoured resistance. Among journalists Wladimir d'Ormesson in Le Temps at the beginning of 1933 warned of the duplicity of the Hitler regime, which, he argued, wanted war. He not only stressed the importance of resisting every German demand, but also, and significantly, emphasized that French diplomacy should avoid the pitfall of isolation.[25] Within the army high command both General Weygand and General Gamelin wanted the strengthening of France's military defences. Weygand was opposed to the disarmament plan presented by the British Prime Minister, Ramsay MacDonald, in March 1933 and later in that year argued that France should reoccupy the bridgeheads of the Rhine. Neither Gamelin nor Weygand, however, were imaginative enough to pursue the proposals put forward by Captain de Gaulle for the transformation of the French military machine into a body capable of resisting German aggression.

De Gaulle dismissed fortification as an adequate means of defence and deterrence. The Maginot Line, a system of fortified zones along the Franco-German frontier begun in 1928, was in the mind of de Gaulle no substitute for a professional and modernized army of 100,000 men that should be well-equipped, motorized and armoured.[26] The central difficulty, however, with de Gaulle's *Vers l'armée de métier*, published in 1934, was that it conflicted with the traditional view of the army as the nation-in-arms, with the republican concept of the citizen army, the *levée-en-masse*. Moreover, there was a further problem with a small professional army. It was felt by some that such an organization might empower the right to carry out a coup. As the socialist leader, Léon Blum, suggested, national independence might be safeguarded at the price of liberty.

French diplomats also, such as André François-Poncet, the French ambassador in Berlin, were well aware that the only effective way to stop Germany rearming was by war. This, though, Poncet realized, was impossible for France, because such action would have to be taken in isolation and would end in isolation. Instead he proposed that France should endeavour to limit the extent of German rearmament by agreement. Jean Dobler, the French consul-general in Cologne, in a sense summarized the feelings of the resisters when, reporting on the plebiscite in Germany of 12 November 1933, called to endorse Hitler's decision to withdraw from both the Disarmament Conference and the League of Nations, he wrote: 'The world can only save itself and Germany from a bloody fate by making this mass – which is already recklessly on the move – feel a sense of danger, because it has lost the idea of risk.'[27]

It was, however, the politicians who clearly illustrated the limitations of resistance. The French foreign minister in 1933, Paul-Boncour, was a man whose inclinations towards the use of force were never far below the surface. Over the issue of the Saar Territory he opposed any kind of arrangement with Germany and even suggested, together with General Weygand, regarding the plebiscite to be held to determine the future of the Saarlanders, that all efforts should be made to persuade them to vote against reunion with Germany. Edouard Herriot too advocated firmness and André Tardieu in *L'Illustration* argued the case of internal recovery through constitutional reform and external recovery through a tough policy towards Germany. But virtually every politician who advocated firmness shied away from the only means that would have stopped German rearmament, namely, preventive war. This was well illustrated in Georges Mandel's great speech in the Chamber of Deputies in November 1933 in which he presented a frightening picture of German rearmament and suggested that the government inaugurate an investigation of German armaments under article 213 of the treaty of Versailles. Mandel, however, did not propose a preventive war. As Henry Lemery put it: 'Preventive war, no one thinks of it and the very word fills us with horror.'[28]

The real problem with firmness in France in the 1930s was that those who advocated it saw British support and co-operation as essential. This, however, was not forthcoming for the British would not until the very end of the 1930s assume further commitments on the continent and declined to respond positively to French invitations to co-operate against German rearmament. General Weygand illustrated the fundamental problem for the advocates of firmness when he proposed a preventive war, but insisted upon the necessity of British moral or naval support. Nevertheless, the tradition of firmness enabled the French government to join with the British in resistance in September 1939, despite the continuation of pacifism and division in French society. Moreover, as the crisis of the 1930s progressed some individuals and groups abandoned their previous pacifism and joined the resisters.

In France the communists led by Maurice Thorez were alarmed at the way in which Hitler destroyed the German communists and during 1934 began to advocate a common front with the socialists against fascism. Left-wing socialists such as Marceau Pivert and Jean Zyromski responded with enthusiasm and in this way the Popular Front was created. This action by the French communists was given official approval by the seventh and final Comintern (Communist International) Congress that took place in Moscow in the summer of 1935.[29] By 1935 the socialist leader Léon Blum was beginning to realize the impossibility of peaceful coexistence with fascism. Having previously opposed provocative alliances, he came to support the Franco-Soviet Pact which Laval concluded in April 1935 and after that year voted for military appropriations. He also supported sanctions against Italy when she invaded Abyssinia on the grounds that it was the morally correct thing to do, for resistance to Italy might also deter Germany in the future. There remained, however, within the French Socialist Party a strong pacifist tendency that was not finally defeated publicly until the national congress of the party in December 1938. While Blum and the Socialist Party endorsed the Munich Agreement in early October of that year, in contrast with the communists who would have nothing to do with what they regarded as 'an act of brigandage,' the socialist leader had been initially reluctant to see Czechoslovakia destroyed. Blum's early opposition to the German threat to Czechoslovakia was founded not merely on the fact that France was committed to defend that country and the justice of the defence of Czechoslovak liberty. What Blum perceived in the German attitude towards Czechoslovakia was a menace to the freedom and independence of the whole of Europe. In the post-Munich period this perception reasserted itself and Blum now argued strongly in favour of a close relationship with Britain and the Soviet Union. German and Italian fascism were to be checked by a democratic bloc. On the left of the Socialist Party, Zyromski went even further. He was prepared to use force and to employ all means to bring international fascism to a halt. At the Socialist Congress on 24 and 25 December 1938 the resisters outvoted the traditional pacifists by 4,322 votes to 2,837.

But, whatever the mood in France, what determined whether or not France in fact ultimately resisted was determined by British policy. There were many reasons why France had become reliant upon Britain. Financial crisis in the mid-1930s was one. Within France, fear of a Popular Front government and a desire to take advantage of an economic upturn in the United States, provoked a flight of capital from France during the mid-1930s.

From May 1935 until June 1936 between eleven and thirteen million francs were exported from France. At a crucial point, therefore, the French holders of capital deprived France of the resources necessary for her real political independence. This had the effect of making French governments both financially and politically dependent on Britain and America. By the end of 1938 the French financial crisis was over, but it is not unreasonable to ask whether or not this was an additional reason why France had been forced 'to resign herself, willingly or unwillingly, to the appeasement favoured by the British'[30].

What was appeasement? For many years it was accepted that appeasement was a policy associated with the government of Neville Chamberlain who became prime minister in May 1937. In the public mind it was indelibly connected with the Munich Conference and the shameful sacrifice of Czechoslovakia to the demands of German policy. Appeasement and Chamberlain became synonymous with concession and weakness. Unavoidably appeasement was seen thereafter in terms of Munich rather than Munich being considered, as it ought, in terms of appeasement. Without seeking to minimize its drama and public impact, the Munich Conference was only an episode in the policy of appeasement and cannot in isolation properly indicate the aims of the British government during the 1930s. In addition, appeasement was not a phenomenon peculiar to Neville Chamberlain or the 1930s. It would indeed be misleading to imply that there was any change in the fundamental aim of British policy during the inter-war years. The basic aspiration of British policy – the organization and maintenance of world peace – remained constant throughout the 1920s and 1930s and a settled Europe free from tension and strife was essential to any global regime of peace. Moreover, the means of attaining that end – revision of the peace settlement as and when necessary –remained unchanged. From the moment the Treaty of Versailles was signed, British policy was revisionist. What happened after 1930 was that the British government increasingly envisaged the necessity of revision on an hitherto unprecedented scale, deemed that an active role on its part was essential to this process and perceived that the time for enacting these revisions was short. In doing this, the British government was not merely reacting to events in Europe, but also acting on the advice of those in Britain who had condemned the deficiencies of the Treaty of Versailles and their impact on European stability from the beginning.

Prior to the signature of the Treaty of Versailles, British reservations concerning the peace began to manifest themselves. John Maynard Keynes, a member of the British treasury team at the Paris Peace Conference, resigned his position over the terms of the draft treaty. He later published his reservations in his book, *The Economic Consequences of the Peace*: he envisaged nothing short of total economic dislocation in Europe as a consequence of the deliberate impoverishment of Germany. Although Keynes was strong in criticism of the part played by Lloyd George in determining the peace settlement, the position of the British prime minister was in truth not far from his own. In his *Fontainebleau Memorandum* of March 1919, Lloyd George warned of the dangers of treating Germany unfairly. She could turn bolshevik or worse if the peace arrangements could not commend themselves as just to the German population.

In Britain feelings of indignation were soon aroused once the peace terms were published. A reaction soon set in in academic and journalistic circles that began to doubt atrocity stories, theories of German war guilt and to question the whole climate of anti-Germanism. H. N. Brailsford had been in Germany in the early months of 1919 and in 1920 he published his depressing predictions of the consequences of Allied treatment of Germany in a book entitled *After the Peace*. According to Brailsford the Treaty of Versailles was an impediment to the success of democracy in Germany; those who signed it would come to be regarded as traitors. The well-known historian of Germany, W. H. Dawson, began a campaign for the revision of the peace settlement in Germany's favour that lasted throughout the inter-war years. During the early 1920s he was hopeful of a tripartite pact of reconciliation between Britain, France and Germany based on concessions by the former two on reparations and territorial, economic and commercial issues. He argued that if this were done Germany 'would at once undergo a peaceful transformation and the outlook for all Europe improve as a consequence as by magic'[31].

Dawson's views represented, although often in extreme form, the convictions of many among the foreign policy-making elite in Britain. These convictions were not based exclusively on sentiments of fair play. As a trading nation Britain's economic recovery during the 1920s and after the depression was directly connected with world recovery for which a climate of peace was essential. This was precisely expressed in the British Defence White Paper of 1935 which stated: 'The first and strongest defence of the peoples, territories, cities, overseas trade and communications of the British Empire is provided by the maintenance of peace.' For writers such as J. L. Garvin and Norman Angell the importance of a revived and contented Germany to a restored world economy and peace was axiomatic. The most influential exponent of this line of thought though was Keynes. In *The Economic Consequences of the Peace* he emphasized that European economic prosperity was contingent upon German economic prosperity. On the other hand, he argued, the peace arrangements only served to impoverish Germany.[32] Keynes' simple and compelling arguments soon provoked a revolution in British attitudes. Within the educated section of British society the peace settlement found few supporters and many opponents.

In many ways nothing better illustrates the attitude of the educated classes towards the problems of peace and war in the inter-war years than the foundation of the *Royal Institute of International Affairs* [RIIA]. For the founders of this organization, people such as Lionel Curtis and Lord Lothian, war was an abomination that could be eliminated by the scientific (by which they meant impartial and academic) study of international affairs and the communication of the results to the widest possible public. Foreign policy, they felt, could no longer be left safely in the hands of the exclusive elites that staffed the foreign ministries of the various nations. Education and information were the means by which effective democratic control of foreign policy could be asserted. Thus the RIIA, or Chatham House as the organization became colloquially known after its acquisition of those premises in St. James's Square in the late 1920s, began publishing numerous scholarly studies on international problems. Its permanent and continuing work, however, was the publication of annual volumes of *Surveys* and *Documents on International Affairs*. These were edited by Professor Arnold J. Toynbee, who was the director of studies at Chatham House until the 1950s. In addition Chatham House published a journal, *International Affairs*, which contained the records of the discussion group meetings at the RIIA that were attended by journalists, members of parliament and other influential personages.[33]

Toynbee was an individual whose life had been very much affected by the First World War and his personal experience of the Greco-Turkish conflict at the beginning of the 1920s. In his memoirs he later recalled that the human waste and misery he had witnessed compelled him to devote his life to work that would contribute to the avoidance of future wars. This was how he regarded his work on the annual *Surveys*: by providing the materials necessary for informed discussion, he was assisting in the creation of an atmosphere in which relationships between states could be conducted upon a rational basis.[34] This sounds very naive today, but it would be wrong to belittle the extent to which Toynbee's contemporaries believed that frank discussion and concession between governments would preserve peace. Indeed this was the very assumption on which visits to Hitler by British ministers in the 1930s was based. Revision of the Peace Settlement, therefore, based upon economic self-interest and morality lay very much at the bottom of the appeasement mentality in Britain during the inter-war years.

It took time, however, for appeasement to enter fully into the practice of government in Britain. In the years after 1919 the British government sought to gain international co-operation for the creation of a peaceful climate in Europe that might provide the basis for the resumption of normal economic activity. This led the British government into a revisionist posture as far as the economic and financial aspects of the peace were concerned. Inevitably this resulted in a certain degree of involvement in the affairs of Europe that was not always to the liking of politicians, for whom the empire was Britain's most pressing and primary care. After Locarno it was hoped that Britain could safely leave Europe to solve her own problems, but by the early 1930s it was clear that detachment could not attain the objectives of British policy. The European situation worsened and Britain in her own interests was compelled to involve herself in the affairs of the continent.

Within the British foreign office, two officials, Orme Sargent and Frank Ashton-Gwatkin, outlined the implications of such involvement in a cabinet paper of November 1931. It was argued that the security of Europe could be left to France and her Allies, which would mean the maintenance intact of the present system and the exaction from Germany of further concessions through the application of economic and military pressure. This though could not result in long term security and confidence. In the short term it would certainly mean the paramountcy of France, but ultimately the continued friction and tension would merely create more insecurity. On the other hand, there was the possibility of general international agreement and action in which all European states, including Britain, would make further contributions towards an atmosphere of confidence and security. There were risks in such a course for Britain, but geographical and economic factors made it inevitable.

This paper had been specifically written in connection with the opening of the Disarmament Conference in 1932. Its major theme was the contention that disarmament could not be considered in isolation. Political, economic and financial issues were now inescapably intertwined. The authors offered the following analysis of world problems:

> The present world 'confidence crisis' can be analysed as a series of interlocking problems, ranging from the purely financial and monetary problem at the one end to the purely territorial problem created by the Peace Settlements at the other end. The links in the chain fall together more or less in the following order. The *monetary crisis* leads inevitably back to the *economic chaos* in Europe. The economic chaos and all attempts to deal with it, involve in their turn the political questions of *reparations and war debts*. These are linked by the United States with the question of *disarmament*, and the latter, in the eyes of the French Government, depends upon the problem of *security*. The problem of security in turn raises the question of the *territorial status quo* in Europe . . . which brings us to the *maintenance of revision of the Peace Settlements*. We thus have a whole range of interlocking problems, and, no matter at what link we touch the chain, we cannot find any satisfactory halting place until we have reviewed this whole series of problems.

For Sargent and Ashton–Gwatkin the broadening of discussion should be welcomed, for in that way disarmament might be successful. They identified the aims of British policy as peace and the restoration of confidence and world trade; the object of French policy was security. But the success of both British and French policy rested upon the fate and future of Germany. Germany was the pivot of the European economy, but until she had sufficient capital to mobilize her own economy there could be no improvement. They wrote: 'World recovery . . . depends on European recovery; European recovery on German recovery; German recovery on France's consent; France's consent on security . . . against attack.' Thus the two officials recommended what in effect was a general revision of the peace settlement: an ' "all–in" settlement', the minimum for which would be a very substantial reduction in reparations, disarmament, guarantees of security and the rectification of frontiers.[35]

The connection between these ideas and those advanced by journalists and expert commentators during the 1920s is evident. In essence the argument was based upon the notion that extremism in Germany was the consequence of Germany's economic strangulation. Nazism and fascism were the manifestations of an economic disease: eradicate the disease and its political symptoms would disappear. These concepts as presented by Sargent and Ashton–Gwatkin were, however, too all–embracing to be taken up by the British government immediately. But, as the crisis provoked by Hitler's assumption of power deepened, the government was compelled to consider precisely the approach recommended by the officials rather than the policy of dealing with the German problem on a piecemeal, case by case basis, as had hitherto been the practice. The aims of Hitler's Germany were anticipated as being much the same as those of previous German governments, although it was accepted that they were now being more urgently and vigorously advanced. Hitler had in fact brought the totality of the peace settlement into question in an unprecedented manner and British policy had to respond to this fact. Encouraged once again by the foreign office, it became the basic principle of British foreign policy from the end of 1935 onwards to seek a *European and general settlement* that would in effect replace the peace settlement of 1919 and bring all the European states into satisfactory treaty relations with one another. This was what was meant by appeasement: the pacification of Europe through discussion and negotiation. Germany was, of course, the focus of such a policy which was intended to create the circumstances in which Hitler could behave like the bourgeois German politicians of the 1920s. Fundamental to the policy was the notion that nazi belligerence could be defused by offering Germany economic prospects that would lead her to prosperity. It was Anthony Eden as foreign secretary who first introduced this policy in 1936. He anticipated that Germany could be induced to agree to a disarmament convention, to return to the League and to renounce all further territorial claims in return for the remilitarization of the Rhineland, some measure of colonial satisfaction and economic priority in the Danube basin. In the subsequent development of this policy Neville Chamberlain, as chancellor of the exchequer, played a significant part and he continued it during his premiership. It was not a policy based upon surrender, but rather one based upon the application of reason to international affairs. This is not to say that perceptions of British weakness and German strength and the desire to play for time until Britain was suitably rearmed played no part in the formulation of this policy.[36] On the other hand, if war came Britain would fight. But war for Britain would in all probability mean world war because of her global commitments: a war of attrition and of long duration the cost of which would be potentially ruinous. War, therefore, should be avoided.

There were, however, serious flaws in this strategy by the mid-1930s. It presupposed that Hitler would himself want to maintain the peace and be susceptible to the traditional bargaining and compromise of international affairs. Secondly, it assumed that nazi extremism was fundamentally economically motivated. On both counts the formulators of British policy grievously miscalculated. The Nazi Party might have been carried into power on a tidal wave of economic discontent, but in essence it was a purely political movement and its political objectives were strikingly different from those of its immediate predecessors. Economic concession could never have deflected it from its course, nor political concessions diverted Hitler from the path he had rigidly prescribed German foreign policy should take under his leadership. But just as British policy-makers miscalculated, so did Hitler. His assumption that Britain's friendship was attainable on the basis that Germany would be allowed an effective hegemony in Europe, in return for the recognition of British imperial predominance, seriously offended the British sense of the balance of power.[37] Once the British government apprehended that the brutal domination of Europe was what Hitler intended, the resistance of Britain was inevitable. In a very real sense the war that came in 1939 was based upon the mutual misperceptions made in

London and Berlin in 1933 and thereafter, regarding each other's foreign policy, and the mutual miscalculations based upon those misperceptions.

The Attitude of the United States

So far the examination of the democratic response to the fascist challenge in the 1930s has focused upon its European aspect. It is, however, important also to consider the response of the United States to the phenomenon of fascism, because the foreign policy that the United States adopted in the 1930s was a material factor in determining the policies that Britain and France were to pursue. The knowledge that the First World War could not have been won by the Allies without the enormous financial power of the United States was a sobering influence once the United States Congress in the 1930s began to pass neutrality legislation.[38]

Although writers such as William Appleman Williams have forcefully argued that *isolationism* is an inappropriate term to describe the foreign policy of the United States during the 1920s[39], 'a pronounced isolationist tradition endured in the 1920s and gained strength in the 1930s.'[40] Led by isolationist politicians, such as Senators Vandenberg and Nye, and encouraged by press magnates, a very substantial sector of American opinion was more than ever disinclined to involve America in European affairs. This situation was not improved by the default of Britain and France on war debt payments. In 1934 Congress passed the Johnson Act, under which the extension of credit by the United States government was forbidden to states continuing to fail to meet their obligations to American creditors. Inevitably this made it difficult for Britain and France to facilitate their rearmament by purchasing weapons and machine tools in the United States.[41] The Johnson Act was supplemented by neutrality legislation between 1935 and 1937 which, in addition to banning all arms sales to belligerent states, precluded them from raising loans or credits in the United States for the purchase of other materials.[42]

The isolationism of the United States at this juncture was also reinforced by the impact of the world economic recession at the beginning of the 1930s. In January 1933 Franklin D. Roosevelt assumed office as President of the United States. He was himself very much an Anglophile and in the ideological struggle in Europe during the 1930s his sympathies were not neutral; the European democracies, Britain and France, were clearly preferable to the nazi dictatorship with its racialist doctrines. On the other hand, he was primarily occupied during his first term in office with the New Deal, the programme of domestic recovery from the depression, and the restoration of economic confidence. What, therefore, tended to characterize American foreign policy at this time in both Europe and Asia was 'drift and indecisiveness'[43].

In Asia the Roosevelt administration continued the policy of non-recognition of changes brought about by aggression that had been instituted by its predecessor. This meant that the puppet state of Manchukuo, created by the Japanese following their conquest of Manchuria in 1931–2, would continue not to be recognized by the United States and that the American government would continue to uphold the policy of maintaining the 'Open Door' in China and preserving her territorial integrity. Nevertheless, the passage of the Silver Purchase Act in the United States in 1934 was scarcely calculated to strengthen China, for by authorizing the United States treasury to purchase silver at an artificially high price this Act damaged the Chinese currency which was based on silver. The metal drained out of the country and the Chinese yuan lost its metallic base. The United States government naturally had not intended this to happen, but the episode indicates the lack of direction that was characteristic of the administration's dealings in Asia and elsewhere at the time. As far as Europe was concerned, there was much moral condemnation in America of national socialism and even demands that Germany should be subjected to a trade boycott. However, the administration did little. Besides, there was little it could do decisively to buttress the European democracies against the fascist dictatorships, even had the will to do so existed in the Congress and the country at large, for the American armed forces throughout the 1930s were inadequate for the task. The United States Navy was of a similar size to the Royal Navy, but deployed mostly on the Pacific coast. There was no independent air force and the army was pathetically short of motorized equipment, having to make do with make-believe tanks in training manoeuvres as late as 1940. While America was capable of assisting the democracies economically and financially, 'military intervention was not an option available to the American administration before Pearl Harbor'[44].

Generally speaking, it is diffcult to disagree with the view that the first Roosevelt administration 'echoed the isolationist sentiment of the public and emphasized the avoidance of trouble . . .. The world was becoming unhinged, and America was not assigning itself the task of resuscitating it.'[45] For the British government the American attitude was alarming. In January 1936, Sir Robert Vansittart, the permanent under-secretary of state at the foreign office, indicated in a minute just how alarming it was. He wrote: 'We only just scraped through the last war with Germany with every assistance we could get from the USA. The deduction is plain . . . In any crisis of life and death . . . this might well mean our "death".'[46] Although from January 1937 onwards, the second Roosevelt administration began to become more active in international affairs, the nature of a possible American contribution to the containment of fascism remained vague in the minds of Europe's democratic leaders. In July 1937 President Roosevelt suggested to the British prime minister, Neville Chamberlain, that he visit the United States to discuss international affairs. The latter rejected the idea with the celebrated words: 'It is always best and safest to count on nothing from the Americans but words.' The damage had been done. In formulating policies towards the dictatorships in the 1930s the democracies assumed that there would no help from the United States. This explains to a large degree why they were to leave no stone unturned in their quest for peace.

5

The International System
Challenged, 1933–1936

Hitler's main preoccupation on achieving power was not the communication of the precise details of his foreign policy programme to the citizens of Germany and the governments of Europe. On the contrary, he proceeded with considerable restraint and deliberately concealed the reality of his regime's intentions. As the minister of propaganda, Joseph Goebbels, put it in a confidential statement to the German press on 5 April 1940: 'When we were asked in [1933–4] how we intended to solve this or that problem, we always answered that we didn't yet know. We had our plans but we didn't subject them to public criticism'. To have revealed the intentions of the regime, as Goebbels observed, would merely have created enemies and stiffened resistance.[1]

This was important because the nazi dictatorship was not consolidated overnight, however much this might seem to have been the case in retrospect. Hitler's government in the first instance was dominated by conservatives. In addition to Hitler, as chancellor, only two other nazis sat in it: Frick, Reich minister of the interior, and Göring, Reich minister without portfolio and Prussian minister of the interior. This latter position made Göring the most powerful individual in the cabinet after Hitler. Nevertheless, Hitler had to proceed cautiously in the early stages of his regime in order not to offend his conservative partners. The process of *Gleichschaltung*, or coordination, in essence the foundation of Nazi totalitarianism, took just under two years. At a very early stage, however, totalitarian control was established over journalism and publishing. The Berlin newspaper correspondents were daily instructed by the Reich minister of propaganda, Joseph Goebbels, in the Nazi version of reality. Moreover, the news agencies and film companies were nationalized, or, as the press was, taken into party ownership. The *Schriftleitergesetz* (Law on Editors) of October 1933 bound editors in duty to the state and effectively deprived publishers of any control.[2] Meanwhile, Göring's position as Prussian minister of the interior gave him control of the police in Germany's largest state. His *Schießerlaß* (Shooting Decree) of 17 February 1933 directed police officers to deal with organizations hostile to the state in the most severe manner: firearms were to be used regardless of the consequences and failure to do so would incur disciplinary action. Given that the nazis and conservatives were united on the need to wipe out marxism once and for all, there was no opposition within the government to such blatant use of the police for what were in fact nazi party purposes.[3] During the following year effective control of all police functions in the Third Reich began to pass to Himmler and the SS. By this time Himmler was already in control of the political police forces in all states except Prussia. On 20 April 1934, however, Göring appointed Himmler inspector of the Prussian secret state police, the *Gestapo*, and from this time onwards Himmler was in *de facto* control of the entire political police in Germany. Two years later in a decree of 17 June 1936 Himmler was empowered to integrate under his command all the police functions of the state. He was now *Reichsführer SS* and chief of the German police in the Reich ministry of the interior. In effect, the police had been taken over by the SS.[4] Through the *Gestapo* a system of auto-policing, or auto-surveillance developed that precluded any effective revival of the left within Germany.[5]

As a means of exerting social and political control, national socialist domination of the media and the police was reinforced after the Reichstag fire of 1933, by the destruction of the political parties and the elimination of the trade unions. On 27 February 1933 the Reichstag was set on fire by the former Dutch communist, Marinus van der Lubbe. The following day the cabinet endorsed, under the emergency provisions of Article 48 of the Weimar Constitution, a presidential decree 'For the Protection of the People and the State.' This suspended all democratic rights and freedoms for an indefinite period. In practice this state of emergency was to last for the duration of the Third Reich.[6] It gave the regime considerable powers to emasculate opposition by permitting the indefinite detention of political adversaries. The communists rapidly disappeared as a threat as they were interned, fled abroad, or went underground. In the Reichstag elections of 5 March the national socialists and their conservative allies improved their electoral position polling between them over fifty per cent of the vote (NSDAP 43.9 per cent, DNVP 8 per cent). There followed on 23 March the passage of the Enabling Act which permitted the government to enact legislation without reference to the Reichstag and without presidential approval. The remaining political parties during June and July were now put under ban or dissolved themselves, with the trade unions being dissolved and their members absorbed into the German Labour Front the previous May. Within six months all organizational forms of political opposition, potential and actual, had, therefore, been removed. During April 1933 a law was introduced that permitted the elimination of political and racial undesirables from the state bureaucracy and in January 1934 the states of Germany were finally deprived of their legal sovereignty, their political independence having been crushed the previous March and April when national socialist governments and Reich governors were installed in them.

By January 1934 Hitler had destroyed all organized opposition outside the government and party, but there remained within the nazi movement a potential source of opposition, the SA led by Ernst Röhm. Furthermore, the army, or rather the army leadership, remained an independent power group. Events during 1934 enabled Hitler to solve the first problem and to ensure that the army (and bureaucracy) would in future swear personal loyalty to him as the expression of their obligation to the state.

If Hitler's foreign policy was to be successfully accomplished it would mean war and the backing of the army. He, therefore, valued the support of the German army more than any other organization. The army, however, perceived a threat to itself in the form of the SA and its ambition to become, as a militia, the main military arm of the Third Reich. This was resented by the army and was no less unacceptable to Hitler. The army too was alarmed, along with the rest of bourgeois society, by wild talk among the SA of a second revolution and the need for further political and social reform: the SA seemed to many like a beefsteak, 'brown on the outside, red on the inside'[7]. Hitler thus determined upon ruthless action that would crush the SA as a centre of power within the Nazi movement and at the same time gain for him the support of the army. On the 'Night of the Long Knives', 30 June–1 July 1934, the SA leadership was arrested by the *Gestapo* and SS and shot. On 2 August, President Hindenburg died and Hitler seized the opportunity to make himself head of state in addition to head of government. He was now *Führer* and Reich chancellor. The army demonstrated its gratitude to Hitler by readily agreeing that in future soldiers would swear their oath of allegiance to the Führer personally.

In subsequent years national socialist control in Germany was further consolidated by command of the German economy, first through the minister of economics and president of the Reichsbank, Hjalmar Schacht, who managed to increase economic activity and raise employment statistics in a closed economy, and secondly, from 1936 onwards, through Hermann Göring and the Four Year Plan. Schacht, who disapproved of what he correctly perceived to be the nature of Hitler's foreign policy, fell out of favour and was easily outmanoeuvred by Göring. In early 1938 Hitler's control of the army became total when he decided to do away with the post of war minister, in the wake of a scandal involving the war minister, Blomberg, who had married a former prostitute with the Führer and Göring as chief witnesses. The old guard of Blomberg, General Werner von Fritsch (the commander-in-chief of the army, who was falsely accused of homosexuality) and General Beck were compelled to resign. Hitler himself became supreme commander of the Armed Forces, while the war ministry was transformed into the *Oberkommando der Wehrmacht* (OKW) with General Keitel at its head. General Walter von Brauchitsch replaced Fritsch as commander-in-chief of the army. Parallel with these changes was the ousting of the conservative Freiherr von Neurath as foreign minister and the installation of the Hitler sycophant, Ribbentrop, as his successor. By 1938, therefore, Hitler's control of the machinery of state was as total as it could be. All centres of resistance and opposition to the Nazi state had been destroyed or immobilized. The conservative, bureaucratic opposition was condemned to futile clandestine plotting, given the moral reluctance to contemplate assassination, and Hitler's hold over the younger elements in the population had been achieved by propaganda and indoctrination.

However brutal at times Hitler may have been in achieving complete control in Germany and however rapid that achievement had been, it is, nonetheless, equally true that Hitler's actions were usually guided by caution until the opportune moment arrived. Similar tactics were to be applied to foreign relations and Hitler was to appear reassuring rather than threatening when necessary. Nevertheless, the public knowledge of Nazi beliefs and Hitler's statements and actions after he took office indicated that the international system in Europe would be subjected to a greater challenge than any so far experienced.

German Rearmament and the Remilitarization of the Rhineland

The German generals can have been under few illusions as to what the Nazi takeover meant for them. On 3 February 1933 they were told by Hitler that his regime probably meant war. The basis of Germany's foreign policy remained the complete undoing of the Treaty of Versailles and in the short term his government would endeavour to secure for Germany equality of rights in the disarmament negotiations then being conducted at Geneva. This did not, however, mark the limits of Germany's ambitions. Referring to the current economic situation, he emphasized the need to save German agriculture and simultaneously to find work for the unemployed. This could not be achieved by an export-led boom, but only by what he referred to as *settlement*. What he meant by this was the acquisition of fresh territory. At the opening of his address, he had stated that the 'sole aim of general policy' was '*the regaining of political power*'. He now stressed that the most important prerequisite for this was the reconstruction of the armed forces and he quickly explained why this should be so:

> How should political power be used when it has been gained? That is impossible to say yet. Perhaps fighting for new export possibilities, perhaps – and probably better –the conquest of new living space in the east and its ruthless Germanization.

Conquest could only mean war and, as if to underline the point, Hitler stated that if France had any statesmen she and her allies in Eastern Europe would attack Germany before it was too late. German rearmament, therefore, was inevitable from the moment that Hitler became chancellor.[8]

Hitler, however, was not going to announce the reality of his ultimate goal to the world. In foreign policy the early months of his regime were marked by caution. The major item on the international agenda at that time was the Disarmament Conference. In 1932 Germany had already withdrawn from these negotiations on the ground that she was being denied 'equality of rights'. But she had been persuaded to return to the conference table by the promise of equality of rights within a regime of security for all nations.

In essence this implied that French forces would be reduced while Germany's would be increased until parity had been attained. In March 1933 the British prime minister, Ramsay MacDonald, and the foreign secretary, Sir John Simon, presented a new plan to the Disarmament Conference which allowed Germany a certain measure of equality. It was proposed that the German Army be increased from 100,000 to 200,000, with a reduction in the size of the French Army. Initial reactions seemed encouraging, but the Germans were soon making difficulties. They disliked the proposed standardization of continental armies on a militia basis, demanding instead a professional, regular army, which naturally would be unacceptable at Geneva. Moreover, it was clear to Brigadier Temperley of the British war office that Germany had surrendered herself to 'the most blatant and dangerous militarism'. Besides which Hermann Göring had been charged with 'the mission of raising a military air force'[9]. Nevertheless, Hitler temporarily revived hopes of some success by a moderate speech on 17 May 1933. He was merely temporizing though. There was no inclination in Germany to contribute to genuine international disarmament: only a willingness to use the Disarmament Conference as a cover for clandestine rearmament during the delicate early stages when Germany was still vulnerable.[10]

That this was so is revealed in Hitler's response to the French counter-proposals for a disarmament convention that were evolved in the summer of 1933. Under this scheme there was to be an initial trial period during which Germany would not be permitted quantitative and qualitative equality of armaments until she had demonstrated her good faith. Furthermore, an effective scheme of supervision would be tested. This was, of course, totally unacceptable to Hitler and the subsequent endorsement of the French proposals by the British, who had been confronted with clear evidence of German rearmament and bad faith, ensured the end of Germany's participation in the disarmament negotiations. It had been clear to the British government for some time that Germany would spin out the discussions for just as long as it suited Hitler's policy of gradual rearmament. Neither the Disarmament Conference nor the League of Nations could any longer suit Hitler's purpose and in October 1933 Germany withdrew from both.

The expansion of Germany's armed forces in the 1930s was indeed prodigious. The Rapallo relationship between Germany and the Soviet Union during the time of the Weimar Republic had been particularly useful from the point of view of the development of German air power and provided a basis for the spectacular advances made during the Third Reich. As early as December 1932, plans which had been formulated during the 1920s for the expansion of the army from 100,000 to 300,000 were activated. By 1935 Germany's infantry divisions had been increased from seven to twenty-one and in March of that year the announcement of the introduction of conscription, in breach of the terms of the Treaty of Versailles, was accompanied by a decision to reorganize and expand the army to a force of thirty-six infantry divisions. Expansion of these dimensions was inevitably to give rise to deficiencies in equipment and training; even so it marked Germany's transition from military weakness to a position of potentially

overwhelming military strength within Europe. Likewise the expansion of
the German Air Force, the *Luftwaffe*, was spectacular and overt. By 1934,
although with the disapproval of the defence and foreign ministries,
squadrons of military aircraft were displaying themselves in the German
skies in defiance of Versailles. Germany's aircraft industry which in 1932 was
comparatively insignificant had by the time of the announcement of the
existence of the *Luftwaffe* expanded its workforce from just over 3,000
workers to 125,000 and supplied almost 2,500 new aircraft. When one
considers that in 1932 the German armed forces disposed of only just over
two hundred aircraft, most of them converted civilian types, this represented
a startling increase in German air strength. Much of this increment was
undoubtedly obsolete, or designed for training. Even so it provided a firm
basis for future development.[11]

Government spending on armaments usually has a deleterious impact
upon the economies concerned. It appears, however, that rearmament in
Germany in the 1930s assisted in the general recovery of the economy from
the recession, although not to the extent that it was at first thought. By the
middle of 1932 the German economy had begun to move out of recession and
between March 1933 and March 1934 unemployment fell by two million.
Clearly a recovery was taking place that was more or less coeval with the
early stages of the National Socialist regime. By 1938 the German economy
was experiencing rates of growth not achieved since 1913 and throughout the
1930s the German economy grew faster than the world economy as a whole.

Table 2 Statistics relating to the economic recovery in Germany 1932–8.

	1928	1932	1933	1934	1935	1936	1937	1938
GNP in RM bn	89.5	57.6	59.1	66.5	74.4	82.6	93.2	104.5
GNP 1928 prices	89.5	71.9	73.7	83.7	92.3	101.2	114.2	126.2
National Income in RM bn	75.4	45.2	46.5	52.8	59.1	65.8	73.8	82.1
Industrial Production 1928=100	100	58	66	83	96	107	117	122
Unemployment in millions	1.4	5.6	4.8	2.7	2.2	1.6	0.9	0.4[12]

The recovery of the German economy in the 1930s has been subjected to
many interpretations, but there is no single one that is sufficient in itself. It is,
however, evident that demand in the German economy shifted from
consumer goods to capital goods and that there was also a high level of
government expenditure. Therefore: 'The main explanation for increases in
demand lies with the increase of public investment and policies designed
directly or indirectly to stimulate demand.'[13] Rearmament must, of course,
have played a part in switching demand from consumer to capital goods, but
just how important its role was remains a subject of some controversy. Early
commentators, such as Thomas Balogh, writing in 1938, and R. Erbe in the
1950s, argued strongly that rearmament was the single biggest factor in
Germany's economic recovery. This, however, was later challenged by Alan
Milward who claimed that rearmament played a much less significant role.

According to Milward, rearmament was deliberately maintained at a low level throughout the 1930s, partly because the *Blitzkrieg* (lightning war) wars that Hitler intended fighting did not require massive expenditure on arms and partly because Hitler did not wish to curb too much non-military consumer spending.[14] Both arguments contain a substantial degree of truth, but cannot be made to fit the facts over the entire period of the Third Reich. During the period 1932 to 1935 military expenditure was relatively low, accounting for 17 per cent of government spending and only 1.3 per cent of GNP. It was after 1936, with the introduction of the Four Year Plan, that government expenditure on rearmament came to play a more important role. It is, though, difficult to escape the conclusion that 'in terms of the recovery period itself the linkage effects generated by rearmament were less than those generated by other forms of expenditure'[15].

Nevertheless, rearmament did take place in the early years of the Third Reich and it was naturally disturbing to the governments of Britain and France. Some of its more obvious manifestations were, of course, easily observed and the British and French intelligence services provided incontrovertible evidence of the more clandestine operations, sometimes exaggerating the achievement out of all proportion with the reality. Hitler, however, was careful not to reveal the ultimate purpose for which this rearmament was intended. On the contrary, he did everything he could to neutralize opposition by adopting as cautious a policy as was practicable. Thus in his speech of 17 May 1933 he gave the British disarmament plan a tentative welcome, offering even to 'renounce all aggressive weapons of every sort' if such a gesture was reciprocated. 'Germany,' he stated, 'has only one desire, to be able to preserve her independence and defend her frontiers'. He added:

> The German Government wishes to come to a peaceful agreement with other nations on all difficult questions. They know that in any military action in Europe, even if completely successful, the sacrifice would be out of all proportion to any possible gains.[16]

Likewise Germany did all she could to foster an image of international co-operativeness by willingly participating in the innocuous Four Power Pact negotiations of 1933 which had been initiated by Mussolini. Then, in January 1934, Germany concluded a pact of non-aggression with Poland that promised, at least for its eight year duration, to guarantee the German–Polish frontier, a course that would have been unthinkable for the political leadership of Weimar Germany. Moreover, between 1933 and 1936, Hitler consistently announced Germany's unwillingness to enter into imperial competition with Britain by pursuing a policy of effective renunciation of the colonies Germany had lost in 1919. If colonies were offered to Germany unconditionally, she would accept them, but otherwise Hitler was unconcerned. There was, of course, a practical motive here. In accordance with the foreign policy plan Hitler had conceived in the 1920s, Anglo-German friendship was a necessary prerequisite of the conquest of the Soviet Union and the achievement of *Lebensraum* in the Ukraine. Hence also Hitler's readiness in 1935 to enter into a naval agreement with Britain that restricted Germany's surface vessels to 35 per cent. of the British tonnage, which Hitler considered to be the first stage of his desired Anglo-German alliance.[17]

The caution displayed by Hitler during the first three years of his regime was, however, also accompanied by acts that were potentially menacing and disruptive. Significantly, the Russo-German Rapallo relationship was terminated by the end of 1933 and in October of that year Hitler risked reprisals when Germany left the League of Nations. It was a calculated gamble though. On 17 October he told a conference of ministers:

> . . . the political situation had developed as was to be expected. Threatening steps against Germany had not materialized nor were they to be expected . . . The critical moment had probably passed. The other side will look for a way to get in touch with us again.[18]

This set a pattern for the many crises that would be provoked by Hitler in the years ahead and undoubtedly the whole episode increased his confidence that his ambitions would not be resisted if he chose the right moments to advance them.

The attempted *Anschluß* of July 1934, was, on the other hand, resisted. In June 1934 Hitler and Mussolini met for the first time in Venice. There Hitler had mistakenly understood that Mussolini had no objection to his five point plan for Austria. This proposed the replacement of the Austrian chancellor by a person unaffiliated to political parties, a general election and the inclusion thereafter of Austrian national socialists in the government. As a result he was disinclined to curb the exuberance of the Austrian Nazis, who, intoxicated by the Röhm purge in Germany at the end of June, attempted a coup in Vienna on 24 July. This resulted in the death of the diminutive Austrian chancellor, Dollfuss (known as *Millimetternich*), and an immediate and hostile reaction on the part of Mussolini, who announced his support for an independent Austria. The *Duce* (the title assumed by Mussolini as leader of Fascist Italy) reinforced his words by mobilizing the Italian Army.[19] Added point was given to this warning by the presence of Italian troops on manoeuvres in the Alps. It was the view of the American ambassador in Vienna that Mussolini's action was critical in putting a stop to what would have been a nazi takeover.[20] Mussolini was furious with Hitler and began referring to him disparagingly.[21] Subsequently, the Austrian clerical-fascist regime quickly re-established itself under the chancellorship of Schuschnigg. Hitler naturally disclaimed any responsibility for these events, but they were a foretaste of the Nazi manner of doing business in international affairs.

Also prophetic of the future was Germany's rejection in 1934 of a French scheme for an *Eastern Locarno* that would ensure the security of the states of Eastern Europe. Germany would not participate in any such scheme while she was denied equality of rights in armaments, for to do so, it was claimed, would be to her military disadvantage. The view of the German government was that security was usually best achieved in arrangements of a bilateral character. Hitler later informed the British ambassador that Germany could have nothing to do with a multilateral security scheme involving the USSR. The deployment of Soviet troops in the defence of Germany he likened to opening a box of plague bacilli at the front: they might well kill the enemy, but they would also inflict untold damage upon one's own troops. In view of Hitler's long term plans the continued isolation of the USSR was naturally preferable to her integration into an international system. It can be little wonder also that Germany objected to the Franco-Russian treaty that was to form a part of the Eastern Locarno arrangements.[22]

Germany's reluctance to contribute to the security of Eastern Europe was disappointing, but in March 1935 and March 1936 Hitler took action that was manifestly disturbing. By this time he clearly felt that Germany was strong enough and her adversaries sufficiently divided and lacking in resolution to reassert her sovereignty in military affairs and in the Rhineland. In March 1935 Part V of the Treaty of Versailles, which provided for the disarmament of Germany, was unilaterally denounced by Hitler when, in defiance of Germany's treaty obligations he announced the reintroduction of conscription, the expansion of the German Army and the existence of the *Luftwaffe*. This met with the condemnation of the British, French and Italian governments when they met at Stresa and denounced the unilateral abrogation of treaty obligations. This was the so-called Stresa Front. But by the time Germany remilitarized the Rhineland, which flouted both Versailles and Locarno, Hitler was able to contemplate such a step in the clear knowledge that the Stresa Front had cracked and that Italy would no longer align herself with Britain and France. The most that Germany would have to deal with was a flurry of diplomatic exchanges. The winter of 1935–6 had indeed witnessed a diplomatic revolution in which Italy had transferred herself from the allied camp to that of the dictators.

The Italian Invasion of Abyssinia

The crucial event in this diplomatic revolution was the decision by Mussolini to invade Abyssinia in pursuit of Italian imperial grandeur. Not only did it shatter the Stresa Front; it also ruined the credibility of the League of Nations as a force for maintaining the peace of the world. The Manchurian crisis of 1931–2 had questioned the ability of the League to maintain the territorial integrity of its members, the Abyssinian crisis now demonstrated its complete dereliction in that respect.[23] Collective security through the League of Nations was no longer realistic.

The Italian state had long coveted Abyssinia as an area for colonial expansion. By the end of the nineteenth century these aspirations had even been endorsed by the British government in an agreement of 1891 which recognized almost all of Abyssinia as an Italian sphere of influence. Indeed the Italian prime minister, Crispi, claimed that the Treaty of Ucciali between Italy and the Emperor Menelik of 1889 had already turned Abyssinia into a protectorate of the Italian crown. Italy's ambitions were, however, thwarted in 1896 when an Italian force was routed in the battle of Adowa. The stigma of this defeat rankled the Italians for many years, as did the fact that Italy's colonial possessions in Africa seemed incommensurate with Italian pretensions to greatness. Nevertheless, the Italians gained in 1906 an important diplomatic victory with the conclusion of the Anglo-Franco-Italian Treaty of that year, which defined the interests of the three powers in Abyssinia, in order to prevent an unregulated scramble for Abyssinian spoils in the anarchy which it was confidently anticipated would follow the death of the Emperor Menelik. Under the terms of the treaty, Britain was to have security for an unimpeded flow of the sources of the Nile, which was important for both Egypt and the Sudan, by then effectively under British control; the French Addis Ababa–Djibouti railway line was to be inviolable; and most of the rest of the country was designated as an area for the expansion of Italian influence. During the First World War the Italian government endeavoured to advance Italian colonial ambitions in the Treaty of London, which secured Italy's participation in the war on the allied side. Under its terms Britain and France promised specifically to increase Italy's interests in East Africa should they themselves make colonial gains at Germany's expense. These pledges were not redeemed in the peace settlement of 1919. For the Italians it became the *mutilated peace* and Italy assumed the status of a profoundly dissatisfied colonial power, with Abyssinia still the focus of attention. In 1924 the British attempted to redress the situation by the cession of Jubaland to Italy, but, although, in addition, the following year a British note to the Italian government recognized Italy's interest in Abyssinia, this was not the kind of compromise likely to satisfy her appetite. Furthermore, frustrated colonial ambition remained at the centre of the chronically bad Franco-Italian relations that persisted throughout the 1920s and into the 1930s.

During the 1920s Italy sought to secure her aims in Abyssinia through friendship. Abyssinia joined the League of Nations in 1923 with Italian sponsorship and in 1928 an Italo-Abyssinian Treaty of 'Friendship and Arbitration' was concluded. But meagre progress was made in the political and economic penetration of the country. Moreover, in 1930 Ras Tafari, who was determined to defeudalize and modernize Abyssinia, was crowned Emperor Haile Selassie I. It was his objective to reduce to order the prevailing anarchy in the country. As the Italian foreign ministry official, Raffaele Guariglia, commented, this was inconvenient from the point of view of Italian interests in East Africa.

By the end of the 1920s the French, agitated by the prospect of the revival of German power, were prepared to make an effort to end their differences with Italy. In 1928 Philippe Berthelot, the non-political head of the French foreign ministry, suggested to Sir Austen Chamberlain that Italy might be permitted to realize some of her ambitions in Abyssinia. This met with a sharp rebuff from the British foreign secretary. Four years later though France and Italy were actually negotiating over Abyssinia and Berthelot mentioned to the British ambassador in Paris that he was going to propose to Laval, the French prime minister, that Italy be allowed a *free hand* in that country. For the time being nothing happened, but in January 1935 Laval, now French foreign minister, visited Rome where a number of Franco-Italian agreements were concluded. There were two colonial agreements: one was public, but the other was kept secret. Publicly it was announced that France had ceded modest amounts of worthless land to the Italian colonies of Libya and Eritrea, while in a secret exchange of letters France declared her economic disinterest in Abyssinia.[24]

There was, though, an even more hidden agenda. Mussolini was later to claim that in a private and unrecorded conversation Laval had offered Italy a *free hand* in Abyssinia, which justified its military conquest. Laval for his part denied that he had used this expression in this sense; rather he had intended it to apply to economic matters. It seems likely, however, that the term *free hand* was used unqualified, as Berthelot had used it earlier, resulting in a deliberate ambiguity. While Laval may not have anticipated the war that broke out, it seems probable that he at least wanted to convey to Mussolini the impression that France would accept some degree of Italian political and economic domination of Abyssinia.[25] But whatever the truth of this matter the Laval visit to Rome was regarded by Mussolini as a green light for the realization of his plans of conquest of that country which had been seriously considered since 1932. Following the frontier dispute at Walwal on the border between Abyssinia and Italian Somaliland in December 1934, Mussolini defined Italy's objective in Abyssinia as its total subjugation and he now thought he had secured the acquiescence of France.

The autumn of 1935 had been regarded for some while as the most likely date for the commencement of this operation, but, apart from the seeming complicity of the French, what also determined Italian action at this time were Italy's diplomatic failures of the preceding two years and the clear inability of Germany for the present to threaten Austria. In 1933, on Italian initiative, Britain, France, Germany and Italy had initialled a Four Power Pact. Its purpose was the preservation of peace in Europe, but it also provided for revision of the peace treaties, which naturally alarmed the states of Eastern Europe. In the event the Four Power Pact was never ratified. Secondly, the meeting between Hitler and Mussolini in Venice, during June 1934, had from the Italian point of view an unfortunate sequel. Austria had during the 1920s become an Italian sphere of influence and Mussolini resented the coup staged by the Austrian nazis which ended in the murder of chancellor Dollfuss. He was soon referring to Hitler as a 'horrible sexual degenerate, a dangerous fool'. In a telegram to the leader of the Austrian *Heimwehr*, Starhemberg, he stated that the death of Dollfuss had been a source of 'profound sadness'. More importantly, though, he emphasized: 'The independence of Austria for which he has fallen is a principle which has been defended and will be defended even more ardently by Italy in these exceptionally difficult times'.[26] With Italian support Austrian independence, as has been indicated, was for the present maintained.

But it was clear to Mussolini that if he wished to risk a war in Africa, he would have to do so before German strength had revived to the point at which a German threat to Austria could only be contained with great difficulty. As he stated to Marshal Badoglio on 30 December 1934, the prospective agreements and rapprochement between France and Italy had removed 'the danger of a renewed German attack upon Austria'. This comment was reinforced by the conclusion in June 1935 of a secret military agreement between France and Italy that provided for the joint defence of Austrian independence. Moreover the French and Italian general staffs discussed a joint strategy for a war against Germany. It appeared, therefore, that the policy initiated by Louis Barthou, French foreign minister in 1934, of securing friendly relations with Italy was coming to fruition. Finally, the disapproval of Germany's rearmament registered by Italy, Britain and France at the end of the Stresa Conference of April 1935 and the emergence of the anti-German Stresa Front also served to boost Mussolini's confidence that he could proceed with his Abyssinian adventure without complications.[27]

The British government too wanted to preserve good Anglo-Italian relations and to maintain Italy in the Allied camp. Whether or not Abyssinia remained independent probably did not agitate many British ministers as a principle. The problem for the British government was that a substantial section of British opinion was devoted to the concept of collective security and the principles on which the League of Nations was based. Although this was primarily a phenomenon of the left in Britain, the results of the Peace Ballot that were announced in June 1935 confirmed the strength of pro-League feeling. Ninety-four per cent. of respondents supported the application of non-military sanctions against aggressors, while 74 per cent. were prepared to resort to war if necessary.[28] It was, therefore, manifestly difficult for the British government to pursue a *free hand* policy for Italy in Abyssinia. The Maffey Report of June 1935, produced by a secret, interdepartmental committee of the British government under the chairmanship of Sir John Maffey, a copy of which soon found its way into Italian hands, might well have concluded that no British interest would be served by resisting an Italian attack on Abyssinia, but it is doubtful if British opinion would have subscribed to such a view.

Although the Abyssinian question was not formally discussed at the Stresa Conference, the Italians were warned by the British delegation of the uncertain consequences of the conquest of that country. The line that Vansittart, the non-political head of the foreign office, took with the Italian officials was that the agreements reached at Stresa would 'all go for nothing, if he [Mussolini] embroils himself for nothing'. Even so Vansittart himself was inclined to buy Mussolini off with British Somaliland. If this course was not followed he predicted the destruction of Abyssinia, the emasculation of the League and another Italian 'volte-face into the arms of Germany'. During the summer of 1935 British efforts at mediation in fact took place: a part of British Somaliland would be ceded to Abyssinia giving her access to the sea and in return Abyssinia would cede parts of the Ogaden to Italy. These negotiations, however, proved unproductive and in October 1935 the Italian invasion of Abyssinia commenced. Mussolini was able to contemplate this action secure in the knowledge that France had committed herself to military arrangements with Italy regarding Austria. Moreover, serious differences had arisen between France and Britain over the Anglo-German Naval Agreement of June 1935. Because it contravened the Stresa declaration regarding infractions of the disarmament clauses of the Treaty of Versailles, the British government had not informed the French of their decision to allow, in effect, a significant measure of German naval rearmament.[29]

The consequence of Mussolini's action was the imposition of League sanctions. The British government took the lead in this with the French following reluctantly. The French government, with Laval now prime minister, could not, however, afford to ignore pro-League sentiment in France because of the delicate parliamentary situation. In November 1935 sanctions were agreed, but these excluded the prohibition of the export of oil to Italy. This would have been particularly effective, but the British government did not want to take action likely to result in an Anglo-Italian war and, of course, Italy could always acquire oil from the USA, a country not bound by the decisions of the League. These public displays of disapproval of Italian action were, on the other hand, matched by private efforts to persuade the Italians to withdraw through the formulation of a compromise scheme. These culminated in the Hoare–Laval Plan of 8 December, finalized while the British foreign secretary since June 1935, Sir Samuel Hoare, was in Paris *en route* to a skiing holiday in Switzerland. Under the terms of this plan Abyssinia was to cede to Italy some two-thirds of her territory, while the truncated, yet ethnically consolidated, Abyssinian state was to receive a corridor to the sea. The plan, however, was leaked in Paris and in the resulting furore was scrapped. The crisis also claimed the resignation of the unfortunate Hoare, whose position became untenable because of opinion both within and without the House of Commons. Whatever the rights and wrongs of the Hoare–Laval Plan, it marked the last point at which the Abyssinian crisis could have been resolved without the total subjugation of Abyssinia, which was achieved in May 1936 when Haile Selassie fled into exile and the King of Italy was proclaimed Emperor of Abyssinia. It also marked the final parting of the ways regarding the Stresa Front.

Mussolini's inclination to change course in foreign policy and align Italy more with Germany than with the democratic countries had been developing for some time prior to the eruption of the Abyssinian crisis. Under the influence of Count Ciano, Mussolini was gradually convinced that Italy's foreign policy and overseas ambitions might best be secured and achieved in alignment with Germany. In May 1935 he was already informing the Germans of his leanings in this direction and during the following August the British foreign office learnt that the Italians had approached the German government with a request for diplomatic support in the Abyssinian question in exchange for Italian support for Germany's colonial aspirations. The failure of the Hoare–Laval Plan now gave this process an irreversible impetus.[30] In essence, Mussolini now realized that 'only a revanchist Germany would back the Italian challenge to Anglo-French hegemony in the Mediterranean and help Italy become a Great Power.'[31] On 6 January 1936 Mussolini informed the German ambassador in Rome that Anglo-Italian relations were bad and not likely to improve for some time to come. In these circumstances, Italy, he suggested, would have no objection if Austria was to become a German satellite, provided that Austrian independence was preserved. Italo-German relations now underwent rapid improvement, to such an extent that Hitler determined upon carrying out the remilitarization of the Rhineland a year in advance of his intentions. On 22 February

Mussolini informed the German ambassador that should this take place Italy would not honour her obligations under the Locarno treaty. Fortified in his conviction that the British and French, preoccupied with the Abyssinian crisis, would not effectively oppose the remilitarization of the Rhineland and that Italy had to all intents and purposes dissociated herself from the Stresa constellation, Hitler on 7 March 1936 ordered units of the German Army to occupy the Rhineland demilitarized zone. Thus, by 1936 an important diplomatic revolution was taking place which was to end Germany's isolation; the League had been defied and discredited as a force for maintaining peace and the integrity of small states; and Germany had laid down the gauntlet to the rest of Europe.[32]

The Reaction of Britain and France

The Peace Settlement of 1919 had consisted of a number of treaties that seemed to endorse the supremacy of Britain and France in Europe and the wider world. However much this may have belied changing economic and strategic realities, that was the contemporary perception. It was probably less true of France than of Britain. French politicians in the 1920s had been more conscious of French vulnerability, hence their enthusiasm for European integration which would have lessened the menace of a revived Germany. On the other hand, the British still preserved an image of themselves as the invulnerable imperialists. The impact of the world economic recession injected a certain degree of realism into British attitudes, but the *hauteur* and self-belief remained. Still, Hitler and Mussolini challenged Anglo-French supremacy between 1933 and 1936 in an unaccustomed manner and the reaction of Britain and France was to be important from the point of view of determining the strategy that these countries were to employ in the long term and the leadership of the democratic bloc in Europe.

Prior to Hitler's assumption of power Sir Robert Vansittart outlined for the British cabinet the alternatives facing British policy in view of the deteriorating position in Europe. The quarrels in continental Europe, he thought, were to some degree nothing to do with Britain. If the major powers could not agree amongst themselves the point might well have been reached where Britain would have to absolve herself of responsibility for what happened there. If, however, Britain counted the achievement of stability on the continent as more important than the benefits of isolation and imperial commitment, the key to the pacification of Europe lay very much in her hands. This implied the leadership of Europe, which in turn required a 'practical contribution' in the form of assistance in the revision of the Peace Settlement, or Versailles System, and maybe territorial concessions by Britain herself. Ultimately the British government found itself compelled by events and by conviction to play a dominant role in the affairs of Europe.[33]

This naturally arose partly from the inability of France to maintain such diplomatic leadership herself. Scandals such as that provoked by the Stavisky affair[34] in 1934 and the accompanying threat of civil war did nothing to create the image of unity and strength that would have been necessary for such a task. Neither did the French parliamentary system which resulted in chronic ministerial instability. These circumstances in themselves precluded a preventive war, which in retrospect the advent of Hitler might seem to have required, but such a course, as has already been indicated, would only have ended in France's isolation and would not necessarily have led to a change in Germany's mood and attitudes. The British certainly did not want a repetition of the occupation of the Ruhr. Besides which, the forcible ejection of the nazi regime by a foreign power would merely have served to reinforce the perception within Germany of external coercion which was one of the grievances that the Nazi movement nourished to ensure its political success.

The Disarmament Conference brought the French no relief. By the time Hitler came to power the concession to Germany of equality of rights meant essentially the legalization of a degree of German rearmament. But French suspicion, rightly, of German good faith in this matter was instrumental in driving Germany away from the Disarmament Conference. In April 1934 the French government brought it to a *de facto* end in a memorandum to the British government which pointed out that military spending in the German Reich for the year 1933–4 had risen by 352 million marks and that clandestine rearmament had continued unabated. Pointing out that 'France must place in the forefront of her preoccupations the conditions of her own security', the memorandum stated: 'The experience of the last war, the horrors of which France had to endure more than any other country, imposes upon her the duty of showing prudence. Her will to peace must not be confounded with the abandonment of her defence.'[35] It was not until September 1936, however, that a meaningful programme of rearmament was introduced by the Popular Front government of Léon Blum, with an expenditure of 31 billion francs over the three years 1936–1939. Nevertheless, problems with industrial adjustment and efficiency meant that rearmament was not as quick and as thorough as it might have been.

Consciousness of the danger presented by the recrudescence of German power stimulated French efforts to end the friction between France and Italy that had been a feature of international affairs in Europe since the end of the First World War. They were made all the more necessary by French agreement to Mussolini's Four Power Pact proposals of 1933. Although the Four Power Pact was never ratified, its endorsement of the principle of treaty revision alarmed the small states of Central and Eastern Europe. These had formed part of the French security system in the 1920s. But in January 1934 Poland sought to solve her security problem with Germany by concluding a non-aggression pact with her neighbour, thus rendering the French security arrangements in Eastern Europe virtually useless. This gave added impetus to the policy of coming to terms with Italy, a course enthusiastically originated and pursued by the French foreign minister, Louis Barthou, prior to his collateral assassination at Marseilles in October 1934, when a Croatian terrorist succeeded both in assassinating King Alexander of Yugoslavia, then on a state visit to France, and in mortally wounding Barthou who was escorting the Yugoslav monarch. The relevant negotiations culminated in the Rome Agreements of 1935 and the *misunderstandings* that preceded the invasion of Abyssinia. In other words, France ultimately lost both the substance of her security system in Eastern Europe and Italian friendship which by the summer of 1935 had seemed so securely achieved. Britain would not guarantee the Peace Settlement in Eastern Europe and so French policy came to an impasse.

There had, however, existed for French policy one further option. As early as October 1933 the French government began to think of the possibility of bringing the Soviet Union into the League of Nations and of concluding a mutual assistance convention with the USSR. On 18 September 1934 the Soviet Union was admitted to the League by its Fifteenth Assembly. In his first speech to the League Assembly, Maxim Litvinov, the Soviet commissar for foreign affairs, implicitly referred to the threat to peace represented by the national socialist regime in Germany when he stated:

> It needed . . . one great dominating common aim to prove incontestably to all nations, including those of the Soviet Union, the desirability – nay, the necessity – for closer co-operation between the Soviet Union and the League of Nations, and even for the entry of the Soviet Union into the League. The discovery of such a common aim has been greatly facilitated by the events of the last two or three years.[36]

During 1934 the French government also elaborated a scheme for an Eastern Locarno security pact. This ultimately collapsed because of Germany's objection to being associated with the Soviet Union and Poland's reluctance to enter into a security arrangement for Eastern Europe that did not include Germany. One aspect of it, however, survived, namely, the Franco-Soviet pact. This was signed on 2 May 1935, but it was not accorded the same priority as the contemporaneous arrangements with Italy and there were no staff talks. Moreover, the process of ratification took an unconscionable time. It was not until the end of February 1936 that the French Chamber of Deputies took the appropriate steps, which then had a surprising sequel. Claiming that the Franco-Soviet Pact violated the terms of the Locarno Agreement, Hitler proceeded to the remilitarization of the Rhineland. The diplomacy of this crisis was to reveal clearly that France had lost all initiative in dealing with Germany.

The initiative had by this time passed irrevocably to Britain. It was not, however, a position assumed by the British government immediately upon Hitler's installation as chancellor. Rather it was a gradual process, which was accompanied by the formulation of plans for a *General Settlement* that would replace the Peace Settlement of 1919. Germany's reasonable demands would be met and, it was hoped, she would settle down to reasonable treaty relations with the rest of Europe. Nevertheless, the triumph of nazism in 1933 did not immediately alter the British strategy for peace which was based upon a successful outcome of the Disarmament Conference. It was hoped that this would lead to a wider detente in Europe. It may, however, be doubted whether the British government necessarily interpreted success in the sense of general disarmament. Rather it was hoped that a measure of British rearmament, in terms of tanks and aircraft, would be legitimized within an overall arms limitation agreement. Success, in terms of general disarmament, would have meant compensating the French government for any arms reductions they agreed to make by offering guarantees additional to those contained in the Locarno arrangements. As Sir Robert Vansittart informed Sir John Simon, the newly appointed foreign secretary, in December 1931:

> If His Majesty's Government take the Disarmament Conference seriously, then they must take seriously the question of the security guarantee also. If we are not seriously considering the question of the security pact, then our attitude towards the Disarmament Conference is not wholly sincere. We are giving lip service only – knowing in our hearts that it is bound to fail.

The British government, however, steadfastly refused to entertain such commitments, partly because it did not wish to encourage the French in too resolute an attitude towards the Germans and partly because, as the British wanted to improve their position with respect to tanks and aircraft as a result of the disarmament negotiations, they were not really interested in general disarmament. But there was also a desire on the part of the British government not to be held responsible for the failure of the Disarmament Conference, which explains the presentation of the British disarmament plan in March 1933, described by one historian as a stop gap, 'designed not to achieve disarmament but to prop up a conference which everyone knew to be disintegrating'[37].

The disarmament negotiations did not survive Germany's simultaneous withdrawal from the conference and the League in October 1933. Still, Sir John Simon, the foreign secretary at the time, tried to gain some advantage from the changed situation by advocating recognition of German rearmament in return for German resumption of active membership of the League. He justified this view in the following manner:

> Germany would prefer, it appears, to be 'made an honest woman'; but if she is left too long to indulge in illegitimate practices and to find by experience that she does not suffer for it, this laudable ambition may wear off.[38]

At the end of January 1935 the French prime minister, Flandin, and his foreign minister, Laval, arrived in London for talks to discuss this new approach. The Anglo-French communiqué of 3 February gave public expression to it. What was proposed in this document was the negotiation of a general settlement of limited type composed of regional security pacts, Germany's return to the League, a 'reciprocal agreement' against air attack that would be supplementary to the Locarno Pact, and the legitimization of German rearmament.

Meanwhile the first steps towards rearmament had taken place in Britain. As early as 1931 Sir Maurice Hankey had been calling for the termination of the rolling Ten Year Rule because of clear evidence of clandestine German rearmament. It was, however, the extension of the fighting to Shanghai in January 1932 during the course of the Manchurian Incident that finally provoked its cancellation. But little was done immediately to realize the implications of this cancellation for fear of doing anything that might damage the Disarmament Conference. This situation changed in October 1933 when Germany left both the conference and the League. A sub-committee of the committee of imperial defence, the defence requirements committee [DRC] was now constituted to review defence deficiencies. But the DRC's proposals for a balanced rearmament programme were drastically revised by the politicians in the summer of 1934. The preoccupation of the public at large and government with the threat of aerial bombardment and the 'knockout blow' led to the bulk of the money available, two thirds of what the DRC thought necessary, being spent on the Royal Air Force and the formation of a strategic bombing force equal to that which it was presumed Germany possessed. Throughout the inter-war years it was universally held that there was no adequate defence against the bomber, which, according to Stanley Baldwin, would 'always get through'. Deterrence, therefore, was considered to be the only realistic form of defence.

While naval construction suffered as a result of this priority, it was the army that was most badly affected. It was decided that there could be no British Expeditionary Force capable of commitment to the field on the continent for the time being and the funding proposed for the army by the DRC was reduced by 50 per cent. The reluctance at this time to consider any further military commitments of land forces to the continent was partly rooted in political calculation and the belief that a continental field force would be politically unacceptable. The memory of the blood bath of the First World War was still very fresh in the minds of the electorate and, of course, a field force could do little to negate the fear of the bomber. Moreover, as in the debate over security compensation for the French in a scheme of general disarmament, it was felt unwise to do anything that would encourage the French to be obdurate in their relations with Germany.

As already indicated, the British government cut the funds proposed for overall rearmament by the DRC by a third. The need for budgetary restraint, therefore, played a significant part in the pattern of British rearmament after 1934. In terms of spending on rearmament it meant that Britain spent in the five years from 1933 to 1938 probably a third of what Germany spent on rearmament in the same period. There were several reasons for this. The economic collapse of September 1931, which resulted in a coalition National Government and sterling being driven off the gold standard, had been a traumatic experience for the treasury and the Bank of England. Throughout the 1930s the bank's major preoccupation was to be the restoration of the credibility of London as a financial centre. There was also concern in the treasury over the balance of payments. Imports were now persistently exceeding exports and remedying this situation was regarded as a high priority. Massive public spending on arms would have cut across both these objectives and thus would have threatened economic recovery. There were also potentially severe political consequences to be feared from increasing taxation and diverting resources from welfare programmes to pay for arms in the circumstances of a depressed economy. Finally, government borrowing for this purpose was to be avoided because of its inflationary impact, the consequent damage to foreign confidence in sterling and the effect on the balance of payments. The ultimate virtue, though, in limiting peacetime expenditure on arms was to be found in the concept of finance as the 'fourth arm' in Britain's defence in addition to the three armed services. It was considered important to enter into a war in which Germany was likely to be the principal adversary with the 'war chest' as full as possible. Such a war was likely to be a long war of attrition in which the economic and financial strength of the British Empire could prove decisive against a German economy it was assumed was incapable of lasting the course. The main consequences of the decisions taken by the British government in 1934 in respect of rearmament were that an added impetus was given to the perceived need to bring Germany into a *General Settlement* and that the foreign policy based upon this premise would be backed up by the deterrent of a strategic bomber force.[39]

By 1934 there were additional reasons, concerned with the world outside Europe, why such a foreign policy should have proved attractive and been pursued. In the United States the passage of the Johnson Act effectively denied the British access to the American arms and loans markets. This meant that in a putative war against Germany, Britain might find herself in the position of having to finance and produce arms for a European coalition, while maintaining her labour for munitions' production. The effects of the Johnson Act were to be intensified by the neutrality legislation of subsequent years. Furthermore, the situation in the Far East was showing few signs of improvement. There had been little that Britain could do to halt the flow of events in China following the beginning of the Manchurian Incident in September 1931. Military or economic sanctions against the Japanese were ruled out by sympathy for Japan amongst the British community in China, the bonds of friendship with Japan that existed among the political and business elite in Britain, and the advice of military and naval experts. Moreover, Britain could not have anticipated any help from any other western power with interests in the Far East. Not only was France disinclined to act in the region, there were rumours in the spring of 1932 of a possible Franco-Japanese alliance! Finally, it gradually became clear that the most that the United States was prepared to offer was little more than moral condemnation.

Had the League of Nations decided, once China appealed for assistance under the League Covenant, to impose sanctions and had they led to war, Britain would have had to have borne the major part of the military and naval burden. This situation was, however, avoided and the League of Nations saved from complete helplessness by the Japanese suggestion that the League should send a commission of inquiry to Manchuria. Herein lay the origins of the commission chaired by Lord Lytton which reported on the 1 October 1932. In addition, by this time the League of Nations had followed the lead given by the United States the previous January in refusing to recognize international changes brought about by methods that contravened the League Covenant or the Pact of Paris of 1928 (the Kellogg–Briand Pact). This was done at a special meeting of the League Assembly convened on 3 March 1932 on a resolution drafted and proposed by the British foreign secretary, Sir John Simon. Thus both the member states of the League of Nations and the United States refused to recognize the Japanese puppet state of Manchukuo, 'ruled over' by the last of the Manchu Emperors, Henry Pu-yi.

While the Lytton Report recognized that the Japanese had certain legitimate grievances against the Chinese, it nevertheless took the view that the Japanese action in overrunning Manchuria was not justified, that the state of Manchukuo was not independent and that a solution to the crisis could be found in the establishment of an autonomous Manchuria under Chinese sovereignty. The acceptance of this report by a special League Assembly in March 1933 led to the withdrawal of Japan from the League of Nations.

Although hostilities between China and Japan were brought to a temporary end by the Tungku Truce of May 1933, the crisis in the Far East was by no means over, as evidenced in Japan's decision at the end of 1934 to give notice of her intention to withdraw from her obligations under the Washington and London naval limitation treaties. Japan now wanted to achieve naval parity with Britain and the United States. In these circumstances it was argued by the British treasury that there was much to be said for attempting to revive the old Anglo-Japanese relationship, particularly now that Germany was considered the major threat. Both the permanent head of the treasury, Sir Warren Fisher, and the chancellor of the exchequer, Neville Chamberlain, believed that it was possible to come to an arrangement with Japan over access to the Chinese market and that in a more relaxed atmosphere it would be possible to reach a satisfactory agreement on naval limitation. A conciliatory, or appeasing, posture in the Far East was, though, challenged by the foreign office. There was no guarantee that it would have the desired effect and it would give rise to grave offence in the United States. In the end, the Japanese decision to reject the naval limitation agreements and the failure of the British treasury mission, headed by Sir Frederick Leith-Ross, that was sent to the Far East in 1935–6, with a view to assisting the Chinese in overcoming their economic difficulties in collaboration with the Japanese, ensured that the strategy favoured by Fisher and Chamberlain came to nothing.[40] However, no other effective strategy was adopted either. Deterrence and containment were ruled out as Britain strove to avoid a breakdown in relations with Japan while simultaneously holding out to China minimal material aid supplemented by moral support.

The lack of definition in British policy in the Far East was, naturally, partly conditioned by the worsening situation in Europe, characterized by Italy's attack upon Abyssinia and the continuing difficulties that the German government provoked. The Anglo-French communiqué of 3 February 1935 was to remain the basis of British policy towards Germany and its publication was to lead directly to the visit to Berlin on 25 and 26 March 1935 by Sir John Simon and Anthony Eden. The visit, however, was almost fated never to take place. The announcement of the existence of the *Luftwaffe* and the introduction of conscription in Germany could have been used to cancel the visit, but, while Sir John Simon thought there should be protest, in his opinion,

We should not retort by saying that now we will not go to Berlin. After all, what *ultimate* end would that serve? It will not alter the German decision and it will break down whatever contact is left and destroy finally any prospect of agreeing about anything. It would be quite a different matter if excommunicating Germany would lead to a combination to stop her. On the contrary, it would have quite the opposite effect.[41]

The more serious threat to the visit though was the publication of the British Defence White Paper of March 1935, the nature of which owed much to the palpable failure of the Disarmament Conference and the report of the defence requirements committee, which identified Germany as the 'ultimate potential enemy' and stipulated that Britain's defence preparations should be completed within five years. On 30 January 1935 it was decided to issue the Defence White Paper for a debate in parliament that would precede the debates on the service estimates. While attempts were made to tone down the language of this document on the ground that 'if you want to do business with a fellow it is a bad plan to start slinging mud in his face', the views of Sir Warren Fisher, the permanent under-secretary at the treasury, and Vansittart prevailed. The document proved 'downright in expression' and unequivocally named Germany as the source of European tension and the cause of British rearmament. The publication of the Defence White Paper infuriated Hitler, who postponed the visit of the British ministers by the fabrication of a diplomatic illness. Nevertheless, the visit eventually went ahead.

In the event it was not very successful. As Hitler had unilaterally announced Germany's rearmament, the basis of the talks that Simon and Eden were to have with Hitler, the Anglo-French communiqué of 3 February, was effectively shattered. In effect, in return for the *legalization* of German rearmament, Germany was being asked to make a number of concessions to the Anglo-French point of view. Simon, however, could no longer offer to do what Hitler had done for himself and the Führer was uncompromising. The only positive response he made to the British enquiries concerned the proposals for a multilateral Air Pact, aimed at deterring surprise aerial bombardment, and a bilateral naval agreement between Britain and Germany. It seemed eminently prudent to take advantage of Hitler's offer voluntarily to limit German naval rearmament. The Washington–London naval treaty system under which Japan's naval power was restricted was manifestly collapsing. As has already been noted, the Japanese government had given notice of withdrawal from the Washington and London naval treaties in December 1934. Anything, therefore, that restricted the naval threat to Britain would be helpful. Accordingly, the Anglo-German Naval Agreement was very quickly concluded. By an exchange of notes of 18 June 1935 Germany agreed to limit her surface tonnage to 35 per cent. of that of the Royal Navy. Germany was permitted submarine equality, but agreed not to exceed 45 per cent. of Britain's submarine tonnage without notice. Attempts to make further progress by negotiations for an air pact met, however, with evasion.

Until this time the British approach to the German question can be described as piecemeal: Germany's grievances were to be resolved one by one. Moreover, the concept of a general settlement remained limited. Arms limitation, security pacts, the legitimization of German rearmament, and

Germany's return to the League were about as far as it went. But by the end of 1935 it was clear to the officials in the foreign office that this policy was a failure. Anthony Eden, who became British foreign secretary in December 1935, was forced to the same conclusion. Early in 1936 he and the cabinet began to consider the more comprehensive strategy that was now thought to be necessary if the grave problems presented by the recrudescence of German power were to be peacefully settled. In essence this represented a return to the scheme for an 'all-in' settlement that the officials Orme Sargent and Frank Ashton-Gwatkin had outlined at the end of 1931. With the help of another official, Ralph Wigram, they now initiated further debate. Their views were supported by reports from Sir Eric Phipps, the British ambassador in Berlin. Throughout 1935, he observed, Germany's foreign policy objectives had remained unchanged. These he identified as absorption of all Germans into one Reich, expansion in the east and recovery of the former colonies. The only uncertainties concerned the methods and timing of the realization of these aims. Friendship with Britain for the moment remained the keystone of German policy, but there was some disillusionment with this. On the other hand, Hitler would not make any move until the Abyssinian crisis had further untied his hands. Phipps commented:

> If Hitler's heart could be searched to-day his policy would doubtless be found to be very simple. He will keep his powder dry, bide his time and put his trust partly in Wotan, but chiefly in his own mysterious good fortune that has led him, at times unexpectedly, *per aspera ad astra*.[42]

A mood of urgency now began to manifest itself in the foreign office.

In January 1936 Eden circulated a review of ambassadorial reports from Germany since 1933. In a covering memorandum he identified European hegemony as the basic aim of German policy. So far Hitler had been successful in all his ventures. Eden concluded that Britain should not only rearm rapidly, but also make every effort to arrive at a *modus vivendi* with Germany that might reduce European tension. Vansittart supported this and urged the government to deal with Germany on a European level. The object of policy should not be an Anglo-German agreement, but a comprehensive, European settlement. Germany would require an inducement in the form of some sort of territorial concession and a sympathetic consideration of Germany's colonial claims might be the solution. As a corollary of this, Eden observed that the British government was faced with a dilemma. Germany was suffering severe economic distress, which could lead to an explosion, and the obvious answer seemed to be to assist Germany's recovery. This, however, might not be a cure in the case of Germany. Despite this reservation, Eden took the following view:

> On balance . . . I am in favour of making some attempt to come to terms with Germany, but upon one indispensable condition: that we offer no sops to Germany. There must be no concession merely to keep Germany quiet, for that process only stimulates the appetite it is intended to satisfy.

The type of agreement Eden had in mind was a replacement of the Locarno Treaty by an air pact, in which France and Germany would guarantee Britain besides one another, and in which the demilitarized Rhineland zone would disappear; there would be an arms limitation agreement; Britain and France would recognize Germany's preponderant interest in Central and Eastern Europe, provided her aims there were peacefully accomplished; and Britain would do what she could not to impede the expansion of Germany's export trade. This was to form the basis of British policy towards Germany during the coming two and a half years.[43]

Cabinet approval of this policy was rapid and it was decided that a start might be made by yet again sounding the Germans as to the feasibility of an air pact. As, however, in the previous year, at the point at which the British government was about to embark upon an initiative which was intended to lead Europe to peace, the German government had already resolved upon action that was to weaken severely the force of such an attempt. On 7 March 1936, Hitler remilitarized the Rhineland.

The response of the British and the French to such an eventuality had been determined in advance. The British government had decided that there was nothing that could be done effectively to counter such action and the French were disinclined to proceed forcibly. As early as February 1936 the British government had come to the conclusion that the maintenance of the demilitarized zone was not vital to British interests. Furthermore, when the Cabinet discussed the possibility of German action in the Rhineland, there was broad agreement that 'the reality of the situation was that neither France nor England was really in a position to take effective military action against Germany in the event of a violation of the Treaty of Locarno'. It was felt that the French should be 'put up against this reality'. There was little need for this. On the same day, Flandin, now French foreign minister, informed the French ambassador in London, that Eden had already been advised that in the event of a violation of the demilitarized Rhineland zone, France would not take 'isolated action,' but would only act in accord with the other signatories of the Locarno Pact. The subsequent management of the Rhineland crisis showed how much the initiative had passed to Britain and the degree to which the decision as to whether or not Europe went to war in the future was now contingent upon the decisions taken in London and Berlin.[44]

6

The Deepening Crisis, 1936–1938

The remilitarization of the Rhineland and its aftermath confirmed the diplomatic revolution that to a considerable extent had made it possible. Relations between Italy and Germany became steadily more intimate to the extent that the two countries gradually began to adopt identical attitudes on outstanding international issues. An important catalyst in cementing this relationship was the Spanish Civil War and in the succeeding two years dictatorial solidarity was further expressed publicly by Italy's adherence to the Anti-Comintern Pact and her withdrawal from the League of Nations. The British government reacted to these developments by attempting to bring into effect a *general settlement* along the lines worked out prior to the remilitarization of the Rhineland and by endeavouring to re-establish Anglo-Italian friendship, which, it was hoped, would split the dictators.

The Spanish Civil War and increasing Italo-German Solidarity

The main issue dividing Italy and Germany was Austria. But in January 1936 Mussolini had taken the first steps towards liquidating this problem. It would be wrong, however, to suggest that Italy ran headlong into the arms of Germany as soon as Britain and France applied sanctions during the Abyssinian crisis. There was always, on the Italian side at least, a certain degree of mistrust of and even contempt, mixed with fear, for national socialist Germany. While Mussolini was, therefore, prepared to concede the primacy of Germany in Austria, he still wished to maintain the latter's independence. Thus the Duce was very gratified and reassured by the Austro-German *Gentleman's Agreement* of 11 July 1936. Under its terms Germany recognized the full sovereignty of Austria; both states undertook not to interfere in the internal affairs of the other; and Austria agreed to conduct her future policy on the basis of the fact that she was a German state.

Clear evidence of Italo-German intimacy came in a speech made by Mussolini in Milan on 1 November 1936 when he stated:

> One great country has recently gathered a vast amount of sympathy among the masses of the Italian people: I speak of Germany. The Berlin conversations have resulted in an understanding between our two countries over certain problems which have been particularly acute. But these understandings which have been sanctioned in fitting and duly signed agreements, this Berlin–Rome line is not a diaphragm but rather an axis around which can revolve all those European states with a will to collaboration and peace.[1]

The Berlin conversations to which Mussolini referred were those between the Italian foreign minister, Count Galeazzo Ciano, and the German foreign minister, Baron von Neurath, which had taken place the previous month. Ciano's visit to Germany terminated with a visit to Berchtesgaden and a conversation with Hitler. The end product of these conversations were the so-called *October Protocols* signed at Berchtesgaden, but not made public to the world. In essence they provided for Italo-German collaboration in respect of South-East Europe and Spain. Ciano's conversation with Hitler is interesting also in that Ciano presented the latter with a copy of a confidential British document, procured from the British embassy in Rome, entitled *The German Danger*, which had been written by Eden in January 1936. This contained a reference to Hitler and Mussolini as 'adventurers' and, while advocating an agreement with Germany, urged the intensification of Britain's rearmament. While this probably did, as Ciano attested, create 'a profound impression on the Führer', it is not necessarily the case that from this time onwards Hitler pursued an anti-British line. Nevertheless, Mussolini saw fit to announce to the world after these conversations that a certain identity of view existed between Rome and Berlin.[2]

Further evidence of this was provided during the winter of 1936–7 by the German and Italian responses to British efforts to renegotiate a western pact to replace the Locarno arrangements that had been destroyed by Germany's remilitarization of the Rhineland. These efforts had their origins in the offer made by Hitler that accompanied the German action: this consisted of proposals for a demilitarized zone on both sides of the Franco-German Rhine frontier; a non-aggression pact of 25 years duration with France and Belgium, guaranteed by Britain and Italy and supplemented by an air pact; and a German return to the League of Nations. This offer excited the interest of the British government because it went some way towards meeting the criteria that they had formulated in respect of the general settlement they wished to negotiate. Accordingly they were anxious to explore these proposals further. This and the British desire for a wider agreement in general were revealed in the reply of the Locarno powers other than Germany of 19 March, which also proposed arms limitation and economic co-operation. Hitler rejected these suggestions and in a memorandum of 31 March the German government produced alternative proposals of their own. They were, in fact, an amplification of the original German memorandum of 7 March. The British government, however, were not convinced that all processes of conciliation had been exhausted and on 6 May they forwarded a questionnaire to the German government seeking further clarification of the German viewpoint. No reply was ever received to these enquiries and the negative attitude of the German government to them was rather brutally conveyed to the British ambassador, Phipps, verbally by von Neurath in July.[3]

Even so the main thrust of British policy during the winter of 1936 remained the attempt to achieve a new western security pact. The British were encouraged in this by the Belgian prime minister, Van Zeeland, who urged upon them a fresh conference of the Locarno Powers as a prelude to a joint approach to Germany that would offer Germany a further opportunity to co-operate. Thus on 23 July 1936 a Three Power Conference took place in London with the result that the British, French and Belgian governments invited the other Locarno powers, Germany and Italy, to a conference that would negotiate an agreement that would replace the old Locarno Rhine Pact and also act as prelude to a general settlement. The two dictator powers agreed to this in principle by the end of the month. On 18 September the British government suggested that the proposed conference be held at the end of October, but the replies of the German and Italian governments, of 14 and 20 October respectively, were disappointing. In reply the British government in a note of 19 November attempted to take matters further, but neither the Germans nor the Italians replied until 12 March 1937 and when they did their replies were identical in substance. Their basic proposition was that Germany should have a free hand in Eastern Europe; in addition the independence of Belgium was to be guaranteed by Britain, France, Italy and Germany and there was to be a Franco-German non-aggression agreement guaranteed by Britain and Italy, although without an element of reciprocity in favour of the two latter powers. These negotiations inevitably now gradually lapsed.[4]

By this time Italo-German relations had been further developed as a result of the Spanish Civil War, which broke out in July 1936 when General Franco and the Spanish Army raised the standard of revolt in Spanish Morocco against the Republic and its Popular Front government, elected in February 1936. The revolt spread quickly to the mainland, but it was resisted and the hoped for rapid *coup d'état* became a violent civil war that was to last for three years. The causes of the Spanish Civil War are too complex and profound for even brief analysis here. Simply put, the parliamentary left in Spain, and predominantly the Socialist party, from the beginning of the Second Republic in 1931 introduced a number of reforms that affected the religious and agrarian structure of Spain and thus provoked strong opposition from both the 'legalist' and 'catastrophist' Right. Although the right won the elections of November 1933, an abortive workers' revolution of October 1934 and the victory of the left in a Popular Front in the elections of 1936 demonstrated the 'impossibility of defending traditional [social and economic] structures by means of the legal imposition of a corporative state'. The failure, therefore, of the 'legalist' right led to 'a resurgence of the 'catastrophist' right and the imposition of a corporative state by force of arms.'[5] The loose Popular Front coalition, supported by socialists, anarchists and communists was opposed by right-wing clerical conservatives, nationalists and a small fascist party known as the Falange. This ideological polarization of democracy and socialism pitted against reactionary, dictatorial nationalism and fascism within Spain seemed to many to reflect the growing European conflict. The Spanish Civil War, therefore, rapidly became a *cause célèbre* and there was a widespread fear that it could precipitate a full-scale ideological European war.[6]

It was primarily because of this that the British government quickly endorsed the proposal by the French government that the powers should observe the principle of non-intervention in Spain. Also of substantial importance was the need for Britain to maintain good relations with whichever side won in Spain, a point vigorously pressed upon Eden by the Portuguese ambassador, Armindo Monteiro. Finally, and with an eye to the major source of danger, the British were anxious to re-establish good relations with Italy, following their impairment during the Abyssinian crisis.[7] This could scarcely have been achieved by supporting opposite sides in Spain. The object of policy here was to inhibit the further development of Italo-German relations. Non-intervention was not intended as a friendly act to the Spanish republican authorities. On the contrary it was hoped and anticipated that the Nationalists would win, for there was a fear that a presumed communist victory in Spain would aid the spread of the 'deadly doctrine' to France and possibly elsewhere in Western Europe with all the complications that would flow therefrom for British policy.

When the Spanish Civil War began France too had recently elected a Popular Front government whose leader was the socialist, Léon Blum. It has often been argued that the decisive factor in prompting Blum to propose non-intervention was British pressure. Obviously, there was some, but the French motivation was primarily domestic. Blum's immediate instinct was to support the lawful Republican government of Spain, but it was very soon impressed upon him that such action would have a very divisive effect upon French society which might itself collapse into civil war. With enthusiastic British backing a non-intervention agreement was concluded. Among the signatories were Germany, Italy and the Soviet Union. The Non-Intervention Committee held its first meeting in London on 9 September 1936, but from the first to last it was a charade. The only genuine non-interventionists were the British and even so their intention was hardly to create a level playing field for both sides.

There was no Italo-German collusion prior to Franco's rising, but from the beginning both the Italian and German governments supported the nationalist cause with very substantial military aid. The motive in both cases was ideological: the left, in the form of the Popular Front government, could not be allowed to triumph. In the very early days of the conflict the provision of aerial transport by Italy and Germany was crucial in ferrying the Spanish African Army to the mainland. Thereafter the German Condor Legion, which assured the nationalists of aerial superiority, and the 60,000 Italian volunteers played a considerable part in assisting the Spanish nationalists. On the Republican side the main source of support was the Soviet Union. Here the principal contribution was *matériel* rather than men, although a number of experts and specialists were sent out. But the aid was never lavish and decreased rapidly after the spring of 1937. By the following year it had virtually come to a standstill. Both Hitler and Stalin probably considered that they had derived substantial benefits from the prolongation of the war in Spain. For the German armed forces it was a valuable field for experimentation and on the diplomatic front it bound Italy and Germany still closer, among other things, as a result of co-operation on the Non-Intervention Committee. From the Soviet viewpoint it was a diversion that focused international interest well away from the USSR at a time when the Soviet state had embarked upon a vicious policy of purges which ended in the death and imprisonment of millions and a devastating weakening of the Red Army as the purges devoured most of its high command and corps of field officers.[8]

In September 1937 Mussolini paid an official visit to Germany; it was important on two counts. First, Mussolini was overwhelmingly impressed with German power and from this time onwards he seems to have been geared psychologically to accept a secondary role in the 'Axis' partnership. Secondly, Italo-German relations were further cemented, although the Italians continued to harbour reservations concerning Germany. Still, this did not prevent Italy's adherence to the Anti-Comintern Pact, concluded the previous November between Germany and Japan, on 6 November 1937 and her withdrawal from the League of Nations at the end of that year. Moreover, the growing reality of an 'Axis' bloc in European politics gave an added boost to Hitler's already burgeoning confidence.[9]

In general, German policy after March 1936 gradually became more overtly aggressive, whereas the posture previously had been fundamentally defensive. This was possible because Germany's military strength was rapidly increasing and, as a result of the Abyssinian crisis, her diplomatic position had improved. By January 1936 German planning for rearmament was in excess of the programme laid down in March 1935; in August of the same year military service was extended to a period of two years. The following month at the Nuremberg Rally Hitler introduced the Four Year Plan in order to fulfil the priorities he outlined in a memorandum of August 1936. Describing Germany's economic problems as he saw them, he concluded:

> The final solution lies in extending our living space, that is to say, extending the sources of raw materials and foodstuffs of our people. It is the task of the political leadership one day to solve this problem.

This was a policy that would clearly mean war and Hitler observed that it was better to prepare for this contingency in time of peace. Subsequently he outlined a programme for making Germany self-sufficient in raw materials, oils and fats, the central objective of which was to insulate Germany against the effects of a blockade should she have to fight Britain. He stated in conclusion:

> I thus set the following tasks:
>   I. The German armed forces must be operational within four years.
>   II. The German economy must be fit for war within four years.

Göring, who was put in charge of this plan, read this memorandum to the German cabinet on 4 September.[10]

During the autumn of 1936 Hitler also began to adopt a rather more strident tone in his relations with Britain. He still regarded the co-operation or neutrality of Britain as important for the realization of his long term plans, but, the Anglo-German Naval Agreement notwithstanding, he was patently making little progress in achieving the kind of relationship with Britain that he wanted. Until 1936 he had soft-pedalled Germany's demands for colonial restoration, partly because the overseas ambitions were still a distant aim and partly not to offend or menace the British. However, at the end of 1936 the German colonial organizations and societies were co-ordinated and placed under the direct control of the government and there now commenced a surge of colonial propaganda. One very eminent German historian has argued the case that, having failed to win Britain by kindness, Hitler was now attempting to coerce the British into the kind of relationship with Germany that he desired. Whatever the motive it is clear that a new sharpness began to enter into the German attitude towards Britain.[11]

While the offer of an understanding with Britain, on German terms, still probably remained intact, Hitler was now less inclined to see it as the precondition of the accomplishment of *Lebensraum*. What appeared to him as British weakness over the Abyssinian crisis, the Spanish Civil War and events in the Far East, convinced him that he could realize his aims in Central and Eastern Europe without the agreement of Britain. Moreover, it seemed improbable to him that there would be armed intervention on the part of Britain to prevent German expansion in the region. The failed negotiations regarding the convention of a five power conference that would negotiate a replacement of Locarno were probably also instrumental in causing Hitler to conclude that, although the western powers might not like the idea of German expansion in Eastern Europe, there existed a reluctance to resort to arms to oppose it. In view of the failure of the understanding with Britain to materialize and increasing doubts as to its imperative necessity, it is likely that from the autumn of 1937 Hitler had decided to pursue his continental aims no longer with, but without Britain.

At the famous meeting in the Reich chancellery on 5 November 1937 (recorded in the Hossbach Memorandum) Hitler observed that Germany 'had to reckon with two hate-inspired antagonists, Britain and France, to whom a German colossus in the centre of Europe was a thorn in the flesh'. However, he clearly felt that the British Empire was in a state of decline and beset by internal difficulties that would inhibit Britain from interfering in the German achievement of *Lebensraum*. This would have to be achieved by force by 1943–5, after which Germany's military, position would be comparatively weaker; that Britain was filled with hate did not of itself necessarily betoken serious opposition. During his discourse, Hitler also looked at more immediate possibilities, namely, the annexation of Austria and Czechoslovakia. French involvement in a war with another power, or the collapse of France herself into a state of civil war would be the occasion on which to finish off both these states as independent entities. Significantly, he considered that Britain and France had probably 'tacitly written off the Czechs' and he evidently anticipated early developments. If Hitler had concluded by the autumn of 1937 that the alliance or understanding with Britain was not within his grasp, he apparently was not dissuaded from proceeding towards the realization of his programme and now contemplated the first moves.[12]

Furthermore, by February 1938, his ascendancy over the German military was complete. Following the bloody purge of the SA in 1934, on account of its perceived threat to the authority of the army, all soldiers took an oath of personal allegiance to the Führer, which within the traditions of the German Army was particularly binding and especially so for the officer corps. Early in 1938 Hitler decided to take advantage of a social indiscretion on the part of the war minister, von Blomberg, to perfect his control of the army. At the Hossbach Conference von Blomberg, and General von Fritsch, the commander-in-chief of the army, had both expressed reservations regarding Hitler's views. Subsequently, when it became known early in January 1938 that Blomberg had recently married a former prostitute, Hitler decided to use the scandal as a means of making the army further subservient to his will in a number of personnel and organizational changes (see above p. 99). The war ministry was now disbanded and replaced by the OKW (*Oberkommando der Wehrmacht*), with Hitler as supreme commander of the armed forces. Hitler knew where he wanted to go and he could now compel the army to do his bidding without opposition.

British Attempts to Secure a General Settlement

By the beginning of 1936 the British government had determined to attempt a broad renegotiation of the arrangements that had governed European politics since 1919. In other words they had determined to seek a *general settlement* that would bring about an *appeasement* of the European situation. One of the inducements to be held out to Hitler to co-operate in such a scheme was the right for Germany to remilitarize the Rhineland. Although Hitler's action in remilitarizing the Rhineland for himself deprived the British government of a valuable concession, thereby placing the foreign secretary, Anthony Eden, in a position of disadvantage in respect of the negotiations he now wished to start, it did not mean that these negotiations would be dropped. On the contrary, Eden thought they were now inevitable. As has been described, during the winter of 1937, one of the principal reasons why the British government wanted a five power conference to renegotiate the Locarno arrangements was to use it as a starting point for achieving a general settlement. It was, however, clear by March 1937 that the negotiations for a five power conference were going nowhere. In these circumstances it was decided by the British government to seize upon various proposals that had been made by the German minister of economics, Hjalmar Schacht, the previous August on a visit to Paris as a means of opening general discussions.

The reasons why Schacht took such an initiative remain to some extent obscure. What does seem clear, however, is that he was very anxious about the direction that Hitler's foreign policy was taking. In short, he had begun to perceive the reality of Hitler's intentions. The quest for *Lebensraum*, and the war that would be necessary to obtain it, were not the mere vapourings of an out of office politician, but were meant in deadly earnest. Schacht was not a nazi and never joined the NSDAP. Moreover, despite his unorthodox methods, he was committed to the liberal economic order in international relations. Thus he was opposed to the Four Year Plan and the *autarkic*, self-sufficient economic system that was an essential part of it. He was also opposed to the war that would be its consequence. Schacht's attitude naturally caused him to lose influence and during 1936 he steadily lost ground in economic matters to Göring, who eventually became reich commissioner for the Four Year Plan. It seems, therefore, that in desperation in August 1936 Schacht, on a visit to Paris, attempted to persuade the French government that only a full or partial restoration of Germany's colonies would avert what he referred to as 'an explosion'. Schacht himself was a keen colonial enthusiast and this must partly explain why he advocated this course, but it is probable that his fundamental motive was to inveigle the western powers into making a generous offer of colonial expansion to Germany, which Hitler would be bound to accept and which would make it difficult for him to justify a war in Eastern Europe on the grounds that the Germans were a *Volk ohne Raum* (a people without space). As Schacht explained to his friend, Dr. Jäckh, colonial restoration was the alternative to the Four Year Plan and the war that would result from it. Clearly, the attitude of the British government would be important in this and Schacht urged Blum, the French prime minister, to discuss his suggestions with the British.[13]

The British were very dismissive when first informed of this development. There was the question to be answered of how much authority Schacht had to proceed in this way. In addition, if the German government wanted to discuss broader issues with a view to an agreement, the negotiations then proceeding for the convening of a five power conference seemed the best means of doing so. By the end of the year, however, rumours were circulating to the effect that a negative British attitude had ruined the Schacht initiative. Moreover, when he was more fully informed of what had taken place the previous summer, Neville Chamberlain, the chancellor of the exchequer, who was by this time already becoming a very formidable influence in the formulation of British foreign policy, became somewhat irritated by what appeared to have been a lost opportunity. He, therefore, prevailed upon Eden and the foreign office to explore Schacht's proposals further, if only to remove the impression that the British government were being unco-operative. Consequently, Sir Frederick Leith-Ross, the chief economic adviser to the British government, was sent to Germany in February 1937 to examine Schacht in rather more detail. This visit did not, in fact, reveal much that was not already known. Yet in a memorandum of 15 March Eden circulated the cabinet foreign policy committee with a record of the conversations that Leith-Ross had with Schacht. He claimed that he wanted to consult the committee as to the nature of the reply that should be sent to Schacht. Probably, however, considering the fact that the negotiations for a five power conference had in effect come to an end, he was at last seriously contemplating using Schacht's suggestions and the possibility of a colonial restoration to Germany as a means with which to persuade the Germans to participate in a conference and ultimately in a general settlement.[14]

On 18 March the foreign policy committee surveyed the new situation. Chamberlain remarked that he understood that Eden shared his view that, if 'a full, final and general settlement' could be obtained by the restoration of Togoland and the Cameroons to Germany, then discussions on those terms ought not to be entirely eliminated. At the end of the meeting it was agreed in principle that exploratory talks with the French should be started with the object of a joint approach to Berlin. The task of preparing a draft note to the French was entrusted to Eden and William Ormsby-Gore, the colonial secretary. They were, however, unable to agree upon the terms of the note and it was a draft prepared by Chamberlain that was finally adopted.

In a covering memorandum Chamberlain put forward the view that it was a mistake to put the colonial question too firmly to the fore. No doubt it was a cardinal point with Schacht; but the Germans ought not to be allowed to dictate the programme of discussion. Nevertheless, he observed

> . . . Dr. Schacht's approaches . . . cannot be regarded as anything but an invitation to a general discussion.
>
> Any Government which turned down this invitation without at least exploring the possibilities sufficiently to make sure that there was no possible basis of agreement would incur a very heavy responsibility. Even a slight improvement in the international atmosphere may lead gradually to a general détente, whereas a policy of drift may lead to a general war.

Chamberlain's note outlined the bases of a joint Anglo-French approach to Germany. Significantly, prior to any general negotiations, Germany would have to satisfy Britain and France in advance that she was ready in principle to conclude treaties of non-aggression to replace Locarno, to reassure the states of East and Central Europe, to return to the League, and to sign an international arms limitation agreement. Were the German government to indicate its agreement to these conditions, Britain would reciprocate by examining means of stabilizing the German economic and financial system. If Germany raised the colonial question, Chamberlain thought that Britain and France should have determined their attitude in advance. It was not possible for Britain to cede Tanganyika (former German East Africa); but he considered that the former German colonies in West Africa that had been partitioned between Britain and France, namely, Togoland and the Cameroons, could be returned to Germany. As the French loss would be proportionately greater, Britain would balance the larger French territorial loss by giving Germany guarantees of freedom of access to colonial raw materials and markets. Clearly, Chamberlain's strategy was to push the colonial question into the background, for if such a contentious issue were to be given a position of prominence, it could easily jeopardize the commencement of general discussions.[15]

Preliminary soundings were made in Paris, but the French were, by this time, less enthusiastic about plans for colonial readjustment, particularly as France was being asked to make most of the territorial sacrifices involved. It was the view of Sir Eric Phipps, now British ambassador in Paris, that it would be prudent not to press the matter. For the moment the efforts to engage the Germans in negotiations for a general settlement had perforce to be abandoned.

In May 1937 a fresh impetus was given to the conduct of British foreign policy when Neville Chamberlain became prime minister. His strong personality would unquestionably have made an impact even had he not quite deliberately decided to have a greater say in the formulation of foreign policy than his predecessor. There were, however, reasons other than his desire to be in command which explain his determination. During the early days of the Third Reich it had been assumed by British intelligence agencies that Germanic 'thoroughness' and 'efficiency' would mean a rather slow rearmament. This complacency, however, did not long survive the reports of the industrial intelligence centre (IIC) and those of Malcolm Christie, a retired group captain resident in Germany. Through the work of the IIC, the scale of German aerial rearmament was gradually apprehended; Christie revealed a German plan for an air force of 11,732 aircraft by December 1938. By the end of 1936 British air intelligence had to accept that they were confronted with a *Luftwaffe* that was expanding without pauses for consolidation. Simultaneously the war office recognized that the German Army and its industrial base had expanded beyond what were regarded as 'legitimate and acceptable' limits. Accordingly, from 1936 until the end of 1938, as the chiefs of staff and the intelligence directorates perceived the gap that had opened up in British and German rearmament, the pessimism that the situation engendered was intensified by the preparation of 'worst-case' scenarios that wildly overestimated actual German capacity. The impact of such reports upon British foreign policy was inevitable and is evident. Germany had to be brought into a stable international framework that was acceptable to her and the principal European powers.[16]

But despite much discussion and effort, Britain was no nearer to getting Germany into a settlement. Sir Alexander Cadogan, who was being groomed as Vansittart's replacement at the foreign office, was moved to complain testily

> I'm quite sure that one needs a long spoon in dealing with the Germans, but by resolutely refusing to come to the table even, we are letting them get all the soup. It can't be said that our 'policy' so far has been successful. In fact, we haven't got a policy; we merely wait to see what will happen to us next.[17]

This was not quite correct. There was a policy, but it was not being boldly presented and there was a clear reluctance to engage the real sources of power in Nazi Germany. Thus when in May 1937 Sir Nevile Henderson, Britain's new ambassador to Berlin, told Cadogan that whatever the foreign office thought he was going to make contact with the Führer and his court, the latter thought the ambassador had the right approach. It would be unfair to blame Eden for having failed to bring a perverse negotiating partner such as the German government into meaningful negotiations, but it must have been clear within the cabinet by this time that Eden was bad in a crisis and indecisive at crucial moments. Increasingly it had been Neville Chamberlain who had led the cabinet foreign policy committee at critical points and it was Chamberlain, as chancellor of the exchequer, who had taken the initiative in ending the disastrous economic sanctions against Italy when they could no longer save Abyssinia. Indeed on the eve of his premiership, Chamberlain had acquired a position of dominance in the cabinet in the field of foreign policy that it would have been difficult to reverse. This was not resented by Eden and all the evidence suggests that far from being apprehensive about the new prime minister Eden was very favourable.[18]

The international situation in the summer of 1937 was gloomy. The era of annual crises precipitated by Hitler seemed to be over; but he had made no contribution to peace. Italo–German relations were progressing towards greater intimacy and an anti-comintern pact had been signed by Germany and Japan. The nightmare of British policy was unfolding: that of being threatened simultaneously in Europe, the Mediterranean and the Far East. A chiefs of staff memorandum warned:

> The intervention of Italy against us would at once impose conflicting demands on our fleet. Our policy must be governed by the principle that no anxieties or risks connected with our interests in the Mediterranean can be allowed to interfere with the despatch of a fleet to the Far East.[19]

Eden had already made it clear that Hitler had seized the initiative from the very first. If the British government was to succeed in its policy of obtaining a general settlement, it would have to secure the initiative for itself and to control events meant to set the pace. Convinced that it was urgent to reach agreement with the dictators and if possible to divide them, Chamberlain was determined to use every opportunity that might bring about that result.

During the summer of 1937 Sir Nevile Henderson had a number of friendly conversations with Hermann Göring. These, however, produced little that indicated that German thinking was likely to make a reality of the British concept of a general settlement. As Göring described it, the German concept of an Anglo–German agreement consisted of two clauses: namely, German recognition of British maritime predominance and British recognition of Germany's primacy in Europe. Moreover, the effort to entice Italy away from Germany had one grave disadvantage: Eden believed that it would be impossible on satisfactory terms. For Eden, Mussolini was the 'anti-Christ' and likely to incline to whichever side offered the greatest advantage. Undoubtedly, in retrospect and on the basis of contemporary evidence there was much to commend Eden's view, but Eden also felt piqued and personally humiliated by Italy's and Mussolini's success in defying the League over Abyssinia. The Italian conquest of Abyssinia became an obsession that obscured from this incorrigibly vain man the danger to Britain stemming from close Italo–German relations. If Germany was ever to be tied down to an agreement she would have had to have been isolated, which implied, however unpalatable it might have been, concessions to Italy. Eden disliked such a prospect intensely which provoked increasingly bitter feelings between himself and the prime minister as Neville Chamberlain began to take personal initiatives with the Italian leader of which the foreign secretary strongly disapproved.

By December 1937 the problems between Chamberlain and Eden appeared to have been overcome as a consequence of the visit of Lord Halifax to Germany. Halifax had been invited in his private capacity as a master of hounds by Göring, the Reich game warden, to attend a hunting exhibition in Berlin. Neville Chamberlain encouraged the visit, which he thought could be useful from the point of view of making contact with the German leaders. Anthony Eden objected when he learnt that Hitler would only receive Halifax at Berchtesgaden, an arrangement he thought resembled grovelling if accepted, but later took the view that the visit might do good. The talks with Hitler left Halifax with the impression that there could be no satisfactory basis for a rapprochement between Britain and Germany unless the colonial question was settled. Halifax told Hitler that, while Britain was not pledged to maintain the *status quo* in Eastern Europe in perpetuity, change would have to be accomplished peacefully. Hitler responded that the colonial question was the only issue between Britain and Germany; he hoped an agreeable solution could be found. According to Halifax this could only be effected within a genuine settlement that would accomplish a real relaxation of the current tension. In his personal record of the talks, Halifax wrote:

> ... while I think he [Hitler] wants to be on friendly terms with us, he is not going to be in any hurry to consider the question of League of Nations return – regards disarmament as pretty hopeless, and, in short, feels himself to be in a strong position and is not going to run after us. He did not give me the impression of being at all likely to want to go to war with us over colonies, but, no doubt, if he cannot be met on this issue, good relations, under which I suppose we might exert a good deal of influence ... would remain impossible.

He urged further examination of a colonial settlement with Germany, which he thought might be used as a lever with which to secure a general settlement.[20] Following the Halifax visit consultations took place in London between Chamberlain and Eden and the French prime minister and foreign minister, Chautemps and Delbos, which resulted in an identity of view on a number of points. It was particularly agreed that the two governments would be willing to examine the colonial question. Consequently, early in the new year it was decided by the British government to make a direct approach to the German government regarding a general settlement that would have a colonial dimension.

Fresh urgency was added to the necessity for such an approach from the point of view of Neville Chamberlain as governmental discussions over the cost and pace of British rearmament reached a critical stage in the period December 1937 to February 1938. In December 1937 the minister for the co-ordination of defence, Sir Thomas Inskip, presented his *Interim Report on Defence Expenditure in Future Years*. Inskip's post had been a new creation and was largely the consequence of serious criticism of the government's conduct of rearmament policy that had surfaced in the wake of the crisis caused by the Hoare–Laval Plan. This criticism was first voiced in the quality press and then taken up by Conservative backbenchers. The main thrust of the arguments put forward by the critics was that the current system, whereby the three armed forces were responsible for their own planning and supply, resulted in inefficiencies, duplication and damaging competition. It was argued that this situation could be improved by the creation of a ministry of defence that

. . . would diminish the overlapping of function and effort, and allow economies to be realized through the joint purchase of common stores . . . [and] foster the development of a unified and well-integrated defence policy by forcing the commands of the three services to work together rather than compete . . .[21]

During February 1936 a private member's bill proposing the creation of a ministry of defence was defeated in the Commons, but the debate revealed the profundity of the disquiet on the backbenches regarding the government's handling of defence issues. Therefore, while the government remained opposed to the idea of a ministry of defence on the grounds that it would superimpose a further layer of bureaucracy and infringe prime ministerial and treasury control of defence-related matters, it was deemed prudent to compromise and create the post of minister for the co-ordination of defence. The primary function of the appointed minister 'would be to serve as a coordinator of defence policy, sitting on all committees dealing with defence matters and acting as a surrogate for the prime minister when he could not attend'. In short, the minister for the co-ordination of defence was to be 'a trouble shooter in the defence organization, making it more efficient without altering its basic method of operation or upsetting the prevailing balance of power within it'. Inskip's appointment to this post provoked a flurry of sarcasm – the most extraordinary appointment, it was said, since Caligula made his horse a Consul – but the surviving evidence shows him to have been competent and efficient.[22]

The problem which Inskip was to address in the autumn of 1937 had its origins in the Defence White Paper of 1936 which set out the figure of £1,500 million as the sum that should be allocated to defence spending over a five year period. Throughout 1937 this was the sum to which the treasury wished to adhere, while agreeing, significantly, that £400 million of it could be raised by borrowing.[23] The difficulty, however, lay in the fact that by 1937 expenditure on defence and rearmament by the three armed services was already exceeding these limitations.[24] Shortly before becoming prime minister, Neville Chamberlain, then chancellor of the exchequer, warned his colleagues at a cabinet meeting of 3 April 1937 that: '. . . we were approaching the time when he would have to propose a fixed limit to which the Services would have to conform'. He, therefore, proposed a further examination of the entire problem.[25] This was precisely the issue that Inskip was called upon to resolve and he was to do so with the assistance of Sir Horace Wilson, Sir Maurice Hankey and Arthur Robinson in what came to be known as the Inskip Committee.

Further increases in expenditure on rearmament were considered within the treasury for various reasons as very undesirable. There was great resistance to any increases in income tax to pay for rearmament as it was felt that the current rate of five shillings in the pound (25 per cent) was excessive and already threatening economic recovery; further increases would only lead directly back to depression. Cuts in social services were also to be avoided as a method of paying for rearmament, on the ground that they would merely foster social unrest which the government wished to avoid. This left borrowing, which the treasury now reluctantly accepted as necessary, but not in excess of national savings, which it was held would lead to inflation. Seen from the treasury, therefore, definite limits had to be imposed on spending on rearmament, animated as that department was by the belief that the costs of rearmament constituted a far graver threat to the social and political order in Britain than the German military threat posed to the national security.[26] Treasury rationale was very well encapsulated in a memorandum of May 1937 by Sir Richard Hopkins, which stated:

> There is a grave danger that we may find at the end of the rearmament period that we have built up our armed forces to a level that is far beyond our capacity to maintain. There is no more certain way of drifting into bankruptcy than to borrow for a temporary capital purpose and then to continue borrowing . . . for normal current requirements.

Thus it was deemed necessary to ration the armed services on the basis that:

> We must face the fact that we cannot do everything which we should like to do; that there is a limit to the amount of money that can be made available for defence measures and that the money available for defence must be allocated to those purposes, which, on a broad review of the whole situation are regarded as of prime importance.[27]

This thinking found its way into Inskip's interim report of 15 December 1937. Security was not merely a matter of war *matériel*. Resources of manpower, industry and financial and economic strength were also vitally essential, as was social stability. Nothing, therefore, should be done to impair Britain's economic and social stability in advance of a conflict. At the heart of this argument was the treasury's concept that finance constituted the fourth arm of Britain's defence services. Inskip's report stated:

> The maintenance of credit facilities and our general balance of trade are of vital importance not merely from the point of view of our strength in peacetime, but equally for purposes of war. This country cannot hope to win a war against a major Power by a sudden knockout blow; on the contrary, for success we must contemplate a long war in the course of which we should have to mobilize all our resources and those of the Dominions and other countries overseas . . . Germany is likely to be the aggressor and will endeavour 'to exploit her superior preparedness by trying to knock out Britain rapidly, for she is not well placed for a long war in which the Sea Powers, as in the past are likely to have the advantage.' We must, therefore, confront our enemies with the risks of a long war, which they cannot face. If we are to emerge victoriously from such a war, it is essential that we should enter it with sufficient economic strength to enable us to make the fullest use of resources overseas, and to withstand the strain. While, therefore, it is true that the extent of our resources imposes limitations upon the size of the defence programmes which we are able to undertake, this is only one aspect of the matter. Seen in its true perspective, the maintenance of our economic stability would more accurately be described as an essential element in our defensive strength: one which can properly be regarded as a fourth arm in defence, alongside the three services without which purely military effort would be of no avail.[28]

It is evident from this report that the stability of sterling and the British economy were considered to be of vital importance in a long war of attrition, in effect a world war. Britain's credit had to be good to enable her to buy arms and supplies before her economy was fully converted to war production; hence the importance of not dislocating the economy in advance of hostilities. Based upon this premise, the priorities for defence were to be, first, military preparations sufficient for Britain to repulse an attempted knockout blow from the air; secondly, the preservation of trade routes essential for the supply of food and raw materials; thirdly, the defence of British territories overseas against land, sea and air attack; and finally, co-operation on the defence of the territories of any power or powers with whom Britain might be allied.[29] The implications of the Inskip interim report for the army were the elimination of the preparations for any continental field force; for the air force the Inskip report ultimately meant priority being accorded to the construction of a fighter force and the relegation of the concept of the deterrent bombing force to second place. Quite apart from the fact that the provision of fighters was cheaper than the creation of a large bomber force, this new priority could now be scientifically justified on the ground of the development of radar which made possible the successful interception of invading bomber squadrons. Nevertheless, this new emphasis was in downright contradiction to the received wisdom within the air ministry where the priority of bombing and bombers was firmly entrenched and arguably almost incurred Britain's defeat in the Battle of Britain. In the event, priority was given to fighters just in time to save the country. The impact of Inskip's report on the navy was by and large neutral. While continuing to deny the rearmament of the navy on the two-power or new standard, the completion of existing programmes was not affected.

When the cabinet discussed the Inskip interim report on 22 December 1937, it was agreed to adhere to the figure of £1,500 million over a five year period, but this was to prove very difficult to achieve in practice. The inadequacy of the figures submitted by the armed services in October 1937 made it very difficult to establish firm budgetary limits for each service. Consequently, the services were asked to submit fresh figures in January 1938, after which Inskip was to present his final report. In the end, however, the treasury had to impose cuts on the service estimates. The central problem with which Inskip grappled was that of reconciling treasury limits with the costs deemed necessary by the armed forces for the adequate defence of the nation. These totalled some £1,926 million without the two-power navy standard and £1,968 million with it. Inskip's ultimate proposal was a recommendation for a total allocation to defence spending of £1,570 million over a five-year period, with the additional provision of £80 million for air raid precautions. While Inskip had been anxious to remain within treasury limitations, he was also very well aware that negotiating with potential enemies to avoid war had to be done from a position of at least apparent strength. Hence the proposal for a modest increase in funding and the recommendation that the bulk of the spending should be undertaken in the first two years of the five-year programme.[30] On 16 February 1938, Inskip's final report was endorsed by the cabinet.[31]

This debate on defence expenditure naturally had implications for foreign policy. Since the summer of 1937 the treasury had been demanding a more positive attitude on the part of the foreign office with regard to Germany.[32] These demands now became much more strident. By December 1937 Edward Hale, a treasury official, was hoping that Britain's negative policy towards Germany would be replaced by a friendly one. Furthermore, he argued:

> If this friendly feeling with Germany can be promoted there should be a real chance of obtaining a settlement of most of the major troubles which beset us, and of obtaining relief from the intolerable and growing burden of armaments.[33]

To these pressures from the treasury should be added those from the chiefs of staff. In a review of Britain's military strength relative to other powers as at January 1938, they concluded that:

> . . . Naval, Military and Air forces, in their present stage of development, are still far from sufficient to meet our defensive commitments, which now extend from Western Europe through the Mediterranean to the Far East. Even today we could face without apprehension an emergency either in the Far East or in the Mediterranean, provided that we were free to make preparations in time of peace and to concentrate sufficient strength in one or other of these areas . . . So far as Germany is concerned, as our preparations develop, our defence forces will provide a considerable deterrent to aggression. But the outstanding feature of the present situation is the increasing probability that a war started in any one of these three areas may extend to one or both of the other two. Without overlooking the assistance which we should hope to obtain from France, and possibly other allies, we cannot foresee the time when our defence forces will be strong enough to safeguard our territory, trade and vital interests against Germany, Italy and Japan simultaneously. We cannot, therefore, exaggerate the importance, from the point of view of Imperial defence, of any political or international action that can be taken to reduce the numbers of our potential enemies and to gain the support of potential allies.[34]

The nature of the problem presented by the chiefs of staff was graphically illustrated in the second half of 1937 when the Sino–Japanese war resumed and precipitated a worsening in Anglo-Japanese relations. Hostilities rapidly spread to Shanghai 'where the value of British investment exceeded that of any comparable area outside the United Kingdom'[35]. A Japanese victory, or even a stalemate, was bound to inflict irreversible damage on British interests in the area. There was little that the British government could do about this; as Neville Chamberlain observed, it would have been 'suicidal' to have forced a confrontation with Japan at a time when the situation in Europe was so grave. The clear limitations of what could be achieved in the Far East were revealed during the Brussels Conference of November 1937, which had been called so that the powers signatory to the Nine Power Treaty could discuss the situation in the Far East. The British foreign secretary, Anthony Eden, allowed himself to be persuaded by the American representative, Norman Davis, that the United States would participate in economic sanctions against Japan. Accordingly, he instructed the foreign office to inform the United States government that Britain would be willing to join in economic sanctions provided the United States would assist in the defence of British territories in the Far East should the Japanese attack them by way of reprisal.

The response of the American government was to indicate that Davis had exceeded his function. There were, therefore, no consequences to Eden's action.[36] This vindicated the view of Gladwyn Jebb in the foreign office who commented on the contents of a foreign office memorandum the previous October: '. . . sanctions would almost certainly mean war [with Japan] and the USA is not prepared to fight, even with the British Empire as an ally. Therefore there will be no sanctions.'[37] Jebb's view coincided very much with that of the prime minister. The United States, Chamberlain thought, would always be full of good will if somebody else was prepared to do the fighting; as he wrote to his sister, Ida Chamberlain, 'the Yanks . . . hadn't the remotest intention of touching . . . [sanctions] . . . with the end of the largest imaginable barge pole'[38].

During December 1937 British and American naval and commercial vessels located in the Yangtze river were subjected to attack by Japanese artillery and aircraft. HMS *Ladybird* was hit by Japanese guns, while the USS *Panay* was sunk and three vessels belonging to Standard Oil were put to fire by Japanese aircraft. This Yangtze Incident was once again to illustrate the difficulties that faced the British government in responding to such outrages and inhibiting further such excesses. Prior to this the British had tried to involve the United States government in joint action to restrain Japanese interference with Chinese maritime customs, which were important for the servicing of China's foreign debts, but without success. Nevertheless, given the nature of these most recent atrocities, a further effort was made to involve the United States in a display of force that would have involved the despatch of as many as nine British capital warships to the Far East, provided that the Americans were prepared to make an equivalent gesture. On the last day of 1937 Captain Ingersoll of the United States Navy arrived in London for staff talks, but, despite the hopes aroused by this, the British government was brought back to earth on 10 January when the US under-secretary of state, Sumner Welles, informed the British ambassador in Washington that the American government could only participate in the most modest gestures until the Japanese did something really outrageous to provoke American opinion.[39]

If the help that Britain could expect from the United States was minimal, equally little could be anticipated from the imperial dominions, namely, Canada, Australia, New Zealand and South Africa. That had been made clear during the Imperial Conference in London of May/June 1937. The Canadian prime minister, Mackenzie King, had spoken of growing opposition in Canada 'to participation in war, any war . . .' and of the deep impression made there by the 'isolationist swing in the United States, its renunciation of war profits and neutral rights in order to keep out of war . . .'. The Australian statesman, R. G. Casey, speaking for the Australian delegation, had argued that Germany should be allowed to incorporate the territories of all German-speaking populations within the Reich. Hertzog, the South African prime minister, had blamed Britain's association with France for the ills of Europe and had warned that 'South Africa could not be expected to have any share or part . . . in a war' that arose from an 'unwillingness to redress the wrongs' of the Treaty of Versailles. M. J. Savage, New Zealand's prime minister, had been the only dominions premier to argue the case for a tougher policy in Europe combined with a co-ordinated imperial foreign policy that would give a lead to the world.[40] The brave words spoken by Savage were not, however, reinforced by a commitment to support such a position with a concomitant expenditure on defence by New Zealand, especially in the Pacific where the antipodean dominions were opposed to any appeasement of Japan. New Zealand in 1937–8 was spending less than one per cent of her national income on defence as opposed to the 5.6 per cent of national income spent by Britain. The corresponding figure for Australia was one per cent. It has been demonstrated that had these dominions committed themselves to a defence expenditure equivalent of that of Britain it would have been sufficient over a period of years to have created in the Pacific a very formidable imperial naval presence. As it was Britain was left to shoulder in effect the entirety of the burden of imperial naval defence in the Far East, the Mediterranean and Europe, which inevitably weakened her position in Europe.[41] It is unlikely that the Imperial Conference of 1937 and its aftermath precipitated on its own the course that British foreign policy took during 1937 and 1938 – and there is no archival evidence to support such a contention. Undoubtedly, however, the nature of the observations made by imperial statesmen at the conference, coupled with the reluctance of the dominions adequately to fund their own defence, the uncertainty of American policy, the deteriorating situation in the Far East and the limitations imposed upon British defence spending all contributed to a conviction on the part of Neville Chamberlain that further attempts at conciliation with Germany and Italy were better advised than confrontation.[42]

The exacerbation of the international situation in the Far East by Japanese action and the continuing reluctance of Washington to commit itself to anything more than the most anodyne gestures, clearly contributed to the British sense of being stretched in all parts of the globe without the prospect of adequate assistance. It was precisely this perception that the German government wished to encourage as in the new year of 1938 it moved towards closer relations with Japan and attempted to give the Anti-Comintern Pact concluded with Japan at the end of 1936 greater substance. Until the end of 1937 Germany maintained a position of effective neutrality between China and Japan, even refraining from recognizing Manchukuo. The nub of the matter was that Germany derived too many benefits from cordial relations with China. After 1927, when Soviet military advisers were expelled from China, and throughout the 1930s, Germany stepped into the shoes of the Soviets and supplied the Chinese government with military assistance in the form of advisers and armaments. Moreover, Germany also developed a substantial trade with China which increased in volume by 300 per cent between 1931 and 1937 and of which arms supplies formed an important part. China clearly offered German exporters a valuable market and in return Germany could acquire raw materials essential to her rearmament. By the beginning of 1938, however, the Germans began openly to side with the Japanese as they pondered the impact of successful Japanese expansion in the Far East on the ability of Britain and the Soviet Union to resist Germany in Europe as she began herself actively to embark upon her own programme of expansion. The installation of Ribbentrop as foreign minister in February 1938 coupled with Hitler's declared intention of recognizing Manchukuo in a speech on the fourth of that month signalled the victory of this thinking in Berlin. As yet caution tended to prevail in Tokyo over closer ties with Berlin, but within the Japanese foreign office an 'Axis faction' emerged around the former ambassador to Sweden, Shiratori Toshio, that maintained close contact with the Japanese army and with the army tended to see Japan's objectives as being more easily realisable through open association with the Fascist Powers, Germany and Italy, against both the democracies and the Soviet Union.[43]

On the basis of the information and recommendations contained in Inskip's *Interim Report*, it was decided by the cabinet at its meeting on 22 December 1937 that the question of policy towards Germany would be examined by the cabinet foreign policy committee early in the new year. On 24 January this committee met. Chamberlain outlined a new approach to Germany. The colonial question was now placed in the forefront. This did not, however, indicate a change of policy. The colonial question could not be settled 'independently of . . . other issues and the examination of the colonial question could only be undertaken as a part and parcel of a general settlement.' At a subsequent meeting of the committee on 3 February it was decided firmly to go ahead with an approach to Germany that was tantamount to an invitation to participate in a general settlement.[44]

By the time this approach was made there had been a crisis in the British government as a result of which Eden had resigned as foreign secretary and been replaced by Lord Halifax. In the past Eden's resignation has been presented as a principled act of opposition to the follies of the *appeasement* that had been introduced by Neville Chamberlain. But Eden did not resign over policy towards Germany. He resigned because, while he was on holiday, Chamberlain had rejected a secret initiative on the part of the American President. Roosevelt, had proposed the convening of a conference in Washington that would address the world's underlying economic problems, which were held to be the fundamental cause of international tension, and establish recognized rules for the conduct of relations between states. Chamberlain had declined Roosevelt's proposal because he felt that such an initiative would merely serve to confuse his own proposed initiatives and because by this time he was confirmed in his belief that the United States would contribute very little of a practical nature to the resolution of the current international crisis. Had Roosevelt's initiative not been confidential, it is probable that Eden would have resigned in January 1938 because he considered the American action, in conjunction with Captain Ingersoll's presence in London, to be the prelude to real American involvement in European affairs. He had, however, to wait until Neville Chamberlain's continued private diplomacy with the Italians, and the prime minister's readiness to obtain an agreement with Mussolini by offering *de jure* recognition of Italy's conquest of Ethiopia, provided him with both an issue on which to disagree and an opportunity to claim that he had been by-passed and his function usurped by the prime minister. When Eden resigned in

February 1938 it was not over some great principle regarding the appeasement of Germany in which he himself was complicit, but on the relatively
minor issues of Anglo-American and Anglo-Italian relations.[45]

The initial British approach to Germany, transmitted by the British
ambassador in a personal interview with Hitler on 3 March, was an
immediate disappointment. It was all the more a disappointment because this
was the first and last time prior to the outbreak of war in 1939 that the British
attempted to deal with Germany on a broad basis that was intended to lead
ultimately to the renegotiation of the entire *Versailles System*. Henderson told
Hitler that Britain was prepared to satisfy Germany's colonial claims and he
asked Hitler what Germany could contribute towards the wider interests of
peace and detente in Europe. Hitler's response was scornful. Nothing could
be done in Anglo-German relations until the hate campaign against him in the
British press was brought to an end; he would not tolerate interference by
third parties in Germany's relations with Central European states; and he
could wait a decade for colonial satisfaction.[46] The following month the
conclusion of an Anglo-Italian agreement, the consequence of the prime
minister's dealings with the Italians, which provided for British recognition
of the Italian conquest of Ethiopia and the withdrawal of Italian 'volunteers'
from Spain, seemed to suggest some improvement in Anglo-Italian relations. But, in the meantime, on 12 March, Hitler had achieved the *Anschluß* of
Germany with Austria. With the effective German annexation of Austria
peace now looked much less secure.

The *Anschluß* and the Munich Crisis

In the military orders at the end of 1937 and in his speech of 5 November of
that year, Hitler laid emphasis upon projected attacks on Czechoslovakia and
yet the first victim of the Nazi juggernaut was to be Austria. There is no
evidence to suggest that at the end of 1937 Hitler was thinking of effecting the
Anschluß by violence. On the contrary the evidence available suggests that
Hitler still wanted the 'evolutionary' course to be pursued. Under the terms
of the 'Gentleman's Agreement', Schuschnigg, the Austrian chancellor,
agreed to include members of the 'National Opposition' in his government;
in November 1936, the nazi sympathizer, Glaise-Horstenau, was appointed
minister of the interior. Moreover, the *Heimwehr*, pro-Italian and the only
organization in Austria capable of resisting the nazis, was dissolved. The
following year, the nazis made further advances with the elevation of the
nazi, Seyss-Inquart, to membership of the Austrian state council. With the
policy of gradual nazi infiltration of the Austrian government succeeding,
Hitler had every reason to discourage nazi agitation in Austria and he did so.

However, by the end of 1937 it was becoming clear that Schuschnigg was
playing for time which naturally increased the impatience of enthusiasts for
Austro-German Union. Schuschnigg's main source of trouble sprang from
the illegal activities of the Austrian nazis which even the injunctions of Hitler
could not stop. In January 1938, the Austrian police raided the nazi
headquarters and found plans for a rising. Consequently, Schuschnigg asked

for an early meeting with Hitler. This took place at Berchtesgaden on 12 February, where Schuschnigg was bullied outrageously. Nevertheless, he made no more concessions to Hitler than those he had decided to offer in advance, of which the Führer had been informed by Seyss-Inquart. It was finally agreed that Germany and Austria would follow common foreign and economic policies, that Seyss-Inquart would enter the Austrian government as minister of the interior, and that Austrian Nazis would be given freedom and be included in the Fatherland Front. In return Hitler repudiated the Austrian nazis' illegal activities and agreed to accept unwanted Austrian nazis in Germany.[47]

The news of what had taken place at Berchtesgaden very soon spread around the capitals of Europe. In Rome the Italians were prompted to speed up their negotiations for an agreement with the British, which had been initiated by Neville Chamberlain with the objective of breaking the Axis. This did not mean that Mussolini had abandoned friendship with Germany in favour of a pro-British policy, or that he thought the *Anschluß* could be prevented by such a shift. On the contrary, Mussolini believed that the *Anschluß* was now inevitable, but he hoped that Hitler would allow sufficient time for Italian opinion to be prepared for Italy's *volte-face* in acquiescing in this. The interval between the 'fourth and fifth acts of the Austrian affair' was also to be used to bring the negotiations with Britain to a successful conclusion, for if an Anglo-Italian Agreement were concluded after the *Anschluß*, the Italian foreign minister, Count Ciano, observed 'it would be impossible to prevent the entire world interpreting our policy of *rapprochement* with London as a journey to Canossa under German pressure'. Mussolini's interest in such an agreement was partly rooted in a desire to reassure British anxieties, besides which there were benefits to be had such as British recognition of the Italian Empire in Abyssinia in exchange for and conditional upon the withdrawal of Italian 'volunteers' from Spain. As already observed, an Anglo-Italian agreement was ultimately and paradoxically concluded on 16 April 1938, after the *Anschluß*, and ratified the following November.[48]

Hitler's plans regarding Austria were, however, to receive an unanticipated check for Schuschnigg, anxious to arrest the course that events were taking in Austria and, if possible, to reverse them, began to revive Austrian nationalism in a speech of 24 February. This was followed on 8 March by an announcement of a plebiscite on the issue of Austrian sovereignty. Hitler's strategy was in ruins. He either had to act rapidly and achieve the *Anschluß* by force, or see the plebiscite, which might go against him, carried out. The German Army was alerted to be ready to invade Austria by 12 March at the latest. In spite of the cancellation of the plebiscite by Schuschnigg the operation went ahead and, in the intoxication of success, Hitler decided on 13 March that henceforth Austria would become an integral part of the Third Reich. In all this, Hitler had been careful in his regard for Italian susceptibilities and he solicited the approval of the Duce, to whom, in return for his acquiescence, he said he would be forever grateful.

The British government had for some time accepted that a closer connection between Austria and Germany was inevitable. Eden told the

German ambassador, Joachim von Ribbentrop, this on 2 December 1937. But the manner of the *Anschluß* created unease and resentment. When the British ambassador, Henderson, agreed with Göring that Schuschnigg had 'acted with precipitate folly', he was immediately reprimanded by Lord Halifax.[49] Moreover, Halifax told Henderson not to mention the written reply Hitler promised on 3 March to the British proposals because any action that the British were likely to contemplate in the colonial sphere had 'receded under the influence of recent events'. Finally, on 24 March, Neville Chamberlain warned of the dangers of a war starting in Europe in the speech to the House of Commons mentioned in the introduction to this book. But it was not possible for the British government to cease all contact with the German government, for the *Anschluß* had created an immediate threat to another Central European state, with a substantial German minority, Czechoslovakia.

The Sudeten German minority in Czechoslovakia was by the 1930s taken over by the same mood of nationalist exaltation that infected Germans everywhere. Whether without the rise of the nazi party in Germany the Sudeten Germans would have adjusted to their situation will never be known. What, however, is clear is that with the rise of nazi popularity in Germany in the early 1930s, nazism and nationalism were also stimulated in the Sudeten districts of Czechoslovakia. In October 1933 the Czech authorities banned the NSDAP, but it reappeared under the leadership of Konrad Henlein as the *Heimatsfront*. By the middle of the 1930s it commanded more votes than any other party and Henlein in 1937 was calling for Sudeten autonomy. With the realization of the *Anschluß*, relations between the German community and the Czechoslovakian authorities reached an impasse. In March 1938 Henlein visited Hitler and the latter approved his tactics which were defined thus: 'We must always demand so much that we never can be satisfied.' Publicly, at Karlsbad, on 24 April, in an eight point programme, he demanded total autonomy for the German-speaking districts of Czechoslovakia and total freedom for national socialism.[50]

These were public manifestations of the problem besetting Prague and the governments of the major powers. Clandestinely Hitler was, from the conference of 5 November 1937 onwards, conniving at the destruction of Czechoslovakia. In December 1937 Operation Green was drafted providing for an attack on Czechoslovakia, giving it priority over the defensive posture in the West (Operation Red). Still, this military directive referred to this action being possible when 'Germany has attained full preparedness for war in all spheres . . .' and no date was proposed for such an attack. Moreover, the general international situation would be of some importance because it was stated that the government would try to avoid provoking a war on two fronts or putting Germany into a situation for which she was not 'militarily nor economically equal . . .'. Planning for such an offensive continued throughout the winter of 1937. But on 20 May 1938, when a new draft for Operation Green was issued, Hitler was still not determined on immediate action against Czechoslovakia unless the political conditions were right. Undoubtedly, Hitler felt much less secure concerning the action he was contemplating following a visit to Italy earlier in the month when he failed to obtain a German–Italian alliance. In the wake of the *Anschluß*, Mussolini was still very angered by SS propaganda in the German-speaking South Tyrol and he had, of course, the recently concluded Anglo-Italian Agreement as a means of exercising a certain independence in respect of Germany.[51]

On 30 May, following firm Anglo-French action in the mounting Czech crisis, the Führer had changed his mind. In response to rumours of German Army movements on Czechoslovakia's northern border on and around 20 May the Czech government called up one class of reservists. This was accompanied by a British *démarche* in Berlin and a public French announcement that France would stand by Czechoslovakia if she was invaded by Germany. In what many historians interpret as a fit of pique, Hitler now irrevocably committed himself to the destruction of Czechoslovakia in 'the near future'.[52] Emphasis, however, was still being laid on the creation of suitable circumstances by the political leadership. This was still substantially the case with the *General Strategic Directive* of 18 June. From October 1938 onwards Hitler was determined to solve the Czech question, but, the document states:

> I shall, however, only decide to take action against Czechoslovakia if, as in the case of the occupation of the demilitarized zone and the entry into Austria, I am firmly convinced that France will not march and therefore Britain will not intervene either.[53]

Whatever interpretation is put on these military orders, it is clear that at this time the destruction of Czechoslovakia was Hitler's major preoccupation. Hitler had laid great stress upon the right conditions for the dismemberment of Czechoslovakia. These to some extent were to be provided for him by British and French policy during the summer of 1938 and Germany did not need to resort to force.

On 15 March the French military authorities decided there was nothing they could do to assist directly in the defence of Czechoslovakia. Three days later Neville Chamberlain made the same observation to the cabinet foreign affairs committee, which discussed the German threat to Czechoslovakia extensively. The prime minister thought that Hitler wanted satisfactory treatment for the German areas of Czechoslovakia and that if he could get what he wanted by peaceful methods he might be satisfied. The committee also had before it a chiefs of staff report which warned that neither Britain nor her allies could prevent the defeat of Czechoslovakia and that a war over Czechoslovakia was likely to escalate into a world war with Italy and Japan. Chamberlain's reaction to this 'melancholy' document was to propose that the British government pursue a policy that avoided war: the Czechs were to be persuaded to achieve a direct settlement with the Sudeten Germans and the French were to be asked to assist in this.[54] At the end of April the British leaders met the prime minister of the new French government, Daladier, and the foreign minister, Bonnet, in London. Daladier struck a fighting pose: France would fulfil her treaty commitments and defend Czechoslovakia. But the primacy of Britain's position is revealed in that it was agreed to make ambassadorial representations in Prague early in May with a view to getting the Czechs to make concessions. There was, however, a wider dimension to Britain's policy. The Czech question was arguably the only remaining obstacle in the way of Germany being brought into a general settlement. Once removed, the powers could concentrate on the wider issues that had inspired Britain's earlier approach to Germany in March 1938 and would provide a basis for permanent peace. This was to be a constant refrain in Anglo-German exchanges over the next few months.

But the Czech crisis steadily worsened. At the end of May, in response to rumours of German troop manoeuvres on the Czech border, the British and French governments reacted firmly: France would stand by her commitment to defend Czechoslovakia and Britain's neutrality could not be regarded as a foregone conclusion. As has already been indicated Hitler responded to this *humiliation* by changing the military orders in a manner such as to suggest an imminent German attack upon Czechoslovakia. The British, in the wake of the May crisis, redoubled their efforts to bring about a mediated solution and in July Lord Runciman was sent to Czechoslovakia to help resolve the matter. The urgency of this was made plain to the Czechs when on 20 July Bonnet confidentially informed them that France could not regard the issue of the Sudeten Germans as one for which she would fight.[55]

In September the crisis finally came to a head. On 5 September Benes, the Czech President, called the bluff of the Sudeten Germans when he conceded the Karlsbad demands almost in their entirety. The rejection by the Sudeten Germans of this offer and the riotous circumstances that ensued revealed that union with Germany and not autonomy was what was in fact being demanded. Simultaneously, the annual nazi rally was taking place at Nuremberg. On 12 September Hitler delivered a speech that was violent in its support for the Sudeten Germans. The result was predictable. Inflamed passions led to riots, which were soon put down; but the discontent in Czechoslovakia and Hitler's mood seemed to point to a war. On 13 September Chamberlain decided to see Hitler personally in Germany in order to avoid a catastrophe. It is significant that while the French were kept informed of this, they were not consulted. On 15 September Chamberlain saw Hitler at Berchtesgaden and agreed in principle to the transfer of the Sudeten areas to Germany. On 18 September Daladier and Bonnet visited London where they endorsed the plan. The Czechs, after a ministerial crisis, accepted it too on 21 September. On 22 September Chamberlain flew to Godesberg to convey the agreement to the cession of the Sudeten areas in person. But for Hitler this was no longer enough. The Poles and the Hungarians too had claims against Czechoslovakia and the Sudeten areas had to be occupied at once, a condition which he later modified to 1 October. In London, cabinet and Anglo-French discussions revealed that these terms were intolerable and a war crisis ensued. Britain even agreed to declare war if France went to war in support of Czechoslovakia.

Eventually the situation was saved by a proposal for a conference from Mussolini, who was less enthusiastic about a war than his fellow dictator. His mediation though was a sham, for the Italian plan had been drafted in the German foreign office. On 29 September a four power conference met at Munich. The powers represented were Britain, France, Germany and Italy.

Czechoslovakia, whose fate was in the balance, was excluded. So was the Soviet Union. In retrospect it is easily understandable that both Germany and Italy should have wished to keep the USSR at arm's length from this crisis, given their ideological dispositions and the nature of Hitler's objectives. On the other hand, the attitude of Britain and France requires a little explanation. The most recent English language study of Soviet policy during the 1930s unequivocally claims that

> ... it was Moscow's view that what would save Czechoslovakia and the peace was a determined stand by the USSR, Great Britain and France. This stance carried with it the risk of war with Germany but it was a risk the Soviets were more than willing to share.[56]

Clearly, the substance of this assertion can never be completely tested until the Soviet archives have been fully opened and exploited. Assuming, however, it is accurate, why did neither Britain nor France bring the Soviet Union into the frame, particularly in the light of the fact that the USSR was bound to Czechoslovakia by a treaty of 16 May 1935? The answer must lie partially in the fact that the Soviet military capacity was held in low esteem in the west, especially after the purges. According to the British chiefs of staff it was doubtful, despite the USSR's vast resources of manpower and equipment, including aircraft,

> ... whether her military staff would consider her organization sufficiently developed to enable her to embark on an offensive war with confidence. The Soviet forces have as yet made little progress in tactical training with the modern arms which they have acquired. The armament industry is still young and has fundamental weaknesses which influence output. In war it could not yet maintain for any length of time the maximum forces that the U.S.S.R. can mobilize.

Furthermore, the Soviet Navy, with the exception of submarines, was regarded as insignificant and it was believed that the Soviet Air Force would disintegrate once it began to suffer severe casualties as the ability and training of reserve pilots were poor.[57] French assessments, such as that of General Schweisguth, were equally disparaging and together with a political distaste for having any dealings with the Soviets, reinforced by British admonitions against military involvement with Moscow, were effective in depriving the Franco–Soviet alliance of May 1935 of any meaning.[58] On practical grounds there was, therefore, no perception of military advantage to be gained from involving the Soviet Union in the crisis of 1938. But, had there been a military advantage, the Soviet Union would still have been excluded, for there was a political agenda too. In 1938 Sir Alec Douglas-Home, prime minister from 1963 to 1964, was Neville Chamberlain's parliamentary private secretary. He later revealed in 1988 that, according to Chamberlain, the Soviet Union had to be inhibited from intervening on behalf of Czechoslovakia on the ground that a successful intervention would leave Eastern Europe exposed to 'Russian penetration'[59].

In the early hours of 30 September agreement was finally reached at the Munich Conference. The Sudetenland was to be occupied by Germany between 1 and 10 October; Polish and Hungarian claims were to be settled; an international commission was to determine the final frontier; and a four power guarantee was to protect the territorial integrity of the rump Czech state.[60]

War had been avoided, but that was not the end of the business at Munich. For the British the resolution of the Czech question had in essence been the prelude to a more far-reaching agreement. That Chamberlain still hoped to achieve the much sought after general settlement is revealed in the private conversation Chamberlain had with Hitler on 30 September that resulted in the celebrated Anglo-German Declaration. This stated:

> We, the German Fuhrer and Chancellor and the British Prime Minister, have had a further meeting to-day and are agreed in recognizing that the question of Anglo-German relations is of the first importance for the two countries and for Europe.
>
> We regard the agreement signed last night and the Anglo-German Naval Agreement as symbolic of the desire of our two peoples never to go to war with one another again.
>
> We are resolved that the method of consultation shall be the method adopted to deal with any other questions that may concern our two countries, and we are determined to continue our efforts to remove possible sources of difference and thus to contribute to assure the peace of Europe.[61]

For Chamberlain this was the real success of Munich. On his return to London he stated that it was 'peace for our time'. In reality it was peace for a time.

7

The Outbreak of War in Europe

In September 1939 war broke out in Europe. Although it began with Germany's unprovoked attack on and conquest of Poland, and involved Britain and France from the start, what it was in essence was, as Professor Watt has recently reminded us, the second Anglo-German war. As, however, the Anglo-German Declaration at Munich intimated, Anglo-German relations were critical for the whole of Europe. If these two countries went to war then other countries would inevitably become involved and a European war would have begun. At first the European war was quite limited in scope, but during 1940 the aggression of Germany extended it to the whole of Western Europe. The following year Hitler decided to attempt the realization of his fundamental aim, the destruction of the USSR and the achievement of *Lebensraum* in the Ukraine. Virtually the entire continent was now engulfed in a conflict the future development of which would be determined in a global rather than continental context.

Britain, Germany and September 1939

The Munich crisis revealed the extent of French subordination to British policy. From this time onwards the crucial decisions in respect of Germany would be taken in London as indeed they had been for some time. Chamberlain's wish, and that of the foreign office, in the immediate aftermath of the Munich Conference was to resume the attempt to achieve a general settlement which had been broken off in the wake of the *Anschluß*. Within the foreign office it was surmised that colonial concessions to Germany might be traded for British naval superiority and economic co-operation. The resulting consensus was contained in a memorandum that suggested dealing with Germany through an international conference once the principal European colonial powers had agreed the nature and extent of the colonial concessions that were to be made to Germany. But, by the middle of November 1938, the prime minister was making it public that there could be no question of colonial concessions to Germany. He did so because it was the British view that colonial concessions could only be made within a general settlement. On 15 November he told the cabinet: '. . . such a settlement was . . . clearly impossible in existing circumstances . . . it followed that there could be no question of a return of colonies to Germany'.[1]

This decision was reached not merely because British public opinion might oppose colonial concessions, but mainly because the domestic and external conduct of the German government since the Munich Conference had made it clear that Germany could not be contained within any rational international system. The vicious pogrom unleashed on German Jews in early November, known as the *Kristallnacht*, because of the glass smashed in Jewish retail premises, caused revulsion in Britain. Hitler had already been making anti-British speeches and in response to British complaints he had declared that Germany would not suffer under the tutelage of governesses.[2] Later it was to be reported through Britain's Berlin embassy that in a private conversation with journalists Hitler had stated that he no longer placed any importance on friendship with Britain. For a time Britain seemed to fare better with *dictator minor*, Mussolini. The Anglo-Italian Agreement was ratified in November 1938 and in January Chamberlain and Halifax visited Rome, but the practical results were nil.

January and February of 1939 saw a revolution in British policy. This was to some extent aided by the intelligence that the British government was receiving. Whereas down to the end of 1938 intelligence had tended to stress the superior capacity of the German armed forces, the joint planning sub-committee in January 1939 produced an appreciation that was much more positive. In terms of land and air forces Germany and Italy were presented as having a superiority over Britain and France of around 2:1. On the other hand, looked at from the point of view of defence against air attack, morale and ability to sustain a long war the picture was much less gloomy. The most favourable war for the Axis powers would be one of short duration; a long war would favour the British and French. Provided the Allies could withstand the initial onslaught and lengthen the war the advantage would pass to them. The apathy toward war displayed by the German population during the Munich crisis was contrasted with British morale should an attack occur. Perhaps though the issue that was central to the tone of this memorandum was the estimation of British economic strength and durability compared with the weaknesses of the German economy. The industrial intelligence centre estimated that, within a year of the start of a war, blockade and foreign currency shortage would have a dramatic impact on the German war effort. In terms of access to the raw materials necessary for a war of attrition Britain was much better placed. Inevitably the intelligence picture now boosted confidence during the coming crises.[3]

In January 1939 the British government received reports that suggested an imminent German attack in the west against the Low Countries and Britain. On 1 February the cabinet decided that an attack on the Netherlands or Switzerland would compel British military intervention because of the threat posed thereby to British security. On 6 February Chamberlain publicly declared that if France were threatened by any power, Britain would come to her aid. By the end of the month the cabinet accepted the logical corollary of all this: should war come Britain would have to establish a large continental army. Britain had now accepted the continental commitment.[4]

Undoubtedly, this pleased the French. The damage done to Czechoslovakia by the Munich Conference had effectively deprived the anti-dictatorial forces in Europe of thirty-five divisions. In the view of General Gamelin, the French chief of general staff, this implied a serious swing in the balance of power towards Germany which could only be remedied by a full Anglo-French alliance. From October 1938 onwards the French government emphasized its view regarding the need for the creation by Britain of a continental field force and the introduction by her of conscription.[5] Although the British government had made it clear during the Munich crisis that Britain would support France if she was compelled to go to war with Germany, French policy did not rest upon this reassurance and remain static thereafter. War was to be avoided, not least because, in the view of Bonnet, the French foreign minister, it could only result in the *bolshevization* of Europe. When Ribbentrop visited Paris on 6–7 December 1938, a Franco-German Declaration was signed which emulated the Anglo-German Declaration at Munich. It expressed mutual goodwill and promised consultation on issues of common concern, but was in essence a rather anodyne document. Ribbentrop later claimed that the hidden agenda was the French concession of a free hand for Germany in Eastern Europe, but there is no evidence of this. And in any case Munich was itself the admission by all of Germany's paramountcy in the region. French desire to assuage the dictators did not though extend to Italy, despite British urgings. Franco-Italian relations steadily deteriorated with public Italian demands for French territory in North Africa and equal determination on the part of the French against conceding them.

The new determination in the British attitude was not to find public expression until March 1939. Although Hitler had agreed at Munich to participate in an international guarantee of the remainder of Czechoslovakia, he had no intention of honouring this commitment. On the contrary, he was preoccupied with destroying Czechoslovakia as soon as he could. Moreover, in the separatist Slovak movement he had the ideal means of wreaking its destruction from within. In October 1938 the Slovak deputy prime minister, Durcansky, saw Göring and emphasized the desire of the Slovaks for full independence, which he claimed a plebiscite would confirm. Göring thought that the Slovak independence movement should be encouraged, for: 'A Czech State minus Slovakia is even more completely at our mercy.'[6] Subsequently, German military orders in October and December 1938 stressed the need for the German armed forces to be ready to eliminate Czechoslovakia should she try to pursue an anti-German policy. By February 1939 Hitler was directly encouraging the Slovak nationalists to declare independence. The following month, between 6 and 10 March, President Hacha attempted to arrest the internal decomposition of Czechoslovakia by dismissing the governments of Slovakia and Ruthenia, where the Germans had also been fomenting unrest, and proclaiming martial law. Hitler now intervened by summoning the deposed Slovak prime minister, Monsignor Tiso, to Berlin where he virtually ordered the latter to declare independence, which Germany would guarantee, or suffer occupation by Poland and Hungary. Accordingly, on 14 March the Slovak parliament declared independence. The Czech president and foreign minister now requested a meeting with Hitler. Their object was to persuade Hitler to agree to the continued existence of Czechoslovakia. The Führer, however, had other plans. In humiliating circumstances Hacha and Chvalkovsky signed away Czechoslovakia's independence in the early hours of 15 March. The same day the German Army entered the Czech provinces of Bohemia and Moravia, which were converted into a *protectorate* of the German Reich.[7]

These events created a profound sense of shock in Britain. It now seemed that Hitler's aims were unlimited. Was he seeking domination of the whole continent, or even the globe? While Hitler had been annexing German-speaking countries and regions, it had been possible to justify his actions, but now that he had started to engulf other nationalities the time had come to stop him. This was given added point on 23 March when Germany seized the city of Memel in Lithuania. True, it was a German-speaking enclave, but the manner of its annexation provoked further alarm. Chamberlain's speech in the House of Commons on 15 March was rather bland in its condemnation, but by the time he spoke in Birmingham on 17 March and in the cabinet on 18 March his tone was more combative. In the days prior to the destruction of Czechoslovakia, Neville Chamberlain had been quietly confident that Germany's economic weakness would compel Hitler to seek an agreement with Britain. The Führer's speech on 30 January had been more moderate than anticipated and he had himself emphasized that Germany must 'trade or die'. To some extent, therefore, the rape of Czechoslovakia took him unprepared even though he had been adequately informed by the secret intelligence service of its imminence. For a moment Chamberlain lost touch with a very real revolution in opinion in the country which revealed itself in the mood of the press and the Conservative party. Prodded, however, by Lord Halifax, he changed the thrust of the speech he was to give in Birmingham. He would speak on foreign policy rather than concentrate on economic recovery and the social services.[8] In his Birmingham speech Chamberlain publicly asked a number of rhetorical questions. Was the destruction of Czechoslovakia the beginning of a new phase of German policy? Would other small states now be attacked? More ominously, was this 'a step in the direction of an attempt to dominate the world by force?' He warned that because Britain opposed war as absurd and barbarous, that did not mean that Britain would flinch from resisting 'such a challenge if it ever were made'.[9]

Another scare now played a part in transforming British policy towards Europe. On 17 March Virgil Tilea, the Rumanian minister in London informed Halifax of a German ultimatum to Rumania demanding a monopoly on her exports in exchange for a guarantee of her frontiers. In effect, Rumania would become an agricultural satellite of Germany. Rumanian oil and agricultural produce would naturally have increased Germany's economic strength. The scare proved ultimately to have been bogus, but it galvanized Britain's attitude. On Saturday 18 March, Chamberlain was even more forthright in his remarks to the Cabinet:

> The Prime Minister said that up till a week ago we had proceeded on the assumption that we should be able to continue our policy of getting on better terms with the Dictator Powers, and that, although those Powers had aims, those aims were limited. We had all along at the back of our minds the reservation that this might not prove to be the case, but we had felt that it was right.
> . . . He had now come definitely to the conclusion that Herr Hitler's attitude made it impossible to negotiate on the old basis with the Nazi regime . . . No reliance could be placed on any of the assurances given by the Nazi leaders.

Chamberlain thought that the next step should be to ascertain who would join, with Britain, in resisting aggression. Poland, it was felt, was the essential element in the situation. Two days later the cabinet again met and a draft declaration of agreement to consult, by interested powers, in the event of further threats to the independence of European states was discussed. Chamberlain emphasized:

> The real issue was that if Germany showed signs that she intended to proceed with her march for world domination, we must take steps to stop her by attacking her on two fronts. We should attack Germany not in order to save a particular victim but in order to pull down the bully.

Herein lay the origins of the policy of guarantees pursued by the British government during the spring and summer of 1939. It was a commitment to go to war should Germany carry out a further unprovoked act of aggression.[10]

Poland was not a state with which the British government had much sympathy in the autumn of 1938. The Poles had taken advantage of the Munich crisis to settle their own frontier disputes with the Czechs. Yet Polish independence was the issue which finally brought Britain into conflict with Germany and thus precipitated the Second World War. How did this situation come about? In addition to planning the destruction of Czechoslovakia, Hitler during the winter of 1938 was preoccupied with negotiating an agreement with Poland over Danzig and extraterritorial rights in the Polish Corridor. It was also hoped to bring the Poles into the Anti-Comintern Pact. This indicated the main object of policy which was to convert Poland into a German satellite which would willingly participate in the war against the Soviet Union, which was, of course, Hitler's principal aim in the medium term, for this would secure *Lebensraum* and German hegemony in Europe. In October 1938 Ribbentrop informed the Polish ambassador that Germany wanted to settle all outstanding points of difficulty between their two countries. He proposed, therefore, that Danzig be returned to the Reich; that Germany should have extra-territorial rail and road rights in the Polish Corridor; that Germany and Poland recognize each other's boundaries; that Poland accede to the Anti-Comintern Pact; and that the Non-aggression Treaty between the two states be extended for up to twenty-five years. Throughout the 1930s the Poles had pursued an independent policy in respect of Germany and the Soviet Union. Had they accepted these German proposals they would, in effect, have acquiesced in a status of subordination to Germany and risked a conflict with the USSR which they did not want. On 19 November the Polish government virtually rejected these proposals and neither a visit to Hitler by the Polish foreign minister, Beck, to Hitler, nor a visit to Warsaw by Ribbentrop had advanced the situation by the end of January 1939. The Poles were not going to budge, however firm the pressure from Berlin. Moreover, they were determined to fight rather than surrender.[11]

The British policy of guaranteeing states under potential threat of German aggression became public at the end of March 1939. Scares to the effect that Poland was shortly to be attacked prompted the British government on 30 March to offer Poland a guarantee of her independence. The Poles immediately accepted and the French too guaranteed Poland. On 31 March Chamberlain publicly announced the fact of the guarantee to the House of Commons. During a visit to London by the Polish foreign minister on 4–6 April it was agreed that this should be converted into a reciprocal Anglo-Polish alliance for which negotiations lasted until the eve of war.[12]

The international situation now steadily deteriorated when on 7 April Mussolini, piqued that Hitler had not informed him in advance of his intention to destroy Czechoslovakia, carried out his own act of international gangsterdom by invading and annexing Albania. This prompted, on 13 April, Anglo-French guarantees of Greece and Rumania and on 26 April the British introduced conscription. Two days later, in an address to the *Reichstag*, Hitler denounced the German–Polish Non-Aggression Pact and the Anglo-German Naval Agreement. The following month on 22 May the Italians, who previously had fought shy of a formal alliance, concluded the Pact of Steel with Germany which virtually committed them to go to war with Germany in any circumstances. Although both Mussolini and Ciano, the Italian foreign minister, had emphasized that Italy would not be ready for war until 1943, Italy was committed to assist Germany even if the latter embarked upon an offensive and unprovoked war, which Hitler was currently preparing.[13]

On 26 March the Polish ambassador had finally made it clear to Hitler that there was no possibility of the Polish government endorsing his proposals for resolving the so-called difficulties in German–Polish relations. The outward and visible sign of worsening German–Polish relations was increased tension between Warsaw and Berlin over the status of Danzig. This predominantly German-speaking Baltic port had been made a free city under the auspices of the League of Nations in order to provide the reconstituted Polish state with free and unimpeded access to the sea. The status of Danzig not surprisingly became a source of frequent disputes between its inhabitants and the Polish government throughout the 1920s until the German–Polish Non-Aggression Treaty of 1934 gave rise to some stability. Throughout the 1930s, however, Danzig was nazified. When, therefore, the Polish government on 5 May 1939 replied to Hitler's denunciation of the German–Polish Non-Aggression Treaty by pointing out that Germany's non-negotiable demands were 'incompatible with the vital interests and dignity of Poland'[14] the activities of the Hitler Youth and nazi para-military formations in the city increased. By the weekend of 1–2 July it was rumoured that *Gauleiter* Albert Forster would openly demand the reversion of Danzig to the Reich. Danzig, though, was only the symbol of a much wider ambition. The first draft of the military orders for an attack upon Poland, Operation White, was ready by the end of March 1939 and on 3 April a directive instructed the armed forces to prepare for an attack on Poland at any time after 1 September. Operation White stressed the need for the isolation of Poland and the limitation of hostilities to a Polish–German conflict.[15] Clearly the Pact of Steel with Italy, from Germany's viewpoint, was a valuable means of achieving this end. Moreover, during the summer of 1939 negotiations with the Soviet Union were to culminate in the Nazi–Soviet Pact of August 1939 which made the outbreak of the Second World War almost inevitable.

The role that the Soviet Union would or would not play during the forthcoming crisis over Poland was also of importance for Britain. On 3 April 1939 the British chiefs of staff considered the implications of British guarantees to Poland and Rumania. They had before them a report of the joint policy sub-committee which stated:

> when considering the question of any form of guarantee to Poland and Rumania it must be borne in mind that Great Britain and France could afford them no direct support by sea, on land or in the air to help them to resist a German invasion. Furthermore, in the present state of British and French armament production, neither Great Britain nor France could supply any armaments to Poland and Rumania who would have to depend for assistance in this respect solely upon the U.S.S.R.[16]

This clearly highlighted the central problem for the British government in forming a European front against German aggression particularly in Eastern Europe. Although the USSR had entered the League of Nations in 1934 and the following year concluded a pact with France, there had been little development in the Soviet relationship with the west. At Geneva Maxim Litvinov preached the virtues of collective security, but in 1938, as has been shown, the USSR was carefully kept out of the Munich Crisis. It is impossible to ascertain whether or not the Soviet government would actually have fought to defend Czechoslovakia if that contingency had arisen, but the problem of transporting Soviet forces to the theatre of engagement with the enemy was never solved. Both Poland and Rumania were reluctant to concede transit facilities for Soviet forces on the ground that if they entered their territory they were likely to stay. The Rumanians did make one concession: Soviet transport aircraft could fly over their territory at a height of over 3,000 metres where their anti–aircraft guns were not effective![17] This problem was to surface again in the summer of 1939.

Between April and August 1939 negotiations were conducted between the British, French and the Soviet Union for an alliance to deter nazi aggression. They began on 14 April when Britain proposed to the Soviet Union that she publicly offer assistance to neighbouring states subjected to an act of aggression. On 18 April the Soviet Union countered with proposals for a three power alliance pledging Britain, France and the USSR to assist Poland and Rumania if they were attacked; the alliance was to be supplemented by immediate staff talks. The French were inclined to accept the Soviet view, the British reluctant and generally slow to respond in the subsequent negotiations. Gradually, however, the British government gave way to the Soviet view that a political treaty and military convention should be signed and agreed on 23 July that military talks should begin. Nevertheless, prior to the commencement of these talks the issue of *indirect aggression* had not been defined. This related to circumstances in which internal subversion within a country connived at by another state resulted in the annexation of the former. The British government were very disinclined to allow the Soviet government to determine the conditions which justified their intervening in the affairs of another state for fear that such intervention would lead to Soviet annexation, particularly of the Baltic republics. The British showed no urgency about sending a military delegation to the USSR, taking the view that a political treaty could be concluded in advance of military talks, in contrast with the Soviets who wanted the treaty and talks simultaneously. Eventually an Anglo-French delegation, the British section headed by Admiral Sir Reginald Plunkett-Ernle-Earle-Drax, left Tilbury on 5 August arriving in Moscow on 11 August. The slow means of transport, namely, the ship the *City of Exeter*, and the blimpish sounding head of the British delegation, have often been taken as indications that the British government was not serious. Drax, though, was a man of considerable acumen and there were sound diplomatic, security and naval reasons for using a passenger ship rather than an airplane. The fact of the matter was that the dilatory responses of the British in the preceding negotiations had created a bad impression already and one which the arrival of the delegation without a plan, elaborated in advance, and without full power to conclude a convention on the spot did nothing to eliminate.[18]

These factors in themselves must have convinced the Soviet authorities of a certain lack of enthusiasm on the part of Britain when the talks opened on 12 August. What, however, proved crucial was the failure of Britain and France to persuade the Polish government to allow Soviet troops to enter Poland. Accordingly the talks collapsed, although the final session was not to take place until 25 August, two days after the conclusion of the Nazi–Soviet Non-Aggression Pact had rendered them a meaningless formality. Undoubtedly the British had committed an error of judgement in not doing everything required to achieve an Anglo-Franco-Soviet Pact, but the Soviets too had made a mistake in considering that Britain needed their help more than they needed Britain's. Subsequent events, namely the German invasion of the Soviet Union in 1941, were to prove the error of this, but men are not blessed with foresight. Neither could Stalin truly have appreciated the central message of *Mein Kampf*, for had he done so he could never have concluded the Non-Aggression Pact.

Some Soviet officials had previously attempted to improve relations with Germany in the winter of 1936. Certain writers have alleged that this is evidence of the fundamental wickedness of the Soviet regime; an indication that Moscow would do down the democracies given the chance and seek an accommodation with Berlin. It is much more likely though that the Soviet officials concerned were merely attempting to keep their options open, for the policy of collective security, primarily associated with the commissar for foreign affairs, Maxim Litvinov, was showing few signs of success. Litvinov appears to have remained mistrustful of any dealings with the Germans,[19] but Munich appeared to have confirmed the failure of collective security. The dilemma confronting Soviet policy was publicly revealed in Stalin's speech to the Eighteenth Party Congress on 10 March 1939. He announced that Soviet foreign policy was non-ideological; the USSR would support peace and the development of business relations with all countries who wished to maintain similar relations with the Soviets. Appeasement was condemned as craven; the democracies were excoriated on the ground that they were conniving at a Nazi–Soviet war from which they would derive the benefit.[20] Strangely, the coded import of this speech, that the Soviet Union was prepared to do a deal with Germany, was lost upon British officials.

Not so the Germans. Early in April a middle-ranking German diplomat in Berlin, Karl Schnurre, head of the economic section of the German foreign ministry, began making tentative suggestions about improved Soviet–German relations. This appears to have been a 'straightforward initiative' by an official who, along with colleagues in the German embassy in Moscow, understood the implications of Stalin's speech. It would not necessarily have been seen of significance in itself by Soviet officials, for it would have been well 'known that . . . [Schnurre] . . . had no importance and significance in the formulation of Nazi foreign policy'. It is, however, evident that by the end of March 1939 meaningful political contacts 'between some Germans and the Soviets were in progress . . .' which continued to develop during the following months.[21] Correspondingly, in the second half of April 1939 the Soviets intimated their readiness for the improvement of relations with Germany culminating in the dismissal on 3 May of Litvinov, who besides being the champion of collective security was also Jewish. He was replaced as commissar for foreign affairs by Molotov. At the end of May Soviet –German negotiations for an economic agreement were resumed; these, however, proceeded in a fairly leisurely fashion until 19 August when the agreement was concluded. By this time, of course, and on German initiative, political discussions were in full swing. On 26 July, and on Ribbentrop's instructions, the German economic negotiator, Schnurre, suggested to Astakhov, the Soviet chargé d'affaires in Berlin, a far-reaching Soviet –German agreement. Time was getting short. On 12 August General Keitel was given orders for the army to be prepared for an attack on Poland on 26 August. Simultaneously the Soviet government agreed to political negotiations taking place in Moscow. It was suggested on 20 August that Ribbentrop could visit on 26 or 27 August. This did not suit Hitler's timetable. At his request it was agreed that Ribbentrop's visit be advanced to 23 August. On that date the Nazi–Soviet Non-Aggression Pact was signed.[22]

The public aspect was a straightforward agreement not to attack each other, or to lend support to third parties attacking the signatories. It was to last ten years. It was, however, the Secret Protocol that provided the substance of the Pact. This was a definition of German and Soviet spheres of influence. Poland was to be divided between the two powers along the line of the rivers Pisa, Narev, Vistula and San. The USSR was conceded a free hand in Finland, Estonia and Latvia and her interest in the Rumanian province of Bessarabia was recognized. For the moment Lithuania was recognized as falling within Germany's zone, although it was later conceded that the Soviet Union should have primacy there too.

The Nazi–Soviet Pact sealed the fate of peace and Poland. It is tempting to suggest that a display of urgency and enthusiasm on the part of the British in the negotiations for a three power pact would have precluded this development. But it is probable that the moment had passed with Munich. Did the Western powers really intend to resist Hitler? And, if they did, were they capable of doing so effectively? If the answer to either of these questions was even vaguely negative, the Soviet Union, through too close an association with the democracies, could have found herself at war with Germany without credible allies in the west. This would have been particularly embarrassing militarily for in 1939 a state of undeclared war existed between the USSR and Japan in the Far East which might ultimately have resulted in a debilitating war on two fronts. On the other hand, the German offer was very attractive. It certainly meant the postponement of war from the Soviet point of view; it implied the possibility of being able to emerge as the *tertius gaudens* from a conflict between the capitalist powers; and allowed the extension of the USSR's defensive lines into Eastern Europe and the Baltic littoral. Stalin opted for the certainties of an accommodation with Hitler, rather than the uncertainties of a tie with Britain and France.

If the Nazi–Soviet Pact was a disappointment for Britain, it at least assisted in lightening the pressure on Britain in another part of the globe. As so often during the 1930s crisis in Europe was accompanied by a corresponding crisis in the Far East, this time involving the British concession in the Chinese city of Tientsin, some eighty miles distant from Peking, and home to some 3,000 expatriate Britons. Following the resumption of the Sino-Japanese War in 1937, the Japanese Army was by the middle of 1939 fully in control of all the ports and cities in North China and most of the rest of the coast as far south as Canton, with the exception of the foreign concessions, and was in a position to exert formidable pressure on these territories. The crisis over Tientsin was provoked initially by the murder there of the manager of the Japanese puppet Federal Reserve Bank in April 1939. Thereafter the Japanese demanded that four suspect Chinese terrorists be handed over to them for trial. During the following weeks the advice of the man on the spot, consul-general Jamieson, and the British ambassador in Tokyo, Sir Robert Craigie, was that it would be prudent to comply with the Japanese requests, lest the Japanese take the most formidable and hostile measures against the concession. This advice was contradicted by the Far Eastern department of the foreign office and the ambassador to the Chinese government of Chiang Kai-shek, Sir Archibald Clerk-Kerr, who argued that nothing should be done to weaken Chinese resistance to the Japanese advance on mainland Asia. British prevarication resulted in the Japanese politely, but firmly, requesting the surrender of the terrorists by 7 June. Failure of the British to comply brought about a full-scale Japanese blockade of the British concession on 14 June, accompanied by the most humiliating treatment of British nationals entering or exiting the concession, several of whom, male and female, were made to strip naked at the point of a bayonet.

Until the crisis erupted neither the foreign secretary, nor the permanent under-secretary, Sir Alexander Cadogan, had given adequate attention to this matter which had been allowed to get completely out of hand. Thus to the mounting threat of war in Europe was added the threat of war in the Far East, or at the very least, a confrontation that was likely to have as its consequence the full adherence of the Japanese to the Axis of Italy and Germany, now cemented by a full alliance, for which the Japanese army and the group connected with Shiratori, by this time Japanese ambassador in Rome, were pressing. On the eve of the outbreak of war in Europe, the Tientsin crisis once more revealed the massive problems with which Britain was confronted in terms of her ability to discharge fully all her defence commitments throughout the globe and the ease with which a war started in Europe could assume global dimensions. Even without war the difficulties generated by Tientsin were serious. The British embassy in Berlin warned the foreign office that the Far Eastern crisis was giving rise to the impression in Germany that Britain would do nothing about Danzig.[23]

A meeting of the cabinet foreign policy committee on 19 June indicated the limits of what Britain could do in the Far East without American assistance. The prime minister warned that if Britain retaliated with economic sanctions this was likely to provoke a war; as Britain was not ready for war, there could be no sanctions. Later that day, a cabinet colleague, Lord Runciman, advised Chamberlain: 'In the absence of a certain promise of active naval and military help from the USA my view is emphatically against any step calculated to lead to war.'[24] The following week the foreign policy committee again discussed the Tientsin crisis and the narrow options in front of Britain were once more thrown into sharp relief in a climate in which the Danzig crisis was worsening daily. Of Britain's fifteen capital ships only seven could be sent to the Far East against Japan's nine. It was thought that because of 'oriental inefficiency' the British seven would be a match for the Japanese nine, but any dispatch of the fleet to the Far East was ruled out by the fact that it was likely to encourage Hitler to take action over Danzig where a coup was likely during the coming weekend.[25] Britain was rapidly being 'confronted with the possibility of a world war' without any prospect of American or Soviet support. Lord Halifax tried to enlist the aid of France and the United States, but the former would not act without the latter and Washington would not stir.[26] *Faute de mieux*, Halifax had to leave the resolution of the Tientsin crisis to Sir Robert Craigie, the British ambassador in Tokyo.

Craigie's own position was essentially conciliatory. He thought it prudent not to do anything that would allow the Japanese Army and its supporters to triumph regarding the direction that Japan's foreign policy should take. The consequence of that would have been the conclusion of a German–Japanese alliance. By patient and skilful diplomacy Craigie assisted in the peaceful resolution of this crisis with minimum loss of face for Britain. In the Craigie–Arita Accord of 24 July 1939, Britain agreed not to interfere in or subvert Japanese control of the parts of China occupied by the Japanese Army, but Craigie had successfully avoided committing Britain to anything like an endorsement of Japan's New Order in East Asia[27] which had been demanded. In subsequent negotiations Craigie prevented the conversion of the Tientsin concession into a Japanese police protectorate, an agreement being reached on police matters on 12 August. There remained the Japanese agenda of obtaining acceptance of the banknotes issued by the Federal Reserve Bank in the concession and the transfer to Japan of silver to the value of one million pounds sterling deposited in the Bank of Communications in Tientsin. Both these demands, if conceded, would have had the effect of undermining the *fapi*, the currency of the Chinese government. These matters were not, however, resolved when the negotiations with the Japanese were adjourned *sine die* on 20 August. The four terrorists had to be surrendered to their fate, but Craigie had avoided an occupation of the concession and the worst complications that the crisis could have thrown up.

By this time considerable firmness had come to characterize the British attitude towards Japan and Tientsin. This was the consequence of two dramatic developments. First, the United States on 26 July 1939 clearly began to adopt a firmer attitude in respect of Japanese aggression, when the Japanese government was given notice of the termination of the Japanese–American Commercial Treaty. There now developed in London a view that if the United States was ever to be enlisted fully in support of the maintenance of British power and independence, then Britain had to demonstrate a willingness in the first instance to resist and avoid compromises with dictators. The government was encouraged in this by the advice of the British ambassador in Rome, Sir Percy Loraine, who pointed that any compromises would be regarded as humiliations and confirm the belief that Britain would 'always give way rather than risk . . . the use of force, however grave the provocation.' Thus, any concession over Tientsin that might be perceived as weakening China was held to be unlikely to strengthen Britain's position in the Far East in the long term in the sense of encouraging American commitment. For this reason, if no other, Lord Halifax, against Craigie's advice opposed transferring the Tientsin silver to Japan. As R. A. C. Parker observes: 'In 1939, in the Far East, weakness paradoxically dictated a policy of resistance designed to win United States support for British ends.' It was one of the first statements of a refrain that would be repeated throughout the course of the twentieth century, namely, that of 'the subordination of British policy to that of the United States in attempts to exploit American resources for British purposes.'[28] Finally, the conclusion of the Nazi–Soviet Pact on 23 August 1939 deprived the group in Tokyo anxious to exploit the Tientsin crisis of the object of their policy, which was an alliance with Germany directed at both the Soviet Union and Britain. For the time being this could not be an option and the main thrust in Japan behind a forward policy over Tientsin receded. Furthermore, what exacerbated the shock of the Nazi –Soviet Pact in Tokyo was the fact that it violated the secret protocol of the Anti-Comintern Pact under which Germany was committed not to conclude any political agreement with the Soviet Union.

With the conclusion of the Nazi–Soviet Pact, however, the way now seemed clear for Hitler to attack Poland. In his speech on 28 April in which he had denounced the German Polish Non-Aggression Pact, Hitler had also publicly demanded the return of Danzig and a road and rail link through the Polish Corridor to East Prussia. In a private address to the German generals on 23 May, however, Hitler revealed his true purpose. Danzig was not the real objective, but rather the destruction of Poland and the expansion of German *Lebensraum* in the east, which alone could secure Germany's food supplies. There would be no re-run of Munich: there would be war. The political task was to isolate Poland. A simultaneous conflict with Britain and France was to be avoided. His past experience of British and French responses to the numerous crises that he had precipitated must have made him confident of achieving this. With the imminent conclusion of the Nazi –Soviet Pact he thought he had done the trick. On 22 August he again addressed the generals at his mountain retreat, the Berghof. Poland was to be depopulated and Germanized. The decision to attack this country had been taken in the spring. No resistance from the west was to be expected; their leaders were 'poor worms'. They might attempt a blockade, but Germany could survive because of her autarchic economic policies and the assurance of Soviet raw materials. The attack was to begin on 26 August. The speech ended with thanks and a primitive display by Göring, who danced upon a table (given his vast bulk, it is perhaps surprising that there was one capable of sustaining him!).[29]

The attack, however, was postponed. There were two reasons for this. On 25 August the Anglo-Polish Alliance was finally concluded. Hitler had always assumed that the delay in doing this was evidence of Britain's fundamental reluctance to become involved on the part of an East European state. This was where he misunderstood the nature of Britain's commitment in 1939. It was not necessarily a commitment to preserve the territorial integrity of a single state, but rather a commitment to destroy the Nazi menace. Had she been fully armed, it would have been difficult for Britain to render immediate and effective assistance to victims of aggression in Eastern Europe. It was axiomatic to British military planners that if war began in Europe it was likely to become a world war of long duration. That was Britain's deterrent effect: the threat of dragging Europe into such a ruinous conflict.

Hitler could not perceive this, but he did apprehend the inconvenience of the Anglo-Polish Alliance. Britain, against all his expectations, might indeed go to war. Point was added to this by the rejection of his offer, made in a hectoring manner to the British ambassador, to guarantee, within a comprehensive settlement, the existence of the British Empire and to support it with German power, if the British acquiesced in the resolution of the questions of Danzig and the Polish Corridor and accepted German hegemony in Eastern Europe. This offer was made slightly in advance of the conclusion of the Anglo-Polish alliance; it was not received until after it had become a fact. Nonetheless, it was recognized as a means of dividing the opposition. Suggestions of this kind had been made by Hitler and rejected on several occasions during the preceding six years; they were rejected now.

If Hitler's guess had been that Britain would not fight when the crunch came, that was not the perception in Rome. Between 11 and 13 August Ciano visited Salzburg where he had talks with Ribbentrop and Hitler. It was now made clear to the Italians that Germany definitely intended to go to war over

Poland and Danzig. Under the terms of the alliance they had made with the Germans three months before, they would be committed to go to war too. Italy was not ready for war. Moreover, Ciano considered that if Britain and France intervened a major conflict would result which the Axis powers were likely to lose. Ribbentrop disagreed. Britain would not intervene and even if she did she would lose. The Italian foreign ministry now worked to convert Mussolini to neutrality. Thus in the early evening of 25 August the Italian ambassador, Attolico, informed Hitler directly that Italy could not go to war because of lack of military preparation and lack of raw materials. The Führer was shaken. At 7.30 that evening the orders for the attack upon Poland the following day were withdrawn.[30]

The delay proved to be of short duration. Hitler was by now too committed, too determined to implement his programme, to go back. In the end he was prepared to risk a war with Britain and France. Moreover, it remained evident that the western powers were still anxious to avert a conflict over Poland and might yet decline to honour their commitments. Some pressure was put on the Poles to compromise; there was last minute shuttle diplomacy between London and Berlin by the Swedish businessman, Birger Dahlerus; and on 31 August Mussolini proposed a conference on 5 September. But the essential facts of the situation remained unchanged. Germany was determined to go to war and Poland was determined to resist. Neither Britain nor France could have escaped their obligations with their honour intact. The Germans had decided that 2 September was the last date for the commencement of a campaign against Poland that could be completed in good weather. The attack in fact took place a day earlier, on 1 September. On 3 September Britain and France issued ultimata to the German government demanding the withdrawal of German forces from Polish territory; failing a positive response a state of war between them and Germany would exist. The Germans did not agree to withdraw and Britain went to war with Germany at 11.00am on 3 September and France followed at 5.00pm on the same day.

The Collapse of Western Europe and the Isolation of Britain

The war unleashed in 1939 was not, of course, immediately a world war. It was not even a European war. Only four of the states of Europe were involved and of these it was the decisions of two that were critical. Germany had decided to attack Poland as a preliminary to the achievement of *Lebensraum*; Britain had decided to resist not so much to defend Poland, but because it was suspected that Germany was at least aiming at hegemony in Europe, which could pose a long-term threat to her empire, and because Hitler's international conduct had become intolerable. In a very real sense it was, therefore, principally an Anglo-German war. Almost certainly Hitler did not intend it to be a world war. The programme of German expansion was to be undertaken by lightning strikes, *Blitzkriege*, that were to accomplish their objectives before resistance could be mounted. Hitler, however, had miscalculated the consequences of his actions. The resistance of the British was what determined whether or not the war was going to be a world war. Britain was a world power and its government had always anticipated that a war starting in Central or Eastern Europe could have global consequences. It had to be assumed that if Britain was drawn into a conflict over Central or Eastern Europe, then ambitious and aggressive powers such as Italy and Japan, whose expansionist inclinations were evident in the conquest of Abyssinia and Manchuria, might take advantage of Britain's predicament and threaten British imperial interests in the Mediterranean and the Far East. It was not certain in 1939 that two years later a European conflict would become a global catastrophe, but Britain's decision to fight in 1939 set in train a series of events that made it likely. Britain's global interests, therefore, implied world war and, as opposed to the *Blitzkrieg*, the long haul, in which she could rely upon her extra–European connections for support.

This was already evident in September 1939, for, although Britain's worldwide interests made her vulnerable, they were also a source of strength. While in 1937 the dominions had been unsupportive of any inclination on the part of Britain to use force against Germany, appeasement had reassured opinion in them of Britain's peaceable intent and confirmed the reality of the national socialist threat. Thus on the morning of 3 September 1939, a few minutes after Neville Chamberlain's broadcast, the Australian prime minister, Menzies, announced 'Britain is at war therefore Australia is at war.' New Zealand's loyalty was predictable and just before midnight on 3 September the New Zealand Cabinet decided to go to war. Although Canada did not declare war until 10 September, because the declaration had to be passed by the Canadian parliament, 'in effect Canada was at war as soon as Britain as all measures were in full operation'. In South Africa the position was less clear cut and involved a change of prime minister. The Germanophile premier, Hertzog, who favoured neutrality, found himself outnumbered in his own cabinet by seven to six. The deputy prime minister, J. C. Smuts, in a debate in the South African Parliament on 4 September moved that South Africa sever relations with Germany, a motion that was carried by 80 to 67. Critically, the governor-general, Sir Patrick Duncan, refused Hertzog's request for a dissolution of Parliament and an election and asked Smuts to form a government. Had Duncan agreed to Hertzog's request it is probable that the latter would have won an election and South Africa would have stayed out of the war. In India the Viceroy declared war immediately, a decision which was resented in the sub-continent. But, whatever the divisions in South Africa and the reservations in India, the war from its beginning had acquired an extra-European dimension and a large part of the Earth's surface was hostile territory as far as Germany was concerned.[31] Of the dominions, only Eire opted for neutrality.

Neither Britain nor France was able to render meaningful assistance to the Poles and by 5 October Poland had been subjugated and partitioned between Germany and the USSR. But the democracies did not waver in their resolution. A peace offer made by Hitler on 6 October was rejected. Adverse weather conditions now postponed Hitler's planned November offensive in the west until the spring of 1940. The posture of the British and French was essentially defensive in these early phases of the war, but an attack by the

Soviet Union on Finland gave rise to consideration by the British and French governments of schemes for the economic strangulation of Germany by assisting the Finns.

Why did the USSR go to war with Finland? In addition to seizing the eastern half of Poland after the outbreak of the war, the Soviet Union also effectively turned the Baltic states, Estonia, Latvia and Lithuania into satellites by Treaties of Mutual Assistance that conceded to her military, naval and air bases and the right to occupy them should they be menaced by Germany. This was essentially a defensive move. The partition of Poland had created a military frontier between Germany and the Soviet Union on the German side of which stood a recently victorious and formidable army. It was essential, therefore, that the Soviet government attempt to improve its strategic position in the Baltic region, by preventing the Baltic states becoming German satellites or protectorates. It was from defensive motives also that the Soviet government subsequently proposed a territorial exchange to the Finnish government that would have the effect of improving the defence of Leningrad, which was situated fifteen miles from the Finnish border. The Finns declined to co-operate; the USSR went to war to secure her aims. There was considerable sympathy in the west for the plight of Finland and a desire to aid her defence and simultaneously to weaken Germany's economic capacity to wage war. To do this effectively would require rights of passage through Norway and Sweden, which would terminate their neutrality and enable the interdiction of iron ore supplies reaching Germany from Scandinavia, which was the major aim of the British government. The French, given the opposition to the war of the formidable French communist party, were much inclined to the notion of an anti-Bolshevik crusade and less reluctant than the British to provoke direct hostilities with the Soviet Union. They contemplated a bombing strike on the Soviet oilfields at Baku from bases in Syria and even a military thrust through the Caucasus to secure them, which would also deprive the Germans of oil. The Norwegians and Swedes, however, would not agree to their involvement in these schemes, wishing to preserve their neutrality. Even so it was decided by the British and French to go ahead and an Anglo-French expeditionary force was assembled. What saved them from this madcap scheme at the last was the capitulation of Finland on 12 March 1940.[32] The defeat of Finland outraged French opinion and Daladier was replaced in France as prime minister by Paul Reynaud who concluded an agreement with Britain under the terms of which Britain and France agreed not to make a separate peace with Germany.

The following month Hitler at last resumed the offensive, but not against France. In February 1940 the German supply vessel, the *Altmark*, had been boarded by a British vessel in Norwegian territorial waters and British prisoners, who were being taken to Germany, released. The British action had been a violation of international law. It aroused fears in Germany that Britain might attempt to occupy Norway as a means of tightening the blockade on Germany by prohibiting the use of the Norwegian port of Narvik as a conduit in the winter months for the supply of Swedish iron ore. It was, therefore, decided to pre-empt the British and in a swift campaign beginning on 8 April Denmark and Norway were invaded and occupied. The British and French endeavoured to eject the Germans from Norway, but it was a disastrous undertaking.

There now followed, in the wake of the fall of Norway, a change of prime minister and government in Britain. Although Winston Churchill, as first lord of the admiralty, had had much more to do with the Norwegian campaign than any other minister, it was Neville Chamberlain who became the focus of criticism for its failures. On 10 May Winston Churchill succeeded him as prime minister. The same day the Phoney War ended when Germany attacked the Low Countries and France simultaneously. Holland was defeated in five days, Belgium in just over two weeks. More depressingly France was compelled to seek an armistice on 17 June and to accept the occupation of two thirds of her territory by its terms five days later. Fortunately for Britain a large part of the British expeditionary force had been evacuated from Dunkirk by 2 June. This was not an act of kindness on the part of Hitler towards the British. He wanted to thrash them in order to convince them of the hopelessness of continuing the struggle. His mistake was in granting to Göring and the *Luftwaffe* the task of closing Dunkirk as a point of evacuation rather than allocating it to armoured units. Bad weather aided the British and 338,226 men escaped captivity. It was a triumphant reverse, but it could not conceal the deteriorating position of the British. In the dark days at the end of May even Churchill contemplated a compromise peace with Germany that would have included a colonial settlement. But the moment soon passed. Hitler though, despite wanting to administer a beating to the British at Dunkirk, still wanted peace with Britain. In a speech to the Reichstag on 19 July he stated:

> A great empire will be destroyed. A world empire that I never intended to destroy or even damage. But it is clear to me that the continuation of this struggle will end with the complete destruction of one of the two opponents. Mr. Churchill may believe that this will be Germany. I know it will be England. At this hour I feel compelled by conscience once more to appeal to reason in England. I believe I am in a position to do this because I am not the vanquished begging favours. As victor, I am speaking in the name of reason. I can see no reason why this war should go on.[33]

But the war did go on and its scope continued to expand. It seemed now as though Britain, isolated in Europe, would have to face alone a German Reich that had assumed mastery of the continent.

Seeing the balance of power in Europe steadily drifting towards Germany, Italy ceased her neutrality on 10 June and declared war on Britain and France. Mussolini had been confidently predicting a German victory for some time and the events of April and May 1940 hardened his convictions. He could no longer remain inactive and delay his 'appointment with history'. It seemed as though a nazi victory was imminent and Italy had to secure her place at the Peace Conference. His immediate reward on 24 June was Nice and a portion of Savoy. The impact of Mussolini's action was to extend the war to the Mediterranean and North Africa. But Italy soon proved a liability to the Axis. In October 1940 Greece was attacked, but without success. Only when

Germany decided to intervene in April 1941 were the Greeks, and simultaneously the Yugoslavs, overrun. Spectacular British successes in North Africa
against the Italians also compelled German intervention which began when
Rommel arrived in Tripoli in February 1941.

The United States and the War

In the months following the fall of France events took place that were to
embroil the future super-powers, the USA and the USSR in the conflict.
Throughout the 1930s the United States had embarked upon a course of
avoiding war by the enactment of neutrality legislation. But the fall of France
came as a profound shock. Moreover, it seemed likely that Britain could no
longer survive. It was suddenly brought home to American opinion that
insulating the USA against political forces inimical to their own democratic
traditions was not so easy. A Europe totally dominated by Germany and Italy
would be a profound threat to America's long term security. This did not,
however, manifest itself in a sudden surge of military and economic help for
Britain. On the contrary, from mid-June 1940 until early the following
August, America provided little assistance to Britain. This was partly
because the conviction of the possibility of British defeat was so well rooted
in Washington that it was felt that further assistance could not materially alter
the outcome of the war. Moreover, naval equipment sold to Britain might, in
the event of Britain's defeat, eventually be used against the United States.[34]
There was also the need to consider the defence of the western hemisphere.
Sales of equipment in early June had left the USA with greatly diminished
stocks. Finally, in 1940 President Roosevelt was seeking election for a third
term and did not wish to expose himself to attacks from the Republican
candidate, Wendell Willkie, that he was involving the United States in a war.
But if only one in five Americans prior to the Japanese attack on Pearl Harbor
in December 1941 supported American entry into the war, the overwhelming majority wanted the defeat of Hitler.

Roosevelt's first administration from 1933 to 1936 had substantially
reflected the isolationism that gripped the United States in the years after the
depression. From the beginning of Roosevelt's second administration
onwards, however, the United States was clearly indicating a greater
readiness to play a significant role in international affairs. A sequence of
events during 1936 showed how formidable the twin threats of war and the
imposition of totalitarian tyranny were becoming and how the world was
dividing into opposing camps. The Spanish Civil War, the Anti-Comintern
Pact between Germany and Japan and the declaration of the Rome–Berlin
Axis all suggested a coalescence of anti-status quo states into a single bloc. In
China, on the other hand, the collaboration of the nationalists and
communists against the Japanese following the Sian Incident in 1936[35]
foreshadowed the type of coalition that would confront them throughout the
world. Following his re-election in 1936, Roosevelt revealed his awareness of
the possible impact of the developing world crisis on the Americas when he
opened in Buenos Aires in November of that year an inter-American

conference for the maintenance of peace. He declared publicly that should any foreign state attempt to extend its power into the New World, it would meet the determined resistance of the United States and other American republics. It should not, however, be imagined that the United States suddenly and in an organized manner responded to a palpable challenge. During both 1936 and 1937, for example, further embellishments were added to American neutrality legislation. Rather a number of crises after 1936 compelled the United States government gradually to readjust its outlook on foreign affairs.

But, for all that Roosevelt and his secretary of state, Cordell Hull, were aware of the growing dangers of fascism and dictatorship and were deeply antipathetic to these political systems, they had to take account of the profound isolationism of opinion in the United States that wanted to avoid war at all costs. This was very well revealed in the narrow failure of the Ludlow Amendment in the House of Representatives in 1938. Following the *Panay* Incident in December 1937,[36] which many Americans felt had almost led to war, Representative Louis Ludlow from Indiana found a majority prepared to discuss his constitutional amendment that the United States could only declare war following a popular referendum. Leverage from the White House secured the failure of this amendment, but the fact that the measure's defeat required the employment of such heavy intervention by the administration well illustrated the depth of anti-war feeling in the country. Prior to this, Roosevelt had already experienced a rough ride from the isolationist press in the wake of his Chicago 'Quarantine Speech' of 5 October 1937, in which he had suggested that the peaceful states of the world should subject manifestly aggressive states to a 'quarantine', such as that imposed by communities on individuals suffering from highly pernicious and contagious diseases. Roosevelt felt bound to emphasize that no new policy initiative was intended by this speech, but this did not inhibit the subjection of his words to the closest possible scrutiny by a critical press. Throughout the later 1930s and into the early war years Roosevelt as far as foreign policy was concerned was between a rock and a hard place. He was aware of the growing threat of international violence and the determination of American opinion to remain aloof from it; aware of the need to do something and aware of the electoral dangers of doing it.

Nevertheless, the 'Quarantine Speech' does mark something of a watershed. The United States did participate in the Brussels Conference of November 1937 regarding the Far Eastern crisis; in January 1938 Roosevelt proposed the convening of an international conference that would endeavour to bind all nations to recognized rules for international conduct; and in the aftermath of the *Anschluß* Roosevelt endorsed an increase in the tempo of American rearmament by supporting the Vinson Naval Expansion Act of May 1938 which provided for the augmentation of the United States capital tonnage beyond that previously agreed in the naval disarmament treaties. This, though, was a symbolic gesture rather than a threatening one for it was thought that it would take a decade to build the US Navy up to the new levels. During the Munich crisis Roosevelt urged all parties to the dispute to resolve the crisis peacefully.

Thus far, American action had been verbal more than anything else, but from November 1938 onwards the United States government began to take action that demonstrably began to favour the democracies. Following the monstrous brutalities of the *Kristallnacht*, the American chargé d'affaires was removed from the Berlin embassy and the United States was to remain without senior ambassadorial representation in Berlin for the rest of the pre-war period. A conference of American states held in Lima in December 1938 likewise passed a resolution condemning Nazi race doctrines. Moreover, at the end of 1938 Roosevelt approved the sale of American aircraft to Britain and France with the deliberate intention of equipping them for a possible war against Germany. This, though, was not in breach of the neutrality legislation as war had not yet broken out in Europe.

Already, however, a tougher attitude had been apparent in the Far East where a decision had been taken as early as March 1938 not to invoke the neutrality legislation in connection with the Sino–Japanese War. This meant that China could buy arms in the United States. Japan had the same privilege, but this was increasingly opposed in the United States by bodies such as the American Committee for Non-Participation in Japanese Aggression. Thus in July 1938 the state department announced a moral embargo on the sale of aircraft to Japan. This was not legally binding, but was an indicator that Japan could not count on the United States in the long term as a source of supply. Moreover, when in November 1938 the Japanese prime minister, Prince Konoe, announced unilaterally the *New Order* in East Asia, which effectively rejected the *Washington System* and the 'Open Door' in China, the United States government responded in the most robust terms. Finally, there could have been no doubting the United States displeasure with Japan when in December 1938 Washington made available to China the small, but important loan of $25 million.

More was to follow. In his address to the nation of 4 January 1939, President Roosevelt stated: 'There are many methods short of war, but stronger and more effective than mere words, of bringing home to aggressor governments the aggregate sentiments of our own people.' He pointed out that the neutrality legislation was defective in that it 'may actually give aid to an aggressor and deny it to the victim.' His message concluded: 'Once I prophesied that this generation of Americans had a rendezvous with destiny. That prophecy comes true. To us much is given: more is expected.'[37] What Roosevelt intended was revealed the following day when he submitted his budget for the fiscal year 1940. Fifteen per cent of a total budget of $9 billion was to be devoted to defence and rearmament. This commitment was quite without precedent in peacetime and the actual expenditures in practice were to be more than specified in the budget, for the administration subsequently requested and was granted by Congress additional appropriations. The United States was now embarked upon an imposing programme of rearmament as part of a programme of deterrence, for it was not intended that rearmament should be the prelude to the involvement of the United States in war. Rearmament was rather seen as an earnest of America's commitment to play a more active part in international affairs, to defend the United States against aggression and to supply potential victims of the aggressor powers. During the rest of the year the administration endeavoured to amend the neutrality legislation, but without success until after the outbreak of war in Europe. In November 1939 Congress relented when it permitted the purchase of arms by belligerents, provided they paid cash for them and conveyed them from the United States in their own vessels. In the Far East the denunciation in July 1939 of the Japanese–United States Treaty of Commerce by the Roosevelt administration, effective from January 1940, was a very significantly hostile measure and created considerable alarm in Tokyo.

It is, of course, important that this transformation of American foreign policy took place before the outbreak of war in Europe and in the context of a debate amongst America's foreign policy-making elite stimulated by a book published by the journalist, Livingston Hartley in 1937.[38] Hartley's book firmly countered the intensification of isolationism and pacifism, that the growth of nazism and Japanese aggression had partly induced in the United States, by demonstrating that the domination of Europe by Germany and Asia by Japan could lead to the destruction of Britain and the British Empire, the resources of which could be used by these powers separately or in combination to threaten the security of the United States. For Hartley, the conclusion was obvious: the United States and Britain had such an identity of democratic interests that America should be prepared to ally herself with the latter. Gradually this thinking acquired more and more adherents and was promoted by scholars such as Nicholas Spykman and Felix Gilbert. The message was compelling. If the United States deemed it necessary to frustrate the total victory of Germany and Japan in their respective spheres, then America's resources should be used to their fullest extent for the defence of the existing world order. But more than that, there was the reality

> that whether the United States wanted to be or not, it was involved in global power politics by virtue of its very existence with its enormous size, population, resources and productivity. This being the case, it had no choice but to assert its role in international affairs rather than passively responding to developments elsewhere.[39]

Nevertheless, there was no question in 1939 of Roosevelt defeating isolationists and non-interventionists in Congress, or of mobilizing American opinion in support of armed intervention anywhere. In the United States the recently introduced Gallup Polls showed in April 1939 that 95 per cent of those polled opposed the idea of American intervention in a European war and 66 per cent were hostile to supplying assistance to any of the belligerents in such a war. Moreover, during 1939 the percentage of those polled who opposed American intervention against Germany rose from 83 per cent in March to 94 per cent in September.[40]

The following year, 1940, was a presidential election year and Roosevelt had to balance in his speeches his perception of America's defence requirements in a worsening international environment with the need to say nothing that would endanger his prospects of re-election. But it was not possible to adopt an even-handed attitude to the war in Europe, the culture and civilization of which he cared about passionately.[41] On 10 June 1940, on the day when Italy declared war on France and when the fall of France was clearly imminent, Roosevelt, in a speech at Charlottesville, Virginia, stated:

> In our American unity we will pursue two obvious and simultaneous courses; we will extend to the opponents of force the material resources of this nation; and, at the same time, we will harness and speed up the use of those resources in order that we ourselves in the Americas may have equipment and training equal to the task of an emergency and every defence.

In a politically courageous and lurid manner, he referred to Italy's attack on France: '. . . the hand that held the dagger has struck it into the back of its neighbour'[42].

The policy of 'All Aid Short of War' towards the opponents of aggressors was one that found support in the United States as the founding in May 1940 of the Committee to Defend America by Aiding the Allies shows. It was also a policy that a majority of Americans now favoured. There was, though, powerful opposition. In September 1940 the 850,000 strong America First Committee was established which opposed aid to the Allies on the grounds that it denied the USA essential resources for its defence and that the Allies were destined to be defeated anyway. The America First Committee boasted a number of prominent isolationist Senators, but its leading member was the charismatic aviator, Charles Lindbergh. Interestingly, German funds financed the publication of anti-interventionist literature, including the 'German White Paper,' which claimed to show that Roosevelt had actively connived in the outbreak of war in Europe. German funds also aided the 'Keep America Out of the War' lobby that attempted at the Republican Convention of June 1940 to secure the nomination of an isolationist presidential candidate.[43] In the event the Republican Convention nominated neither of the isolationist Senators, Taft and Vandenberg, but the nominal internationalist, Wendell Willkie.

Willkie's position on foreign policy was very close to Roosevelt's, but, as the election approached, he inclined to play upon isolationist sentiment. It was, therefore, more than ever necessary for Roosevelt to reassure the electors that aid to Britain was not only morally justified, but would also keep America at peace. Rather incautiously for him, he stated: 'I have said this before, but I shall say it again and again and again. Your boys are not going to be sent to any foreign wars.'[44] Undoubtedly, this was his intent. That he wanted to avoid war if he could clearly motivated his sending of under-secretary of state, Sumner Welles, to Europe in March 1940 to ascertain the possibilities of bringing the belligerents to a lasting peace. The failure of the Welles mission made it clear that the war would run its course, but Roosevelt hoped now that a victory for democracy and the security of the United States could be assured by the provision of substantial aid to the one resisting democracy, Britain.

It was becoming clear in London by the late summer of 1940 that Britain could not achieve victory over the Axis powers without American assistance. If the United States could be brought into the war that would, from the British point of view, be preferable, but the minimum that was needed was substantial military and economic aid. From the moment he became prime minister, Churchill strove to involve the United States more fully on the side of the Allies. In November 1939 the American neutrality legislation had been revised so as to allow military and non-military sales to the belligerent states on a cash-and-carry basis. This had been principally to the advantage of the Allies because of their sea power and foreign exchange reserves. Now Churchill sought something more. At first Roosevelt had been reluctant to let Britain have the American destroyers of First World War vintage requested by Churchill. During August 1940, however, the American president was gradually convinced of Britain's ability to survive as the Royal Air Force contained the onslaught of the *Luftwaffe* in the Battle of Britain. On 2 September 1940 America agreed to transfer to Britain fifty destroyers in exchange for leases of six bases in the Western Atlantic and a promise, in the event of defeat, not to surrender the British fleet. In his memoirs Churchill described the Destroyers Deal as a development that brought the United States closer to war. In the context of the American presidential election it represented for Roosevelt a very substantial political risk and could be interpreted by his opponents as action likely to involve the United States in war.[45] This was almost certainly not the intention of Roosevelt. He certainly wanted the defeat of Hitler, but Britain was to do it as America's proxy. He was still bent on keeping America out of the war if he could, but two things now made it more difficult. Germany, Italy and Japan saw in the Destroyers Deal the beginnings of an Anglo-American alliance and, secondly, Britain was rapidly becoming bankrupt.[46]

The desperate nature of Britain's financial situation was already becoming clear by May 1940 when the chiefs of staff compiled a memorandum on Britain's position in the event of the fall of France. This emphasized the importance of the United States being 'willing to give us full economic and financial support, *without which we do not think we could continue the war with any chance of success*'. A subsequent memorandum prepared for the British ambassador in Washington, Lord Lothian, stated unequivocally: 'Without the full economic and financial co-operation of the whole of the American Continent the task [the defeat of Germany] might in the end prove too great for the British Empire single-handed.'[47] After the elimination of France from the war in June 1940, there was no longer any point in conserving foreign currency reserves, as it was necessary to acquire the means of survival and to trust that the United States would continue to supply once the money ran out. In October 1940 Britain placed a massive order in the United States for military equipment and aircraft totalling $5,000 million. Consequently, by December 1940 Britain's gold and dollar reserves were virtually depleted.

Following his re-election in November 1940 Roosevelt had been approached for rather more substantial assistance by Churchill and the American president now saved Britain's situation by the idea of Lend–Lease, which he likened to lending a neighbour a hose to put out a fire in his house. The good citizen would not require to be paid the cost of the hose before passing it to his unfortunate neighbour, but say: 'I don't want fifteen dollars [the cost of the hose] – I want my garden hose back after the fire is over . . .'[48]. The relevant Act of Congress came into force in March 1941. Under its terms Britain was able to place orders for equipment with the

American government which would pay American businesses for the relevant goods. Thereafter they would be lent or leased to Britain with payment deferred until after the end of the war. Aid under Lend–Lease totalled some $31 billion and accounted for over 50 per cent of Britain's payments' deficit during the war's course. This assistance took the form of US government credits, rather than the private loans that had characterized American aid during the First World War and had resulted in the international payments tangle of the 1920s. Lend–Lease, though, was not a charity. The price to be paid was Britain's acceptance of America's view of the post-war economic world. The 'consideration' that the president was authorized to negotiate under the Lend–Lease legislation as defined in a draft submitted to the British on 28 July 1941 comprised 'a firm British commitment to abandon Imperial Preference and financial controls after the war, in return for a promise of radical reductions in US tariffs'. The Lend–Lease Consideration Agreement was signed on 23 February 1942. This committed the parties to discussions on post-war economic problems which continued throughout the war. On the issue of imperial preference the British proved highly resistant. On currency matters, however, there was more agreement and the war-time discussions resulted in the Bretton Woods Conference of 1944, which agreed that a regime of fixed exchange rates should come into force in the post-war world, coupled with an International Monetary Fund that would assist countries suffering temporary balance of payments crises.[49] After Lend–Lease, however, there was still no intention in Washington of becoming involved in war if it could be avoided. Writing to Francis Sayre in December 1940, Roosevelt specifically stated this, while adding that if the United States became involved in a war with Germany or Japan it would be as a consequence of their actions.[50] But, inevitably, the United States had moved closer to belligerency.

Barbarossa

Following the fall of France, Hitler's most pressing problem was that of continued British resistance. During the winter of 1940–41 that resistance was clearly being stiffened by increased Anglo-American intimacy. For a time Hitler toyed with the idea of invading Britain, but the technical difficulties in the way of the invasion plan, Operation Sealion, were insuperable. Moreover, Britain's victory in the air denied Germany the aerial superiority necessary for success. In September 1940 the plan was discreetly abandoned. Hitler now turned to another possibility. As early as the beginning of 1938 the German government contemplated bringing about a tripartite alliance between Germany, Italy and Japan as a means of checkmating Britain by applying pressure in all the areas where Britain had vital interests. This, however, had proved unsuccessful because of division in Japan over the nature of such an alliance and whether one should be concluded at all. The army was willing to accept an alliance with Germany that would be directed against Britain and France as well as the Soviet Union. On the other hand, Admiral Yonai, first as navy minister and subsequently as prime minister, argued that the inclusion of Britain as one of the targets of a putative alliance effectively meant including the United States too. It was his view that the very fact of a German–Japanese alliance would in all probability provoke an Anglo-American alliance that would have disastrous consequences for Japan if Germany started a European war in which Japan was obliged to participate. Younger naval officers, however, embraced the possibility of war with the democracies as a means of justifying large increases in naval expenditure. Similar divisions existed in the foreign ministry between the 'moderates' and the 'Axis faction.' Neither was Hitler immediately successful with the Italians. He was only able to secure the alliance of Italy in May 1939. On 27 September 1940, however, success was eventually achieved when Germany and Italy recognized Japanese leadership in Asia, Japan recognized the leadership of Germany and Italy in Europe and all three agreed 'to assist one another with all political, economic and military means when one of the three contracting parties is attacked by a power at present not involved in the European war or in the Sino-Japanese conflict.' The Tripartite Pact did not mention the United States by name, but that was the power to which it referred. Hitler hoped that Japan would now be stimulated to attack British possessions in the Far East and that the Pact would intimidate the USA into neutrality through the threat of a two front war.[51]

There remained the problem of the Soviet Union. In November 1940 Molotov was invited to Berlin for talks with Ribbentrop and Hitler. The Führer spoke grandly of the collapse of the British Empire and proposed a division of the world between Germany, Italy, the Soviet Union and Japan. In responding to the blandishments of Hitler and Ribbentrop Molotov was dour and even sarcastic. He asked inconvenient questions about the presence of German troops in Finland and proposed that the Germans revoke their guarantee of Rumania, recognized by Germany in 1939 as a Soviet sphere of influence, which Hitler declined. The Führer was also interrogated about the status of Bulgaria. On 13 November, Ribbentrop and his hosts, at a gala banquet in the Soviet embassy, were compelled by a British air raid to retire to the German foreign ministry. There the German foreign minister revealed a draft treaty converting the Tripartite Pact into a Quadripartite Pact by the adherence of the USSR. The four powers would 'respect each other's natural spheres of influence' and settle any disputes amicably; and agree not to join or aid any bloc 'directed against one of the Four Powers'. A secret protocol allocated the USSR's portion of the globe as parts of Central Asia abutting the Indian Ocean. Molotov's response remained impassive. The Soviet Union was not interested in the Indian Ocean, but rather about matters affecting her security in Eastern Europe.[52]

What was Hitler's purpose in proposing this scheme? Did it mean that he had finally abandoned his ambition to destroy the Soviet Union and achieve *Lebensraum* in the Ukraine? Almost certainly it did not. When Hitler had addressed the generals at Berchtesgaden on 22 August 1939, he had stated: '. . . in a few weeks hence I shall stretch out my hand to Stalin at the common German–Russian frontier and with him undertake to redistribute the world'. This did not though constitute a finality for Hitler. The arrangement he was going to make with the Soviet Union (the Non-Aggression Pact) was a tactical ploy only. He explained:

> My pact with the Poles was merely conceived of as a gaining of time. As for the rest, gentlemen, the fate of Russia will be exactly the same as I am now going through with in the case of Poland. After Stalin's death – he is a very sick man – we will break with the Soviet Union. Then there will begin the dawn of the German rule of the earth.[53]

Now with the Quadripartite Pact he was playing for time: time with which to bring Britain to her knees. Ribbentrop spelled it out to Molotov. The central point was this: was the USSR prepared to co-operate in the destruction of the British Empire? Molotov retorted that this assumed that Britain was already defeated. It had been stated to him by Hitler that Germany was involved in 'a life-and-death struggle' and he observed sarcastically that he construed this as meaning that 'Germany was fighting "for life" and Britain "for death"'. To Ribbentrop's constant assertion that Britain could no longer resist, Molotov asked why it was that he and Ribbentrop were discussing these matters in an air raid shelter and whose bombs were falling on Berlin.[54] Clearly the Soviet Union had doubts about the defeat of Britain. Although Stalin replied positively to these overtures in November, he did so on terms, such as the evacuation of German troops from Finland, that were unacceptable to Hitler.

Ideally, Hitler had wanted to neutralize Britain before attacking the USSR. He now decided to reverse his priorities. In July 1940 the first discussions concerning a German attack on Russia took place among the army leadership without the prompting of Hitler. On 31 July, however, he emphasized to military and naval chiefs that one of the reasons why Britain was continuing to resist was the possibility that the Soviet Union could ultimately be brought into the conflict against Germany. He stated:

> *Britain's hope lies in Russia and the United States. If the hopes pinned on Russia are disappointed then America too will fall by the wayside,* because the elimination of Russia would tremendously increase *Japan's power* in the Far East . . . *Russia is the factor on which Britain is relying the most.*
> *Something must have happened in London!*
> The British were completely down; now they have perked up again. Intercepted telephone conversations. Russia is painfully shaken by the swift development of the Western European situation . . .
> *With Russia smashed, Britain's last hope would be shattered.* Germany will then be master of Europe and the Balkans.[55]

Serious planning for the destruction of the Soviet Union began in August and on 18 December Hitler issued the directive *Operation Barbarossa*. This required the preparation of the army for an attack on the Soviet Union even before the defeat of Britain. In other words, Hitler was now ready to attempt the medium term priority of his foreign policy programme, the subjugation of the USSR and the achievement of *Lebensraum*, without the neutrality or acquiescence of Britain. Indeed, the defeat of the USSR was now regarded as the means of realizing that objective. He was confident of winning because it would take at least eighteen months for the British to open a second front, which meant that the mission could be accomplished without the danger of a two front war. Moreover, the racial and military superiority of the German over the Slav would ensure a rapid victory.

Following a delay caused by the need to bail out the Italians after their disastrous attack upon Greece and to conquer Yugoslavia, after a coup had installed a pro-British government in Belgrade, the German attack on the USSR began on 22 June 1941. Despite warnings from the British and American governments and from his own agents, most notably Richard Sorge in Tokyo, Stalin and the Red Army were unprepared for the onslaught. But the initial successes of the German Army were perhaps not quite as spectacular as is often claimed. On parts of the front the Red Army fought not only bravely, but cleverly, exacting a heavy toll in men and equipment. By August 1941 it was clear to General Halder that Germany had underestimated the Russian colossus.[56] Arguably, Hitler attacked the USSR when he did in order to end the war in Europe, but now virtually the whole of Europe was engulfed in a conflict and Germany embroiled in a war on two fronts with two world powers. The world community was halfway to a global conflict.

The Atlantic War

One of the post-war superpowers was now involved in the Second World War and the other, the United States, had by this time determined her strategic priorities should she become, against her will, a belligerent. Moreover, by the time of the Japanese attack on Pearl Harbor in December 1941 she had already entered into a state of virtual undeclared naval war with Germany in the Atlantic. The conclusion of the Tripartite Pact in October 1940 impacted in Washington by inducing in American policy makers and strategic planners the conviction that Germany, Italy and Japan were co-ordinating their policies. During the autumn of 1940, therefore, there was general agreement in Washington that the time had come to define America's strategic priorities. In the absence of clear instructions from the White House, it was the chief of naval operations, Admiral Stark, who bore the main responsibility for devising what came to be known as Plan D, or Plan Dog. Both Stark and the army chief of staff, General George C. Marshall, were of a mind that given American involvement in a two front, or two ocean, war, the Atlantic theatre should have priority over the Pacific theatre. In other words, the United States should remain on the defensive against Japan, or even avoid war with her, until the defeat of Germany. It was, in fact, a major assumption of Plan D that Germany could only be defeated by committing substantial American land and air forces to the European continent. Stark's plan, produced on 11 November 1940, was implicitly, but not formally, endorsed by Roosevelt in January 1941.[57]   Added point was given to the priorities of Plan D by the implications of Lend-Lease. In his fireside chat broadcast of 29 December 1940, Roosevelt described the function of the United States as that of 'the arsenal of democracy'. It was in the United States' interest to supply Britain, the focal point of resistance against powers determined upon world conquest. He emphasized: 'If Great

Britain goes down, the Axis powers will control the continents of Europe, Asia, Africa and Australia and the high seas.' There was not much point however in being the arsenal of democracy if the supplies were constantly being sent to the bottom of the Atlantic by German submarines and surface raiders. Within Washington there were powerful advocates of the view that the United States should do everything to secure the safe delivery of supplies to Britain. These were men such as Henry Stimson, the secretary for war, Henry Morgenthau, the secretary of the treasury and Admirals Knox and Stark. By the spring of 1941 some 500,000 tons of shipping was being lost to German wolf packs and the pressure upon Roosevelt to do something became intense.

From almost the start of the war the United States had conducted a policy in the Atlantic that was advantageous to Britain. At the conference of American states held in Panama in September 1939 it was agreed to establish a neutrality zone in the Western Atlantic that extended between 300 and 1,000 miles to the east of the coast of continental America with the exception of Canada. In this zone, naval action by belligerent powers was to be forbidden. Ostensibly an act of neutrality, the zone favoured Britain rather than Germany. It meant, in theory at least, that U-boats were excluded from the Western Atlantic and that the patrolling of these waters by American naval vessels would release Royal Navy vessels, which otherwise would have patrolled these waters, for duty elsewhere. Moreover, Roosevelt authorized US Navy patrols to inform their Royal Navy counterparts of the whereabouts of German vessels with the clear intention that they should move in for the kill.[58] In April 1941 civilian hawks in Washington and US Navy chiefs pressed Roosevelt to authorize the escort of British shipping in the Atlantic. At first willing to agree, Roosevelt later withdrew because of the opposition of public opinion and within Congress to escorting and the conclusion of the Russo-Japanese Neutrality Pact which for the time being made it imprudent to consider the redeployment in the Atlantic of vessels stationed in the Pacific. Roosevelt did, though, later agree to extend the neutrality zone eastwards to the longitudinal line of 26° west, which included Greenland in the north and the Azores in the south. US Navy patrols were authorized to inform the British of the presence of enemy vessels so that convoys could take evasive action.

This decision was bound to have serious implications for the future course of German–American relations, for in March 1941, in response to pressure from Admiral Raeder, Hitler had agreed to extend the German combat zone in the Atlantic to a line west of Iceland up to Greenland's three mile limit. Within this area it was agreed that neutral as well as belligerent merchant shipping could be sunk on sight. Hitler had been reluctant to concede Raeder's actual demand for non-recognition of the American neutrality zone or, at least, recognition only as far as three hundred miles east of the coast of the western hemisphere, on the ground that he did not want complications with the United States prior to the subjugation of the Soviet Union, planning for which was at an advanced stage by then. Even so, Roosevelt's new delimitation of the neutrality zone overlapped with the German combat zone which meant inevitably that incidents involving German and American vessels were now likely to occur.

Roosevelt, however, still evaded the important issues of repeal of the neutrality legislation and escorting merchant shipping. On 27 May 1941 he made a storming speech and spoke of the administration's resolution to take the necessary 'additional measures' to ensure that supplies reached Britain. But, at a press conference on the following day, he made it clear that there would be none. Clearly, the president was not prepared to move too far ahead of American public opinion, 76–79 per cent of which still wished America to stay out of war according to polling conducted in June 1940. Polling conducted the previous month showed that while 76 per cent of opinion favoured helping Britain even at the risk of war, a bare majority, 55 per cent, wished to risk escorting.[59] Nevertheless, by the end of August Roosevelt had ordered escorting to become effective on 1 September. Undoubtedly, the German attack on Russia pushed him in this direction, as did the American occupation of Iceland in July 1941. Earlier in the year, America had taken Greenland under its protection to pre-empt its use as a German base. The American occupation of Iceland was undertaken with the same end in view. It had already been agreed the previous March that the British division stationed in Iceland would be relieved by American troops in September 1941 to make it available for deployment elsewhere. The action was advanced by two months, however, on account of suspicious German submarine and aerial activity. The American occupation of Iceland was carried out in agreement with the Icelandic government which had effectively declared its independence from Denmark in May 1940, following the German occupation of the latter the previous month. The Icelandic representative body, the *Althing*, entrusted the powers of the Crown to the Regent, Sveinn Bjornsson. Although relations between Denmark and Iceland had been good, the Icelanders had already determined not to renew the Iceland–Denmark Treaty of Union of 1918 when it came up for renewal in 1943. On 17 June 1944, Iceland became an independent republic. The American occupation of Iceland was also greeted with enthusiasm in the United States. Roosevelt now on 11 July overreached himself: he offered US Navy escort to vessels of any nationality that joined American and Icelandic convoys bound for Iceland. A week later, however, his usual caution returned and he withdrew the protection offered to non-American vessels. Nevertheless, the American commitment had gone a stage further, for the US Navy was now directed to hunt and destroy any vessels threatening American merchantmen.

What, however, was probably most critical in convincing Roosevelt of the need for US Navy escorts for British merchant vessels, was the fact that Britain could no longer sustain the current level of losses and remain in the war. This was made clear to Roosevelt by the joint army-navy board on 11 September. Moreover, the Soviet Union's continued, but unexpected, survival after the German onslaught of June 1941 meant that the resources of the Royal Navy were further stretched by the need to escort supplies to Murmansk and Archangel along the Norwegian coast. The conclusion was obvious: if Britain was to stay in the war America had to replace Britain's shipping losses and provide more protection in the Atlantic. Finally, rendering as much help as possible to Britain might be the only way of keeping America out of the war. During the staff conversations in Washington in March 1941, British representatives had argued that the blockade of Germany plus aerial bombardment might be enough to defeat Germany. This was a view that appealed to Roosevelt; but it was one that the American soldiers and sailors strongly contested, believing that only the entry of the United States into the war by committing land forces in Europe and Africa could for certain bring down Hitler's Germany. This view was very forcibly put to Roosevelt by the joint army-navy board in September. Avoidance of such an eventuality by assisting Britain in the Atlantic and ensuring that supplies reached her seemed preferable to Roosevelt. Moreover, it was a course that would entail minimal risk: while Hitler was still preoccupied with the Soviet Union, he would take little action against the United States.

Precisely why and when Roosevelt took the decision to provide American naval escorts for British merchant shipping will probably never be known, but what is certain is that at the historic meeting between Churchill and Roosevelt at Placentia Bay, Newfoundland, from 9–12 August, arrangements were made for the escorting of both British and American merchant vessels as far as Iceland with effect from 1 September. On the other hand, Roosevelt was not very candid about this with American public opinion until the American destroyer, the USS *Greer*, was attacked by a German submarine on 4 September. This now allowed the President to indulge high dudgeon as he justified the new policy, which, with reference to the 80 per cent of Americans who were against war, he carefully emphasized was not an act of war. Nevertheless, American naval vessels were now under instructions to destroy U-boats and surface raiders without waiting to be fired at. During the following month crucial sections of the neutrality laws were repealed by Congress so that American merchant vessels could be armed, enter combat zones and carry war freight directly to friendly ports. The votes, however, were very close, despite the fact that the debates took place in a context in which two American vessels, the USS *Kearney* and the USS *Reuben James*, had been attacked, and one sunk, by German submarines with considerable loss of life. The votes had been so close that Roosevelt felt that a presidential request for a declaration of war would be heavily defeated.

Nevertheless, America was now as close to war with Germany as it was possible to be without a declaration of war. Probably Roosevelt wanted to keep it that way. Probably he still hoped that America's contribution to the war would be 'arms rather than armies'. Probably, he did want to complete his third administration 'without war'. Probably, as he himself observed, Japan unexpectedly took the matter 'out of his hands'[60].

8

Crisis in the Far East

In the autumn of 1941 it must have seemed as though American support for Germany's enemies, which now included the Soviet Union,[1] and the activity of the United States Navy in the Atlantic must soon bring about war between Germany and the United States. As far as the United States was concerned, priority continued to be accorded to the war in Europe. It was, however, to be the attack upon the American Pacific fleet at Pearl Harbor in Hawaii on 7 December 1941, which was accompanied by simultaneous attacks on British possessions in the Far East,[2] which brought the United States into the war and created a state of total global warfare. How did this situation come about?

Japan in the 1920s

During the 1920s it could easily have been assumed that Japan was developing her own form of westernized government based upon parliamentary institutions. Within the Diet, the Japanese parliament, there were two principal parties, the *Seiyukai* and the *Kenseikai*. It was the leader of the latter party, Kato Komei, a man committed to parliamentary rule, who provided the main impetus for political reform. In 1924 he was able to form a government following elections which had largely been brought about because the politicians refused to accept the nomination of a non–party figure, the army man Kiyoura Keigo, as prime minister. Kato argued powerfully the case for responsible party governments in which the prime minister would be appointed from the largest party. He forced a dissolution of the Diet on this issue and, having won the following elections, formed a coalition government. From August 1925 until his death in January the following year he was able to continue in office on the basis of *Kenseikai* support alone. Once in office, Kato carried through electoral reform when in 1925 the Universal Manhood Suffrage Act was passed, conferring on males of twenty-five years of age and over the right to vote. This had the effect of expanding the Japanese electorate from three to thirteen million. Kato also trimmed the Japanese bureaucracy by reducing its establishment by 20,000 posts. Similar economies were made in the armed forces by reducing their budget share from forty per cent to under thirty per cent. This resulted in the reduction of the army by four divisions and the premature retirement of two thousand officers.

On coming to power, Kato appointed three men to senior ministerial posts who were to play important parts in the political life of Japan over the next eight years. These were the home minister, Wakatsuki Reijiro; the finance minister, Hamaguchi Osachi; and Baron Shidehara Kijuro, the foreign minister. Shidehara had formerly been Japanese ambassador in Washington and he came to office with an internationalist foreign policy that set him and the government of which he was a member some distance apart from the Japanese Army. Shidehara agreed that China was of great importance for Japan, but he was opposed to advancing Japan's interests on the mainland of Asia by coercive measures. Shidehara believed in proceeding by conciliation and compromise. The maintenance of good relations with the United States he thought imperative. In 1924 he wrote:

> In our restricted islands we suffer from a population increase of 700,000–800,000 annually. There is, therefore, no alternative but to proceed with our indus-trialization. It follows from this that it is essential to secure overseas markets and this can only be done by adopting an economic diplomacy. If we try to cure our economic problems by territorial expansion, we will merely destroy interna-tional cooperation . . . Japan, being closest to China, has an advantage by way of transport costs and she has also the greatest competitive power because of her wages [low production costs]. It must therefore be a priority for Japan to maintain the great market of China.[3]

Much more, he thought, could be achieved by winning the goodwill of the Chinese and he vigorously opposed interference in the political affairs of China.

Both in the sphere of domestic policy and that of foreign policy Japan must have appeared to be inclining towards western norms, particularly when, in 1927, the government of prime minister Wakatsuki, who had succeeded Kato on his death in 1926, was forced to resign mainly because of a crisis in the banking world. The incoming *Seiyukai* government, headed by Tanaka Gi'ichi felt it necessary to call elections in order to strengthen its position in the Diet. In Japan's first ever elections held on the basis of universal male suffrage, the government succeeded in its objective and gained a majority of two seats. There were, though, disquieting features in all this. Wakatsuki's government had fallen largely because of a banking crisis, but it is significant that objections, spearheaded by the army, to Shidehara's foreign policy, which was stigmatized as weak, played their part. Equally, while Kato had achieved universal male suffrage, the trade off had been the Peace Preserva-tion Law under which any individual who advocated the abolition of private property or amendments to Japan's 'unique' national structure would be liable to imprisonment for up to ten years. This legislation was considered essential by Japanese conservatives to minimize the impact of Japan's recognition of the Soviet Union in 1925. Moreover, while Tanaka won the elections of 1928, the police harassed the opposition party during the electoral process and other forms of intimidation were employed by the government. (Following a merger between the *Kenseikai* and the other opposition groups, the opposition was now known as the *Minseito*.) Finally, Kato had not been able to curb the influence of senior bureaucrats, or reform the House of Peers. In fact, the Meiji Constitution and its conservative and elitist bias remained largely intact.

Until 1945 the linchpin of the Japanese political system was indeed the Meiji Constitution, which was an integral part of the modernizing process instituted by the Meiji Restoration. By 1885 the central organ of government in Japan was the cabinet. It was presided over by a prime minister who had received an 'imperial mandate to form a government'[4] and it was responsible for all major governmental decisions. During the course of the next five years a constitutional system was fully elaborated, beginning with the establishment of a privy council in 1888, the function of which was to render advice to the emperor on important matters of state. Finally, after several years of study and drafting, the lead in which was taken by Ito Hirabumi, the Meiji Constitution was on 11 February 1889 handed by the Meiji Emperor to the prime minister, Count Kuroda, coming into force in November 1890. This constitution laid down the legal foundation for governmental activity. It provided for a Diet with an elected lower House and a House of Peers composed of a nobility that had been created in 1884 and which was inevitably supportive of the regime of the Meiji Oligarchs. These arrangements were certainly not democratic: the franchise was restricted and the unelected upper house had equal power with the elected body. Moreover, the government, and the ministers within it, were not responsible to the Diet, but to the throne. The principle on which governments were formed was not parliamentary: cabinets 'were "transcendental" and non-party, appointed by the emperor not necessarily from the majority party in the diet'. Even the freedom of the cabinet was restricted by the requirement that all important decisions be submitted to the privy council for ratification. Equally beyond parliamentary control were the armed forces which were solely responsible to the emperor, their leaders enjoying 'direct access to the emperor and complete autonomy from the cabinet regarding defence matters'[5].

A fundamental objective of the constitution was the maintenance of the power and influence of the those who had made the Meiji Restoration, namely the Meiji oligarchs. This in essence was effected through the person of the emperor who stood at the apex of the constitution. It was he who had 'bestowed' a constitution on the Japanese people. Sovereignty resided in him totally and he was 'sacred and inviolable'. He was also head of the government and in theory was possessed of vast legislative, executive and military powers. In reality, though, these powers were exercised by the elites who had presided over the Meiji Restoration. As David Titus has written:

> Far from being his personal decision-making powers . . . the emperor's prerogatives were the source of authority for rule by others – at first, by the statesmen who had engineered the Restoration and created the institutions of prewar Japanese government; later, by the leaders produced by the new institutions that grew to maturity under the constitution of 1889. In short, the

imperial prerogatives laid down in the constitution became institutionalized in a government structure over which the emperor reigned but did not rule: the civil and military bureaucracies, the imperial legislature and the courts. The emperor was once again a transcendental prisoner, but in a new and different political system: a constitutional monarchy based on imperial prerogative.[6]

What made the Meiji state stable were the *Genro*. These were men who, as a consequence of long and distinguished service to the nation, had become intimate and permanent counsellors of the emperor. By the end of the Meiji period (1912) the most notable of the Meiji Oligarchs, Ito Hirabimi and Yamagata Aritomo, had become *Genro*. The fundamental source of the power and influence of the *Genro* lay in the fact that it was on their advice that the emperor chose the prime minister. They also influenced the composition of governments and the nomination to important posts outside the cabinet. Thus it was they who determined appointments to non-elective bodies such as the privy council and the House of Peers. They also had a decisive say in appointments to the most senior posts in the bureaucracy and the armed services. The important point, though, is that all these appointments were imperial prerogatives exercised on the basis of the advice of the *Genro*, who 'were the glue that held the Meiji state together'[7]. While the authority of the *Genro* remained intact, the Meiji state would continue to function steadily and smoothly, the more independent-minded elements such as the armed forces being held in check by the respect that a man such as Yamagata could command within the upper echelons of the army. The last appointed and longest serving of the *Genro*, Prince Saionji Kimmochi, would until his death in 1940 remain a force for moderation.[8] Once, however, the authority of the *Genro* began to disintegrate the weaknesses inherent in the Meiji Constitution would begin to manifest themselves.

Japan emerged from the First World War as a victor, her position as a leading world actor seemingly having been confirmed. But in the eyes of many Japanese, Japan remained a pariah. Until 1919 organized nationalism in Japan was a minority activity.[9] This did not mean that patriotic feeling did not exist, for all Japanese were deemed to be patriotic. From the end of the First World War onwards, however, nationalist societies began to proliferate leading to the phenomenon of *double patriotism*. The *double patriots*, the advocates of extreme nationalism, were deemed to have twice the patriotism of the ordinary Japanese.[10] The stimulus for this development lay in a perception that Japan was not being treated as an equal in the international community. The failure of the Paris Peace Conference to incorporate in the covenant of the League of Nations a statement endorsing the concept of racial equality was a significant blow to Japanese self-esteem and was intensified in its impact in 1921–2 by the failure of Britain to renew the Anglo-Japanese alliance. The reasons for the British decision have already been discussed,[11] and they had nothing to do with an Anglo-American desire to exclude Japan, or an Anglo-American conspiracy of any kind. It is, on the other hand, significant that many Japanese to this day believe that is precisely what it was.[12] Yet more humiliation was in store in 1924 when the United States Congress enacted immigration legislation that excluded the Japanese from the new quota system. This was gratuitously offensive because under the pre-1914 'Gentlemen's Agreement' the Japanese government had voluntarily restricted Japanese immigration into the United States in a system that worked well. The inference, however, that the Japanese were unsuitable for American citizenship, taken in conjunction with similar restrictions on Japanese immigration into Australia and Canada, once more aroused fears of a white conspiracy against Japan. The feeling of disgrace was such that one Japanese ritually disembowelled himself in the grounds of the United States embassy in Tokyo.

The perceived need for Japanese emigration because of overpopulation lay behind the desire to have the concept of racial equality written into the League Covenant. Underpopulated areas of the English-speaking world might then become accessible to Japan's surplus population. By the 1920s the hopes that population pressure would be relieved had not been realized by Japanese emigration to Korea and Formosa (under direct control) or Manchuria (under indirect control). Despite substantial encouragement on the part of the government, emigration to mainland Asia proved unattractive to the Japanese. By the middle of the 1920s only a quarter of a million Japanese had settled in Manchuria. But even here it seemed that the international community was endeavouring to frustrate Japan's expansionism. Over Shantung Japan had given way to American opinion and simultaneously had withdrawn from a four-year occupation of Siberia without any gains. It appeared that Japan was being confined and isolated in a manner that was not applied to comparable powers.

Discriminated against racially by the English-speaking world, Japan by the end of the 1920s was also experiencing discrimination from the same quarter in respect of her trade. During the First World War Japan and America developed a mutually beneficial commercial relationship. American exports to Japan multiplied by a factor of five, Japanese exports to the United States by a factor of three. This relationship continued to blossom into the 1920s when the United States remained Japan's largest trading partner. Just how critical this relationship was from the Japanese point of view can be gleaned from the fact that most of Japan's motor cars, industrial machinery and oil were imported from America. Furthermore, forty per cent of foreign investment in Japan was supplied by American banks. As a market for Japanese exports, the United States was also critical taking some forty per cent of Japan's total exports and ninety per cent of raw silk exports.[13] This relationship was, though, badly affected by the depression. The collapse of purchasing power in the United States caused the price of silk to fall and a catastrophic reduction in the volume of silk exports, bringing ruin to many of Japan's peasant producers. The effects of the depression were intensified by organized boycotts of Japanese goods in the United States and the introduction of the Hawley–Smoot Tariff in 1930, which imposed duties averaging 23 per cent on Japanese imports. Similarly, the British attempted to exclude Japanese textile exports from their colonial markets in India and Africa. The social distress caused by the depression and the economic discrimination encountered by Japan only served further to intensify the Japanese nationalism that had burgeoned during the 1920s.

For all its force Japanese nationalism was a divided phenomenon. By the

1930s there were, for example, over seven hundred nationalist societies. They and their predecessors since 1919 were, however, often transient organizations brought to a swift end by internal rivalries and lack of money. Some of these organizations, such as 'The Japan National Essence Society', *Dai Nippon Kokusuikai*, were devoted to containing the impact of socialism and the growth of organized labour. The appearance in Japan of left-wing societies such as the *Shinjinkai*, 'The Association of New Men', also provoked the formation of anti-liberal organizations such as Professor Uesugi Shuinkichi's 'League for the Study of Statesmanship', or *Keirin Gakumei*. Uesugi's principal associate was Takabatake Motoyuki, a socialist writer whose ultimate thought reflected national socialism. According to Takabatake, 'the evils of capitalism would disappear if the great financial and industrial magnates surrendered their assets to the Emperor – to the state, in other words'. Action of this type would 'knit the Empire together into an economic as well as spiritual unity'. This was Takabatake's view of state, or national socialism.[14] Ultimately, Uesugi and Takabatake were to disagree causing the dissolution of the *Keirin Gakumei*. Takabatake became an advocate of radical, revolutionary nationalism, while Uesugi remained representative of a more conservative nationalism enshrined in the *Keirin Gakumei's* successor the *Kokuhonsha*, or 'The National Foundations Association'. This organization emphasized Japan's unique religious character; the need to reform anything in Japan contrary to the moral principle on which the nation was founded; the acceptance of Japan's special mission in Asia; and the complete rejection of any identification of European fascism with Japanese nationalism.[15]

The most influential thinkers among the ultranationalists were Kita Ikki and Okawa Shumei. Kita was originally a socialist and lived in China both before and during the First World War. In the end he became convinced that Japan could only assist China against the west if Japan reformed herself first and he ultimately advocated that Japan should reform herself on the basis of a national socialist economic system. In 1919 he published *An Outline for the Reconstruction of Japan*, which argued the case for a blend of socialism and Japanese imperialism.[16] Together with the nationalization of vast areas of Japan's economic life – manufacturing, banking, shipping, railways and land above a certain value, Japan was also to undertake a massive rearmament programme in order ultimately to seize territory currently administered by the British Empire and the Soviet state. According to Kita, this could be justified on socialist grounds, claiming that Japan was one of the internationally disadvantaged with a prescriptive right to seize land from the advantaged in the name of justice. It was a forerunner of the 'have/have-not' debate of the middle 1930s. He wrote:

> Justice is the proper demarcation of interests. As the class struggle within a nation is waged for the readjustment of unequal distinctions, so war between nations for an honourable cause will reform the present unjust distinctions [between nations]. The British Empire is a millionaire possessing wealth all over the world; and Russia is a great landowner in occupation of the northern half of the globe. Japan with her scattered fringe of islands is one of the proletariat, and she has the right to declare war on the big monopoly powers. The socialists of

the West contradict themselves when they admit the right of the class struggle to the proletariat at home and at the same time condemn war, waged by a proletariat among the nations, as militarism and aggression . . . If it is permissible for the working class to unite to overthrow unjust authority by bloodshed, then unconditional approval should be given to Japan to perfect her army and navy and make war for the rectification of unjust international frontiers. In the name of rational social democracy Japan claims possession of Australia and Eastern Siberia.[17]

These objectives could not, of course, be achieved without conferring upon the armed forces the requisite supreme power within the state and Kita did not shrink from the advocacy of a *coup d'état* to realize this.

Kita ultimately returned to Japan through the assistance of the other major ultranationalist figure, Okawa Shumei. At first they worked closely in the *Rosokai*, 'The Society of the Young and Old', and then in a propagandist group known as the *Yuzonsha*. Eventually, however, the two men parted company because Okawa could not support Kita's revolutionary domestic programme, although he accepted that Japan had a mission to liberate Asia.[18] This led to the dissolution of the *Yuzonsha*, which spawned in its turn several right-wing groups, some of which were to be important, not only for the ideas they developed, but for their contact with the army. First, the *Gyochisha*, 'The Activist Society', founded by Okawa in 1925, is important because of the concept of a *Showa Restoration* that became associated with it. The reigns of Japanese emperors were not signified by the actual name of the sovereign, but by the title that the emperor wanted to give to the period of his reign. Thus Mutsuhito styled his reign from 1852 to 1912 as Meiji. His son, who reigned from 1912 to 1926 chose the title Taisho; while, in turn Hirohito, who reigned from 1926 to 1989 elected for Showa or 'Enlightened Peace'. The *Restoration* that took place under the Meiji Emperor referred to the revolutionary, or purification process in which the feudal Tokugawa regime had been overthrown and the Emperor restored to his rightful authority. That, of course, was not the actual historical reality[19] and what the proponents of a *Showa Restoration* wanted was the exact reverse of such a process. The theory of a *Showa Restoration* demanded the restoration by the capitalists and the political parties of their powers to the emperor and therein lay the actuality of what was intended.

> For those who advocated a 'Showa Restoration' usually had in mind a military dictatorship, in which the Emperor in fact, if not in name, would be no more than a sacred puppet . . . So far as the Emperor was concerned such would be the very reverse of restoration", in the sense in which the term was used for describing what happened in 1868.[20]

What also was important with respect to the *Gyochisha* was that it forged a relationship with the younger, junior officers in the army and promoted terrorism as a political weapon. One of the first signs of this was the formation in 1927 of a group known as the *Kinkikai*, or 'The Society of the Imperial Flag', which included junior officers from the general staff headquarters. Kita too was involved in the *Gyochisha*, but his main associate now was Lieutenant Nishida Zei who was on the army reserve list. Through

Nishida, Kita had access to army officers both on the active and reserve lists and both men were instrumental in forming the small terrorist group, the *Hakurokai*, or 'Society of the White Wolf.' which, like the *Kinkikei*, had serving army officers among its members. The development of ultranationalism in the army was reinforced by changes in the class structure of the officers following the First World War. More and more junior officers now came from the lower middle classes of small landowners and small shopkeepers, approximately thirty per cent of them by 1927 coming from this segment of society. They were, therefore, by 1930 very familiar with the privations of peasant farmers and small traders brought about by the depression. Inevitably this further radicalized their outlook.

There was by the end of the 1920s, therefore, a considerable gulf between the internationalism of men such as foreign minister Shidehara, and the ultranationalism of elements within the army. This ultimately was to reveal itself in the Manchurian incident of 1931. What lay behind this was the fear among certain groups in the army that Shidehara's internationalism might threaten Japan's position in China and that China might regain the substance and not merely the shadow of sovereignty in Manchuria.

Japan's presence in Manchuria was the consequence of her victory over the Russian Empire in 1905, when she gained the Kwantung leasehold. But more than that, it was the consequence of the progressive decline of the Manchu Dynasty in China. The overthrow of the Manchu Dynasty in the revolution of 1911 did not, however, result in the formation of a strong central government that would unify the country and resist the encroachments of the foreigner. On the contrary, the chaos that was China continued. The nation was wracked by civil war and dominated by warlords. The powers continued to recognize a government in Peking, but it had no authority over the warlord regimes. In Manchuria, the bandit, Chang Tso-lin, became the effective native ruler and he also dominated a portion of North China south of the Great Wall. His rule, though, was contingent upon the approval of the Japanese and he functioned largely as their client. In the south, Sun Yat-sen's *Kuomintang*, or the Nationalist Party, based upon Canton represented the only potentially viable Chinese government. Sun Yat-sen had been very much the spiritual influence behind the Chinese Revolution of 1911, but he lacked the support necessary to make him president of the republic. In 1912, however, he founded the *Kuomintang* and civil war ensued the following year. But, although the revolution had been undertaken with a view to curbing foreign interference in the affairs of China, none of these authorities was able to break the humiliating regime of the *Unequal Treaties*, which conferred upon Japanese, European and American businesses in China economic and legal privileges.

The process of reintegration might be said to have begun when Sun Yat-sen decided to approach the Soviet Union for help. The Washington Conference of 1921–2, besides addressing matters of naval disarmament, had also concluded the Nine Power Treaty, which, while recognizing Chinese territorial integrity and administrative control, had not conceded full sovereignty.[21] The Soviets, on the other hand, had not been party to the Nine Power Treaty and had in any case prior to the Washington Conference

renounced extraterritorial rights in China inherited from the Russian
imperial regime. Moreover, they were keen to enlist allies in their anti-
imperialist cause. Thus it was that in 1924 agents of the Communist
International (Comintern) were sent to Canton to assist in restructuring the
Kuomintang so that it would become a disciplined revolutionary body in
alliance with the Chinese Communist Party, founded in 1921. It was hoped
that it would become the spearhead of a mass movement that would liberate
and unify China. In 1925, however, Sun Yat-sen died. Chiang Kai-shek,
appointed commandant of the Soviet-financed Whampoa Military Academy
in 1924 and very much associated initially with Sun Yat-sen's leftist leanings,
eventually became the new dominant personality in the *Kuomintang*. Under
his leadership the *Kuomintang* was declared the national government of
China. In 1926 fighting between the warlords in North China destroyed even
the semblance of government in Peking and on 4 July of that year Chiang
announced his 'Northern Expedition' the purpose of which was the
unification and liberation of China. By the summer of 1927 the *Kuomintang*
was in control of Shanghai and Nanking, the latter becoming the capital of
the *Kuomintang* regime. At the same time, and reflecting a rightward drift on
the part of the *Kuomintang* leadership, Chiang effected the independence of
the *Kuomintang* by brutally suppressing the Chinese communists and
expelling Comintern agents from China. This undoubtedly was connected
with a perception that the United States was now a better bet as an ally than
the USSR. Quite apart from the fact that there was a growing mood of
sympathy in the United States for China, which one must not exaggerate at
this juncture, secretary of state Frank Kellogg in January 1927 announced that
the United States would be willing to grant tariff autonomy to China if a
strong central government were established that was based upon the support
of the Chinese population and which could guarantee the property and lives
of American nationals. Peking finally fell to the *Kuomintang* in July 1928 by
which time it was in control of most of China and the United States
government fulfilled its promise. In exchange for a most-favoured-nation
agreement, in which China and the United States agreed to impose upon each
other's exports the most minimal tariffs, the United States accorded China
unilaterally tariff autonomy.

To Japanese ultranationalists and expansionists these developments were
most alarming, for Japan's interests in China and Manchuria now appeared to
be seriously threatened. By the 1920s Japanese industries, including the
zaibatsu, huge financial conglomerates such as Mitsui, Mitsubishi, Yasuda
and Sumitomo, which dominated many of the new manufacturing and
financial enterprises, had very substantial interests in the Chinese textile
industry. Ninety per cent of all inward investment in China came from
Japanese sources and China took twenty-five per cent of Japan's exports.
China's status as a Japanese economic colony was, of course, maintained by
the institution of restrictions on China's ability to impose tariffs on foreign
imports without the consent of the powers and the other extraterritorial
privileges that the Chinese had conferred on foreign powers in the *Unequal
Treaties* of the nineteenth century. Chiang's regime threatened all this. By
1929 the Chinese leader was announcing his determination to set China's

own tariffs in defiance of treaty obligations and organized boycotts of Japanese goods, a regular occurrence in China in the 1920s, were already in full swing. Furthermore, the *Kuomintang* government announced that it would construct in Manchuria a railway to compete with the Japanese-owned South Manchurian Railway and would encourage Chinese emigration to the province. Finally, on 29 December 1928, Manchuria was formally reintegrated into China.

This last event would have appeared to the more radical elements in Japan, particularly in the army, as very ominous indeed. It was, however, the indirect consequence of action by such elements, centred upon Colonel Komoto Daisaku, who wished, on the contrary, to effect Japanese total control of Manchuria. In 1927 the Wakatsuki government based upon *Kenseikai* support in the Diet and with the conciliatory Shidehara as foreign minister fell and was replaced by one based upon the *Seiyukai*. Since 1925 the leader of the *Seiyukai* had been General Tanaka Gi'ichi. He now became both prime minister and foreign minister and his government also had the support of the army. Having previously attacked the flaccidity of Shidehara's foreign policy, he declared that he would proceed forcibly with the Chinese in order to protect Japan's rights in China.

Tanaka is probably best remembered for the statement that bore his name, the so-called *Tanaka Memorial*. This document, of unknown authorship and undoubtedly a forgery, claimed to contain the views of Tanaka as conveyed to the emperor shortly after his appointment as prime minister. It was later published by the Chinese for propaganda purposes. What the document claimed was that Manchuria and Mongolia would first have to be conquered, if Japanese control of China was to be established. Japanese control of China would, however, only be secure if the United States were defeated. Japan should, therefore, throw off the fetters of the Nine Power Treaty and, using trade and commerce as a blind, extend her influence throughout China. China would ultimately be the base from which Japan would conquer the world.

But Tanaka's foreign policy scarcely resembled the prospectus that bore his name. He was certainly openly vigorous in the protection of Japanese rights and nationals in Manchuria and North China. What agitated Tanaka was the fear that the *Kuomintang* might, if it gained control of Manchuria, threaten Japan's interests there. Thus he decided to attempt to curb Chiang Kai-shek's northern advance by action in Shantung that was intended to be monitory rather than minatory. Japanese forces were sent there as an indication of Japan's determination to protect her interests on the mainland. The Japanese commander, however, exceeded his instructions and provoked a Chinese resistance that united the *Kuomintang* and its domestic opposition, ending up in a boycott of the Japanese and their trade. This clearly had an alarming impact on Japan's industrialists and bankers many of whom supported the *Seiyukai* financially. Moreover, the decision to send military units to Shantung elicited protests from Britain, the USSR and the United States. Tanaka was anxious to proceed without offending world and American opinion and by the beginning of 1929 had decided to come to an agreement with Chiang Kai-shek. In November 1927 Chiang Kai-shek had,

in fact, been in Tokyo where he had spoken with Tanaka and the foundations
of an understanding between Japan and China had been laid. It appears to
have been unofficially suggested that in return for China respecting Japanese
rights in Manchuria and Shantung, Japan would recognize *Kuomintang* rule
throughout the rest of China. Early in 1929 Tanaka decided to move towards
formal recognition of the *Kuomintang* regime in Nanking, to accept China's
new tariff schedule and to withdraw from Shantung.[22] Tanaka's China
policy was, therefore, coming more and more to resemble Shidehara's at
precisely the point where China seemed to be reasserting her authority and in
a manner likely to prejudice Japanese interests. Why was this?

The truth of the matter was that by the beginning of 1929 Tanaka's China
policy was in tatters. During the first half of 1928 Chiang's northward
advance, despite the Japanese occupation of Shantung, was coming to a
successful conclusion and by the middle of the year the fall of Peking to the
Kuomintang was imminent. The problem for Tanaka was that Japan's client in
Manchuria, Chang Tso-lin, who himself had aspirations to rule the whole of
China, was in occupation of Peking. What Tanaka, who the previous
November had tacitly agreed to recognize the authority of the *Kuomintang*
outside Manchuria, wanted to avoid was fighting between Chiang Kai-shek
and Chang Tso-lin in order not to compromise his private agreement with
Chiang. During June 1928 he finally prevailed upon Chang Tso-lin to
withdraw into Manchuria.

Chang now fell victim to a plot devised by an officer of the Kwantung
Army, Colonel Komoto Daisaku. Alarmed by the concessions made by
Tanaka to the *Kuomintang* and fearful of the implications of this for Japan's
interests in Manchuria, certain officers calculated that the assassination of
Chang Tso-lin would lead to disturbances that could be used by the Japanese
as an excuse to occupy the entire province. On 3 June 1928, Chang Tso-lin's
train departed Peking for Mukden where it was blown up on that city's
outskirts. This event, however, did not have the desired effect. Chang's son
and successor, Chang Hsüeh-liang maintained discipline among his followers and continued an orderly withdrawal. Strenuous efforts were made to
place the blame for this incident on the Chinese, but it was very soon apparent
that it had been the work of the Kwantung Army. Accordingly the
inclination was now very strong on the part of Chang Hsüeh-liang to throw
in his lot with the *Kuomintang*. Despite the heavy pressure put upon him not
to do so by Tanaka, Chang did precisely this on 29 December 1928 when he
recognized the sovereignty of China in Manchuria. As Professor Nish has
observed: 'In a disastrous way, Tanaka's desire to insulate Manchuria from
China proper . . . had for the moment failed. The ill-judged military
conspiracy of Komoto had gravely embarrassed Tokyo and thwarted his
(Tanaka's) objectives.'[23]

The assassination of Chang Tso-lin resulted in first-rate political scandal in
Japan. Its consequence was the fall of the Tanaka *Seiyukai* government in July
1929. The Showa Emperor, Hirohito, was quite clearly displeased and
Tanaka himself was in favour of punishing those involved. Subsequent
events, however, revealed the growing power of the army, which conducted
an internal enquiry of its own, but declined to make its findings public.

Colonel Komoto was put on the retired list, but no further disciplinary action was taken. Tanaka felt obliged to inform the emperor that the army had not been involved in the assassination. This was known to be a falsehood and, along with general feelings of dissatisfaction with Tanaka's government, it led directly to his government's collapse.[24]

The Manchurian Incident

A *Minseito* government succeeded that of Tanaka, headed by Hamaguchi Osachi. It marked also the return to office as foreign minister of Shidehara Kijuro. The Japanese ultranationalists by this time were naturally anxious about Japan's position in Manchuria and Shidehara's continued policy of a conciliatory approach to the Chinese problem did nothing to allay their fears. In March 1930 the Japanese recognized China's tariff autonomy and in exchange China agreed only to impose light duties on Japanese imports. Worse, though, was to follow, for at the London Naval Conference of 1930 Japan failed to gain agreement to her requirement of a cruiser and auxiliary craft fleet seventy per cent the size of that of the United States.

At the Washington Conference of 1921–2, it had been agreed that the United States, Britain and Japan should possess fleets of capital ships based respectively upon the ratio of 5:5:3. In other words, Japan's capital fleet should be in terms of tonnage sixty per cent the size of the American capital fleet. At the time this agreement had been most strongly opposed by Admiral Kato Kanji. Basing their calculations on the battle of Jutland in 1916, it was assumed by Japan's naval authorities that an attacking force would require a superiority of 40 per cent to defeat Japan's naval forces in the Western Pacific. To be secure, therefore, Japan should possess a fleet at least seventy per cent the size of that of the United States, the USA being considered Japan's most serious potential naval rival. A navy any smaller than this would mean that Japan would forever have to defer to the United States in respect of policy towards China and mainland Asia.[25] Having been thwarted in 1922, Admiral Kato, chief of the naval general staff, was determined to prevent a recurrence of this mistake at the London Naval Conference of 1930.

The London Naval Conference sought to extend the 5:5:3 ratio to cruisers and auxiliary vessels. The American view was that Japan could be conceded no more than 60 per cent. Giving evidence to the Senate Committee on Naval Affairs, Rear Admiral Pringle stated:

> I estimate that with the five to five to three ratio, we would have a chance of conducting a successful campaign, but the minute this ratio began to be altered in favour of the Japanese, our chances are reduced thereby and became less than what you would possibly call an even chance.[26]

On the other hand, Japan had been conceded supremacy in the Western Pacific under the Washington Naval Treaty and if it was in order for the Hamaguchi government to seek endorsement of that supremacy at the London Naval Conference then a demand for a cruiser fleet seventy per cent of that of the United States was not unreasonable. The United States would

not, however, concede this request. The furthest the United States would go
was represented in the so-called Reed–Matsudaira compromise. Under this
scheme Japan would be accorded, in terms of percentages of the United States
Navy, 60.2 per cent of America's large cruiser fleet, 70 per cent of the small
cruiser fleet, 70.3 per cent of the destroyer fleet, and parity in submarines.
This would give an average percentage for all these classes of 69.75. In an
effort to make this compromise even more attractive, it was agreed that the
United States would also delay the building of her cruiser programme so that
'in terms of fleets-in-being, Japan would possess a *de facto* 10:7 ratio at least
until the 1936 conference on naval limitation.'[27]

Admiral Kato was vehemently opposed to this arrangement, but opinion
in the navy generally was divided. Admirals Yamamoto and Saito were
prepared to accept this compromise, as was the vice-navy minister
Yamanashi. Outlining the situation to the Japanese cabinet on 1 April 1930,
Yamanashi agreed that the Reed–Matsudaira proposals compromised the 70
per cent requirement. On the other hand, he felt that the effects of this could
be mitigated through technological ingenuity and increasing the naval air
force. Furthermore, it was clear that the *de facto* seventy per cent would exist
until the next naval conference when the claim could be pressed for *de jure*
recognition of the 10:7 ratio. On this advice, the Japanese cabinet decided to
accept the Reed–Matsudaira compromise that would fix the sizes of the
American, British and Japanese fleets in the categories discussed at the
London Naval Conference in the ratio of 10:10:6.975 respectively. This
created uproar in Japan. The *Seiyukai*, the Reservist Organization, the
popular press and numerous patriotic clubs and nationalist societies excoriated the government and supported the opposition of Admiral Kanji, who
expressed in an audience with the emperor the view that the Reed
–Matsudaira compromise violated the right of supreme command under
Article 11 of the constitution. In other words, he argued that the decision to
accept the outcome of the London Naval Conference had been taken in
disregard of professional advice. Nevertheless, the government ratified the
London Naval Treaty. The mood of ultranationalist opposition to the
government, and the desperate measures to which it was willing to have
recourse, was revealed in November 1930 when the prime minister,
Hamaguchi, was mortally wounded by a fanatic on the grounds that
Hamaguchi had indeed violated the right of supreme command. In the
Japanese press Hamaguchi's assassin was celebrated as a patriot and his cause
attracted considerable support at mass rallies. The internationalist foreign
policy of Shidehara was under constant criticism.

The return of Shidehara as foreign minister in the Hamaguchi government had from the beginning promised a termination of the bilateral Sino-
Japanese approach to solving Japan's problems with China in favour of an
attempt to internationalize the Chinese problem by involving the western
powers in a multilateral co-operative venture that would bring peace,
progress and wealth to the Far East. In January 1931 Shidehara in a speech
reiterated the need for Japan to co-operate with Britain and the United States
and to seek a peaceful solution of Sino-Japanese problems. He anticipated the
complete dismantlement of the *Unequal Treaties* with China, but he warned

that China would first have to effect constructive reforms in her government and adopt a foreign policy that respected the complementary needs of China and Japan.[28] What Shidehara was hinting at was 'some type of new confirmation of Japanese rights in Southern Manchuria, especially in terms of the South Manchurian Railway'[29]. Nevertheless, by the summer of 1931 Shidehara's China policy was suffering setbacks illustrated by Chinese attacks on the Japanese and their property. Internationalism of Shidehara's stamp did not appeal to the Japanese Army. There was now a general feeling in military circles that the time had come to put pressure on the politicians to adopt a more assertive attitude. There was, in effect, a conviction among the military that the moment had arrived to stimulate the revival of the nation through violence.

This was very much the nostrum of the army officers who formed the *Sakurakai*, or Cherry Blossom Society. As has already been observed, in the case of the assassination of Chang Tso-lin, there was an inclination within the Kwantung Army to sever Manchuria totally from China and to establish Japanese rule there. From 1930 onwards the *Sakurakai* planned precisely that. This was, of course, contemplated in order to forestall the effective reestablishment of Chinese authority in Manchuria, but it was directed no less at terminating Japan's flirtation with westernized institutions and systems. Over the years the indoctrination of the Japanese military with the *Bushido* code of the *Samurai* inculcated a profound and mystical respect for Japan's imperial institution and a duty of absolute loyalty to it. Correspondingly there developed also a pronounced anti-liberalism and anti-socialism. This was also accompanied by a distaste for western-style capitalism. By 1930 Japan was experiencing the catastrophic effects of the economic depression: high urban unemployment and unsustainable falls in rice and silk prices which led to acute rural distress. Given the large number of army officers who now came from those sectors of Japanese society most seriously affected by the economic collapse, it is not surprising that they were easily seduced by idylls of pre-industrial and non-westernized Japan. What they hankered after was a regime allegedly more in tune with the country's history and traditions; one that was martial and authoritarian.

In March 1931 the *Sakurakai* almost carried out a *coup d'état* which was designed to bring about the fall of the *Minseito* government and establish a government of national reconstruction under the war minister, General Ugaki. Despite encouragement from Okawa Shumei to carry out the *Showa Restoration*, Ugaki at the last minute elected not to go ahead.[30] Although the emperor and the senior palace officials were apprised of this matter by the late summer of 1931, the army succeeded in closing ranks and hushing up the affair as they had previously done in the matter of the assassination of Chang Tso-lin. This March Affair had been very much a conspiracy contingent upon the active participation of senior officers for its success. These were, in fact, debarred from membership of the *Sakurakai*, which was open only to officers of the rank of lieutenant-colonel and below. Its abandonment was a severe disappointment to middle-grade officers such as Lieutenant-Colonels Hashimoto and Shigeto who now determined to press on with their plans for governmental change and, more importantly, direct action in Manchuria.

During the autumn of 1930 Okawa Shumei had been on a lecture tour of the Tohoku area of Japan. Financed by the ministry of war, his lectures were an invitation to a forthright approach to the Manchurian problem. Manchuria, he pointed out, was a vast underdeveloped region to which Japanese farmers should emigrate. The possibility of this, though, could soon be closed down by the *Kuomintang* and Chang Hsüeh-liang. Pointing out that when Chang had seized the Soviet-controlled Chinese Eastern Railway in Manchuria, the Red Army had swiftly dealt with the situation, he argued that Japan could only secure and develop her interests there by similar resolute action. His recommendations were seized upon by both staff officers of the Kwantung Army, led by Colonel Itagaki Seishiro, and sympathizers in Tokyo. The conspirators were further encouraged by the disappearance in Manchuria during the summer of 1931 of Captain Nakamura, an intelligence officer, who was murdered, together with his three assistants, while on a mission in the north of the province. In Tokyo the government discovered rather late that elements in the Kwantung Army were about to take direct action and it was decided to attempt to forestall them by sending Major-General Tatekawa to Manchuria with instructions to inform the officer commanding there, Lieutenant-General Honjo, that the emperor wished that discipline be restored and maintained in the Kwantung Army. Honjo was also to be instructed to prevent any unauthorized incident. Unfortunately, Tatekawa was party to the conspiracy and delayed conveying his messages until after the beginning of the *Manchurian Incident*.

At about 10 pm on the night of 18 September 1931 a Japanese railway maintenance worker was compelled at the point of a sword to detonate a small section of the South Manchurian Railway track just north of Mukden. The damage amounted to less than a metre in length and was so slight that the express train from Changchun traversed the gap with only a slight wobble, arriving on time at Mukden. Nevertheless, it was this that served as the excuse for the Kwantung Army to run amok in Manchuria. Alleging the detonation to have been the work of Chinese saboteurs, the Japanese forces fell upon the Chinese garrison in Mukden. Reinforced by Japanese units sent from Korea without the approval of the government in Tokyo, the whole of Manchuria was subjugated by February 1932. Given the rapid success of the conspirators there was little that those who wished to stop the Army, such as Wakatsuki, prime minister in succession to Hamaguchi, and foreign minister Shidehara, could do. The army had calculated correctly that Shidehara could not disown Japanese armed forces once they were involved in fighting. The occupation of Manchuria proved popular throughout Japan and ultimately more cautious elements in government were compelled to accept the *fait accompli*. Shidehara's foreign policy was at an end and so was the *Minseito* government of Wakatsuki which had resigned, Shidehara along with it, by the end of 1931.

In January 1932 the Japanese extended the war to Shanghai, following skirmishes there between the Japanese Navy and the Chinese Nineteenth Route Army in which the former received the worst of the exchanges. This resulted in military reinforcements being sent from Japan and a major assault on Shanghai, where the district of Chapei was subjected to fierce bombing and bombardment. Eventually the Chinese were compelled to retreat and both sides after six weeks accepted a truce and mediation. This episode was, however, a defining moment for with the bombing of Chapei there began the process of the alienation of world opinion by Japan and the growth of sympathy for China.[31] Neither did the creation of the new state of Manchukuo on 1 March 1932 help the image of Japan. Allegedly brought into existence to restore the right of self-determination to the people of Manchuria, Manchukuo was a blatant Japanese satellite or colony, ruled over by the last Manchu Emperor, Henry Pu-yi. These acts merely served to stiffen international opinion and precipitated the first steps in what was a process of self-isolation from the rest of the world community.

The International Reaction

The problem for the Japanese Army and the governments that succeeded Wakatsuki's was that the rest of the world declined to acquiesce in Japan's action. From the beginning the Chinese played their hand as best they could to encourage international sympathy. They were very active diplomatically and equally had a good eye for public relations. In Nanking, the *Kuomintang* government appealed to both the League of Nations and the United States. There was, however, little that the League of Nations could do physically to restrain Japan: Britain, on whom the responsibility for such action would have devolved, was neither militarily nor navally equipped for such a task. Neither was the United States, which, in any case, had very substantial business interests in Japan to consider. Moreover, there was in the west considerable sympathy for Japan and even admiration for what she had done to develop Manchuria. The chaos that was China contrasted badly with this. The Japanese presence in Manchuria was also regarded as a block to bolshevik expansion in the Far East. Finally, and as a whole, the western economic stake in both China and Japan was high and there was a reluctance to take reckless action that might damage such interests.

In the circumstances, the country to take the most forward action was the United States. Under the leadership of secretary of state Henry L. Stimson, it was decided to pursue a policy of non-recognition and to do so in such a way as to leave it open to any other country to associate itself in this with the United States. On 7 January 1932, Stimson addressed a note to the Japanese government declaring that the United States

> does not intend to recognize any situation, treaty, or agreement which may be brought about by means contrary to the covenants and obligations of the Pact of Paris of August 27th. 1928, to which Treaty both China and Japan, as well as the United States, are parties.[32]

This was, of course, a reference to the Kellogg–Briand Pact of 1928 which outlawed war. Stimson had hoped that the British would immediately associate themselves with this effort, but they decided not to on the ground that it was inopportune to move so quickly. This was not intended as a rebuff, but was interpreted as one by Stimson. Later the British foreign office official, Sir John Pratt, was to explain: 'Rightly or wrongly we attached little importance to the démarche. Non-recognition was a peculiarly American technique . . . wholly out of harmony with the British tradition in international affairs.'[33] Stimson's action, however, was ultimately to prove to have been of critical importance for US–Japanese relations and put the United States in 'the forefront of the nations opposing aggression . . .'.[34] Arguably from this time onwards Japan and the USA were locked into postures that in due course would lead to war, for Japan would not back down and neither would the USA accept the changes in the Far East that the Japanese had imposed and wished to impose by force.

The following month Stimson tried yet again to associate the British with the non-recognition policy, which he considered essential if it was to have any force and attract the support of other nations. Between 11 and 15 February 1932 Stimson tried to persuade the British foreign secretary, Sir John Simon, in a number of telephone conversations of the virtues of such a course. Simon, however, took the view that Britain, as a member of the Council of the League of Nations, was bound to act with the League, which Stimson accepted with great regret. Accordingly, the American government acted alone in the form of an open letter from Stimson to Senator Borah of the Senate foreign relations committee. This letter, dated 23 February, appealed for international support for the policy of non-recognition and, moreover, emphasized the complementarity of the treaties concluded at the Washington Conference of 1921–2. Thus, infringement of one treaty affected the continuing validity of them all: Japan had infringed the Nine Power Treaty and thus the United States in respect of Japan could not feel bound by the Naval Treaty. Stimson wrote:

> The willingness of the American government to surrender its then commanding lead in battleship construction and to leave its position at Guam and in the Philippines with further fortifications was predicated upon, among other things, the self-denying covenants contained in the Nine Power Treaty.[35]

This was a threat to renew the naval arms race. Meanwhile, on 16 February the League Council issued a declaration to the effect that the League of Nations would not recognize any changes brought about in violation of Article X of the League Covenant, an action that was endorsed by a special meeting of the League Assembly on 3 March.

It was at this time also that the commission of inquiry appointed in November 1931 by the League arrived in Yokohama. Named after its chairman, Lord Lytton, the Lytton Commission was charged with the duty of investigating the background to the *Manchurian Incident* and recommending a settlement. This was, however, pre-empted by the Japanese creation of the puppet state of Manchukuo. Nevertheless the commission continued with its work publishing its report in October 1932. The Lytton Report was a fair-minded document that analysed the origins of the dispute between Japan and China in terms that were by no means unfavourable to the former. Even so, the report had to recognize that, however well-merited her claims, Japan had been the aggressor. In accepting the Lytton Report in March 1933 the

League effectively condemned Japan, to which the latter replied by withdrawing from the organization.

For the time being, though, the conflict between China and Japan had to be brought to a halt. Having penetrated China north of the Great Wall, the Japanese began to find Chinese resistance more severe. Consequently, a truce was concluded between China and Japan. The Tangku Truce of May 1933 recognized the Japanese presence to the north of the Great Wall and a demilitarized zone to the south of it. The truce did not refer to the new status of Manchuria. It did, however, offer Chiang Kai-shek and the *Kuomintang* a breathing space in which China could be further unified and the Chinese communists, located in Kiangsi province, destroyed. Eventually the communists were forced out, reestablishing themselves in the west of China after the Long March.

The Renewal of the Sino-Japanese Conflict

In March 1933 the Hoover administration in the United States was replaced by the New Deal presidency of Franklin Delano Roosevelt. Given the severity of the economic problems confronting the new administration, foreign policy was bound to be secondary to the needs of domestic recovery from the depression. The installation of the new administration did not, however, signify any fundamental change of policy on the part of the United States towards the events that had taken place in the Far East. Roosevelt's presidency continued the policy of non-recognition inherited from the previous administration.

The attitude of Roosevelt towards foreign policy has long been a matter of some debate. In his early career he was much influenced by the conviction of President Theodore Roosevelt that the United States must be active in world affairs. This attitude was reinforced by his experiences in the Wilson administration and as a consequence he became an emphatic supporter of American membership of the League of Nations. During the presidential campaign of 1932, however, Roosevelt retracted his views on League membership. It seems unlikely that this represented a genuine conversion and was more probably a political manoeuvre connected with the exigencies of the internal political situation, in which New Deal supporters tended to favour American isolation in foreign affairs. Roosevelt himself was an unconvincing conviction isolationist.

A man of his cosmopolitan and urbane character would inevitably have understood the dynamics of modern inter-state relationships and the impact of science and technology upon them. The aeroplane, even for a country such as the United States had rendered the equation of isolation with security obsolete. In the circumstances of the 1930s, the United States was plainly subject to threats in both the Atlantic and Pacific Oceans now that hostile powers, through the development of the aircraft carrier, had the means of delivering aerial strikes. Roosevelt himself appears to have been clear in his mind that isolation and neutrality could not be absolute guarantees of peace.

Roosevelt was also aware that in Asia and Europe forces had come to the fore that were inimical to the traditions and interests of the United States. By 1934–5 opinion in the United States had been alienated from Germany by the visible internal brutalities of the Nazi regime, particularly the treatment of the Jews, and the economic policies pursued by Hjalmar Schacht. The unilateral reduction by Germany of interest on borrowed money, such as the Dawes and Young loans, and bilateral and restrictive trading treaties concluded by Germany with the states of Central and South-East Europe, which were designed to create a closed trading area dominated by Germany, were resented in Washington. It was particularly felt that Germany could have continued to pay interest in full had she not given priority to rearmament. All this contrasted with the bilateralism of the American Reciprocal Trade Agreements (RTA) Act of 1934, which was rather directed at the expansion of world trade and global peace, presumed to be the dividend of free trade and prosperity. With the incorporation of the most-favoured-nation clause, the concessions made in specific bilateral trade agreements between the United States and other countries were automatically extended to third parties, provided they did not discriminate against American goods. Although the actual increment in world trade accruing from the RTA was negligible, the philosophy behind it illustrated the gulf that divided the Americans from the European dictatorships and Japan. As the American secretary of state, Cordell Hull, put it: 'unhampered trade dovetailed with peace. High tariffs, trade barriers and unfair economic competition with war.'[36].

The continuation of the policy of non–recognition had not the slightest impact on the Japanese who proceeded with the creation, exploitation and development of the satellite state of Manchukuo. Disagreeable as this was from the point of view of the Americans and disagreeable as was the clear intention of the Japanese to exploit Manchuria economically by exercising a monopoly in that country, the administration did nothing. Nevertheless, Roosevelt mistrusted Japan and he harboured suspicions about her long term aims which he surmised might be of an imperialist and extensive nature. Indeed at the first cabinet meeting of the new administration the practicalities of a war with Japan were debated: it was estimated that it might take the United States between three and five years to defeat Japan after an initial period on the defensive. In many ways this was to prove a remarkably accurate conclusion. In 1933, however, war was not a practical issue: the war between China and Japan was for the time being at least in abeyance and Roosevelt wished to push his New Deal legislation through an isolationist Congress.

Still, the events in the Far East were sufficiently alarming to stimulate in 1933 the beginnings of American naval rearmament. This does not mean that Roosevelt was an advocate of a 'big navy' policy. On the other hand, he was not a believer in 'disarmament by example' and was opposed to 'a policy which left the United States with a navy that was weak relative to those of other countries'[37]. Already in 1932 Carl Vinson, the chairman of the house committee on naval affairs, had attempted to pass a bill through Congress that would have laid the foundations of a substantial naval reconstruction. This had not been successful. On assuming office, however, Roosevelt soon demonstrated a critical awareness of the deficiencies of the United States Navy, particularly in light cruisers and destroyers. Through the agency of Vinson, Roosevelt was able in June 1933 to secure the appropriation of $238 million for the construction of thirty-two vessels. Although substantially less than Vinson had requested the previous year, it was the beginning of a programme of reconstruction that meant that the United States Navy was soon able to equip itself to the levels agreed at the Washington and London Naval Conferences. By 1937 the annual naval appropriation had increased by one hundred per cent. In 1933 Roosevelt was able to justify naval increases as part of the programme of relieving unemployment, the money being allocated from funds devoted to relief. But concern at developments in the Far East had also played a part in the deliberations of Congress. And, as Roosevelt himself explained, the mood in Japan was not such as to inspire confidence in a future of non-aggression.

This should not, however, be construed as implying an exaggerated concern in the United States with the plight of China. Until 1940 China was considered to be Britain's responsibility. It is true that a missionary lobby existed in America that was very alarmed by developments in China, but it did not really begin to win over American opinion until Roosevelt's second term. Moreover, the liberal American vision of a China properly integrated under Chiang Kai-shek and the *Kuomintang* and based upon the American liberal-capitalist system and the romanticism that accompanied it, exemplified in Pearl Buck's novels, *Last Train from Shanghai* and *The Good Earth*, was very much a characteristic of Roosevelt's third term. And even so, this kind of liberal-romanticism never made much political impress. It certainly had very little impress during Roosevelt's first administration. Although, in the wake of the Manchurian crisis, the United States recognized the Soviet Union, partly on the ground that this action might deter Japan, and although Washington attempted to stimulate China's economic recovery in 1933 with a credit of $50 million, naturally with an eye to enabling Chinese purchase of American agricultural surpluses, other aspects of American policy towards China were positively unhelpful and tended to weaken her. In 1934 Congress passed the Silver Purchase Act as a consequence of the activities of certain influential Senators acting on behalf of American silver producers. This act authorized the United States treasury to buy silver at prices above those in the world market; it had a very deleterious effect upon the Chinese currency which was silver-based. Between 1934 and 1935 there was a haemorrhage of silver from China resulting in a fall in the silver reserves of approximately 53 per cent, which drove the yuan off its silver base. Inevitably, this did nothing to help the efforts of the Chinese government to restore the Chinese economy.

The underlying fact of the matter was, though, that in the early 1930s the United States government did not possess the military and naval means successfully to inhibit Japanese aggression nor the support of public opinion for such a course. Furthermore, China represented for America rather small beer; the American economic stake in that vast country was, in fact, rather modest. Indeed the state department even discouraged investment in and trade with *Kuomintang* China. At this time China accounted for no more than three per cent of America's total trade, whereas in 1935 Japan accounted for nine per cent of American trade. In addition, American investments in China in 1931 amounted at the most to $250 million in comparison with investments of some $466 million by 1935 in Japan. For the United States to have damaged her trade by embarking upon a confrontation with Japan while recovering from recession would have appeared imprudent to say the least.

By way of contrast the economic interest of Britain in China was very much greater. In 1931 her investments there totalled £244 million. At the beginning of the 1930s Britain's commercial interest in China just exceeded that of Japan and the two states between them shared 72 per cent of the total foreign investments in China. This did not, however, foreshadow immediate confrontation between the two states regarding Japan's China policy. On the contrary, within Britain there was an inclination to repair the relationship with Japan as a means of enabling Britain to concentrate all her forces in Europe against the German threat. This was a view that received strong support from the head of the treasury, Sir Warren Fisher. In a memorandum of April 1934 he strongly argued that the menace of Germany in Europe made it essential that Britain should seek an accommodation with Japan particularly in view of the fact that no reliance could be placed upon American support in the Far East. If Britain could rely upon American goodwill, by which Fisher meant 'the practical assurance that if we got into difficulties anywhere we could permanently count on the effective support of the United States' rather than 'high-sounding professions', then good Anglo-Japanese relations would assume a less urgent priority. 'But,' Fisher continued, 'the very last thing in the world we can count on is American support . . .'. There was no point in letting relations with Japan drift towards war, because at ten thousand miles distance the defeat of Japan was impossible. Those who wished to try it, he considered 'worse than Don Quixote in his most idiotic moods towards a windmill . . .'. There was, therefore, everything to be gained from an accommodation with Japan that would resemble 'in substance though not in form' the old Anglo-Japanese Alliance. But such a course would have invited strong opposition from the United States and Roosevelt let it be known that, if there were any hint of such dealings with Japan, the British dominions would forcibly be made aware that their future security lay with the United States.[38]

Concern in Britain to improve relations with Japan did not, on the other hand, preclude economic assistance to China, although initially it was hoped to accomplish this with Japanese co-operation. Indeed, in advance of the dispatch to the Far East in 1935 of Sir Frederick Leith-Ross, at the head of a British economic mission, it was decided that the object of policy should be not only to help China, but 'at the same time to foster good relations between Japan and China'. It was thought by Leith-Ross, that having been assisted financially by a loan, the Chinese might be induced to recognize Manchukuo on a *de facto* basis. This was, in effect, an attempt to bring about diplomatic co-operation in the Far East within a modified Washington System. Significantly, Leith-Ross visited Japan, where he had talks with the Japanese foreign minister, Hirota, before arriving in China. What, however, Leith-Ross proposed was rejected. The Japanese were not interested in Anglo-

Japanese partnership in China; what was desired in Tokyo, on the contrary, was the development of Sino-Japanese relations on the foundation of an exclusive Japanese partnership. Throughout 1935 Hirota in fact conducted negotiations with the Chinese for this purpose, but they foundered on Japanese insistence that China should accept the situation in Manchuria. But had Hirota wanted to be more accommodating regarding that which Leith-Ross had proposed, he would undoubtedly have been countermanded by the Japanese military who were by this time very much in the saddle and, despite internal divisions, unanimous in their rejection of any liaison with the British and Americans in Asia. While in Japan, it was suggested to Leith-Ross by the former Japanese ambassador in London, Matsudaira, that the army regarded China as Japan's exclusive sphere of influence; that they viewed the activities of Leith-Ross in the Far East 'with jealousy, if not open hostility; and that the Government was powerless to overrule them.'[39] Nevertheless, Leith-Ross, for all the failures of the Japanese aspect of his mission, proceeded with a programme of assisting the Chinese in the restoration of their economy and currency, as a result of which the Chinese currency, renamed the *fapi* had been stabilized by the end of 1935 by linking it with sterling.

The uncompromising attitude displayed towards Leith-Ross was compounded by the withdrawal of Japan from the London Naval Conference in January 1936. By 1934 the moderate 'treaty faction' in the Japanese naval general staff had almost completely lost ground to the 'fleet faction'. Nevertheless, the Japanese Navy was forced to participate in a further round of naval disarmament negotiations by the refusal of the ministry of finance in 1934 to countenance demands from the military and naval services for a huge military budget. What the Japanese Navy wanted now, though, was the abolition of naval ratios and, in effect, parity with the United States and Britain. The preliminary conference of 1934 ended with the Japanese giving two years' notice of their intention to withdraw from the Washington and London Naval Treaties. When at the end of 1935 the London Naval Conference formally opened the parties were no nearer agreement. President Roosevelt and the American administration would not entertain parity or any major relaxation in the naval ratios, neither would the Americans agree to the compromise suggestions of the British. On 15 January 1936 the Japanese delegation withdrew from the conference. A Naval Arms Limitation Treaty was concluded on 25 March, but Japan was not bound by it and neither would she be bound by the previous Washington and London Naval Treaties by the end of the year. Japan was now free to expand her navy.[40]

Such expansion was of great interest to the feudal-industrial families that dominated the *zaibatsu* conglomerates, Mitsui, Mitsubishi, Sumitomo and Yasuda. Protectionism in the United States following the world economic depression deprived them of American markets as did protectionism in British India and Africa. In these circumstances, they were driven back on the state as a principal customer. Rearmament, therefore, promised them very profitable contracts and the object of rearmament, overseas expansion, opportunity for economic exploitation. Increasingly from 1933 onwards the destiny of Japan was determined by a military–industrial alliance and the economy of Japan geared towards the needs of the army and navy rather than those of a civilian economy. This naturally had serious implications for financial stability and inevitably created further pressure for the consolidation and expansion of Japan's position in mainland Asia in order that she might derive real economic advantages from her interests there. The degree to which the *zaibatsu* profited from their relationship with the military might be gleaned from the following statistics: first, the value of Japanese industrial production leapt from 6 billion yen in 1930 to 30 billion in 1941; secondly, the *zaibatsu* increased their total assets by over 300 per cent in the same period. Given the refusal of the United States to recognize the status of Manchukuo, or any changes in mainland Asia brought about by force, it was widely understood in Japan that the direction in which her foreign policy was tending might embroil Japan in war. It was also widely understood that this would place Japan in a very critical position, dependent as she was on western sources for over ninety per cent of her petroleum supplies, 65 per cent of which was supplied by the United States. The consolidation of the military–industrial alliance in Japan was to follow the Tokyo Mutiny of 26 February 1936, which marked a significant turning point in internal developments in Japan during the 1930s.

The *de facto* conquest of Manchuria stimulated the Japanese ultra-nationalists to even more egregious behaviour and also marked the beginning of the end of party government in Japan and the rise to dominance of the military. Following the resignation of Wakatsuki as prime minister in 1931, Inukai Tsuyoshi, the leader of the *Seiyukai*, was appointed in his place. This did prevent for the time being the installation of a military figure as prime minister, but it could not prevent the growing influence of the army in the *Seiyukai* and even some *Minseito* politicians formed a breakaway group that toyed with the military. The importance of keeping the army on the side of the government was emphasized by the appointment of General Araki Sadao, a leading figure in the *Imperial Way* or *Kodo* faction and favourite of the Kwantung Army as army or war minister. Moreover, the emphatic victory of the *Seiyukai* in the elections of February 1932 indicated the degree of disaffection in Japan from the policies associated with the *Minseito* and the extent of popular endorsement of the actions of the army. What happened to those who did not bend to the will of the ultranationalists was clearly illustrated when Inukai himself was assassinated. Inukai had been acutely conscious of the damaging impact of Japanese actions in Shanghai in 1932[41] on Japan's relations with the west and particularly with the United States. For this reason he had stalled over the matter of formal Japanese recognition of Manchukuo. As a result of this and also the possibility that he intended to obtain an imperial command ordering the Kwantung Army to withdraw to the South Manchurian Railway Zone,[42] he was murdered on 15 May 1932 by a group of young naval officers and army cadets. These had been supplied with funds and other assistance by Okawa Shumei's *Jimmukai* (a revamped version of the *Gyochisha*) and Tachibana Kosaburo's *Aikyojuku*, which promoted the concept of the *Showa Restoration* and agrarian romanticism, in which the village was to become the focus of political and economic life.[43]

Inukai's murder was the third in the so-called year of assassinations. The others were orchestrated by the *Ketsumeidan* led by the demented Buddhist monk, Inoue Nissho. The *Ketsumeidan* was a secret society pledged by a blood oath to kill traitors and exploiters of deprived rural communities. On 9 February a former finance minister, Inoue Junnosuke, a known opponent of the Manchurian adventure, was assassinated. This was followed on 5 March by the murder of the managing director of Mitsui, Baron Dan Takuma. Little wonder that Hugh Byas later described this period as ushering in 'government by assassination'[44]. The evident desperation of the men who committed these crimes and the indulgent treatment of the perpetrators by the courts, which passed risible sentences on the guilty, inevitably caused government ministers to fear for their lives if they advocated anything like moderation in China policy. Indeed the whole climate of terror favoured increasingly army-dominated authoritarian rule in Japan.

Following the murder of Inukai party government came to an end. This was largely because the emperor's liberal advisers feared the consequences of continuing such a practice. It was felt that the continuation of party government would possibly provoke further excesses by ultranationalists in the army, who might carry out a revolution in which all the established institutions in Japan, even the throne, would be under threat. In order to forestall this it was decided to resort to the old practice of non-party government. Cabinets would contain representatives of the principal parties, but would be headed by non-party figures. Inukai was, therefore, succeeded by Admiral Saito Makoto. It was also hoped that the radical elements in the army could ultimately be manipulated by concession. Expansion in Manchuria was accepted and discipline of the army postponed until senior officers felt capable of enforcing it. This was 'control by concession': a policy that ultimately devoured everything it was intended to save.[45] Professor Storry has written of the murder of Inukai:

> The 15th May Incident had a significance for modern Japanese nationalism second only to that of the Manchurian Incident eight months earlier. After 15th May 1932, liberalism as a factor in official life, was a spent force. There could be no turning back from the path of overseas expansion, opened up by the seizure of Manchuria, or from the course of increasing authoritarian control at home.[46]

From now onwards ministers tended to become spokesmen for their ministries and the prime minister an arbitrator between the foreign, war and navy ministers.[47]

The increasingly authoritarian nature of Japan was demonstrated by the Minobe Affair. Minobe Tatsukichi was Professor of Constitutional Law at Tokyo Imperial University. In his writings Minobe presented the so-called 'organ theory' of the throne. According to this view sovereignty in Japan resided in the state and the emperor exercised sovereign power as an organ of the state. This was very inconvenient from the point of view of the military who wished to use the prestige of an absolutist imperial institution in Japan in order to impose their will on the state more effectively. Thus it was contended that Minobe had insulted the dignity of the throne; rejected the divine nature of the sovereign; and besmirched the national polity (*kokutai*). Hirohito himself had no time for such condemnation of Minobe, whom he considered to be a loyal and excellent scholar. He was happy with the 'organ theory' and thought that its opposite, the theory of imperial sovereignty, could only result in despotism. He thought it would be 'lamentable' to 'bury' a scholar like Minobe. The army was, however, determined to do precisely that. In October 1935 Minobe's views were publicly repudiated in a statement issued by the Okada government. From this time onwards in Japan 'political discourse would be predicated on the unquestioned assumption that Japan's was an absolute, not a limited monarchy'. Ultimately, the ministry of education in 1937 issued a document entitled, *Cardinal Principles of the National Polity*. Regarded as an official statement regarding the ideology of the state and widely used in schools, this document characterized the Japanese state as 'aggressively nationalist, imperialist, authoritarian, non-individualistic'[48].

While the period after 1932 certainly marks the ascendancy of the military in Japan as the dominant political authority there were within the army two fundamental factions, both of which anticipated future war. The first of these, the *Kodoha,* the *Imperial Way* or *Kodo* faction, was largely composed of radical young officers who aimed at the restoration of a pre-industrial, non-westernized Japan. The emperor was to be freed from liberal palace officials, while the state as a whole was to be rid of parliamentarianism, opportunist bureaucrats and capitalists. The *Kodoha* emphasized the importance of submission to the divine will of the emperor and what they aspired to in essence was the spiritual reformation of Japan and a return to traditional values, in other words, a *Showa Restoration*. In the field of foreign policy the *Kodoha* believed that war with the Soviet Union was unavoidable and imminent. The leading exponents of this way of thinking were Generals Araki and Mazaki. For a time this faction was in a strong position with Araki as war minister and Mazaki as vice chief of staff. Araki's resignation in 1934, on grounds of ill-health, however, saw the start of a decline in its fortunes. His successor, Hayashi Senjuro, fell under the influence of Major-General Nagata Tetsuzan, a member of the opposing *Toseiha*, the *Tosei* or *Control* faction. Until July 1935 Mazaki held one of the most important of the army's posts, director of military education, but Nagata then procured his dismissal. In turn, Nagata was murdered by one of Mazaki's supporters, resulting in the trial of the assassin and plans to remove the more radical members of the *Kodoha* to Manchuria.

The *Toseiha,* like the *Kodoha,* anticipated war, but not one specifically directed at the Soviet Union. On the contrary, they looked forward to total war and believed that Japan should be organized for it by a system of state controls. They were pragmatists and realists. They were quite willing to work within existing structures, with bureaucrats and capitalists, provided that their priorities were accepted as constituting the national agenda. Moreover, it was clear to them that something more than spiritual renewal was required if Japan was to be successful in war and expansion; they were to find in the *zaibatsu* willing partners.[49] In the long run the *Toseiha*, composed of more senior and sober-minded officers of a practical disposition, was a more lethal force than the *Kodoha*.

The latter, however, frustrated by the situation they found themselves in at the end of 1935 elected to carry out a *coup* on 26 February 1936. During the course of the Tokyo Mutiny some fourteen hundred troops under the command of junior officers occupied government buildings and carried out the assassination of leading officials who it was claimed had hindered political reform. Prime minister Okada escaped assassination because his would-be killers mistook a relative for him. His predecessor, Saito, was not so lucky and neither was finance minister Takahashi, who had indicated strong reservations concerning the vast sums of money the army wished to spend. Other victims were the inspector general of military education and the lord privy seal. Everything the mutineers did, they did in the name of the emperor. This did nothing, however, to rally the nation to their cause and both Generals Araki and Mazaki would have nothing to do with the uprising, which was put down with great ferocity and ruthlessness. In this the emperor himself was very active, feeling later that in this he had exceeded his constitutional function.[50] The consequence of the Tokyo Mutiny was that the *Toseiha* now became dominant in the army, while the influence of the *Kodoha* waned. Henceforth, the influence of men such as Generals Umezu, Tojo, Sugiyama and Koiso would be decisive. In terms of policy towards China this made little difference as both factions were broadly in agreement. Avoidance of conflict with the regime of Chiang Kai-shek, centred on Nanking, and the consolidation of Japan's position in Manchuria were the principal concerns of the army. On the other hand, there were elements in the Japanese Army on mainland Asia that wished to secure Japan's position in the north by establishing separatist Chinese regimes south of the Great Wall. These inclinations were, however, opposed in Japan by some of the army commanders which had the effect of inhibiting further adventurousness in North China for the time being.

This did not indicate a new-found internationalism in Japan as far as China was concerned. Throughout the army there was a widespread view that excluded the notion of Japanese co-operation with Britain and the United States in China. Indeed from the point of view of the formulation of foreign policy the year 1936 in Japan marked the point at which even the semblance of co-operation with the Washington System disappeared. It also signalled a new stage in the stranglehold of the army on the Japanese government. The *Toseiha*, having imposed unity on the army and preserved the country from extremism, could now demand autonomy in military matters and decisively influence the composition of the cabinet. From this time onwards the co-operation of the high command was essential in the formation of all governments. In the wake of the Tokyo Mutiny Hirota Kokei, the former foreign minister, became prime minister, although the real power in the government was the war minister, General Terauchi Hisaichi, who had determined its composition.

One of the first acts of the new government was to decide in March 1936 that in future Japan would refrain from publicly committing herself to the Nine Power Treaty. On the contrary, Japan would from now onwards seek to render it meaningless. Furthermore, in conjunction with the military, two documents were adopted by the government in 1936 which reveal the extent to which those who now controlled the destiny of Japan had decided upon a new course. These were *The Fundamentals of National Policy* and *Foreign Policy*

Guidelines. There were now three fundamental aims: Japan's position on mainland Asia was to be firmly secured and sustained; Soviet encroachments in the Far East were to be resisted; and ultimately Japan was to expand into the South Seas. As General Terauchi put it, Japan's priority was to 'establish the Japanese Empire's leadership in East Asia' and to force the Soviet Union to abandon her 'positive aspirations' in the Far East. China, furthermore, was to be dissuaded 'from depending on European and United States aid' and induced to adopt a 'friendly [by which was meant subordinate] attitude' towards Japan. Britain, because of her interests in China, was now listed as one of Japan's leading enemies.[51]

In November 1936 Japan also concluded the Anti-Comintern Pact with Germany. On the surface this was a response to the call of the Communist International (Comintern) for the establishment of a popular front against fascism and provided for co-operation against communist subversion. A secret protocol, however, also provided that if either of the contracting parties were involved in a war with the Soviet Union the other would remain neutral. Coming after the declaration by Mussolini on 1 November 1936 of the Rome–Berlin Axis, the historical significance of the Anti-Comintern Pact perhaps rests on the fact that Japan was now clearly identifying herself with the revisionist powers in Europe and simultaneously drawing away from the powers who were party to the Washington System.

However, in December 1936 an event took place which seemed ominous from the point of view of Japan's long term goals in China. This was the so-called Sian Incident. Briefly put, forces loyal to Chang Hsüeh-liang, the former Manchurian war lord, arrested Chiang Kai-shek at Sian, the capital of Shensi province in North-West China. Chang Hsüeh-liang was bitterly disappointed that instead of assisting him and his army in the reconquest of Manchuria and North China, Chiang Kai-shek had employed the Manchurians in an anti-communist campaign in Shensi province where the communists had settled after their Long March. This had seemed to some of Chang's forces a senseless proceeding when their only objective was to expel the Japanese from Manchuria, and some had defected to the communists. Chang himself finally met a senior communist, Chou En-lai, in June 1936 and became convinced of the need to end the civil war and create a united front against the Japanese. Chiang Kai-shek, however, remained deaf to Chang's entreaties on this point. In December 1936 Chiang decided to visit Sian to inspect the Manchurian forces there. Learning that the *Kuomintang* leader intended to appoint another commander to direct operations against the communists, Chang Hsüeh-liang decided openly to side with the communists and place Chiang and his entire retinue under arrest. Eventually, Chiang Kai-shek was released presumably on the understanding that the *Kuomintang* would call off its campaign against the communists and establish a united front with them against the Japanese. The Sian Incident did not end cleanly and much remains obscure. Within China there was, however, a broad consensus favouring a united front, in the context of the success of the Leith-Ross economic and currency reforms and continuing German military assistance to the *Kuomintang*, which had steadily improved the Chinese military position against Japan. In these circumstances, Chiang had little option other than to respond positively to Chang Hsüeh-liang's proposals and participate in a united front. Significantly, in August 1937 the Nanking government concluded a Non-Aggression Pact with the USSR.[52]

Whatever the sincerity and solidity of a united Chinese front, Japanese policy had to be predicated upon the presumption of its reality. Consequently, these developments caused the Japanese to have some second thoughts concerning their China policy. The policy guidelines of August 1936 had not crystallized to the point at which they could not be reversed. Within both the civilian and military leaderships consideration was briefly given to an alternative strategy in China that would have involved ending the encouragement of separatism in North China, which had been pursued by the Japanese since the Tangku Truce and which the truce itself facilitated by the provision of a demilitarized zone south of the Great Wall. It was well understood that the unification of China could only be prevented by war, which the Japanese general staff was for the time being unwilling to risk. This period of caution is associated with the government of General Hayashi Senjuro which replaced that of Hirota in January 1937. This government was notable for the fact that it was the last occasion on which the remaining *Genro*, Prince Saionji, 'took responsibility for answering to the throne on a cabinet change'[53]. It was also notable for the fact that its foreign minister, Sato Naotake, was an internationalist in economic terms. Japan's population problem, he considered, could only be solved by industrialization and economic growth, which meant participation in a free, international economic system based upon co-operation and interdependence. He rejected the notion of the acquisition of fresh territory and the creation of a closed, autarchic economic area. Sato's new approach predictably did not commend itself to those within the military who remained firmly wedded to existing policy. Moreover, on the Asian mainland within the Tientsin Army, stationed in North China (under the terms of the Boxer Protocol of 1901), to protect communications between Peking and the coast, there was a firm conviction that any weakness over the autonomous buffer regimes set up under Japanese patronage in North China would not only result in a loss of Japan's position in the region, but also perhaps of Manchuria. For those of this persuasion Chinese nationalism had to be resisted and the Japanese hold on North China further entrenched. The Sato policy, however, disappeared with the politically unpopular Hayashi government in June 1937.[54]

A fateful choice was now made in the appointment of Hayashi's successor, Prince Konoe Fumimaro. Konoe's major asset was that he was trusted by all and respected by the military, many of whose views he shared. It was, therefore, expected that he would be able to control the army to some degree.[55] Konoe, with one major interruption, was to serve as Japan's prime minister until October 1941. He was a leading member of the *Great Asia Association*, which had been founded in 1933 amid a general consensus that the old western-dominated international order was disintegrating. He had long been a critic of the domination of the globe by the western powers and in 1918, prior to attending the Paris Peace Conference, had composed an essay that attacked the League of Nations concept, 'as a convenient instrument for British and American domination of the poorer Asian powers'. Japan, he considered, should only join the League if the western powers abandoned economic imperialism and discriminatory practices towards Asians.[56]

Within the *Great Asia Association* it was assumed that the old international order would be substituted by three power groups: one would be based on Britain and America, the second on the Soviet Union and the third on Asia. 'The Asiatic bloc would comprise Greater Japan, China, the Dutch East Indies and Siam, and under the leadership of Japan it would form a coherent trading bloc.' Japan was to be provided with raw materials by her partners and in turn she would provide them with finished industrial goods.[57] This provided the basis of the concept of the *Co-Prosperity Sphere*, advocated by the Japanese in the late 1930s and 1940s, which was based upon the premise, naturally, that all the nations within it were subordinate to Japan.

It would, however, be wrong to see Konoe purely and simply as mouthpiece for Japan's militaristic *fascists*.[58] He was appointed in 1937 to solve the China problem, hence the importance of his perceived ability to control the military; later in 1941 he was expected to be able to deal with President Roosevelt. On both occasions he undoubtedly attempted sincerely to succeed, but on both occasions failed.[59] There can be little doubt that he wished to avoid a further bout of war with China and later the war with the United States, but, despite his many eminent qualities he was unable to do so. As Professor Nish has observed: 'Konoe indeed was a man caught up in a cascade of events and ensnared in a complicated political scene which he could prescribe for but could hardly control.'[60] There was, though, also a fatal defect in Konoe's character that goes a long way to explain his failure. Professor Maruyama has written:

> As the perfect case of 'weak nerves' most . . . will, of course, think of Prince Konoe. His political career certainly provides a wealth of examples of how a fatal weakness of character can operate at important moments. According to the marquis Kido's evidence 'Whenever any difficult questions arose he frequently said, "I want to give up."'[61]

This judgement may be harsh, but it does much to explain the lack of adequate control of policy in Japan from 1937 to 1941.

Upon accepting office as prime minister, Konoe announced that the present division of the world's resources and land was unjust. There were *have* and *have-not* powers which were bound to conflict with one another until a redistribution had been achieved. Such a redistribution was not in sight. Japan, therefore, had a duty to preserve herself, which justified her policy in China. This, together with the appointment of Hirota as foreign minister, who adhered to the policy of excluding the western powers from China, would probably have ensured Japan's isolation in world affairs in itself. What made that isolation certain was the resumption of hostilities between China and Japan in July 1937, barely a month after Konoe's appointment.

The renewed war was not the consequence of any decision in Tokyo. It began as a chance incident when Japanese troops, legally present in Peking under the terms of the Boxer Protocols for the protection of the Japanese legation, were fired upon by Chinese troops while on night manoeuvres near the Marco Polo Bridge just outside Peking. There was no reason why this trivial incident in itself should have led to a major war that was to last for eight years. Fundamentally, Konoe wished to contain the incident, although he was probably not averse to a short, victorious war that would provide him domestically with the kudos essential for the passage of a raft of reform measures through the Diet. He, therefore, was seduced by the hardliners in the Japanese Army into thinking that a forceful policy towards China might force Chiang Kai-shek to back down and grant concessions. The key man, however, was General Ishiwara Kanji, the head of the army general staff's operations division. In 1931 he had been the driving force behind the conquest of Manchuria, forcing his reluctant superiors to follow on. In 1937, however, he was on the side of caution and led those officers who wanted the Marco Polo Bridge affair settled as quickly as possible so that Japan could continue to concentrate on internal reform and the long-term objective of economic self-sufficiency. Even a short war with China would involve friction with the western powers who were critical suppliers of the goods and commodities required for the strengthening of Japan. Ishiwara, though, like Konoe, succumbed to the arguments of the hardliners: a minimal display of force, they believed, would cause Chiang to back down and North China would be in Japanese hands in a matter of months. Fundamentally, the government was compelled to adopt a forward foreign policy by the force of opinion among significant sections of Japan's foreign policy-making elite.

Although on 11 July a local truce was concluded, the Konoe cabinet on the same day endorsed the despatch of three divisions to the area of the incident. The punitive purpose of this measure was aided by the decision of Chiang Kai-shek to disown the negotiations that had led to the truce and simultaneously to appeal to the signatories of the Nine Power Treaty. On 17 July Chiang called for total resistance to the Japanese and authorized the posting of Chinese troops in the demilitarized zone of the Tangku Truce. The Japanese government responded by calling for a final reckoning with China and an hysterical war fever erupted in Japan.

What shook the Japanese was not only the decision to resist but the valiant conduct of the Chinese in the field. During August fighting spread to Shanghai following the murder of a Japanese naval officer. From this point onwards the war, still referred to by both sides as an 'Incident,' rapidly spread, culminating in the *Rape of Nanking* in December 1937, when the Japanese forces committed a range of atrocities so horrible that to describe them in detail might give offence. Some 250,000 innocent people were raped, tortured and murdered. This conduct, although put in the shade by what was yet to come in Europe, inevitably encouraged international sympathy for China and there was a widespread feeling in the international community that Japan had put herself beyond the pale of civilized society. Apart, however, from a little help with cash and supplies, sympathy was all that China could expect until Japan attacked the United States in December 1941.

9

From War to World War

Whatever the revulsion in the west regarding Japan's conduct in China, Chiang Kai-shek overestimated the amount of assistance that would actually be forthcoming from the powers. While sympathy was never in short supply, the practical support they were prepared to offer China was very limited. By maintaining the fiction that the renewal of Sino-Japanese hostilities was not a proper war, the United States government was able to circumvent the Neutrality Acts which meant that arms could continue to be supplied to China. This though was a mixed blessing as American arms could also be shipped to Japan. From 1937 onwards, however, relations between the United States and Japan steadily worsened as the situation in Europe gave certain elements within Japan confidence to persist in a forward policy which the Washington government was bound to oppose.

Japan and the Axis

Most depressing for Chiang Kai-shek must have been the attitude of the Germans. Since 1933 Germany had been very supportive of China and had demonstrated her friendship practically by supplying to the Chinese aircraft and military advisers. China, as already noted, was attractive to Germany because of the clear potential of the country as a market for Germany's industrial produce; she was also a source of important raw materials vital to German rearmament. On the other hand, the Germans and the Japanese had concluded at the end of 1936 the Anti-Comintern Pact, which, of course, was directed against the USSR. Nevertheless, too much importance should not be attributed to that step at that stage as reservations continued to exist on both sides regarding even closer relations and, significantly, during 1936–7 the Germans actually increased their stake in China. But with the eruption of the Sino-Japanese War Germany now became reluctant to step up her aid to China. Instead she opted for the path of neutrality and offered her mediation to end the dispute.[1]

The consequence of this was that Chiang Kai-shek sought Soviet aid. This was not immediately forthcoming as the Soviet Union was fearful of provoking a military confrontation with the Japanese for which she was not ready. Eventually, however, Moscow conceded half Chiang's request and also concluded a non-aggression pact with China. Strangely, the corollary of this was not a confrontation with the Japanese, but rather a decision by the Japanese government to accept German mediation in their dispute with China, for senior military personnel in Tokyo were anxious about the possibility of Soviet intervention in China and wanted the fighting to cease. By the beginning of November 1937 the Japanese were ready, therefore, to offer terms which included an autonomous Inner Mongolia, a demilitarized zone in North China administered by Nanking, the prohibition of anti-Japanese activities and co-operation against communism. These conditions, however, were a clear violation of the Nine Power Treaty, as they infringed China's sovereignty. Accordingly, Chiang Kai-shek found them unacceptable, wanting rather a return to the position that had obtained before hostilities began.

Chiang's obstinacy was undoubtedly encouraged by certain developments in the international situation. Although the democratic powers were at first inclined to little more than moral condemnation of Japan, there were signs by the end of the year that they were hesitantly moving towards collective action. On 13 September 1937 China formally appealed to the League of Nations, which body responded by constituting an Advisory Committee of twenty-three nations in which the United States also participated. This was followed on 6 October by condemnation of the Japanese action by the League Assembly and a request for the convention of a conference of the signatories of the Nine Power Treaty, which was endorsed by the United States. Indeed on the previous day President Roosevelt had in Chicago made his celebrated 'Quarantine Speech' in which he had called for the quarantining by international action of the nations that were giving rise to 'international anarchy and instability'[2]. Although it would be wrong to interpret this as the beginning of the United States' emergence from isolation, it was a significant development in that for the first time for many years Washington was demonstrating a willingness to act with other nations in maintaining peace. The meeting of the Nine Power signatories at the Brussels Conference, however, soon illustrated the limits of American policy at this time. President Roosevelt judged that American opinion would not endorse anything as adventurous as economic sanctions and so the Brussels Conference ended disappointingly for the Chinese with nothing more than a statement of support for China. For his part, the United States ambassador in Tokyo, Joseph Grew, thought the convening of the Brussels Conference had been a grave mistake. It was obvious from the start that it 'could never in the world agree to take *effective* measures', against Japan and would only serve to encourage Japanese militarists for whom the 'lack of unity and impotence of the Powers' would be made plain.[3] In London there was relief that the Brussels Conference had come to nothing. Anthony Eden had allowed himself to be convinced by the American representative at the conference that the United States was likely to do something positive,[4] but his cabinet colleagues had never been convinced of this and were reluctant to take any kind of action without firm evidence of American support. Quite apart from that, there was a fear that the adoption of coercive measures and participation in international condemnation might well drive Japan into closer ties and collaboration with Germany and Italy.[5]

The rather feeble attitude of the Brussels Conference towards Japan's aggression caused Chiang Kai-shek at the end of November to reverse his earlier negative attitude towards German mediation. This, however, came too late. Shortly after the Brussels Conference ended, it was decided by the Japanese to outflank the Chinese forces defending Shanghai by landing at Hangchow Bay. So successful were the Japanese that the Chinese forces withdrew and retreated to Nanking, whence the Chinese government departed for Hankow and later Chungking in the heart of China. The Japanese thus rapidly occupied the capital of Nationalist China and perpetrated the ghastly atrocities that reverberate until the present day. The horror of these events shook and shocked not only the international community, but also officers of the Japanese Army in other stations who cried with shame when they heard news of these crimes. It has often been alleged that the rape of Nanking was sanctioned by Hirohito, but many scholars now incline to the view that this was not so. The fact was that he could no more control the army in the field than could the general staff.[6] For his part, the American ambassador was of the opinion that the Japanese Army had carried out atrocities 'which the Emperor himself cannot publicly desire or sanction'[7].

Nevertheless, in December the Japanese military for the first time in the course of its operations against the Chinese inflicted casualties on British and American military and civilian personnel in China. The British ambassador's car, although plainly marked, was strafed in August 1937 on the road between Nanking and Shanghai, causing the ambassador, Sir Hughe Knatchbull-Hugessen to suffer severe wounds.[8] Worse, however, was to follow as the Japanese pushed towards Nanking. American and British gunboats patrolling the Yangtze river were fired upon by Japanese aircraft and artillery causing the sinking of the USS *Panay* with substantial loss of life. President Roosevelt's response to these events was to react positively to an earlier British suggestion for Anglo-American naval staff talks with a view to concerting future naval action in the Asian–Pacific area. By the end of the year Captain Ingersoll of the US Navy was in London exchanging information with his British counterparts. This did not, however, lead to any immediate commitment on the part of the United States, the situation not yet being considered sufficiently serious to arouse American opinion.[9] In the meantime, the Japanese government had apologized for the *Panay* incident and agreed to make indemnity payments to the bereaved.[10] The contemporaneous rape of Nanking, however, demonstrated, if demonstration were needed, the complete ruthlessness of the Japanese Army as far as China was concerned.

By the beginning of 1938, the Powers that would ultimately resist Japanese expansion in Asia and the Pacific were, however tentatively, coming together. Theirs was a relationship that would be cemented by every further act of Japanese aggression and expansion on continental Asia. Although Nanking had fallen, this did not end Chinese resistance and the Sino-Japanese war dragged on. As the Japanese would not withdraw from China without defeating Chiang and establishing their position there, this inevitably drew them further into China and ultimately in the direction of the 'southward advance' that would bring them into fatal confrontation with the United States and Britain.

The 'southward advance' was particularly favoured by the Japanese Navy. The Japanese naval high command never had the same hold over the government as their military equivalents; moreover, they were by no means as belligerent. In particular, they were sceptical of the obsession within the army of those who argued the need to fight the Soviet Union. In their view, the so-called 'northward advance' would end in a war of attrition against two land powers, namely, China and the USSR. Rather than pursue that suicidal course, the navy agreed with those in the army who favoured a thrust to the south. As Japan was committed to the subjugation of China, the deployment of superior naval power along China's coast appeared the most appropriate means of achieving this aim. It was believed that control of China's seaboard and the Yangtze river as far inland as the cities of Wuhan would provide Japan with sufficient leverage to ensure China's acquiescence in all her political and economic demands.[11] It would also minimize the danger of a conflict with the major powers. The extension of Japan's naval power southwards was also considered advantageous in respect of the Dutch East Indies (modern Indonesia) which were so rich in the raw materials, particularly oil, essential to Japan. As the army's actions in China began to lead to Japan's isolation and ostracization and an uncertain dependency on the United States for the supply of vital commodities such as oil, the Japanese admirals began to regard the Dutch East Indies as an area vital to them.

Japan, however, was not totally isolated. During the early months of 1938 the German government decided to end its pro-China policy in Asia and transfer its priority to Japan. Undoubtedly the perception in Berlin that Japan would win the war with China played a significant part in this reversal, but it was also connected with Hitler's clear intention, as outlined in the so-called Hossbach Conference of 5 November 1937, to move towards the realization of his objectives in Europe. To have Britain and the Soviet Union preoccupied in the Far East by an expansionist Japan would, of course, facilitate his design. Such a course was one that very definitely appealed to Joachim von Ribbentrop, who was to become the German foreign minister in February 1938. Decidedly more anti-British in outlook than Hitler, Ribbentrop thought that closer ties with Italy and Japan were essential for the future. In his speech to the Reichstag on 20 February 1938, Hitler publicly acknowledged the change in policy when he announced that Germany was willing to recognize Manchukuo and paid tribute to Japan's work in fighting communism. From this time onwards there was to be constant talk of a formal relationship between the two countries closer than that of the Anti-Comintern Pact. This was very much supported by sections of the military in Tokyo and the ministry of finance who favoured Japan's identification with the 'have-not' powers, Italy and Germany, against the democracies as a means of distracting them.[12] The Japanese prime minister, Konoe, was, nevertheless, reluctant to move too overtly in this direction for the time being, as he was loath to do anything to offend the United States.

Crisis in Europe and its Impact on the Far East

Japanese policy in China showed no such restraint. In a statement of 16 January 1938, Konoe made it clear that Japan would no longer deal with the government of Chiang Kai-shek. This statement followed an imperial conference held five days earlier. This conference was of critical importance for the future. Since November 1937 there had been a prospect of such a conference, because the emperor himself had considered the need for one in order to define Japan's response to Chiang Kai-shek should he wish to discuss terms. But a conference was demanded no less by General Tada, the vice-chief of general staff and the navy chiefs of staff who '. . . were seeking the support of the throne for . . . [their] . . . approach to the China situation.' From the beginning of the 'China Incident' the previous July, Generals Kanin, Tada and Ishiwara of the army general staff had opposed escalation of the conflict, but invariably the cabinet blamed 'pressure of field armies' for the failure to reach a diplomatic settlement with China. It was Tada's intention now to 'use the Imperial Conference as a way to commit the army, through the supreme command, to a policy which would enable and force the cabinet to intensify its efforts for a negotiated settlement with Chiang Kai-shek.'[13] Those who opposed further escalation of the war with China wanted Hirohito put a question to the conference that would have the effect of opening the subject to debate. The emperor was, however, dissuaded from speaking at the conference by the *Genro*, Prince Saionji, on grounds of the potential constitutional imprudence of such a course, and the prime minister, Konoe, who would present an agreed policy himself. Konoe thus out-manoeuvred the army moderates. Arrogant in his belief that Japan could bring the 'China incident' to a speedy determination by one last push, what he wanted was a hardening of policy towards China.

The result of the imperial conference was that it was agreed, with the implied endorsement of the emperor, that Japan would pursue a policy of annihilation towards *Kuomintang* China, unless, within seventy-two hours Chiang agreed to the following desiderata: formal recognition of the state of Manchukuo; formal renunciation of anti-Japanese policies; the establishment of neutral zones in North China and Inner Mongolia; the creation of new political organs in North China; the creation of an anti-communist and autonomous government in Inner Mongolia; anti-Soviet co-operation in East Asia; Sino-Japanese co-operation in the parts of Central China occupied by Japan; agreement between Japan, China and Manchukuo on customs, trade, aviation and transport matters; and the payment of reparations to Japan. These conditions were intolerable and so on 16 January 1938 Konoe announced that Japan would no longer recognize the *Kuomintang* government of China and would seek instead to assist in the creation of a new regime in China with which she could co-operate.[14] This commitment to a war of annihilation was a gross error, for it committed Japan to a war that she could not win. General Tada informed the foreign minister that it was an act of folly, knowing as he did the very real obstacles in the way of the success of such a venture. Towards the end of his life Konoe himself acknowledged this when he stated: 'The announcement of January 16, 1938, brought no favourable results, a fact of which I am well aware without having anyone point it out to me. I, myself, confess it was an utter blunder.'[15] By June 1938 Konoe wanted a negotiated peace, but could not succeed because of the conditions he himself had created.

The significance of the imperial conference of January 1938 also lies in the fact that it shows that the *Toseiha*, or control faction, in the army cannot be held responsible for the escalation of the 'China Incident'. Moreover, it indicates the extent of the complicity of non-army elements in the cabinet in the further deterioration of Sino-Japanese relations. Konoe was himself very close to a number of the *Kodoha*, or imperial way, generals and in August 1937 attempted to intercede on behalf of Kita Ikki and Nishida Zei when they were sentenced to death for their part in the Tokyo Mutiny of February 1936.[16] In the words of J.B. Crowley: 'One suspects that several members of the cabinet – Premier Konoe, Foreign Minister Hirota, Home Minister [Admiral] Suetsugu, and Education Minister Kido – believed that Japan could and should realize the "principles of co-prosperity and co-existence based upon the Imperial Way" by subjugation of China.'[17]

Toughness in Japan's foreign policy was matched by domestic develop-ments that signified her developing alignment with the Rome–Berlin Axis. The revolution in Germany's Far Eastern policy in Berlin was welcomed by the Japanese Army, because, just as Hitler wanted increasing intimacy with Japan to provide a Far Eastern diversion for Britain and the Soviet Union as Germany began expanding in Europe, so Japan could use the threat of Germany in Europe to immobilize the western powers and the Soviet Union in the Far East. Moreover, Germany's system of government provided a model for the type of order that the Japanese Army wanted to introduce in Japan. The foundation stone of this was laid in March 1938 with the passage of the National General Mobilization Law. Under this instrument all aspects of Japanese life were to be arranged so as to bring the society and economy of Japan to a peak of military efficiency.[18] It was, though, what it portended for the future that was more important than what it achieved. The Japanese political parties in the diet proved not very co-operative and ensured that the Law could only be invoked in time of declared war, which the 'China Incident' was not. This meant that as long as the 'China Incident' lasted the Law was very much dead a letter and that the resources which should have gone into the expansion of Japan's industrial potential for the future were diverted into the Chinese drain. But this Law, as Sir Robert Craigie, the then British ambassador in Tokyo, later pointed out was precursor of developments that would later 'place Japan on a fully totalitarian footing'. Behind this process stood the army. Craigie wrote: '. . . each successive measure of repression added to the political power of the Army, to which the very name of liberty was anathema. For behind the civil Government stood the Army – in those days still an *éminence grise*, but soon to emerge as the undisputed ruler of Japan. Liberties lost to the Japanese Army were lost for good'.[19]

Chiang and the *Kuomintang* simply could not be easily crushed. Although by October 1938 all the major cities in China were in Japanese hands, both the nationalists, from their new base in Chungking, and the communists continued to resist. It would either be necessary, therefore, to continue the war or seek mediation. The latter, however, would clearly involve concessions that the Japanese were not prepared to make and the former alternative would mean a drain on national resources that would affect Japan's ability later to confront the Soviet Union. The cleft stick in which Japanese policy found itself was revealed during the summer of 1938 following the resignation of Hirota as foreign minister in May of that year. He was replaced by General Ugaki. Ugaki considered the 'China Incident' an example of a lamentable failure of statesmanship, which had seriously interrupted Japan's plans for expanding the industrial production base, sucked in costly imports such as machine tools, oils and steel alloys and contributed to the growth of anti-Japanese feeling in the United States whence many of the imports came. Ugaki took office on the understanding that the statement of 16 January no longer applied so that he could attempt to end the war with China. In effect, however, the most he could offer the Chinese was the ending of hostilities. No concessions of any substance could be proposed. At the very least Manchukuo would have to be recognized; North China would for all practical purposes be detached from China proper; and Chiang would have to resign. But even if the Chinese had been prepared to accept a peace based upon such premises nothing would have come of it, for the army minister appointed at the same time as Ugaki was appointed foreign minister was Lieutenant-General Itagaki, who would have found such a peace unacceptable. Itagaki was one of the principal figures in the Mukden conspiracy of 1931 and a hardliner. By the summer of 1938 he and his associates favoured nothing less than the conversion of the whole of China into a satellite state under a puppet government, which meant further escalation of the 'China Incident.' Eventually Konoe succumbed to those in the army who opposed Ugaki's policy and agreed to the creation of an Asian Development, or China, Board, (*Koain*), which would remove China from the responsibility of the foreign ministry. This not surprisingly prompted Ugaki to resign in protest in September 1938.[20]

Konoe now reverted to the stick by first explicitly renouncing the Washington System and secondly negotiating an anti-Soviet military alliance with Germany. It was in this manner hoped to bring the China war to a speedy conclusion on Japan's terms and without leaving Japan isolated. The termination of the 'China Incident' seemed also to have been facilitated by the willingness of Wang Ching-wei, one of the leading figures in the *Kuomintang*, to perform the role of a quisling. Wang had been a close friend of Sun Yat-sen and had been the latter's amanuensis when he had dictated his will. He had, in addition, held high office in the Nationalist government. But he also appears to have been jealous of Chiang Kai-shek. His motives in setting up the pro-Japanese government that Tokyo desired were probably mixed. Undoubtedly ambition was important, as was probably the belief that he was acting in the best interests of China; but he probably thought also that he could outsmart the Japanese.[21] In this he was frustrated and he died bitterly disillusioned and disappointed in 1944. Wang's regime was not to be formally recognized by Japan until 1940.

The explicit rejection of the Washington System was made in a statement issued by Konoe on 3 November 1938. In this statement, it was asserted that the Nationalist government of China had been reduced to a local regime and that Japan's primary objective was the creation of a New Order that would ensure permanent stability in East Asia. In this New Order Japan, Manchukuo and China would co-operate politically, economically and culturally with a view to the defeat of communism and the establishment of a new culture and a new economic union in the region.[22] The East Asian economic union was, of course, to be exclusivist and what was really involved was the domination of other countries by Japan. On the other hand, there can be no doubting the sincerity of those, such as General Tojo Hideki, vice army minister, under Itagaki, who argued the moral validity of the New Order. After the war, he explained to his captors:

> The basic intention was that the raw materials which China possessed in abundance would be contributed by China and the technique, capital and skilled personnel [would] be contributed by Japan for the mutual benefit of both countries. Manchuria would come into the picture similarly . . . The idea of profit or loss did not enter in. The idea of mutual benefit was the main one. It had a moral basis.[23]

In respect of the alliance with Germany, however, disagreements in respect of its scope were ultimately to lead to the fall of the Konoe government in January 1939. There was general agreement that there should be closer ties with Germany and Italy, but, whereas foreign minister Arita, who had replaced Ugaki, and the navy wanted to restrict the scope of the alliance to an anti-Soviet bias, the army wanted, in conformity with German wishes, to cover Britain and France also. These differences among others proved irreconcilable and Konoe, unable to bring hostilities with China to a satisfactory conclusion, resigned in January 1939. He was replaced by Hiranuma Kiijiro, who immediately pledged himself to make China co-operate.

Japan's international position in 1939 weakened: the more she became entrenched in China, the more she provoked American resistance. Furthermore, Chiang Kai-shek and the Chungking regime continued to receive the support and recognition of the democracies. These though were now confronting a serious crisis in Europe, which the Japanese hoped to compound by concluding the German alliance. The negotiations for this were, however, beset by the same problems that had preceded and partly precipitated Konoe's resignation. Elements within the foreign ministry and the navy were opposed to an alliance that would involve Japan in a war with adversaries other than the Soviet Union. The army, for its part, was more inclined to accept the German preference for an alliance without restrictions.

In June 1939 the Japanese Army decided to take advantage of Britain's problems in Europe and embarrass the British by blockading their concession at Tientsin. Alleging that the concession was serving as a base for anti-Japanese terrorist activities, all persons entering it were searched. The real purpose of this activity, however, was to diminish Britain in Asian eyes and, as far as the Japanese Army was concerned, by provoking a crisis in Anglo-Japanese relations to convince the government of the virtues of the German–Japanese Alliance.[24] Because of the deteriorating position in Europe at this time and because of the need to do nothing that would drive the Japanese into a formal alliance with Germany, the British government declined to retaliate and the Tientsin Crisis was resolved peacefully. In the long term, however, incidents such as this could do nothing to improve relations with Britain and the United States, which were already tense, given that the Japanese occupation of Hainan Island and the Spratly Islands in February and March 1939, placed British, French and American interests in South-East Asia under direct threat.

By the beginning of 1939 the United States was manifestly demonstrating its opposition to Japanese policy. In many ways the critical point had been reached with Konoe's announcement of the New Order. The American response was a ringing reaffirmation of the United States' adherence to the Washington System, the 'Open Door' in China and the principles of a multilateral economic and trading system. The unilateral announcement of the New Order was condemned as arbitrary.[25] The response of the Japanese was adamantine. The attempt to apply pre-'China Incident' ideals and principles to the new situation in East Asia would contribute nothing to peace and stability in the area. According to foreign minister Arita it was essential for Japan's security and defence that she exercise control over China's resources and economy from which foreigners were to be excluded. The most astonishing thing in all this was the degree to which representatives of the Japanese government were capable of ignoring the fact that it was Japan's aggression which was responsible for the new situation.[26] Officials in Washington now began to explore the possibility of deterring Japan by economic pressure, which would involve the circumscription or cessation of trade with Japan, and financial assistance to China in the form of loans. The latter was immediately approved by Roosevelt and, although the sums involved were modest, it was an act of great significance for the future. In July 1939, in the wake of Japan's humiliation of the British at Tientsin, the United States finally decided to impose trade sanctions upon Japan by giving the required six months notice of intent to abrogate or cancel the American–Japanese Treaty of Commerce and Navigation of 1911. This was a very serious development as Japan was very reliant upon imports of American oil and scrap metal. It was, in effect, 'a potential blockade' that made Japan's actual blockade of Tientsin 'pale in comparison'[27]. Moreover, it probably represented a very fundamental policy miscalculation in Washington, that was to influence the American attitude right up to Pearl Harbor, namely, that escalating economic pressure alone would suffice to bring the Japanese to reason.

Worse was to follow for the Japanese in the following month. The previous year, in August 1938, a border skirmish took place between Soviet and Japanese troops at Changkufeng on the Soviet–Manchurian border. The result of the fighting was a stalemate, although the Soviet press hailed it as a victory. The message should, nevertheless, have been clearly conveyed to the Japanese military that the Red Army was not to be treated lightly in the Far East. But from July until September 1939 battle was resumed between Soviet and Japanese forces at Nomonhan on the border between Manchuria and Outer Mongolia. Despite severe reservations in Tokyo on the part of Japan's army commanders about this development, the Kwantung Army leadership in Manchuria and their supporters in Tokyo were confident that this venture was fundamentally safe on the grounds that the Soviet Union would be preoccupied by events in Europe and that, given Japan's continuing discussions with the Germans regarding an alliance, Germany would assist Japan if the crisis threatened to run out of control. The immediate requirements of German policy in Europe, however, provoked a speedy rapprochement between Germany and the Soviet Union. The calculations of all those who had advocated the German alliance were now in ruins and the Soviet Union was able to concentrate fully upon the threat in the Far East. By the time the fighting ended, the Japanese losses at 50,000 dead were five times greater than those sustained by the Soviet Union. Moreover, the Soviet forces had shown themselves superior in fire-power and very capable of beating off a serious attack.[28] This, and the fact of the Nazi–Soviet Pact, came as a great blow to Japanese policy. Japan was now left isolated as she proceeded with the 'southward advance' in China that inevitably alienated the western democracies. The failure of Japanese policy by August 1939 culminated in the resignation of the Hiranuma government.

Into the Abyss of World War

During the course of the next two years, from the outbreak of war in Europe to the development of a truly global conflict involving the United States, the situation in the Far East was characterized by the reluctance of the Japanese to surrender their position in China and the absolute refusal of the United States to recognize it. At the end it was these irreconcilable positions that led to Japan's attack on Pearl Harbor. The animus in Japanese–American relations could not be 'healed by the medication of diplomacy' and had to be excised 'by the surgery of war'[29]. It would, however, be wrong to suggest that Japanese policy led inevitably and directly to war with the United States and the democratic powers. Both the Abe and Yonai governments that succeeded that of Hiranuma were determined to keep out of the European war. Moreover, they both attempted to achieve an understanding with the United States. Nevertheless, their reluctance to give up the New Order concept and American determination that they should do so were the immovable obstacles. The Japanese reacted by deciding to solve the problem directly by winning the war in China. This, however, and the formal recognition of the Wang Ching-wei regime in Nanking in November 1940 merely served to stiffen American resistance all the more. A foretaste of what was to come came in December 1939. The Japanese and Americans having failed to reach any agreement by this time, the United States' unilateral abrogation of the

Treaty of Commerce and Navigation between the two countries, notice of its termination having been given the previous July, came into immediate effect at the end of the year.

Nevertheless, the ending of the Phoney War in Europe in May 1940 and the subsequent defeat and subjugation of the Low Countries seemed to offer the Japanese certain advantages in the Far East. With Britain now isolated in Europe, the Japanese attempted to exploit her difficulties in order to strengthen their position in China. Supplies and aid had previously been reaching Chiang Kai-shek through Burma, which was then under British control. In June 1940, however, the British government was forced to succumb to Japanese pressure and close the Burma Road for three months. Equally, the Japanese compelled the new French Vichy authorities to close the route to Chiang through the northern border of Indo-China and to agree to the stationing of a Japanese observer force in the area. Moreover, pressure was put on the Dutch authorities in Batavia (modern Djakarta) to guarantee essential supplies of petroleum, rubber and tin from the Dutch East Indies.

The problems that the Japanese continued to encounter in defeating China and the fact of the Nazi–Soviet Pact precluded now any realistic consideration of the 'northward advance' against the Soviet Union. Nevertheless, this was not necessarily considered in Tokyo to be disadvantageous from the point of view of solving the Chinese problem. On the contrary, it was felt in certain quarters that a rapprochement between Japan and the Soviet Union could impose upon both China and the United States the sort of psychological pressure that might end the war in China. This and Japan's desired closer relationship with Germany were regarded as essential elements in a worldwide, revisionist coalition that could be crucial in assisting Japan's revisionist aims. Little thought was given to the fact that such a power constellation might make American and British resistance in the Far East all the more determined. Thus, when the government of Admiral Yonai fell in July 1940, the succeeding Konoe government pursued such a policy with vigour.

Konoe's appointment signified Japan's further identification with the revisionist dictatorships in Europe. Japan now became a one-party state, with the government committed to national unity. In a radio broadcast, Konoe declared that democracy, liberalism and socialism were all evil aspects of party politics which were 'not agreeable to the national ideas of Japan'. This signified Japan's internal rejection of Anglo-American influence. The attitude of the ancient *Genro*, Prince Saionji, towards this change was caustic. He wrote:

> The talk of a whole nation party is ridiculous. This is no real party . . . It is a real puzzle to me why Konoe wants to lead such an amalgamation. The more I hear, the more I come to feel that Japan is politically underdeveloped. There are no fights between gentlemen, just the petty quarrels with pygmies and there is no trace of understanding of what national politics is . . . Our education policy was, after all, misguided.[30]

In the field of foreign policy, Konoe was equally rejectionist of democracy, internationalism and the liberal-capitalist tradition; hence his belief that Japan should join with Germany and the Soviet Union to end Anglo-American world dominance. Significantly, the new foreign minister in Konoe's cabinet was Matsuoka Yosuke. His perception was that Germany was surely winning the war in Europe; he was, therefore, anxious that Japan should conclude an alliance with Germany as soon as possible as a means of making the United States respect Japan more.

The late summer of 1940 also marked two important developments regarding future Japanese military strategy. It was now accepted that with no prospect of an immediate end to the war in China there could be no question of the 'northward advance' and a conflict with the Soviet Union. Thus the priority of the 'southward advance' was established. The army too now agreed that Japan needed her own secure, economic base, otherwise Japan would be forever dependent upon the United States and Britain. Japanese war planning was, therefore, at this time beginning to contemplate a lightning strike towards the Dutch East Indies before Britain and America could intervene. It was even surmised that with an imminent German invasion of Britain the time had come to finish off the British Empire in Asia for good.

Prior to the formation of his government, Konoe discussed the foreign policy priorities of his government with Tojo Hideki and Yoshida Zengo, the prospective war and navy ministers. It was decided that they should be, first, the strengthening of ties with Germany and Italy; secondly, the creation of the New Order in Asia; thirdly, a non-aggression pact with the USSR; fourthly, the incorporation of British, French and Dutch colonies in Asia into the Japanese sphere of influence; and, fifthly, a rapprochement with Chiang Kai-shek and the Chungking government if they would collaborate in the New Order. The Liaison Conference between the cabinet and the supreme command endorsed this programme, although a split between the army and navy began to emerge with the latter wanting the avoidance of war with the United States and Britain, while the army thought that this was an eventuality that would probably have to be faced.

On 27 September 1940 Matsuoka concluded the Tripartite Pact with Germany and Italy. His fundamental aim was to strengthen Japan against the American led coalition of Britain, the British Commonwealth, China and the United States. He considered this an urgent matter as he feared that, once Germany had defeated Britain, Germany might seek an accommodation with Washington to Japan's disadvantage.[31] Japan's conclusion of the Tripartite Pact with the Axis powers was meant to preclude such an eventuality. Hitler's hope was that Japan would keep the United States preoccupied while Germany defeated Britain. For the Japanese adherence to the Rome–Berlin Axis was one means of avoiding isolation. The other was attachment to the Anglo-American bloc. The latter, however, would mean giving up the New Order and that was decisive in Japan aligning herself with Germany and Italy. This was a most critical turn of events. As Stephen Large has observed:

> Together, the Tripartite Pact and ... [the] ... 'southern advance' linked Japanese aggression in Asia to the European war in a manner which virtually ensured a future collision with the Anglo-American powers.[32]

Fearing precisely this, the emperor, whom Matsuoka had endeavoured to reassure by claiming that the Tripartite Pact would serve the interests of peace by keeping the United States out of the Far East, made the following comment to Konoe: 'I have often heard that in map room problems of the Naval Staff College, Japan is always the loser in a Japanese–American War. Can you reassure me about that?'[33]

Even before the conclusion of the Tripartite Pact, the United States had embarked upon a policy of deterrence. Following its annual manoeuvres in the spring of 1940, most of the United States Pacific fleet was maintained in Hawaiian waters for the duration of the summer rather than returning to base. More action was to follow. The tone surrounding the formation of the second Konoe government had been alarming, as was the decision of the Japanese army to occupy all northern Indo-China in September 1940 following a skirmish with French forces. The United States reacted by prohibiting in July 1940 the sale to Japan of aviation fuel, lubricating oil and certain grades of scrap iron. This was supplemented in September by a decision to ban all sales of scrap iron to Japan.[34] Moreover, in the same month Britain was supplied with practical help from the United States in the Destroyers-Bases deal. As a consequence of these developments and improvements in the European situation, the British felt confident enough to reopen the Burma Road when the agreement with the Japanese expired in October. This inevitably encouraged the Chungking authorities and made the Japanese conquest of China as remote as ever. The ever-increasing commitment of America to the forces opposing the Axis was revealed at the end of the year in the Lend-Lease Agreement.[35] Japanese policy had, therefore, by the beginning of 1941 proved an abject failure.

This did not, however, give the Japanese leadership the slightest pause in their fundamental aim of making the Chinese bow to their will. Moreover, Japanese military planning now extended beyond the confines of China. The navy too had come to see the probable inevitability of a war with the United States because of the latter's use of the economic weapon. In order to secure supplies of essential raw materials such as petroleum, the navy considered access to the produce of the Dutch East Indies essential. The guarantee of such access could probably only be obtained by force, which would mean war with America and Britain. In these circumstances, Admiral Yamamoto began to consider a lightning strike against the Philippines in order to give Japan a tactical advance base against the United States while she achieved her aims in South-East Asia. By December 1940 the Japanese Army too was considering the implications of the 'southward advance' with the Dutch East Indies and Malaya as the main targets.

Concentration on the south implied a need to put relations with the USSR on a steady basis. Matsuoka's solution to this problem was to bring the USSR if possible into the Tripartite Pact. The consequent quadripartite pact he assumed would assist in the establishment of the New Order, end Soviet assistance to China and lead to Anglo-American withdrawal from the Pacific. In the first instance the Japanese foreign minister proposed a non-aggression pact with the Soviet Union. This grand scheme was, however, doomed to failure, for by the end of 1940 Hitler had taken the irrevocable decision to attack the Soviet Union. In March 1941 Matsuoka left for Europe in order to further his design. In Berlin he learnt of the worsening of Russo–German relations which rendered his proposed quadripartite pact impossible. On the other hand, the Soviet authorities, alarmed by the worsening of relations with Berlin, were anxious to negotiate a treaty of neutrality with Japan which was in fact concluded on 13 April. Under the terms of this treaty, Japan undertook not to attack the Soviet Union if she were at war with Germany; Japan also undertook to recognize the territorial integrity of Outer Mongolia. For her part the Soviet Union agreed to respect the frontiers of Manchukuo, which was tantamount to recognition of the puppet regime there.

In reality, though, Japan's international position continued to deteriorate. It should have been clear to Japan by the beginning of 1941 that there could be no reconciliation between her and the United States unless she returned to the *Washington System*. While the Americans were not yet prepared to go to war, they were committed to those resisting aggression in Europe and Asia, namely, Britain and China. The priority for American strategists remained as it was in 1940 the European–Atlantic theatre of war, with a defensive posture in the Pacific. This was the essence of Plan D, or Plan Dog, which was tacitly approved by Roosevelt in January 1941.[36] The underlying assumption was that Japan, contained by economic pressure and the threat of the American Pacific fleet, would probably not resort to force against the Western powers. It did not mean, however, that the United States would reduce its commitments in the Pacific. On the contrary, American policy would continue to stimulate co-operation between Powers opposed to Japanese aggression. In other words, Washington would preside over the creation of the ABCD (American, British, Chinese and Dutch) alliance.

By the spring of 1941 the democratic coalition in Asia and the Pacific was beginning to solidify. Following a number of staff conversations between British and American personnel in Washington, the Report ABC-1 was produced on 29 March. As in Plan D, this provided for concentration on Europe as a priority in the event of a two ocean war and a defensive strategy in Asia and the Pacific, where the Japanese 'southward advance' was to be resisted by economic means and the threat of the US Pacific Fleet. Subsequently, there was a meeting in April of British, American and Dutch officers in Singapore.

The developing power realities in the Pacific suggested to the United States government an eventual Japanese retreat. Indeed the posting of Admiral Nomura, who was known to favour improved Japanese–American relations, to the Washington embassy in early 1941 seemed to hint on this direction. But in the subsequent talks with secretary of state Cordell Hull it became clear that what the Japanese actually wanted was to gain American endorsement of their current position in the Far East and South-East Asia. They had not the slightest intention of giving way to Hull's four principles: territorial integrity, non-interference in the internal affairs of states, equal economic opportunity and the peaceful alteration of territorial arrangements. What the Americans wanted fundamentally was the complete withdrawal of Japan from China. This was not on offer.

Matsuoka's grand design was, of course, ruined by the German attack on the USSR in June 1941, which now placed Moscow in the Anglo-American camp. In these changed circumstances, Konoe argued the case for a policy that would lead to good relations with the United States. This though was not acceptable to the military or Matsuoka. For the army, Konoe's proposals could only lead to a surrender to the American point of view and the abandonment of the China war as hopeless. On the other hand, the army leadership was not prepared to follow Matsuoka's demands for an immediate Japanese attack upon the Soviet Union in the Far East in support of the German ally, generally favouring instead preparations for such an eventuality sometime in the future. Conscious of the losses suffered at Nomonhan in 1939, the Japanese military were understandably cautious about starting hostilities with an adversary of proven redoubtability,[37] preferring, as Tojo put it, to wait until the persimmon was ripe and ready to fall.[38] For its part, the Japanese Navy was still preoccupied by its southern strategy and would only agree to military preparedness against the USSR. It was only Matsuoka who wanted an immediate attack upon the Soviet Union in order to frustrate a firm alliance between Moscow, Britain and America. He reasoned that Germany would soon defeat the USSR and that by the end of 1941 Britain too would be prepared to sue for peace. Japan, therefore, should take the opportunity to assist in the defeat of the Soviet Union and in this way ensure the Anglo-American–Soviet alliance could not be realized.

Japanese foreign policy endeavoured to adjust itself to the changed world realities at a meeting in the presence of the emperor on 2 July. It was agreed that Japan, notwithstanding recent events, should press on with the creation of the *Great East Asian Co-Prosperity Sphere*; that a settlement of the China problem should be attempted; that preparations for southern expansion should continue; and that an attempt should be made to solve the northern problem. On the same day, it was decided that the whole of Indo-China should rapidly be occupied. This was felt to be necessary by the army to break the links between Chungking and Britain, America and the Dutch East Indies. For the navy the move was considered essential given the possibility of an eventual war with the ABD Powers (America, Britain and the Netherlands). The operation was to be completed by 29 July.

For Konoe this action was infinitely preferable to a 'northward advance' on the USSR. Moreover, in a manoeuvre designed to weaken pressure for such a course, he procured the removal of its main advocate, Matsuoka, on 18 July. His replacement was Admiral Toyada, which was a pro-American move; its force, however, was vitiated by a remonstrance on the part of the supreme command on 21 July that the new government strictly adhere to the decisions of 2 July and remain loyal to the Tripartite Pact. Konoe acquiesced. Clearly Japanese foreign policy was losing any room for manoeuvre, which was significant as US–Japanese relations moved into an advanced state of crisis.

The reaction of the United States to the German attack on the Soviet Union, as far as its Pacific policy was concerned, was to warn the Japanese in no uncertain terms that an attack by Japan upon the USSR would not only endanger any future negotiations with Washington, but would also endanger peace in the Pacific. The United States government was from this time onwards quite well-informed of Japanese intentions as the Japanese diplomatic code had been broken by American naval intelligence officers in the spring of 1941. All Japanese dispatches from Tokyo to Washington were now intercepted and read, the process, for security purposes being codenamed 'Magic'[39]. Washington, therefore, was well aware of the intended occupation of Indo-China by Japanese forces which was completed peacefully on 30 July. Five days earlier the United States had reacted by freezing Japanese assets in the United States. Almost immediately afterwards similar action was undertaken by Britain, the Philippines, New Zealand and the Dutch authorities. On 1 August the supply of essential raw materials to Japan from the United States was rendered virtually impossible by the institution of a system of export licences. This amounted to a *de facto* embargo on oil supplies to Japan. The supply of oil from the Dutch East Indies was also prohibited.

For the Japanese Army and Navy this was tantamount to an act of war. For the navy particularly, the 'southward advance' now became a matter of life and death. Any possibility of a war with the Soviet Union now receded; from 9 August onwards the strategy of the Japanese was predicated upon a possible conflict with the ABCD powers. The view of the navy was that war would have to begin by December at the latest because of the depletion of naval oil stocks. It was agreed by both the army and the navy by 22 August that Admiral Yamamoto's scheme, based upon a pre-emptive strike on the United States fleet at Pearl Harbor, would offer the greatest chance of success. With the United States thus immobilized, Japan could subsequently proceed towards the rapid establishment of a Japanese-dominated area in South-East Asia that would include the Dutch East Indies. There were, however, still substantial differences between the navy and the army. In the navy, Yamamoto's strategy was regarded as the best course *if war became inevitable*; the resumption of oil supplies, it was thought, would end the case for going to war. The army, however, generally took the view that negotiation would produce nothing and that Japan should face war immediately. Oil was not, for the army, the central issue: China and South-East Asia were. The United States would not accept Japanese policy in these regions. It was, therefore, necessary to have a timetable for negotiation and war.

The views of the army and navy regarding Japan's future course were brought to a compromise in a document entitled, 'Guidelines for Implementing National Policies,' which was accepted as the basis for national policy at a conference in the presence of the emperor on 6 September. It was agreed at the conference that Japan should be ready for war by the end of October. If negotiation with the United States had not produced terms acceptable to Japan by the middle of October, then Japan would decide to solve her problems by war. The minimal acceptable terms would be the cessation of all Anglo-American military and economic assistance to Chungking; no installation of Anglo-American military facilities in South-East Asia, or increase in their current strength in the region; and the resumption of normal economic relations with Japan. In essence, the 6 September 'Guidelines' were a decision to go to war. There was little likelihood that the Americans would ever agree to such terms and, as Tojo, the war minister, observed the following day, the terms that would be acceptable to the United States would be far too humiliating for Japan to abide by them.

From the point of view of the army any concession to the United States that meant a return to the Washington System would render pointless the efforts that had been expended in Manchuria and China and imply the subordination of Japan to the United States. Tojo put it thus: 'Rather than waiting for extinction with folded hands it is better to face death by breaking through the encircling ring to find a way for existence.'[40] The army, though, thought there was a possibility of success provided that in the early stages of a war Japan could secure her economic base in South-East Asia. The navy concurred in such thinking which, of course, lay at the bottom of the Pearl Harbor strategy.

Konoe and the emperor construed the 6 September 'Guidelines' as meaning that the government could make one last attempt to reach agreement with the United States. As Tojo had predicted, however, the United States was not prepared to make any concessions to the Japanese point of view. Throughout September, secretary of state Cordell Hull made it clear to the Japanese ambassador, Nomura, that any agreement between Japan and the United States would have also to be endorsed by Britain and China. This could only mean that Japan would have to withdraw from and surrender her special position in China. On 2 October, Cordell Hull made this position explicit to Nomura. Three days later Tojo and General Sugiyama, the army chief of staff, agreed that Japan should decide on war or peace on 15 October.

A governmental crisis rapidly ensued. As the time approached when an irrevocable decision would have to be taken, it became clear that Konoe wanted to continue talking to the Americans. He was to some extent fortified in this position by the view of the navy, as expressed by the navy minister, Oikawa, that war with the United States, essentially over the army's position in China, would be foolhardy, particularly when the navy would incur the bulk of the responsibility for fighting the war. The navy, however, was reluctant to press its reservations too overtly for fear of their impact on the army and public opinion. At a meeting at Konoe's residence on 12 October, Oikawa stated that the decision regarding peace or war was one for the prime minister; the navy would do its duty whatever the outcome.

The key to the situation was the attitude of Tojo and the army. Tojo remained resolute and eventually became dominant in the cabinet. His view was that delay was the Americans most important weapon: further talks could only lead to more delay. Moreover, as Tojo was opposed to any concessions, talks with the Americans could bring Japan no advantage whatever. In these circumstances, Konoe and his cabinet resigned on 16 October. The following day Tojo was asked to form a cabinet. Although under the Japanese system of government this development meant that the 'Guidelines' of 6 September were open to review, a momentum had been established which it would have been difficult even for Tojo to reverse.

At a liaison conference between the civilian and armed forces leaderships on 1–2 November it was agreed that the final date for negotiation would be 30 November. The minimal terms that Japan would accept would, however, still leave Japanese troops in China and were predicated upon non-interference by third parties in Sino-Japanese affairs. This, of course, would have been intolerable to the United States. At a conference in the presence of the emperor on 5 November war was accepted as inevitable by most of the participants. In a speech broadcast from a plenary session of the Japanese Diet on 17 November, prime minister Tojo emphasized that Japan stood 'at the crossroads of her two thousand year existence'. Japan would not suffer the interference and obstruction of third parties in the 'successful conclusion of the China affair'. Finally, economic blockade, which was a measure hardly less hostile than armed conflict, had to be brought to an end. Tojo concluded by congratulating Germany and Italy upon their achievements and expressing the hope that the Tripartite Pact powers could establish a new world order that would be based upon justice.

On 5 November the Japanese government despatched to Washington an experienced diplomat, Kurusu, to assist Ambassador Nomura, who was hopelessly out of his depth. In Washington this was received as a positive sign at the time and later represented as an act of treachery. It has to be said, on the other hand, that the Americans knew through 'Magic' intelligence intercepts that the Japanese intended to break off negotiations and on what date. On 20 November, the day the Pearl Harbor task force was ready to sail, Nomura and Kurusu presented the final Japanese offer to Cordell Hull. Six days later Hull replied. Before economic measures against Japan could be lifted and oil supplies resumed, Japan would have to withdraw from Indo-China and the whole of China, which was understood to include Manchuria. Whatever the niceties as to what constitutes an ultimatum, the American note was regarded as such in Tokyo. On 29 November the most important cabinet ministers explained to the emperor that war was unavoidable. Two days later the emperor formally endorsed the decision for war. The task force, which had left base on 26 November, was instructed to attack Pearl Harbor on Sunday 7 December, a day on which it was presumed that the United States Navy would be at rest, back at base and in a condition unlikely to be able to offer meaningful resistance.

Through 'Magic' the United States government knew well in advance that the Japanese would probably attack soon, but the precise date and actual target were not known. Nevertheless, on Saturday 6 December, President Roosevelt sent a final message to Tokyo requesting the withdrawal of Japanese forces from Indo-China as a means of maintaining peace in the region. Because, however, of a request from the Japanese Army, all incoming cables were subject to delay by the censorship section of Tokyo's central telegraph bureau. Roosevelt's message was not, therefore, delivered to the emperor until 3.00 am on Sunday 7 December, two hours after the Japanese task force had passed the point of no return. A similar delay also occurred concerning the Japanese declaration of war on the United States. It had been intended to present it to the United States government thirty minutes before the attack was due to begin at 1 pm Washington time on

7 December. Because of the lengthy note that accompanied the declaration of war and the time taken to decipher and retype it, the declaration of war was not formally delivered to secretary of state Hull until fifty minutes after the commencement of the attack on Pearl Harbor.

Although the United States government had expected an attack, the sense of shock and amazement was undoubtedly real. The scale and devastation of the aerial bombardment that had destroyed a substantial portion of the Pacific Fleet had simply not been anticipated.[41] When Nomura and Kurusu delivered the Japanese declaration of war, they had no idea that hostilities had actually begun. Cordell Hull, the secretary of state, was well-informed. With icy contempt he dismissed the justification of Japanese action as a tissue of mendacity. He stated:

> I must say in all my conversations with you [Ambassador Nomura] during the last nine months I have never uttered one word of untruth. This is borne out absolutely by the record. In all my fifty years of public service I have never seen a document [the Japanese declaration of war] that was more crowded with infamous falsehoods and distortions on a scale so huge that I never imagined until today that any Government on this planet was capable of uttering them.[42]

The Japanese diplomats were motioned to leave without opportunity to reply.

The United States was now at war. In addressing Congress on 8 December, President Roosevelt spoke of an 'unprovoked and dastardly' attack on a day that would 'live in infamy'[43]. He observed in his fireside chat broadcast on the following day: '. . . we must face the fact that modern warfare, as conducted in the Nazi manner, is a dirty business. We don't like it and we didn't want to get into it. But we are in it and we are going to fight with everything we have got . . .'[44]. Roosevelt had been careful not to ask Congress for declarations of war on Germany and Italy also, as they were not, under the terms of the Tripartite Pact, formally required to come to the assistance of Japan. Nevertheless, he had made it quite clear what the United States government thought of nazism. The potential dilemma of the United States was resolved for Roosevelt when on 11 December Germany and Italy declared war on the United States. In fact, Hitler and Ribbentrop had been urging Japan to declare war on the United States by the end of November and had promised that Germany would also declare war upon the United States. The German decision was probably based upon the calculation that if Japan distracted the United States in the Pacific this would assist Germany in winning the battle of the Atlantic, essential if Britain was to be defeated. Moreover, if Japan could keep America occupied in the Pacific throughout 1942, this would help Germany defeat the USSR, after which Germany could turn her attention to the defeat of the United States and Britain. There is some support for this in that on 9 December, when Ribbentrop had last minute reservations about declaring war on the United States, Hitler stated: 'The chief reason is that the United States is shooting at our ships. They have been a forceful factor in this war and through their action have already created a situation of war.'[45]

There could for Roosevelt be only one outcome, total victory. In a radio broadcast on 15 December the President stated: '. . . having taken up arms in the defence of liberty, we will not lay them down before liberty is once again secure in the world we live in. For that security we pray; for that security we act – now and evermore.'[46] By December 1941 the world was truly at war; the result would set the political agenda for Europe and the world for the rest of the twentieth century. In this development, Britain's role as a world, or global, power had been very important. She formed the decisive connection between the two theatres of war. The United States could not afford to see Britain go down in Europe and the Atlantic and by the end of 1941 was to all intents and purposes at war with Germany. Equally, in the Far East, the fates of the two nations were entwined. During the course of the 1930s the situation in that region had increasingly assumed the form of a confrontation between Japan and the United States, but the community of interest between the Anglo-Saxon powers was reflected in the fact that they were simultaneously attacked by Japan, albeit the United States more ambitiously and spectacularly at Pearl Harbor and the Philippines, while the British possessions of Malaya, after a landing at Kota Bharu, and Hong Kong were also subjected to invasion and conquest (the bombardment of Kota Bharu commencing two hours earlier than the attack on Pearl Harbor). Britain's decision to resist Germany in September in 1939 and her continued survival had, however, been the critical factor in setting in train the events that led in December 1941 to total war.

10

Interpretation
and the Changing View

The horrors that are inevitably associated with the Second World War – the murder of six million Jews, the murder of millions of other innocent civilians whose only crime was not to be of German birth, the Bataan death-march and the cruelties of the Japanese prisoner-of-war camps – all of which were revealed in the war crimes trials at Nuremberg and Tokyo, made initial interpretation of the war's origins relatively simple. The peace-loving, liberal-capitalist states of the west that dominated the existing international structure, namely the Versailles and Washington systems, were attacked by three ruthless, expansionist states bent upon transforming that structure in their own interests. Had Neville Chamberlain not pursued the policy of appeasement, had France been more resistant, had American opinion not been so isolationist, events might have occurred differently. There might not even have been a war!

For the first fifteen years of the post-war period this version of the origins of the Second World War was the one that commanded respect. Indeed it was the only one. It was lent distinguished authority by British writers such as Sir Lewis Namier and Sir John Wheeler-Bennett.[1] But, although these men were accomplished historians, their analyses of the war's causes were affected by personal involvement[2]: they were too political, too judgemental. Their writings, as far as Britain was concerned, were infused with a sense of guilt and British official policy was easily condemned as crass and craven. But these accounts were simplistic too, totally ignoring, as they did, the threats to Britain's extra-European interests. What also agitated these men was a fear that another war-guilt controversy might divert American opinion away from the justice of Britain's case. Their works, therefore, exhibited an exaggerated and irrational Germanophobia that excoriated the Germany of Weimar as much as that of Hitler. This was no less true of A. J. P. Taylor, whose book, *The Course of German History* was clearly blemished by an overt anti-German bias.[3] In 1961, however, it was to be Taylor who was to shatter the cosy assumptions of the post-war years when he published his book, *The*

Origins of the Second World War. Despite its many weaknesses,[4] here was an attempt at dispassionate historical enquiry: the study of the origins of the Second World War now ceased to be hysterical and became historical. Taylor was provocative. Hitler's aims were no different from those of other German statesmen: 'His foreign policy was that of his predecessors, of the professional diplomats at the foreign ministry, and indeed of virtually all Germans.'[5] Munich 'was a triumph for all that was best and most enlightened in British life; a triumph for those who had preached equal justice between peoples; a triumph for those who had courageously denounced the harshness and short-sightedness of Versailles . . .'[6]. Anthony Eden's credentials as an opponent of appeasement were questioned. Some of the shrillness that had previously governed investigation of the causes of the war surfaced in the reviews of Taylor's book. Writing in *Encounter*, Professor Hugh Trevor-Roper, who was later to discredit himself by authenticating the fraudulent *Hitler Diary* prior to its forensic examination, stated: 'This casuistical defence of Hitler's foreign policy will not only do harm by supporting neo-Nazi mythology: it will also do harm, perhaps irreparable harm, to Mr. Taylor's reputation as a serious historian.'[7]

Despite such criticisms, the appearance of Taylor's book marked the beginning of a stream of works on the causes of the Second World War, which, while no longer in full flood, shows no sign of abating. In many respects this research has confirmed Taylor's views; in others it has refuted them. It was the introduction of the Thirty Year Rule in Britain during the 1960s, which allowed access to the archives of the British state for the 1930s, and the increasing accessibility of private archives such as those held at Churchill College, Cambridge, and state and private archives in other countries that allowed many of Taylor's contentions to be subjected to further empirical research. Overall the picture of the events that led to war in 1939 and world war in 1941 is now a much more complex one than the monochrome version of the 1950s. If much of the old black and white image remains intact, substantial parts have been modified by various colourings that have given us a more profound perception of the problems that confronted those who acted on the international stage in the 1930s.

The European Axis

The centrality of Hitler and German policy to the origins of the war is little questioned by historians. It would be wrong, however, to suggest that there has been and is no debate about the nature of Hitler's foreign policy. Perhaps the most important issue relates to the question of whether or not Hitler had evolved a clear and coherent foreign policy by the time he assumed office and to which he was to adhere until his suicide in the bunker. The desultory nature of his writings as expressed in *Mein Kampf* and his bizarre views at first made it difficult for historians to construct what could be regarded as an integrated foreign policy programme. Opportunist, Machiavellian expansionism seemed the essential quality of the foreign policy of the Third Reich. There seemed to be no plan. Writing in 1952 Alan Bullock suggested that in

1933 Hitler could not have predicted how events would unfold; on the other hand, 'no man was more of an opportunist' than he and none knew better 'how to turn events to his advantage'. Hitler's foreign policy 'was the logical projection of that unappeased will to power, both in Hitler himself and in the Nazi Party, which, having conquered power in Germany, was . . . eager to extend its mastery further'. Still, Bullock did manage to identify two objectives: namely, the overthrow of Versailles and 'the realization of the Pan-German dream of a German-dominated Europe', with the conquest of Russia as the great prize on which would be built Hitler's New Order.[8] A. J. P. Taylor took broadly the same view, although characteristically in rather more extreme form. A master of the waiting game, Hitler's greatest attribute was 'patience'. There was no need for a plan: 'The greatest masters of statecraft are those who do not know what they are doing.' Hitler's utterances, as recorded in the Hossbach Memorandum, Taylor dismissed as 'day-dreaming': 'There was no concrete plan, no directive for German policy in 1937 and 1938. Or if there was a directive, it was to wait upon events.' Even so, Taylor had to concede that 'Eastern expansion was the primary purpose' of Hitler's policy.[9]

In 1960, however, Hugh Trevor-Roper published in a German academic journal an article entitled *Hitler's War Aims* which suggested that Hitler's foreign policy did have a structure to it. It was suggested that Hitler intended first to establish alliances with Italy and Britain. This would enable him then to neutralize, or crush, France. With Germany's western flank thus secure it would be possible for Hitler to proceed to his central aim of the acquisition of *Lebensraum* – living space – for Germany's surplus population. This would be obtained in the Ukraine at the expense of a defeated and subjugated Soviet Union.[10] This view was later elaborated further by two German historians, Eberhard Jäckel and Dietrich Aigner.[11] According to Jäckel: 'Even a cursory glance at the diplomatic and military history of the Third Reich demonstrates that this program served as an outline of those German policies that were defined by Hitler himself . . . It was, of course, not a timetable or even a detailed prospectus, but a definite and structured list of objectives, priorities and conditions'[12].

The elaboration of these theories was greatly aided by the revelation and publication at the end of the 1950s of *Hitler's Second Book* and other material emerging from the archives. It was now possible to establish a consistency in Hitler's views as presented in *Mein Kampf*. Within a comparatively short period of time another school of thought emerged that, while accepting in essence the policy programme first outlined by Trevor-Roper, ascribed to Hitler more far-reaching aims. Whereas Trevor-Roper and Jäckel saw Hitler's objectives as being primarily Europe-centred, this new body of scholars considered German mastery of the whole globe as his final aim. Once fortress Europa had been established, after the destruction of the Soviet Union, Hitler looked towards a further conflict with the United States which could be regarded as a struggle between Europe and America for domination of the world. It was the German scholars Andreas Hillgruber and Klaus Hildebrand who were the main advocates of this theory.[13] In recent years this 'globalist' standpoint has been questioned by the British historian Geoffrey

Stoakes, who, while accepting the existence of a programme and the attempt to implement it in the 1930s, doubts whether Hitler's ultimate goal extended beyond continental aspirations. He has written: 'In the absence of more concrete evidence . . . it must be concluded that in all probability Hitler did not seriously contemplate German world conquest. What he did hope was that Germany would replace Britain as the pre-eminent world power and the way to achieve this was to acquire *Lebensraum* in Eastern Europe and become master of continental Europe.'[14]

In general, all the writers referred to above belong to the 'intentionalist' school. That is to say, they accept that whether or not Hitler had a plan it was his dictatorial will that was the determining factor in the foreign policy of the Third Reich. On the other hand, by the end of the 1960s another group of writers had emerged who considered that governmental policy in the Third Reich was dictated by the structure of the state; that policy decisions were determined by the functioning of the principal elements of the system. The basis for the 'structuralist' or 'functionalist' school was provided by a number of studies that demonstrated the *polycratic* nature of the nazi state. By the end of the 1960s it was clear that the nazi system was not a monolithic, centralized, efficient dictatorship, but rather an administrative anarchy of competing agencies. Hitler, therefore, was characterized by some writers as a 'weak' dictator who rather than initiating policy responded to the pressures created by the system.[15]

By a different route, writers belonging to the structuralist school have reverted to the view Taylor put forward over thirty years ago. In the opinion of Hans Mommsen, the foreign policy of the Third Reich did not consist of the rigorous pursuit of 'established priorities': there was no plan. It was accepted that the foreign policy had an expansionist dynamic, but there was no ultimate aim. It was 'expansion without object'[16]. Like Mommsen, Martin Broszat could see little evidence of an overall foreign policy plan or scheme. *Lebensraum*, the critical objective of nazi foreign policy for intentionalist historians, becomes for Broszat an ideological metaphor esssential for the sustenance of the dynamic forces released by Hitler and the National Socialist movement. It was employed as an image that accounted for and justified unceasing foreign policy initiatives, unfettered by the normal restraints of diplomatic activity, until the image became attainable. The 'plebiscitary social dynamic' of national socialism, therefore, fed off itself, producing demands for incessant foreign policy activity until foreign policy was no longer susceptible to rational control, resulting in 'self-destructive madness.' In Broszat's view, the fact that Hitler never considered the problem of Poland in relation to the acquisition of *Lebensraum* in the Ukraine is evidence of the absence of concrete planning in Hitler's foreign policy.[17]

Finally, the late, Oxford historian, Tim Mason, took the view that the war that began in 1939 had its origin in the domestic-economic crisis in Germany in the late 1930s. He wrote: '. . . the timing, tactics and . . . also the strategic confusion of Hitler's war of expansion were decisively influenced by the politico-economic need for plunder, a need which was enhanced by the very wars necessary to satisfy it'[18]. According to Mason, while the revolutions that occurred in Europe during 1917 and 1919 indicated 'the domestic political limits of military expansionism,' for the national socialists, the stab-in-the-back concept negated those limits. Social cohesion, essential for successful military expansionism and imperialism, could be attained, from the national socialist viewpoint, by 'the liquidation of the German labour movement, the elimination of its leaders and functionaries, and the radical suppression of its organizations'. In this way, German society could be prepared for wars of conquest and expansion. The legacy of 1918 for national socialism, therefore, was 'a barbarous programme that promised, first, to suspend class conflict and then to eliminate it entirely by involving the whole nation in the building of a colossal imperial system'[19]. This did not mean, however, that Hitler wanted Germany to be involved in a major European war in 1939 with Britain as one of her major adversaries. On the other hand, it is evident that Mason believes that Hitler anticipated that Germany might become involved in a major European war by about 1943 by which time she would be prepared for it. The question to be answered in Mason's analysis is, therefore, why was it that Germany involved herself in a European war in 1939 that included Britain as one of her adversaries? Why was it that Hitler changed his timetable? The answer lies, according to Mason, in the fact that a number of internal problems manifested themselves in Germany after the acceleration of rearmament from 1936 onwards. Accelerated rearmament 'required resources far in excess of those available in (or to) Germany; and the excess of requirements over supplies was magnified by the way in which the regime and the markets distributed economic resources'. A commodity that was in very short supply was labour, particularly at the point where Germany had in June, 1938, and during the winter of 1938–9, decided further to force the pace of rearmament. Other problems confronting the economy were the threat of inflation, budgetary difficulties, the worldwide trade recession of 1937 which circumscribed Germany's export possibilities and hence her capacity to import necessary raw materials, and the condition of the agricultural sector beset as it was by severe labour shortages and strict price controls on agricultural produce. In Mason's opinion, there was one further important ingredient in the domestic crisis of Germany in the late 1930s that caused Hitler anxiety. Full employment and the relative prosperity of the late 1930s had the disadvantage of giving the workers too much potential power and might also cause them to 'lose what he imagined to be their sense of aggressive discipline, militarism and ideological fervour . . .'[20].

Mason concluded that the forced rearmament programme of the late 1930s intensified all the contradictions and difficulties in Germany's domestic situation; contradictions and difficulties that simply could not be resolved by technical adjustments. He wrote: 'In their essence they raised a fundamental problem of the dichotomy between means (the regimentation of people and resources) and ends (further rearmament), and thus tended to develop into a deep crisis of the power and legitimacy of the whole regime which necessarily spilled over into the sphere of foreign policy.' Because of the tensions in Germany's domestic economic and social-political situation Hitler, there-fore, decided that war, but not necessarily a European war, should come sooner rather than later.[21] Throughout 1938 and 1939 Hitler constantly courted the risk of war; wanted war rather than the Munich settlement.[22] Consequently, it seems that Hitler had 'come to see the need for plunder through military conquest as a means of breaking the chains of pressing immediate bottlenecks and dangerous policy choices'[23]. Some substance is lent to these contentions by evidence which shows that without the 1.5 million foreign workers and 1.3 million prisoners of war who were employed in German industry and agriculture as cheap or slave labour in June 1941, Germany would either have lost the war, or, to have continued it, would have had to impose the full burdens of the war economy on the German workers themselves with all that that would have implied for future social stability. By June 1941, 'it was clear that the German war economy would have collapsed in 1939/40 if the occupied areas had not been looted of raw materials, foodstuffs, war *matériel* and production capacity, or if the Soviet Union had not delivered vital supplies.'[24]

Undoubtedly, the work of Mason and the other structuralist historians has enriched historical knowledge of the functioning of the Third Reich and contributed much to a more precise understanding of conditions within it, but there is a difficulty in demonstrating precisely how those conditions impacted on the formulation of foreign policy. In fact, there is hardly any evidence to show that they did. Mason himself throughout his analysis admits the paucity of the documentary base for some of his conclusions. Thus, '. . . the sources do not conclusively prove that the political leadership *deliberately* used the tactic of deferring expansion of its dictatorial powers on the home front until some event in the international arena offered a propagandistically useful pretext . . .'[25]; on the relationship between the domestic situation and the decision for aggression and expansion, '. . . the sources on which to base an interpretation of his [Hitler's] view of the problem are skimpy . . .'[26]; and, in respect of the same issue, 'the documentation is neither ample nor unequivocal . . .'[27]. It seems, in fact, to be the case that it is almost impossible to show that Hitler was motivated in the way described by structuralist analyses. Finally, structuralist interpretations also involve a rather mechanistic view of human behaviour that as far as the Third Reich is concerned does not always conform with the known evidence.

A. J. P. Taylor had, of course, stressed the typical Germanness of Hitler's foreign policy. This was strongly challenged not least by Trevor-Roper.[28] In the year, however, following the publication of Taylor's book, Professor Fritz Fischer published his work *Griff nach der Weltmacht*,[29] which suggested a continuity in aim between the elites of the Second and Third Reichs. Fischer, whose views were innovatory mainly because they were presented in Germany for the first time,[30] argued that the German imperialists in 1914 had realized the mutual compatibility of continental and overseas expansion in their quest for world empire. In the introduction to his book, Fischer wrote that he hoped the work would provide 'pointers to fields wider that its own, for it indicates certain mental attitudes and aspirations which were active in German policy during the First World War and remained operative later. Seen from this angle, it may serve as a contribution towards the problem of the continuity of German foreign policy from the First World War to the Second.'[31] Taylor, therefore, may be said to have been the pioneer of the theory of the continuity of German history from 1871 to 1945, now an accepted element in the literature on the subject of modern German history.[32]

If Germany's role in the origins of the Second World War has given rise to varying interpretations, often held with vitriolic passion, the same cannot be said for her European partner in the Axis, Italy. Nevertheless, the passage of time and the revelation of fresh documentary material has helped to give a rather more complete picture of Italian foreign policy under Mussolini. It is clear that Mussolini was able, and from the beginning, to exploit the resentment felt in Italy at her treatment by other powers, particularly at the Paris Peace Conference. This led to a revisionist posture, which inevitably and from an early stage elevated the importance of Italy's relations with Germany as a means of counterbalancing the British and the French. As early as 1923 Mussolini proposed an Italo-German alliance.[33] Moreover, to further Italy's interest in Germany, the Italian government patronized German nationalist organizations throughout the 1920s, including the developing nazi movement. The latter was of particular importance because of the esteem in which it held the fascist movement and because of its renunciation of the Germans of the South Tyrol in the interests of close Italo-German relations.[34]

With Hitler's accession to the chancellorship in Germany, Mussolini hoped to maintain his revisionism and to control that of Germany within the Four Power Pact which he proposed. He hoped thereby to short-circuit the League of Nations and create a new body for regulating the relations of the European Great Powers. The German revisionism that mattered most to Italy related to Austria and the Brenner frontier between Italy and Austria. Austria was an Italian sphere of influence, which Hitler clearly intended to incorporate into the Reich. The murder of the Austrian chancellor, Dollfuss, in 1934 and the associated attempted nazi *coup* greatly alarmed Mussolini and drove him back towards the democratic powers. As, however, research has shown, it also prompted him to embark upon the expansionist war in Ethiopia that eventually and paradoxically was to lead to Italy's Axis alignment with Germany. What now seems clear is that Mussolini in the wake of the Dollfuss assassination decided to take advantage of what appeared as a favourable moment in the European situation to achieve a spectacular imperial success in Abyssinia before Germany could resume a threatening posture regarding Italy's interests in Austria. What becomes strikingly apparent in, for example, Esmonde Robertson's, *Mussolini as Empire Builder*, is that the Italian government made a thorough assessment of the position in Europe prior to attacking Ethiopia and concluded that a more suitable moment for the realization of this ambition was unlikely to recur.[35] What also emerges from research is the degree to which Mussolini's adventure was provoked by the development of social unrest in Italy as fascism lost its reforming impetus after 1930 and as the effects of the depression began to be felt. In these circumstances the cult of the Roman Empire was used as a means of mobilizing opinion behind the government. The fascist government would now preside over a third Roman Empire in succession to that of the Caesars and the Popes; militarism and imperialism would now become the main features of the regime rather than fascist social transformation.[36]

It is also evident in the literature that from the middle of the 1930s onwards Social Darwinian concepts increasingly infused Mussolini's attitude towards the international situation. Italy would side with the strongest power, which in the 1930s appeared to be Germany. Mussolini had no moral objection to war. When Mussolini stayed out of the war in 1939 it was the lack of economic resources and a deficient fighting machine that principally deterred him. Mussolini's anguish at this state of affairs impelled him thereafter to look for an opportunity to participate in the conflict which Germany's easy victories in the spring of 1940 provided. As Mussolini observed: 'Italy cannot remain neutral for the entire duration of the war without resigning her role, without reducing herself to the level of a Switzerland multiplied by ten.'[37] This was not a position shared by his advisers who tended on the whole to favour neutrality. Among these was Count Ciano whose perception of the war that started in 1939 was very different from Mussolini's. Mussolini thought the war would be of short duration, but Ciano had grasped perhaps more fully than most the implications of Britain's decision to resist. He wrote: 'I am not a military man. I do not know how the war will develop, but I know one thing – it will develop and it will be long, uncertain, and relentless. The participation of England makes this certain. England has made this declaration to Hitler. The war can end only with Hitler's elimination or the defeat of Britain.'[38]

The European Democracies

Ciano's comment in his diary would not have been a very apt one to many of his contemporaries in Britain. The Italian foreign minister's perception was of a Britain determined to resist and to overthrow Hitler by means of a long war of attrition, that is to say, a world war. Ciano might, of course, have been uncertain of a British victory, but he was by no means certain of a German one. This is a far cry from the perception that many of Neville Chamberlain's critics in Britain had of British policy at this time and were to maintain until he was compelled to resign in 1940. Chamberlain, the author of the cowardly policy of appeasement, had been forced into war; his government's conduct of that war was stigmatized as defeatist. The most cogent and sophisticated presentation of that view came in 1964 when Martin Gilbert and Richard Gott published The Appeasers.[39] Yet within a few years the views expressed in it became rapidly outmoded. Indeed in the following year Professor Cameron Watt wrote in The Political Quarterly an article entitled 'Appeasement: The Rise of a Revisionist School' in which he referred to the orthodox view of British policy in the 1930s as now being 'definitely on trial'. As he pointed out, the view of appeasement still current in the 1950s was largely based upon an assessment of it that had crystallized to some extent before 1939 and certainly before the documentation used later to buttress it became available. On the other hand, the diaries of the former US secretary of the treasury, Henry Morgenthau, the memoirs of the former Canadian high commissioner, Viscount Massey, and even the memoirs of Lord Avon (Anthony Eden) all made it clear that the image of Neville

Chamberlain as a pro–German dupe, ignorant of foreign affairs, was now rather less easy to sustain.[40]

By 1966 Martin Gilbert himself began to withdraw from the position he had held in 1964. In a book entitled, *The Roots of Appeasement*, he illustrated that appeasement could no longer be treated as a peculiar characteristic of the government of Neville Chamberlain. Appeasement now became rather the objective of all British governments from the time of the Peace Settlement of 1919. Gilbert, however, asserted that Chamberlain was wrong to continue to apply it during the period of his premiership.[41] Two years later Keith Robbins published *Munich 1938*. Conventional in style and bland in its judgements, the author's intentions marked a change of emphasis compared with previous writing. His was an attempt to examine the development of Munich without the encumbrance of the notion of appeasement; to see Munich in the context of fifty years of Anglo–German relations. He also indicated the identity of view that existed between the appeasers and the so-called anti-appeasers and was right to assert that at the heart of Munich, at least from the British side, lay 'the desire to avoid another war' between Britain and Germany, rather than the desire to achieve peace at any price. Perhaps the author himself most succinctly assessed the importance of his work when he wrote that it was a 'transitional book', that appeared 'to say farewell to the preoccupations and prejudices of the years since 1945 but' left 'open the future direction of research and criticism'[42].

What made it possible for revision to assume a pace and variety that could not have been imagined at the time A. J. P. Taylor's work appeared was the introduction of the Thirty Year Rule in 1968. Throughout the 1970s the gap that existed in the published documents relating to British foreign policy during the 1930s was gradually filled until by 1980 it was possible to analyse with great accuracy British foreign policy in the years between 1934 and 1938. This was particularly useful for discrediting the role that Anthony Eden had cast for himself as a leading anti-appeaser.[43] Indeed by 1971 a now little quoted, but excellent book, by Neville Thompson, *The Anti-Appeasers*, illustrated how inappropriate the appeaser/resister concept was. In many respects there was much more that united the appeasers and anti-appeasers than divided them.[44] What became strikingly evident was that between 1935 and his resignation in 1938, Anthony Eden played a central part in the formulation of the appeasement policy. Moreover, he not only collaborated with Neville Chamberlain in this but allowed the latter, even when chancellor of the exchequer, to play a dominant, if not the dominant, role.[45]

The rehabilitation of Neville Chamberlain began with the publication in 1975 of Maurice Cowling's *The Impact of Hitler: British Politics and British Policy, 1933–1940*.[46] This was a curiously constructed work which sought to interpret British foreign policy in the context of party politics, but it did stress the responsible nature of Chamberlain's policy as one designed to safeguard British interests and to match British commitments and resources. But Cowling's work was not merely significant for what it said about *appeasement* and Neville Chamberlain, it was also significant for what it implied about the decision to go to war in 1939 and, secondly, Churchill and the decision to continue the war in 1940. At the beginning of the 1970s, the Cambridge historian, Corelli Barnett, published *The Collapse of British Power*. In this work, he indicated just how parlous Britain's position was in the summer of 1940 after the fall of France, when the 'assets and liabilities of British power were subjected to the searching audit of war'. The reality was that there was 'an immense disparity' between the land, naval and air forces available for the defence of the British Empire compared with the resources available to Britain's actual and potential opponents. The empire could scarcely defend itself: the combined 'white' population of the dominions, numbering some twenty millions, in terms of naval strength, disposed of only eleven cruisers and twenty destroyers, compared with Britain's twelve capital ships, seven aircraft carriers and fifty cruisers provided from the resources of a population of fifty million. Furthermore, because of uneven and inadequate economic development, the empire could not provide all the resources and strategic raw materials required by Britain, while the dominions and India remained 'almost wholly dependent on British industry for the equipment of their armed forces'. Inevitably, Britain was forced to rely upon the resources of the United States. Barnett stated:

> Unlike Nazi Germany, which could wage war out of the resources of her own industry and the skills of her own technology, or out of the extra resources of countries her armies could conquer, Britain had to turn to American industry and American technology.[47]

There were, though, alternatives. Britain could have accepted the Nazi domination of Europe and made as favourable a peace with Germany as possible, or Britain could have fought a limited war 'commensurate with Britain's reserves of gold and dollars; and by holding a judicious balance between the industrial resources devoted to war and those devoted to paying for it . . . by exports'. Such a strategy would not, of course, have brought about the defeat of Hitler, but would perhaps have held the ring until more friendly and powerful states were compelled to join in on Britain's side. As Barnett observes, however, peace with Hitler was unthinkable while Britain herself remained undefeated and the notion of a limited war was never entertained. Instead, under Churchill's leadership Britain elected in the summer of 1940 to fight for 'victory' by employing means of which she did not dispose. 'Victory' over Hitler in these circumstances would, though, not be 'synonymous with the preservation of British power'. On the contrary, Barnett argues, the decision to wage such a war was a deliberate sacrifice of Britain's 'existence as an independent power . . .'; a decision to become an 'American satellite warrior-state . . .'. He concludes:

> Churchill's policy therefore provided the Americans with the opportunity firstly, of prospering on British orders, and secondly, of humbling British world power, a long-cherished American ambition. From 1940 to the end of the Second World War and after, it was America, not Russia, which was to constitute the lurking menace to British interests which Churchill, in his passionate obsession with defeating Germany, failed to perceive.[48]

It is clear, therefore, that the war that Britain continued to prosecute in 1940 was, in Barnett's opinion, not one that conformed with Britain's long term interests. The British were obsessed with 'honour', the Americans with long term calculation. Implicit in Barnett's analysis was the view that war in 1940 might not have been the best option.

Cowling's book, when it appeared, endorsed Barnett's view of the damage to Britain's world power position occasioned by the decision to fight on and sought to explain how Britain became involved in such a ruinous war from which she could not escape. In terms of domestic politics the problem was that during the 1930s foreign policy became central and 'the form that party conflict took'. From the point of view of the government the fundamental imperative was to keep Labour, which by the middle of the 1930s was showing signs of revival, out of office. Thus in 1935 the national government of Baldwin successfully used support for the League of Nations during the Abyssinian crisis as a means of registering an overwhelming victory in the general election of November of that year. The scandal created by the Hoare–Laval Plan blighted this electoral success, but once he succeeded Baldwin as prime minister, Neville Chamberlain hoped to restore the prestige and credit of the government through a combined policy of appeasement and rearmament. This design was, however, wrecked by Hitler's annexation of Bohemia. By this time an election was due in just over eighteen months and it was perceived by the Conservative leadership, and particularly the foreign secretary, Lord Halifax, that it would be necessary to get tough with Hitler in order to defeat Labour. Chamberlain was, therefore, compelled to pursue a policy of staunch resistance to Hitler which was to lead to a ruinous war, his fall from office and the succession to the premiership of Winston Churchill. Chamberlain fell from power because, after the German occupation of Prague, he had become a 'victim of the fateful collision between a war policy embarked upon in order to restore "honour" to the "Conservative cause" and the damage war would do to the structures the "cause" was intended to protect'[49]. Of Churchill's assumption of the premiership, Cowling was scathing:

> What he [Churchill] had done was creatively opportunistic, uniting hopes and fears which had nothing in common and arriving, through Hitler's instrumentality, where he would have wanted to arrive [the premiership] whether Hitler had shown the way or not. He stood, however, for nothing in particular except the prosecution of a war which was not to be prosecuted and the preservation of an Empire that was not to be preserved.[50]

But it was not just the empire and Britain's world position that was delivered a mortal blow by the decision to fight for 'victory'. What also was encompassed was 'the murder of pre-1941 mentalities'. The political conflict of the 1930s had been to a degree generational: the phasing out of politicians in their sixties, the phasing in of politicians in their thirties and forties. Hitler and Mussolini were locked 'in hostile embrace' by the younger generation and used to discredit the previous generation until success obliged them 'to face up to the crisis which hostility had helped to create'[51]. From May 1940 traditional conservatism was a discredited force and the war was directed by a leadership of a consensus of the centre under the direction of Winston Churchill. Ultimately, the war brought about not only the loss of empire, but also the demise of non-socialist society in Britain. The war and the British politicians who prosecuted it were the midwives of the welfare state.

Whereas the lack of wisdom in fighting on in 1940 was implicit in Barnett's analysis, Cowling was much more explicit. Broadly, Cowling claimed, Chamberlain's policy of appeasement had been correct until Munich. An isolationist foreign policy coupled with rearmament would have been adequate for the protection of British interests and would have preserved the empire, because Hitler posed no threat at all to British interests. At Munich, however, Britain had agreed to participate in a guarantee of the rump Czechoslovak state in order to induce the Czechs and the French to accept the Munich Agreement. This was the fatal step because thereafter Britain was increasingly locked into the position of guarantor of the East European map, thereby abandoning a principle tenet of British foreign policy since the days of Palmerston. This was particularly true of the months succeeding the Prague *coup* in March 1939. Continued isolation would have avoided the questionable duty of going to war over Poland. Cowling wrote:

> Hitler may have wanted to destroy the British Empire. But this was not obvious then and it is far from obvious now. It is at least as likely that he aimed primarily to fulfil promises about Germany's economic and world role and was compelled to attack Britain only by British action in May [May Crisis] and September 1938. Even if it is assumed that his aims were from the start to 'purify' Germany, destroy Russia and colonize the Ukraine, that suggests nothing about his attitude to Britain.
>
> It may be that Hitler was the 'beast from the abyss' whom Britain had a duty to destroy. It may be that victory over Russia would have been followed by an attack upon the West. It is possible to deny the duty, to question the sequence or to believe that success, or failure to succeed against Russia, would have affected the character of the regime in Germany . . .[52]

The message in this opaque prose is simple. It was not axiomatic that Britain should go to war in 1939 and continue as a belligerent in 1940.

In his biography of Anthony Eden, David Carlton, suggested strongly that Britain probably could have obtained from Hitler in June 1941 satisfactory terms for a compromise peace. During the last few days of May 1940, as Hitler's armies were rampaging through Western Europe, the possibilities of peace with Hitler were examined by the British cabinet. At one meeting Lord Halifax supported by Neville Chamberlain argued that Britain had little to lose in joining with the French and asking Mussolini to broker peace terms, which could always be rejected if found to be unsatisfactory. Churchill, however, thought it most unlikely that Britain could accept any terms that Hitler would offer, although, according to Neville Chamberlain, if Britain could get out of the jam she was in 'by giving up Malta and Gibraltar and some African colonies he [Churchill] would jump at it.' The cabinet minutes confirm Chamberlain's record of the event. If peace could be made with Hitler on the basis of the restoration of the former African colonies and 'the overlordship of Central Europe' that would be worth considering, but Churchill doubted if this was what Hitler had in mind. On the basis of this evidence, Carlton concluded that Churchill was not opposed in principle to a settlement with Hitler, but thought that decent terms would not be on offer.

Moreover, he considered Churchill's judgement to have been been faulty: 'For the Führer may well have been interested in establishing a neutral West that would leave him a free hand in the East.' In Carlton's estimation, a compromise peace in 1940 probably collapsed not because of Churchill's determination and resolve, but because of 'a mere failure of communication between London and Berlin . . .'[53].

Carlton's biography of Eden, published in 1981, was followed in 1989 by an article which made it clear that he regarded Britain's decision to go to war in 1939 as a fundamental mistake that stemmed from Chamberlain's failure to call a general election in the autumn of 1938 in the wake of his Munich success. For Carlton, this was 'probably the single most important blunder of [Chamberlain's] entire premiership'. Had he called an election then he would undoubtedly have been returned with a massive majority and for the foreseeable future been able to pursue foreign policy without an eye to its electoral consequences. In an analysis that owes much to the Cowling model, Carlton emphasizes the pressures that were on Chamberlain after the Prague *coup* to alter his policy given the imminence of a general election in 1940. On 17 March 1939, Harold Nicolson wrote in his diary: '. . . the feeling in the lobbies is that Chamberlain will either have to go or completely reverse his policy . . . All the tadpoles are beginning to swim into the other camp . . . The idea is that Halifax should become Prime Minister and Eden Leader of the House.' In this way Chamberlain was obliged to pursue the policy of guaranteeing the states of Eastern Europe with the critical Polish guarantee being given unilaterally on 31 March 1939. Ultimately, Britain went to war for no tangible advantage to herself, the only beneficiaries being the Tory dissidents, or glamour boys, and the Soviet Union. The policy of guarantees, Carlton argues, 'greatly increased Stalin's options and made it likely that the war, initially at least, would be between Germany and the Western Powers rather than between Germany and the Soviet Union'[54].

In 1989 John Charmley published what is perhaps the most complete defence of Neville Chamberlain's reputation to date under the title, *Chamberlain and the Lost Peace*. The main body of the book contained nothing that was exceptionable and indeed said nothing that was startlingly new. The argument that the policy of *appeasement* was justified to the last because Britain's involvement in war with Germany would be ruinous as winner or loser was perfectly reasonable. Had Chamberlain been dealing with a normal statesman in Hitler, not only would there have been much to commend *appeasement*, but the policy would in all probability have been crowned with success. That Hitler was not normal was, of course, only ultimately to be verified through the empirical process of diplomacy and maybe Chamberlain deserves credit rather than condemnation for that. What, though, comes across in the opening and closing pages of the book is the sense that for Britain the war itself was a mistake. Thus:

> Chamberlain saw no gains for Britain in another war, and, despite the pious assumptions of British historians, it is by no means clear that the results of the Second World War were commensurate with the sacrifices it entailed. The old balance between the fascist and communist Powers on the continent was tipped decidedly in favour of the latter, whilst the economic and diplomatic founda-

tions of the British Empire received a mortal blow; nor was the lot of the Poles, on whose behalf war was declared, improved. The world was handed over to a Manichean struggle between America and Russia; was this whither a thousand years of British history were tending?[55]

In defending the reputation of Sir Nevile Henderson, Britain's ambassador in Berlin from May 1937 until the outbreak of war, Charmley also implied that Hitler's Germany represented no threat to British interests. Henderson was a notoriously bad appointment who, in his zeal to ensure the success of *appeasement*, tended to become an apologist for Hitler's Germany. Within the British foreign office, his views were quickly discredited. Charmley, however, argued that it 'is by no means self-evident' that these views were deserving of the 'almost universal and dismissive condemnation which they received . . .'[56]. Moreover, he quoted *in extenso* from Henderson's memorandum of 10 May 1937 to show why Henderson's opinions, although dismissed in the foreign office, were not so easily discounted elsewhere in Whitehall and why Chamberlain had confidence in the ambassador. Among other things, Henderson stated that, although Germany was evidently 'ruthless and troublesome', there was no reason why, provided Germany did not trample too openly on the 'vital principles of the League of Nations', engage in overseas and naval rivalry with Britain, or deliberately threaten Britain from the air, 'she should perpetually constitute a danger of war for us'. There was 'no British possession' on which Germany encroached. According to Henderson, the aims of German policy – the *Anschluß*, absorption of the German minority in Czechoslovakia, expansion in the east of Europe, and the reacquisition of the former colonies – would not 'injure purely British national interests'[57].

It is also clear that it is not simply the loss of empire that Charmley bemoaned. When Chamberlain fell so did a tradition. Under Churchill the country lost its 'greatness' and the Conservative Party was 'never the same again . . .'[58]. Out went the social and economic Conservatism of the 1930s and in came the welfare of the 1940s. The war spelt, therefore, not only the end of the British Empire, but also that 'of the *ancien régime* whose interests he [Chamberlain] and his [Conservative] party embodied'[59]. In a subsequent work, *Churchill: The End of Glory*, Charmley was more explicit about the 'failure of statesmanship,' if not in 1939, certainly in 1940 when Churchill and the rest of the cabinet decided to fight on. He wrote: 'Churchill's leadership was inspiring, but at the end it was barren, it led nowhere, and there were no heirs to his tradition.'[60] Furthermore: 'Churchill stood for the British Empire, for British independence and for an "anti-Socialist" vision of Britain. By July 1945 the first of these was on the skids, the second was dependent solely upon America and the third had just vanished in a Labour election victory.'[61] The Americans 'emerged as the receivers of a bankrupt concern' and Britain became an American protectorate. The war, however, had been fought to maintain Britain's independence and Britain's new status could be 'of little comfort to many Englishmen.' The Conservative politician, historian and diarist, Alan Clark, lent his authority and prestige to Charmley's views in an article in *The Times* claiming that peace could have been obtained from the Germans on 'reasonable' terms in 1940 and 'excellent' terms a year later, an opinion that was robustly rebutted by Professor D. C. Watt in luridly 'nautical' language, in an interview published in the *Observer*.[62]

The works of these revisionist writers are immune to the morality of the decisions to fight in 1939 and fight on in 1940. Everything is interpreted purely in terms of what would have been in the best interests of Britain in the sense of *maintaining and improving Britain's imperial position*. That Britain won the war is irrelevant because she would inevitably lose, and did lose, the peace. The war, therefore, could not have been fought to serve Britain's interests and could not, therefore, be justified. In terms of morality, grappling with nazi Germany, according to a senior journalist who has worked for many years for a right-wing, British newspaper group, did not save a single Jew. Moreover, in the view of the same source, however grotesque the nazi regime was in the late 1930s and early 1940s, the radical figures of the years of political struggle would in the fulness of time, as in Franco's Spain, have been replaced by bureaucratic technicians and the system would thereby have been ameliorated.[63] And a regenerate national socialist regime, according to this line of thought, would no doubt have been a much more congenial international companion for Britain than the Soviet Union; in addition, would probably have destroyed the the USSR to the advantage of Britain and the interests of world capitalism.

The defence of Neville Chamberlain has, therefore, ultimately become bound up in a larger argument: one that is perhaps more political than historical and one that focuses upon Winston Churchill as the villain. Those who support this view argue in essence that once France fell in 1940 the war could no longer be won by Britain; that the decision taken by the government, headed by Churchill, to continue the fight in these circumstances bankrupted Britain and fatally damaged her world position; that the continuation of the war converted Britain into an American satellite; that the war ultimately meant Soviet and communist domination of Eastern Europe; and that the war and the ascendancy of Churchill meant the introduction of the welfare state and socialism into Britain.[64] Indeed, it is impossible to escape the nostalgia felt by these writers for the world of the 'pre-war Tory party, that supine rump of Blimps, Forsytes and Box-Benders who thought [according to one critic] to preserve their rents and dividends by giving "Mr. Hitler" a free hand in Central Europe'[65].

An examination, however, of this 'revisionist' thesis tends to show that the contentions of these writers are misconceived and unhistorical. First, was a peace on offer from Hitler in July 1940 that would have helped in averting Britain's comparative decline? The offer of peace that Hitler made in his *Reichstag* speech of 19 July 1940 was, in fact, not very specific. Moreover, given that Hitler proposed peace to Britain from the vantage point and *reason* of the conqueror, it could easily be construed that what he was proposing was surrender rather than a negotiated peace. In this respect, the 'magnanimous' peace that Hitler had concluded with France the previous month, which left only two-fifths of France independent and obliged her to return 100,000 political and racial (Jewish) refugees, was scarcely encouraging. It is the view of this writer that the terms that Hitler himself might have offered would probably have been comparatively generous, in that it is unlikely that Britain would have had to have compromised her empire, but undoubtedly Britain would have been asked to concede Germany's supremacy and ascendancy on the continent of Europe. It had, on the other hand, been an axiom of British foreign policy for many years to avoid any continental power gaining such an hegemonic position,[66] which would inevitably pose a threat to Britain's world and imperial position. A peace of this character, therefore, would have represented a considerable *volte-face* and would have been unthinkable. It is, however, arguable that Hitler's terms in 1940 would have been much more severe. The Führer was surrounded by anglophobe advisers, such as the foreign minister, Ribbentrop,[67] and the propaganda minister, Goebbels, in addition to which the whole of Germany had been made euphoric by the victories of 1940. In this situation, Hitler's scope for generosity might well have been very much restricted. What, however, is clear is that on the basis of the available evidence the 'revisionists' cannot demonstrate that Britain could have concluded a peace with Germany which would have *maintained and improved her imperial position*. Neither can they show that Hitler's word could have been trusted.

Secondly, would the British public have accepted a peace with Hitler's Germany? Could Winston Churchill have turned British opinion round? There were, of course, by the summer of 1940 those who would have made peace, but they did not constitute an organized lobby. Rather they were a disparate group of individuals. Within the cabinet, the foreign secretary, Lord Halifax, as the cabinet minutes show, clearly thought peace might be best. Within the foreign office, Rab Butler was of a like mind.[68] Moreover, the former prime minister, David Lloyd George, who never lost his illusions about Hitler,[69] was of the opinion that Britain should endeavour to obtain from Hitler an agreement that would preserve all that which Britain had gone to war to secure. He had, however, little support in parliament. In the country at large pro-fascist groups, such as Mosley's British Union of Fascists favoured peace, as did the Communist Party, following the Nazi–Soviet Pact. Furthermore, there were the pacifist activities of the Peace Pledge Union. None of these individuals and organizations, however, were representative of the balance of opinion in the country. Neville Chamberlain in October 1939 might well have informed one of his sisters that in a period of three days he received 1,860 letters out of a total of 2,450 pleading for an end to the war, but in the same month opinion polling showed that while 17 per cent of respondents favoured a negotiated peace with Germany, 77 per cent disapproved. The corresponding figures for February 1940 were 29 per cent for a negotiated peace, 61 per cent against. Despite this increase in the number favouring peace however, opinion continued to be overwhelming in its support for the war. Given that Winston Churchill had effectively been appointed as war leader in May 1940, quite apart from the loss of prestige he would himself have sustained in suing for peace, what credibility would he have had with a public determined to continue the war? So far the 'revisionists' have failed to show how this hurdle could have been negotiated. The fact of the matter was that Churchill shared the opinion of most Britons in respect of nazism: it was regarded as dishonest, duplicitous and considered to offend against all the normal canons of political liberty and decency. It was impossible to make peace with it.

It is, indeed, precisely this that the moral relativism of the 'revisionists' ignores. In July 1940 the British wanted to continue the war against the Third Reich because it was an horrendous political and social structure. It was utterly intolerable. In 1940 it was already evident that Nazi Germany had begun the racial reorganization of Europe: racially inspired policies were already in force in Poland and Bohemia and Moravia, and in 1940 70,000 French people were expelled from Alsace-Lorraine. Moreover, if it was not fully apparent in 1940 that time would never produce an amelioration of the nazi regime, it is now. The SS-trained bureaucratic technicians of the future were likely to have multiplied and magnified the palpable inhumanities of the nazi system rather than to have reduced and diminished them. As for the argument that Britain's belligerency did not save a single Jew, that is, of course, true of those unfortunate human beings who perished in the Holocaust that occurred between 1941 and 1945. It cannot, however, be proved that had Britain made peace with Germany that the position of the Jewish population would have materially improved. It is possible that the nazi regime would have attempted to solve the 'Jewish Problem' by deporting European Jewry to Madagascar. This, though, would not necessarily have been a humane alternative to the extermination camps of Auschwitz, Birkenau, Belzec, Sobibor and Treblinka. How was this island, with its own population, to cope with an influx of millions of deportees? How were they to be sustained and housed in this tropical island ghetto? The reality is that the 'Madagascar Solution' would have just as certainly condemned millions of dislocated Jews to torment, torture and death as the measures that were actually employed in the Holocaust. Had Britain made peace with Germany and had Germany carried out the Madagascar Plan, Britain would have been complicit in the atrocity. That Britain determined to finish the war, historically, meant that ultimately the racial state would be brought down, not least to the advantage of Britain.

In essence, the need to preserve Britain's perceived interests and the morality of the issue, rather than the interests of narrow electoral strategy, were what underlay the British decision to resist Hitler right from the destruction of Czechoslovakia in March 1939 onwards. On 18 March 1939 Lord Halifax told the British cabinet that Hitler was bent on 'world domination' and that Britain was the only state that could organize effective resistance to Germany. A united resistance was essential: 'Otherwise we might see one country after another absorbed by Germany.'[70] Some days later he stated to the cabinet foreign policy committee: 'We were faced with a dilemma of doing nothing or entering into a devastating war. If we did nothing this in itself would mean a great accession to Germany's strength and a great loss to ourselves of sympathy and support in the United States . . . if we had to choose between two great evils he favoured . . . going to war.'[71] These arguments were just as valid a year later. To have made peace with Hitler in 1940 would have had horrendous consequences for the future of Anglo-American relations. Had Germany then been left to conquer the USSR, Britain 'and her Empire' would have been left isolated against a greatly strengthened Germany. Had a German attack on the Soviet Union ended in a nazi defeat, Britain would have been left isolated against a Stalinized Europe. On this latter point, it is futile for the 'revisionists' to argue that Britain's decision to maintain her belligerency in 1940 in the long run was only of benefit to the Soviet Union, for it was not the belligerency of Britain that led to the Sovietization, or Stalinization, of Eastern Europe, but Hitler's decision to attack the USSR in June 1941.

Peace with Germany in 1940 would have meant abandoning all Britain's war aims. Hitlerism would not have been overthrown; democracy in Western Europe would have been finished for the foreseeable future. It would have meant cohabiting with a regime that was economically reordering Europe ruthlessly in Germany's interests; a regime embarked upon Europe-wide plunder and exploitation. It would have meant associating with a regime whose inclinations were incompatible with Britain's long-term interests. It would not have preserved the empire. Hitler, even on the dubious assumption that his 'guarantee' was worth anything, could not have 'guaranteed' an empire that had already begun to feel the impact of centrifugal forces and was beginning to fall apart in the 1920s and 1930s. In the early 1940s the reality was that Britain could only preserve her interests and what was left of her 'glory' by tying herself to the United States.[72] Perhaps it is best to leave the last word on this to Lord Dacre (Professor Trevor-Roper), who cannot by any stretch of the imagination be described as a left-wing historian. Writing on the fiftieth anniversary of the defeat of the Third Reich, he wrote:

> Some historians have argued that we have nothing to celebrate: that the world would be a better place now if we had made peace with Hitler in 1941 and let him conquer Russia, leaving us to rule our empire, if we could, under his protection. Did he not repeatedly "guarantee" the British Empire? He would have given us good terms – for the time being. But when I think through the consequences, I cannot agree. Hitler made . . . 13 treaties of peace and alliance. He broke every one. A British Empire "guaranteed" beyond its natural term by his patronage is not an edifying prospect.
>
> We may have paid heavily for our ultimate victory; but who can deny that its consequences are better for the whole world, and more honourable for us, than that alternative; that we have a right to be proud, and a duty to give, and perhaps even to receive, thanks?[73]

As far as the rehabilitation of Neville Chamberlain is concerned the 'revisionist' defence of Chamberlain tends to vitiate the case for him rather than strengthen it. The case for Chamberlain must rest on grounds other than that he attempted to preserve the British Empire by avoiding war with Germany. The policy of appeasement, the objective of which he understood to be the achievement of a European and general settlement that would secure peace by replacing the Peace Settlement of 1919, was one that was endorsed and modified by the inner core of the cabinet over a period from 1935 onwards. It was also one that originally emanated from the foreign office with the full backing of its head, Sir Robert Vansittart. Secondly, it was Chamberlain, even while chancellor of the exchequer, who stopped the dithering that had characterized British policy towards Germany and gave it direction. Finally, it was Chamberlain as prime minister who led the attempt to engage the Germans in direct negotiations.[74] Even though this ultimately led to Munich, its aftermath was to show the futility of talking to Hitler.

At least one man in the cabinet perceived this. What is now very clear in the literature is the degree to which the foreign secretary, Lord Halifax, became responsible for abandoning appeasement and promoting resistance. His most recent biographer has described the respect that he commanded in the cabinet in the post–Munich period as 'astounding.' Furthermore, 'far from being . . . Chamberlain's faithful Sancho Panza, Halifax was the first politician in the Government to see what was happening and the major force in steering the way from an appeasing to a resisting tack'[75]. The significance of Halifax in the final year of peace was first underlined by Cowling, although he saw Halifax's decision to resist Hitler in the context of a need to resist the Labour Party in the period after the German occupation of Bohemia and Moravia. It is, though, now established that Halifax was moving towards resistance as early as November 1938 after the *Kristallnacht* atrocities and that this occasioned not a little friction with Chamberlain thereafter.[76] Indeed this verity cannot be avoided even in Charmley's eulogy of Chamberlain.[77]

Research has also emphasized the constraints imposed upon British foreign policy in the 1930s. Professor G.C. Peden has, for example, shown that the desire to encourage and maintain business confidence in the wake of the depression imposed limitations on spending on rearmament. The problem here was that too lavish expenditure on this sector might be good for shipbuilding, for example, but would unbalance the budget and generally undermine the civilian industrial base resulting in a run on sterling and political and social crisis.[78] Norman Gibbs' massive and magisterial history of British rearmament policy also stresses the limitations imposed by financial restraint, which was also conditioned by the need for Britain to be solvent if she went to war. Finance would be the fourth arm of defence in the long war of attrition it was expected Britain would have to fight.[79] Rearmament after 1937, when more money was made available, was also impeded, as Professor Shay has argued, by structural weaknesses in industry and the labour force which made it impossible to switch with the desired efficiency to the manufacture of armaments.[80] The fundamental problem regarding rearmament was, of course, the functioning of the British economy and this problem and its connection with British foreign policy in the 1930s is fully explored by Professor Gustav Schmidt in his *The Politics and Economics of Appeasement*. For Schmidt, appeasement is to be regarded as 'a form of preventive diplomacy which was to ensure that economic recovery should be absorbed neither primarily nor totally by preoccupation with rearmament, but should benefit the social services'[81].

Despite this evidence, a recent study of the foreign policy of the Chamberlain government by R. A. C. Parker has argued strongly that there were alternatives to the appeasement policy. The case is very convincingly argued on the ground that by the end of 1938 there was widespread support throughout the political spectrum in Britain, from Churchill on the right, through Lloyd George and the Liberals led by Sir Archibald Sinclair, to the Labour Party and Stafford Cripps on the left, for a policy of military encirclement of Germany that could have been effected under the League of Nations. Chamberlain rejected such a course, although he was compelled in the months following Munich 'to accept, in appearance, much of the alternative policy pressed on his government.' Under Chamberlain's leadership, however, 'effective deterrence' had been avoided and his 'powerful, obstinate personality and . . . skill in debate probably stifled serious chances of preventing the Second World War'[82]. The problem with this interpretation, however, is that it assumes that Hitler could have been stopped. If one accepts that he was determined to gain *Lebensraum* in the Soviet Union then war was bound to ensue sooner or later. Nevertheless, Parker's treatment of Chamberlain, although critical, is balanced and fair. Chamberlain was 'neither a coward nor a fool; he was neither ignorant nor idle. He was a cultivated, highly intelligent, hard-working statesman . . .'[83].

Intelligence also played a part in the course followed by British foreign policy. In a book which brilliantly reconstructs the intelligence picture the British government had of Germany in the 1930s, Wesley Wark illustrates the inaccuracies of this picture and the impact it had on policy. Preconceived ideas about German thoroughness and perceptions of German planning based upon British experience, caused the British intelligence services at first to underestimate the rate of German rearmament. After 1936, however, intelligence began to overestimate the rate of German military development; this and the construction of 'worst-case' scenarios painted a very gloomy picture with obvious consequences for diplomacy. By the end of 1938, however, confidence began to revive as the industrial intelligence centre began to reveal weaknesses in Germany's economic capacity to wage a long war. While the confidence that the industrial intelligence centre began to generate was perhaps a little misplaced, it was, nevertheless, an essential adjunct to the determination to resist in 1939.[84]

Closely connected with intelligence were propaganda and news management. Like intelligence, propaganda and news management have become essential adjuncts of modern government and the 1930s marked important developments in these areas which have been the focus of some important studies. According to the political journalist, James Margach, Neville Chamberlain was the 'first Prime Minister to employ news management on a grand scale'[85]. The object of this activity was to suppress opposition to the policy of *appeasement* and to facilitate its success. A critical figure in this process was George Steward, the head of the Press Office at 10 Downing Street. Through Steward the political journalists at Westminster, who constituted The Lobby, were gradually organized so that they became disseminators of the official line, rather than journalists competitively seeking after news and stories. Steward's briefing meetings became the principal source of a political correspondent's news. In this way, in the opinion of Richard Cockett, the author of *Twilight of Truth: Chamberlain, Appeasement & the Manipulation of the Press*: 'By September 1939, the press had become not so much watchdogs of democracy as the harlots of democracy – at every level forfeiting their independence for power and fortune . . .'[86]. The foreign office through its news department created a similar body of dependent foreign correspondents. This was mainly the work of Rex Leeper, the head of the department from 1935 onwards, whose role has been the subject of a study by Philip Taylor, entitled *The Projection of Britain: British Overseas Publicity and Propaganda 1919–1939*.[87] So successful was he that the veteran correspondent of the *Manchester Guardian*, Robert Dell, was moved to complain that 'the independence of the British Press will be destroyed, and so, as far as foreign policy is concerned, it will become merely a gramophone repeating the F.O. dope . . .'[88]. Leeper's view was that the news department's function ought to be, in addition to the supply of daily news, the education of the 'different organs of publicity along the lines of the foreign policy pursued by the Government'[89]. The news department, however, was also used as a vehicle for the imposition of Leeper's own priorities on the government, most notably during the Munich crisis when he announced that in the event of a German attack on Czechoslovakia that both Britain and the USSR would stand by France and her Czech ally.[90] This almost certainly brought about Leeper's removal from the news department and his temporary exile in the British Embassy in Bucharest. Paradoxically it was often claimed by those who served in the Chamberlain government that they had to pursue *appeasement* because they were constrained by public opinion. It was, however, a public opinion that they themselves contrived to create.

Finally, the impact of events in the Far East on British policy during the inter-war years was the subject of a number of studies during the 1970s.[91] These have recently been supplemented by a study by Antony Best, which clearly indicates how much Britain's dependence upon American goodwill in peace and war deprived her of any real room for manoeuvre in her relations with the Japanese Empire. The issue that divided Britain and Japan was not a moral one, but rather one of power 'and in particular power over the commercial destiny of China.' Once the Sino-Japanese War resumed in July 1937, there was a clear uncertainty about the future of Britain's position in China. Instead of remaining 'a market dominated by British capital,' China could become 'an adjunct of the Japanese Empire . . .' That, of course, was the import of Konoe's 'New Order in Asia' pronouncement of November 1938. From the British point of view matters were complicated further by the transparent inclination of the Japanese to side with the Axis group in Europe. Within the British treasury there was a predisposition to resolve the Far Eastern problem through an understanding with Japan. This was, however, frustrated by the realization of the impact of such an understanding on Britain's relations with the United States. Best writes:

> The American role was crucial in denying Britain flexibility. Washington hung over Britain's East Asia policy like some Victorian morality painting warning of the dire consequences of veering from the road of righteousness. There was a clear understanding in London that any attempt to arrive at a deal with Japan at the expense of China or any undercutting of the sanctity of the Nine Power Treaty would have serious repercussions in the United States which would threaten Anglo-American co-operation not only in East Asia but also in Europe. Britain knew that in a war with Germany it would at the very least require the benevolent neutrality of the United States, and this perception of the necessity to assure American support grew ever greater as the threat to Britain grew ever closer.

In addition, fear that the purpose of Soviet supplies to China might be not merely to drive the Japanese off the mainland, but also themselves, caused the British by the end of 1938 to step up their aid to the Chinese which inevitably tended to exacerbate relations with Japan.[92] For the British government the central problem was that however desirable improved relations with Japan were, the benefits would always be outweighed by the disadvantages.

The shock of the Nazi–Soviet Pact and the outbreak of war in Europe, which denied to the Japanese the possibility for the time being of an alliance with the Axis powers of an anti-Soviet character, theoretically provided an opportunity for improved Anglo-Japanese relations; but Britain's need to inhibit the ability of neutrals to trade with the Third Reich and her intensified control and consumption of the raw materials at her disposal, which in turn denied Japan access to them, were incompatible with good Anglo-Japanese relations in the long term. On her side Japan's determination to bring the war in China to a speedy end led to her demand in June 1940, when Britain's position in Europe became suddenly very precarious, that the Burma Road, through which Britain was supplying Chiang Kai- shek, be closed. This was a turning point in Anglo-Japanese relations, for, thereafter, Churchill was convinced that no lasting deal could be struck with Japan. This conviction was confirmed the following October when Japan adhered to the Tripartite Pact, placing her firmly in the Axis camp.[93] With the objective still of avoiding war, Britain now embarked upon a programme of deterrence through military planning and the co-ordination of economic sanctions with the other three members of the ABCD group, the Americans, the Dutch and the Chinese. Economic sanctions, though, merely stimulated increased Japanese aggression even before July 1941, when the United States dramatically upped the stakes with the freezing of Japan's assets and the prohibition of oil exports to her. It was, in fact, on 16 June 1941 that the Japanese Army and Navy demanded the occupation of southern Indo-China 'by the end of July so that Japan would have the option of a military advance later in the year if the present level of economic pressure had not ceased'[94]. From this point onwards there was a certain inevitability about the clash between Japan and the *status quo* powers, Britain and America, in East Asia which was compounded by Winston Churchill's 'dangerous underestimation of Japan's military capability and overestimation of the deterrent value of British and American forces in the region . . .'[95].

Best concludes, however, that it is perhaps unwise to apportion blame for the outbreak of war in the Far East, in the sense that Japan, as the aggressor, must be inevitably guilty. There was an 'arrogant assumption' on the part of Britain that the power structure in East Asia and the Pacific, which she had helped create and which provided her with advantage was 'the natural, moral order of things'. Thus, despite a willingness to reach an understanding with Japan, if one could be achieved, it was always frustrated by a reluctance to ignore the reality of Japan's rise and an inclination to believe that 'time could be made to stand still, that Britain's wealth could be held for perpetuity'; by a belief that the Japanese could be 'easily dismissed as unwelcome parvenus who did not know their proper place'. He writes:

The sheer complexity of the events . . . shows that the idea of Japanese guilt is hard to apply to the Pacific War – it was rather the result of the never-ending struggle between those who 'have' and those who 'have not'. This does, however, raise the issue of how far *status quo* powers should be responsible for the maintenance of peace. While recognizing the problems that hindered Britain at the time, there is surely a lesson to be drawn about the dangers of refusing to countenance managed change.[96]

There is undoubtedly much to commend this comment, not only in its relevance to Britain's role in the Far East, but also in respect of Britain's reception from 1870 until 1945 of the actuality of the implications of Germany's unification, the last ripples of which might be said to have manifested themselves in Britain's response to the recent reunification of Germany and which continue to reveal themselves in Britain's attitude towards the European Union.[97] What is certain though, is that two world wars have not inhibited the rise to dominance of Germany and Japan and neither have they interrupted Britain's decline.

Writing in English on French foreign policy prior to the outbreak of the Second World War is not as voluminous as that relating to Britain. This is probably because of the secondary role France played in the democratic camp in the events leading to the outbreak of war in 1939. Recent scholarship has, however, given us a better insight into the imperatives on which French foreign policy was based. The work of R. J. Young illustrates the perception of French weakness in respect of Germany that was widespread among France's military leadership. Were Germany to renew hostilities, France could only survive in alliance with Britain and hence the concept of the *war of long duration* to which French military planners were attracted throughout the inter-war years. France because of her inferior population resources in comparison with Germany and because her metallurgical industries were located near the German border would require an effective alliance with Britain. As Professor Young has written: '. . . the historian of France between the wars simply has to accept that the French sense of dependence on Britain has not been exaggerated'. Yet that sense of dependence was not founded on malaise and indifference, but rather upon a practical appreciation of the problems with which France was confronted.[98]

Nevertheless, a sense of decadence continues to pervade analyses of French policy in the 1930s. Indeed, it forms the underlying thesis of Professor Duroselle's work on the subject. Indecision and vacillation, he believes, were the basic characteristics of French policy. This stemmed from the domination of the French legislature over the executive which ensured chronic governmental instability. Moroever, the enormous toll of French lives during the First World War deprived France in the 1930s of men who might have matched the hour.[99] Duroselle's successor at the Sorbonne, René Girault, has added to his predecessor's views by suggesting that a shared perception of French weakness among France's policy makers lay at the root of decadence, in conjunction with an ideologically divided society.[100]

On the other hand, Duroselle himself does not dissent from the view that by 1939 the mood of resistance in France was strong. The French under the leadership of Daladier resisted British pressure for French concessions to Italy as a means of luring the latter away from Germany. Moreover, in the protracted, desultory and ultimately abortive negotiations with the USSR in the summer of 1939, it was increasingly the French ministers, Daladier and Bonnet, who made the running.[101] This resistance was conducted in the context of improved national economic performance and a growing mood of popular opposition to German demands. In an opinion poll taken in the wake of the Munich Conference, it was demonstrated that some seventy per cent of the French population favoured joint Anglo-French opposition to any further demands from Germany. Moreover, thirty-seven per cent of those polled felt that Munich had been a mistake. By June 1939 seventy-six per cent thought that France should go to war with Germany if she attempted to seize Danzig by force.[102]

In some respects it is difficult to escape the impression that the French leadership deliberately opted for a policy of appeasement and in so doing disregarded the strengths of France's position that could have been used in constructive opposition to the Third Reich. This is the theme of Professor Adamthwaite's work. He has argued that the French were not merely coerced into appeasement by the British, but pursued such a course with independence and vigour. When France finally decided to opt for a mood of defiance it was too late. As Professor Adamthwaite puts it:

> Although in urgent need of repair in 1937–8 the alliances with Czechoslovakia, Poland and the Soviet Union still stood. The French army remained a formidable force with more trained reserves than the German army, and the Maginot Line was superior to the then unfinished Siegfried line. In 1939 France produced more fighter aircraft than Germany and over twice as many tanks . . . Different leaders could have given France the upsurge of energy needed to pursue firmer policies towards Germany and Britain. A vigorous effort to repair France's alliances and to establish a full partnership with Britain would have altered Hitler's perception of the international scene. French statesmen feared that resistance to Germany would only deepen internal divisions and weaken yet further France's international position. Daladier's discovery in March 1939 that firmness to friends and foes alike brought personal popularity and a measure of national unity came too late to save France from war and defeat.[103]

In his most recent work, Professor Adamthwaite has restated this case with renewed vigour. He does not see the transformation of victor France in 1918 to vanquished France in 1940 as an inevitable process. He agrees that France paid a heavy price for her victory in 1918, but this did not mean that she was doomed thereafter always to wait upon the initiatives of others and to assume a role of dependence. After 1945 both Germany and Japan recovered spectacularly from the devastation of defeat; equally spectacular was the revival of France under de Gaulle. France, in the view of Adamthwaite, could have recovered just as dramatically from the devastation of victory in 1918. She did not do so because her integration of foreign policy-making and defence policy-making processes was deficient. Neither did the liberal democratic traditions of the Third Republic aid the modernization of the governmental process in this respect. This meant that rivalries between the civilian and military branches of government, suspicion of a strong executive branch of government, governmental instability and mistrust between departments all contrived to deprive ministers and their advisors of 'the proper means to judge priorities and devise solutions'. Moreover, leading French politicians lacked qualities of decisive leadership: Clemenceau was unable to maximize France's position at the Paris Peace Conference; Poincaré's mishandling of the Ruhr occupation led to the failure to establish French hegemony in Europe; French financial strength in 1931 could have provided the leverage on which to pursue a policy of conciliation with Germany, but the 'conservative, unimaginative, overcautious outlook of political and military chiefs blocked concessions', essentially revision of the Treaty of Versailles, necessary to make such a policy successful. Once Hitler was installed in power, no French leader could match him.[104]

Even so, argues Adamthwaite, French leaders could after 1933 have wrested the initiative and maintained French power: 'A policy might have been devised which upheld liberal values and the desire for a peaceful settlement, yet demonstrated determination to defend allies and interests.' To succeed it would have required effective alliances, military preparedness and a determination 'to make the *entente* with Britain work for France.' But, rather than capitalize upon Britain's 'need for a strong France,' the French 'deliberately fostered British tutelage in order to provide a fig leaf for disengagement from east central Europe.' The road to Vichy, though, was not direct: France could have confronted Germany successfully and resumed a role as 'an independent great power'. There was, however, no resolute leadership, no grand design and, above all, no 'self-confidence'. For Adamthwaite, the French crisis of the 1930s is fundamentally about lack of self-confidence. France's leaders simply could not say *merde* to the Germans, a quality which evidently endeared Clemenceau to the French Army in the First World War. Had they been able to do so to Hitler, Adamthwaite believes that the history of the world in the twentieth century might have taken a different course.[105]

The Peripheral Powers and Japan

France had traditionally sought security against Germany in the alliance with Russia. For most of the inter-war years, however, this was rendered impossible by the consequences of the revolution of 1917 and the founding of the USSR. Not until 1935 did France and the USSR conclude a Mutual Assistance Pact. Even then it was rendered virtually meaningless by the French foreign minister, Pierre Laval. Within France the conservatives were horrified by the prospect of close collaboration with the Soviet Union and the pact was not supplemented by military discussions. It is, therefore, easy to see why for many years discussion of the role of the Soviet Union in the events leading to the Second World War was limited in many works to the negotiation and conclusion of the Nazi–Soviet Pact in 1939. The threat of the Soviet Union was, however, ever present in the minds of Europe's bourgeois politicians who, whatever their feelings about Germany, continued to view her as a bulwark against Bolshevism.[106] Indeed it was the western powers that were to a considerable degree responsible for keeping the USSR out of

Europe even after the Soviet Union elected to join the League of Nations in 1934 to pursue a policy of collective security.[107]

Throughout the 1930s British politicians frequently cast doubt upon the motives of Soviet foreign policy. This seemed to be confirmed at the time and subsequently by the conclusion of the Nazi–Soviet Non-Aggression Pact of August 1939. According to one school of thought, Stalin's policy was to embroil the capitalist states of Europe in a mutually destructive war from which the Soviet Union and communism would emerge as the beneficiaries. This has found its most extreme interpretation in the analysis of Robert Tucker who has argued that this was the basis of Soviet foreign policy from 1928 onwards. The scale of Tucker's alleged conspiracy is vast. Stalin's prohibition of an alliance between German communists and socialists was designed to bring Hitler to power; collective security cloaked the real intentions of the Soviet Union which were to bind Hitler into an aggressive relationship; even the purges are interpreted as a means of removing the opposition to a pro-Hitler policy. For Tucker Stalin's policy towards Nazi Germany was a continuation of the Rapallo relationship of the 1920s.[108]

It is, of course, evident that it was Hitler who terminated the Rapallo relationship between Germany and the Soviet Union rather than Stalin. Gerhard Weinberg, in his study of German foreign policy, has argued that, in these circumstances, the policy of collective security was for Stalin very much a second preference and that the fundamental aim of Soviet policy remained that of an agreement with Germany. He cites as evidence the contacts between Schacht and Kandelaki, a member of Stalin's personal secretariat, who was sent as commercial attaché to the Soviet Embassy in Berlin in 1936.[109] Finally, Jiri Hochman has argued that Stalin and Molotov actually conspired to make the failure of collective security certain. There was no desire to strengthen the alliance with France, no intention of coming to the assistance of Czechoslovakia, and no inclination in earnest to obtain for the USSR transit rights through Poland in order that the Red Army might more effectively resist German aggression.[110]

These sinister interpretations of Soviet policy do have flaws. The policy of the USSR towards Germany in the 1930s cannot simply be construed as a continuation of Rapallo. The policy of the Soviet Union towards Weimar Germany, while clearly designed to divide the capitalist west, was also a defensive strategy aimed at avoiding the outbreak of war in Central Europe which might then have involved the Soviet Union. Moreover, if the purges were designed to facilitate the pursuit of a pro-German course, it was the westerners and advocates of collective security, such as Litvinov and Maisky who survived rather than those who favoured the German connection.[111] Finally, those that argue that good Nazi–Soviet relations were the preferred option of the Soviet leadership in the 1930s, have to reconcile the fact that almost the entirety of Soviet diplomatic activity of the 1930s was aimed at something diametrically opposed, namely, collective security against Germany. Was it perhaps that collective security served as a cover for the improbable rapprochement of August 1939?[112] As Geoffrey Roberts has suggested:

. . . for the 'German' school, what are important are a few intermittent, largely informal diplomatic contacts in which the possibility of a Soviet–German détente was raised. Relatively unimportant are the USSR's entry into the League of Nations in 1934, the Soviet pacts of mutual assistance with France and Czechoslovakia in 1935, Moscow's anti-German campaign in the Munich crisis of 1939, the triple alliance negotiations of 1939, and the consistent and persistent fight for collective security and anti-fascism. It is the type of contention that in most areas of history would require some pretty impressive evidence to gain any credence at all. The 'German' school interpretation rests, however, on the flimsiest of evidential bases. In truth it is no more than a series of speculations that benefited from the absence of Russian archival evidence and drew strength from the cold war atmosphere that pervaded post-war western Soviet Studies.[113]

Perhaps the most balanced analysis of Soviet policy in the 1930s is that of Jonathan Haslam. Haslam's meticulous researches tend to support the view that Stalin pursued the foreign policy option that would most effectively guarantee the Soviet Union irrespective of ideological considerations and preferred options. Moreover, Haslam has revealed the diversity of opinion that existed within the Kremlin concerning foreign policy. There were two main factions: namely, those who supported Litvinov and collective security and those, such as Molotov and Zhdanov, whose position he describes as *isolationist*. Isolationism consisted of three main elements: serious doubts as to the viability of a security alliance with the democracies; a desire to return to the convenience and comforts of the Rapallo relationship with Germany; and concern that the Soviet Union should not be dragged into an almost certain war between the imperialist powers. Stalin would choose, however, the option that most closely approximated to the interests of Soviet security. Throughout most of the period from 1933 to 1939 Germany pursued a policy of unremitting hostility towards the USSR which meant that Stalin had no alternative other than to follow a policy of collective security until almost the last. Haslam argues that throughout the Munich crisis Stalin remained committed to collective security and, given that the French too honoured their commitments to Czechoslovakia, would probably have aided the Czechs had they been subjected to a German attack. It was, however, the determination of the British and French to pursue appeasement and British reticence in the summer of 1939 that convinced Stalin that he had no alternative other than to achieve the security of the Soviet Union by an accommodation with the Third Reich. But 'the Nazi Soviet Pact was unquestionably a second-best solution. Even into the autumn of 1939 the rapprochement with Berlin remained an uncertain victory.'[114] Nevertheless, much of this must remain conjecture until historians have complete and free access to the Soviet archives of the 1930s. Until then the way in which decision-making functioned in Moscow during this period, the quantity and quality of the information that reached Stalin, and the use that was made of intelligence information must remain shrouded in mystery.

Just as historically controversial as the role of the USSR in the origins of the Second World War is that of the other post-war superpower, the United States. Was President Roosevelt an isolationist, or an interventionist biding his time? Did Roosevelt know in advance that the Japanese intended to attack Pearl Harbor and contrive the deaths of over four thousand American servicemen in order to gain popular support for American entry into the war? These questions have given rise to endless speculation, some of it very wild indeed,[115] but the precise views and responsibility of Roosevelt remain, in many respects, as elusive as ever.

Another problem in assessing America's part in the diplomacy of the 1930s relates to the fact that it is very misleading to speak of an American policy towards Europe at this time. As David Reynolds has indicated, that would imply 'a unity and continuity of thought and action that did not then exist.' Foreign policy only becomes central and immediate to a state when 'its security is threatened'. This did not happen in the USA until the summer of 1940. Consequently, the formulation of American policy for much of the 1930s corresponded to the model of bureaucratic politics in which there were '. . . a series of initiatives by rival government departments, supplemented by occasional forays by the President, largely unco-ordinated, often at odds with each other and reflecting the different interests and perceptions of the individuals and groups involved'[116].

If the United States had a foreign policy in the 1930s it was fundamentally *economic*. What Washington wished to achieve in the 1930s, as demonstrated by W.A. Williams and Lloyd C. Gardiner,[117] was the restoration of the 'Open Door' economic order throughout as much of the world as possible. It was felt that the withdrawal into protectionism by many countries following the depression was severely damaging to the commercial interests of the United States. What was found particularly irksome in the 1930s was the system of imperial preference within the British Empire created after the Ottawa Conference of 1932. This together with British bilateral trade and payments agreements, with states such as Argentina, were considered artificial means of promoting 'British exports at the expense of American'[118]. In the opinion of secretary of state Cordell Hull, who held that office from 1933 until 1944, the Ottawa System was 'the greatest injury in a commercial way, that has been inflicted on this country since I have been in public life'[119]. It was Hull's aim was to conclude as many Reciprocal Trade Agreements with other states as possible, thereby freeing up trade generally by the reduction of tariffs and the elimination of discriminatory practices. The key to a liberal world economy would, he thought, be the conclusion of an Anglo-American trade treaty which would mark the beginning of the dismantlement of imperial preference. In November 1938 an Anglo-American trade agreement was finally concluded. This and other reciprocal trade agreements, it was believed, would ultimately lead to a global regime of peace through free trade and prosperity and the *freezing-out* of the autarchic states Germany, Italy and Japan.

The American historian Arnold Offner has, however, put all these efforts into an overall context of a policy of American appeasement, which began with American sympathy for Germany regarding the Treaty of Versailles and continued until the spring of 1940 when Sumner Welles, under-secretary of state, was sent on a mission to Europe. For Offner, American policy in the 1930s was not one of isolation, but, on the contrary, a positive policy of appeasement. Roosevelt's proposals of 12 January 1938 for an international agreement on disarmament and equal access to raw materials are considered as an effort to support the attempts of Neville Chamberlain to secure an agreement with Germany. According to Offner the economic argument regarding United States policy in the 1930s has been exaggerated. He states:

> ... the primary decline ... in German–American trade occurred during the the worldwide collapse of 1929–32, and while German–American trade recovery lagged behind world trade recovery in the 1930s, the United States still ranked first in the value of exports to Germany in 1933, 1934 and 1938. The Germans had constant access in critical materials ... and grains through [until] 1938. Further, while the State Department always protested against Germany's subsidizing exports through currency manipulation ... it usually compromised its liberal trade principles to allow American importers and exporters to use clever book-keeping devices to 'barter' American goods ... for German products. By 1939 barter accounted for 50 per cent of American–German trade.[120]

In other words, despite the trading preferences of the American government, the ultimate confrontation between the United States and Germany could not be rooted in economic policy. Rather it was the consequence of a perceived threat to American security following the failure of appeasement that caused the United States in the spring of 1940 'to muster their political and economic power to defeat the new – or Nazi – Germany and its Axis allies'[121].

For Robert Divine, the turning point came much earlier. His book, *The Illusion of Neutrality*, argued that in general Americans sympathized with Britain and France, but also recognized that there was a profound reluctance to become involved in another European war. There were, therefore, significant domestic restraints on Roosevelt's freedom of action. Nevertheless, in Divine's view, Roosevelt's policy begins to change in October 1937 with the *Quarantine Speech*. But isolationist sentiment in America persisted, despite the increasingly clear motives and objectives of the aggressor states; this caused Roosevelt considerable disquiet and amazement. On the other hand, Roosevelt was able to drift away from the implications of neutrality to some extent by refusing to recognize that the resumed Sino-Japanese conflict was a war. In accepting the view that it was an *Incident*, he was able to ignore the Neutrality Acts which would have required a proclamation of Neutrality and an embargo on arms sales to the belligerents. In this way it was possible to maintain a flow of arms supplies to the Chinese government.[122] Robert Dallek too finds that Roosevelt was inhibited by domestic problems and the lack of an enthusiastic response to the United States in Europe and particularly in Britain.[123]

Did Roosevelt, though, intend ultimately that the United States should go to war in defence of the democracies? David Reynolds believes that the president probably as late as autumn 1941 was still only prepared to confront the dictators by proxy. He writes:

> ... Roosevelt could see good reasons for avoiding formal U.S. entry into the war, at least for the moment. In particular, he was afraid that it would lead to a

potentially disastrous cutback in supplies to the Allies as Americans demanded total concentration on U.S. rearmament, and that war with Germany would inevitably mean war with Germany's ally, Japan. If . . . he could do all that seemed necessary to assist Britain and Russia under his existing powers as Chief Executive and Commander-in-Chief why be in a hurry to go beyond limited, undeclared war?[124]

If this argument is sound, it, of course, constitutes a powerful case against those who postulate the theory that President Roosevelt let Pearl Harbor happen as a means of bringing the United States into the war.

The charge that President Roosevelt had conspired to engineer America's entry into the war, while publicly disavowing such intentions, was made early after the war by Charles A. Beard in his books *American Foreign Policy in the Making 1932–40* and *President Roosevelt and the Coming of the War, 1941.* There then followed a rash of similar studies, which culminated in a rather extravagant refutation of the revisionist thesis in Basil Rauch's *Roosevelt: From Munich to Pearl Harbor.*[125] Inevitably a flood of books also appeared accusing Roosevelt of having knowingly left the Pacific fleet vulnerable to attack in order to make American belligerence unavoidable. This argument was initiated during the war by Roosevelt's domestic opponents and given some substance by a statement made by the British minister, Oliver Lyttelton, to the American chamber of commerce in London on 20 June 1944. Lyttelton stated: 'Japan was provoked into attacking the Americans at Pearl Harbor. It is a travesty on history ever to say that America was forced into the war. Everyone knows where American sympathies were. It is incorrect to say that America was ever truly neutral even before America came into the war on an all-out fighting basis.'[126] Although Lyttelton, in response to American indignation, issued a qualifying statement affirming that the Japanese attack on Pearl Harbor had been an act of unjustified treachery, the damage was done and Lyttelton's words thereafter became part of the stock in trade of every extreme revisionist. Typical of the revisionist literature on Pearl Harbor are books by George Morgenstern and and Robert Theobald, which were published in the late 1940s and early 1950s.[127] In 1962, however, Roberta Wohlstetter, published an objective analysis that did not recriminate, but rather illustrated a complete failure of intelligence.[128] A more recent study written by Gordon W. Prange has pointed out that the idea that 'the Navy-minded Roosevelt would have staked out the U.S. Pacific Fleet as a lure for the Japanese' is so 'incongruous' that even the President's most bitter critics were reluctant to use it.[129]

Many theories, though, still abound, perhaps the most fantastic of which is that Winston Churchill knew of the plans to attack Pearl Harbor in advance, but deliberately concealed this intelligence in order that the United States should be forced into the war.[130] Recent intelligence releases by the Public Record Office at Kew would seem, however, to indicate that Churchill could not have behaved in such a dishonourable manner. In August 1941 the British intercepted a dispatch from the Japanese ambassador in Berlin which stated that Hitler had made it clear that, were Japan to go to war with the United States, Germany herself would declare war upon the latter. Churchill wrote on the decrypted intercept: 'In view of the fact that the Americans themselves gave us the key to the Japanese messages it seems probable that the President [Roosevelt] knows this already. But anyhow it is desirable he sh[ou]ld know it.'[131] The real story behind Pearl Harbor is probably one of genuine strategic miscalculation, compounded with sloppy intelligence.'[132] There was also cognitive dissonance. As Admiral Kimmel, the commander-in-chief of the United States Pacific Fleet, later put it: 'I never thought those little yellow sons of bitches could pull off an attack so far from Japan.'[133] This is very much part of Prange's conclusion too. Neither the Americans, nor the Japanese had enough accurate information about each other's characteristics, histories and institutions to assess with reasonable precision the outcome of their policies and actions towards one another. He writes: 'Before the Pacific conflict the United States was woefully ignorant of Japan. Experts on the Mikado's empire, his people, their culture, and language were as scarce as Egyptologists.' There was, therefore, a 'mutual misunderstanding' that resulted in 'mutual underestimation,' which 'even an elementary knowledge of each other's histories would have brushed away . . . and allowed the two peoples to see each other more clearly.'[134]

The Japanese attack on Pearl Harbor was the final event that engulfed the world in war and the culmination of a decade of almost systematic Japanese expansion in the Far East and the Pacific. During the past thirty years numerous books and articles have examined in detail almost every aspect of Japan's road to war. Nothing, however, has changed the fundamental interpretation that the Second World War consisted of two wars, one in Europe and the other in the Pacific. While the origins of the European war can be studied virtually without reference to the origins of the Pacific war, the causes of the Pacific war cannot be treated in isolation from Europe. Professor Akira Iriye has written:

> European powers were deeply involved in the Asian–Pacific region and played an important role in transforming the Chinese–Japanese conflict into a multinational one. Moreover, the United States which too was of little relevance to the immediate causes of the European war, steadily developed into a major Asian–Pacific power so that its position would have a direct bearing on the course of the Chinese–Japanese war.[135]

In the immediate aftermath of the war and the Tokyo War Crimes trial, studies of the origins of the Pacific War tended to accept the view that Japan had followed a programmatic policy of expansion in the 1930s. This was the version contained in works such as Herbert Feis, *The Road to Pearl Harbor*, and W. L. Langer and S. E. Gleason, *The Challenge to Isolation* and *The Undeclared War*. This approach has, however, been modified by subsequent works such as F. C. Jones, *Japan's New Order in the Far East*, which argues against the notion of planned expansion. Moreover, the role of the military leadership has been diluted by the work of J. B. Crowley, who, in his *Japan's Quest for Autonomy*, has also implicated the civilian leadership. R. C. Butow in *Tojo and the Coming of the War* has indicated the limits to Tojo's freedom of manoeuvre in the military and political system of pre-war Japan.[136]

Perhaps one of the most interesting controversies concerning Japan's foreign policy in the 1930s relates to the culpability of the Emperor Hirohito.

In 1971 David Bergamini published a book entitled *Japan's Imperial Conspiracy*, which apportioned a substantial part of the blame for Japanese aggression to the Emperor. This provoked a fiercely condemnatory response from academic circles. Charles D. Sheldon, after examining the diaries of the lord privy seal, Marquis Kido, and the papers of the emperor's senior adviser, Prince Saionji, and his secretary, Baron Harada, concluded that 'the Emperor was absolutely consistent in using his personal influence to induce caution and to moderate, and even to obstruct, the accumulating, snowballing impetus towards war.' The emperor's influence was naturally exercized privately, for a public expression of his views would have committed every government thereafter to his preferences. A government that contradicted the imperial wishes would have weakened 'the Imperial institution' and simultaneously deprived the government of legality: 'It was better for the Emperor simply to exist, and not be involved in politics, at least publicly. And it happened that this political inaction coincided both with Japanese tradition and with the modern idea of a limited constitutional monarchy.' In theory, the emperor was absolute, but, 'in fact, and by understanding among leaders of government . . . the Emperor was a limited constitutional monarch'. There was general agreement that personal rule by the emperor would merely damage the Imperial institution. Indeed, non-involvement in Japanese politics over the centuries had been the key to the survival of the Japanese monarchy.

After the war the Emperor stated:

> It goes without saying that wars must be avoided. Concerning the war, I tried to avoid it as much as possible . . . But in spite of all my efforts, I failed, and we plunged into war. I was truly grieved by this. It is often said that the war was ended by my efforts. If this is so, why did I not prevent the war before it began? Indeed, this seems superficially a reasonable argument. But in fact it was not possible . . . we have a firmly established constitution, and the Emperor must act in accordance with it. According to this constitution there are Ministers of State who are given the power and responsibility over state affairs. The Emperor cannot on his own volition interfere or intervene in the jurisdictions for which the Ministers of State are responsible. Whether in domestic or foreign affairs, if those whom are constitutionally responsible have adopted a policy after careful deliberation, and submit this for Imperial approval in accordance with the provisions of the constitution, I have no choice but to approve it whether I desire it or not.

The situation at the end of the war offered Hirohito scope for initiative because there was a clear division of opinion within the government and the emperor was also asked to take the ultimate decision.

If Hirohito was compelled to submit to the decisions of his ministers, this clearly did not inhibit him from expressing his reservations in the strongest terms. There are numerous examples of this, but perhaps it will suffice to mention his attitude to the Soviet–Japanese clash at Changkufeng in July 1938. According to the record of Prince Saionji, he told the war minister, Itagaki:

> The methods of the Army in the past have been unpardonable. In the Manchurian Incident and also in the doings at the Marco Polo Bridge, at the

beginning of the present [China] Incident, there was complete disobedience to central orders. There are frequent instances where the methods used have been arbitrary and sneaky, which is altogether improper as my Army. This is disgraceful. Nothing like this must happen again.

Itagaki departed very humiliated.[137]

While the tendency of academic writers has been on balance vigorously to condemn Bergamini's analysis and to support those writers who take a benign view of the emperor's role,[138] this did not prevent Edward Behr from reasserting the culpability of Hirohito at the end of the 1980s. According to Behr, Bergamini's error had been to attribute a 'conspiratorial pattern in Hirohito's behaviour, from his earliest years as crown prince, and to try to prove that he deliberately placed a handful of key supporters in top positions in order to plan Japan's militaristic expansion . . .' Nevertheless, Behr argues that the responsibility of Hirohito was deliberately concealed, for fear that the social fabric of Japan might disintegrate if its monarchy were deliberately abolished or compromised. In Behr's opinion, Hirohito was not a mere passive participant in the events of the 1930s, but was, in fact, capable of being energetically active, as was the case during the army rebellion of February 1936. He could, therefore, have intervened more decisively to halt the drift to war. Moreover, Behr alleges Hirohito's complicity in the ghastly experiments carried out on human guinea pigs by General Ishii's Manchuria-based Unit 731, which specialized in research into bacteriological and chemical warfare. According to Behr, Hirohito sanctioned the war against China; believed in Japan's right to hegemony in Asia; held similar views in respect of Germany and Italy in Europe; and thought the Axis powers would ultimately triumph.[139]

Perhaps the most balanced opinion is that recently advanced by Dr. Saki Dockrill. She takes the view that had Hirohito insisted on peace after the appointment of Tojo as prime minister then peace would have followed. The relationship between the Japanese leadership and the emperor was, however, one of interdependence, with the emperor relying upon the leadership for protection. His position was a 'delicate one' because of the complexity of the international problems faced by Japan and divisions within the Japanese leadership. In the end, he endorsed the decision to go to war for three reasons: the paucity of Japan's resources; the note from secretary of state Cordell Hull of 26 November 1941, which was interpreted as an ultimatum more or less requiring Japan to yield all gains since the Manchurian 'Incident' of 1931; and a mood in Japan that seemed to favour war. As Dr. Dockrill comments, Hirohito was 'aware of the possible consequences of a . . . veto – military revolts, internal revolution, the assassination of his close officials and probably himself'. She concludes that the Emperor should be given credit for attempts, however weak, to avoid war, but asserts that 'this does not alter the fact that in the last resort, he was responsible for the decision to go to war.'[140]

The Second World War ended in 1945 and the perceptions of its origins that were then current have been subjected during the last four decades to highly detailed academic research. The last remaining obscurities relate to Soviet policy in the 1930s. Access to the relevant governmental archives in Moscow and similar material has until recently been impossible and remains restricted.

Until monographs based upon these sources appear it will, however, be impossible to state with any precision how Soviet policy was formulated and what exactly it was. In many respects, therefore, this represents the final frontier of the subject. There is also lacking for English-speaking historians any classic treatment of the War's origins from the Chinese point of view. Here, though, the problems of research appear to be most formidable. Nevertheless, the historical achievement of the last forty years has been most impressive. While research has not always been able to provide definitive answers to the questions that emerged from the processes that led to the Second World War, it has enhanced our understanding of the complexities of those processes and, in many cases, revealed the limited alternatives that confronted statesmen and politicians during the 1920s and 1930s.

Conclusion

The Second World War was a vast conflict and it transformed the structure of power throughout the globe. For almost fifty years after its end that structure was a bipolar one with the superpowers, the United States and the Soviet Union, dominating the ideological/economic blocs they led. On the other hand, it would be misleading to imply that that was the only change. The major global power of the pre-war period, Britain, went into manifest decline, while her quondam adversaries, Germany and Japan, experienced prodigious economic growth which left Britain far behind. Defeat and the devastation of war had not in the long run impeded the rise of Germany and Japan to economic and political preeminence and war was proved to have been largely irrelevant to and unnecessary for it. On the other hand, the price these countries paid for their advance in the post-war world was political and social modernization in the context of a liberal-capitalist international community. What they had attempted previously was the imposition of their ascendancy in their respective regions without compromising, or intending to compromise, what they perceived to be their unique national characteristics and traditions. Germany and Japan in the 1930s were dominated by regimes that were nationalistically conservative at home and abroad; that were disinclined to participate in the compromise customary in international affairs. These characteristics had indicated intolerance and domination and, perhaps, amibition without limit.

Neither the United States, nor the Soviet Union, preoccupied as they were with internal reconstruction and domestic political problems, was in a position to take the lead against the dictators and aggressors. By default the task devolved upon Britain: she still possessed the prestige and status for the duty, if not the wherewithal. Inevitably the main focus of Britain's resistance was Germany, for the Third Reich threatened the British Empire at its very heart. Britain could not countenance with equanimity a situation in which Hitlerite Germany, by force, established a hegemonic position in Europe whence she could pose a long-term menace to the survival of the British Empire. This determined Britain's resistance by war, once it seemed that Hitler's aims were not limited to the incorporation of Germans and

German-speaking territories within the Reich. It may well be true that leading the war against Hitler, at least in its early stages, meant ultimately the loss of empire and the loss of position to the United States and the Soviet Union, but in 1939 the reduction of Germany was for many Britons the only guarantee of the continued existence of the British Empire. As for those who argue that Hitler would have guaranteed the survival of the British Empire in an Anglo-German peace, neither the Führer, nor anyone else for that matter, could have stopped the process of British imperial disintegration that had already set in in the 1920s and 1930s. The truth was that Britain was damned if she resisted and damned if she did not. In 1939 Britain chose the honourable path of resistance, rather than the craven course of acquiescence in the further advance of the power of the Third Reich. While, in retrospect, the path of resistance may historically have spelt the end of the British Empire, it also ensured that the rise of Germany and Japan would be accomplished in a manner more suited to the accepted norms of international conduct among the western democratic powers.

British resistance, however, was not lightly undertaken, for it was assumed that, given the global nature of Britain's commitments and the threat represented to them by the members of the Anti-Comintern Pact, war would not be confined to Europe. It is, indeed, the fundamental argument of this book that it was the breakdown in Anglo-German relations caused by Germany's determination to pursue a policy of expansion based upon war and conquest that was critical in determining that the European war that began in 1939 would in all probability become a world war. One historian has recently stated: 'A meticulous inquiry into the origins of the European war of 1939–41 and the world war of 1941–45 would require the investigation of no less than eight distinct wars in the earlier period and four for the latter. They all have direct or direct links with one another but each one also has specific causes.'[1] While this is a perfectly defensible position and unexceptionable in its way, it ignores the critical centrality of the Anglo-German War in 1939. For that to have remained a European war would have required the early defeat of Germany by the Anglo-French combination. That did not happen; was not expected to happen. Inevitably, as German arms seemed irresistible, other revisionist forces were tempted to take advantage of the situation created by German military successes. The world war, therefore, that was implicit in Britain's decision to resist Germany in 1939 was made explicit in 1941.

That is not to say that it was certain in 1939 that world war would ensue, or that British politicians and civil servants wanted the war to assume global dimensions; rather it is to suggest that they anticipated that that would be the outcome. And indeed, just as German policy proved in the end to be the solvent of the European order, so the Anglo-German war which it ultimately provoked proved to be the solvent of the world order.

The introduction to this book mentioned Neville Chamberlain's statement in the House of Commons of 24 March 1938 and this narrative, in a sense, concludes with it. During the evening of the same day, Lord Lothian addressed a gathering in Chatham House on the subject of *Issues in British Foreign Policy*. This was one of a number of lectures given on this theme

during March and April by distinguished speakers and experts such as
A. J. Toynbee and R. A. Butler. What Lothian had to say is interesting in
the light of Chamberlain's speech. He argued that if the 'dynamic totalitarian
regimes' attempted to obtain 'what is unjust by power politics,' they would
finally 'find themselves confronted by what every one of them is most afraid
of, *world war*'. Lothian could not conceive of a single power that would want
to start such a war 'for the reason that nobody could tell what its outcome
would be . . .'[2]. This was an analysis strikingly similar to that of the Prime
Minister and more explicit in that Lothian actually indentified *world war* as the
likely consequence of Germany's continued aggression.

There was a sequel. Following the May Crisis of 1938, Lord Halifax, by
then foreign secretary, suggested to Lothian that he write to *The Times*.
Although Lothian ultimately declined to do so on the ground that it would
have little impact on Germany where it would now be understood that in a
future conflict Britain and Germany were likely to be on opposite sides, the
terms of Lothian's draft are interesting. While emphasizing that Britain
would do everything possible to bring about a solution to the Czech question
and was not averse to modifications in the territorial map of Europe, the draft
insisted that such changes would have to be accomplished by peaceful means.
Significantly, it also referred to Chamberlain's Commons statement of 24
March and referred to the uncertain consequences of a war started in Central
Europe.[3] Arguably, British politicians and members of the establishment
were convinced that British involvement in a European war would
ultimately mean a world war in which the losers would lose totally. In this
respect, September 1939 is as good a date as any to mark the beginning of the
Second World War and probably better than most.

Appendix 1

Prime Ministers, Foreign Ministers and Finance Ministers of the Major Powers, 1918–1941

(a) United Kingdom:

	Prime Minister	Foreign Secretary	Chancellor of the Exchequer
Nov. 1918	D. Lloyd George	A. Balfour	A. Bonar Law
Jan. 1919			A. Chamberlain
Oct. 1919		Lord Curzon	
Apr. 1921			Sir R. Horne
Oct. 1922	A. Bonar Law		S. Baldwin
May 1923	S. Baldwin		N. Chamberlain
Jan. 1924	J.R. MacDonald	J.R. MacDonald	P. Snowden
Nov. 1924	S. Baldwin	Sir A. Chamberlain	W. Churchill
June 1929	J.R. MacDonald	A. Henderson	P. Snowden
Aug. 1931		Marquis of Reading	
Nov. 1931		Sir John Simon	N. Chamberlain
June 1935	S. Baldwin	Sir S. Hoare	
Dec. 1935		A. Eden	
May 1937	N. Chamberlain		Sir J. Simon
Feb. 1938		Viscount Halifax	
May 1940	W. Churchill		Sir K. Wood
Dec. 1940		A. Eden	

(b) France:

	Prime Minister	Foreign Minister	Finance Minister
Nov. 1918	G. Clemenceau	S. Pichon	L. Klotz
Jan. 1920	A. Millerand	A. Millerand	F. François-Marsal
Sep. 1920	G. Leygues	G. Leygues	
Jan. 1921	A. Briand	A. Briand	P. Doumer
Jan. 1922	R. Poincaré	R. Poincaré	Count de Lasteyrie
Mar. 1924			F. François-Marsal

cont.		Prime Minister	Foreign Minister	Finance Minister
June	1924	F. François–Marsal	E. Lefebvre	
June	1924	E. Herriot	E. Herriot	E. Clémentel
Apr.	1925	M. Painlevé	A. Briand	J. Caillaux
Oct.	1925			M. Painlevé
Nov.	1925	A. Briand		L. Loucheur
Dec.	1925			P. Doumer
Mar.	1926			R. Peret
June	1926			J. Caillaux
July	1926	E. Herriot	E. Herriot	A. de Monzie
Aug.	1926	R. Poincaré	A. Briand	R. Poincaré
Nov.	1928			H. Cheron
July	1929	A. Briand		
Nov.	1929	A. Tardieu		
Feb.	1930	C. Chautemps		C. Dumont
Mar.	1930	A. Tardieu		P. Reynaud
Dec.	1930	T. Steeg		G. Martin
Jan.	1931	P. Laval		P.E. Flandin
Jan.	1932		P. Laval	
Feb.	1932	A. Tardieu	A. Tardieu	
June	1932	E. Herriot	E. Herriot	G. Martin
Dec.	1932	J. Paul–Boncour	J. Paul–Boncour	H. Cheron
Jan.	1933	E. Daladier		G. Bonnet
Oct.	1933	A. Sarraut		
Nov.	1933	C. Chautemps		
Jan.	1934	E. Daladier	E. Frot	F. Piétri
Feb.	1934			P. Marchandeau
Feb.	1934	G. Doumergue	L. Barthou	G. Martin
Nov.	1934	P.-E. Flandin	P. Laval	
June	1935	F. Bouisson		J. Caillaux
June	1935	P. Laval		M. Régnier
Jan.	1936	A. Sarraut	P.E. Flandin	
June	1936	L. Blum	Y. Delbos	V. Auriol
June	1937	C. Chautemps		G. Bonnet
Jan.	1938		E. Daladier	P. Marchandeau
Mar.	1938	L. Blum	J. Paul–Boncour	L. Blum
Apr.	1938	E. Daladier	G. Bonnet	P. Marchandeau
Nov.	1938			P. Reynaud
Sep.	1939		E. Daladier	
Mar.	1940	P. Reynaud	P. Reynaud	L. Lamoureux
June	1940	H.P. Pétain (Vichy)	P. Baudouin	Y. Bouthillier
Sep.	1940		P. Laval	
Dec.	1940		P.E. Flandin	
Feb.	1941		F. Darlan	C. Huntzinger
Aug.	1941			Y. Bouthillier

(c) Germany:

	Chancellor	Foreign Minister	Finance Minister
Nov. 1918	Max von Baden	W. Solf	E. Schiffer
Nov. 1918	Government of People's Representatives. Principal members were F. Ebert, P. Scheidemann and O. Landsberg. It overlapped with the Imperial authorities.		
Dec. 1918		Count Brockdorff-Rantzau	
Feb. 1919	P. Scheidemann		
Apr. 1919			B. Dernburg
June 1919	G. Bauer	H. Müller	M. Erzberger
Mar. 1920	H. Müller	A. Köster	J. Wirth
June 1920	K. Fehrenbach	W. Simons	
May 1921	J. Wirth	F. Rosen	
Oct. 1921		J. Wirth	A. Hermes
Jan. 1922		W. Rathenau	
Nov. 1922	W. Cuno	H. von Rosenberg	
Aug. 1923	G. Stresemann	G. Stresemann	R. Hilferding
Oct. 1923			J. Koeth
Nov. 1923	W. Marx		H. Luther
Jan. 1925	H. Luther		O. von Schlieben
Oct. 1925			H. Luther
Jan. 1926			P. Reinhold
May 1926	W. Marx		H. Kohler
June 1928	H. Müller		R. Hilferding
Oct. 1929		J. Curtius	
Dec. 1929			P. Moldenhauer
Mar. 1930	H. Brüning		
June 1930			H.R. Dietrich
Oct. 1931		H. Brüning	
June 1932	F. von Papen	K. von Neurath	L.E. Schwerin von Krosigk
Nov. 1932	K. von Schleicher		
Jan. 1933	A. Hitler		
Feb. 1938		J. von Ribbentrop	

(d) Italy:

	Prime Minister	Foreign Minister	Finance Minister
Nov. 1918	V.E. Orlando	Baron S. Sonnino	F. Meda
Jan 1919	F. Nitti	T. Tittoni	F. Tadesco
Nov. 1919		V. Scialoja	
Mar. 1920			K. Schanzer
May 1920			C. de Nava
June 1920	G. Giolitti	Count C. Sforza	F. Tadesco
Aug. 1920			L. Facta
July 1921	I. Bonomi	Marquis della Torretta	M. Saleri

		Prime Minister	Foreign Minister	Finance Minister
Feb.	1922	L. Facta	K. Schanzer	G.B. Bertone
Oct.	1922	B.Mussolini	B. Mussolini	A. de Stefani
July	1925			Count di Misurata
July	1928			A. Mosconi
Sep.	1920		Dino Grandi	
July	1932		B. Mussolini	G. Jung
Jan.	1935			Count Thaon di Revel
Jun.	1936		Count Ciano di Cortallazo	

(e) USA:

		President	Secretary of State	Secretary of the Treasury
Nov.	1918	W. Wilson	R. Lansing	W.G. McAdoo
Feb.	1920			D.F. Houston
Mar.	1921	W. Harding	C.E. Hughes	A.W. Mellon
Jan.	1925		F.E. Kellogg	
Mar.	1925	C. Coolidge		
Mar.	1929	H.C. Hoover	W.L. Stimson	
Feb.	1932			O.L. Mills
Mar.	1933	F.D. Roosevelt	C. Hull	W.H. Woodin
Nov.	1933			H. Morgenthau jr.

(f) Russia and the USSR:

		Secretary of Central Committee of CPSU	Chairman of Council of People's Commissars and Ministers	Commissars and Ministers for Foreign Affairs	Commissars and Ministers of Finance
Nov.	1918		V.I. Lenin	G.V. Chiherin	I.E. Gukovsky
Apr.	1921				A.K. Krestinsky
	1922	J.V. Stalin			
	1923				G.Y. Sokolnikov
Feb.	1924		A.I. Rykov		
	1926				N.P. Brukhanov
	1930				G.F. Grinko
July	1930			P. Litvinov	
Dec.	1930		V.M. Molotov		
Aug.	1937				V.Y. Chubar
Jan.	1938				A.G. Zverev

cont.	Secretary of Central Committee of CPSU	Chairman of Council of People's Commissars and Ministers	Commissars and Ministers for Foreign Affairs	Commissars and Ministers of Finance
May 1939			V.M. Molotov	
May 1941		J.V. Stalin		

Exact dates cannot always be supplied for the date on which office was assumed. The post of Secretary of the Central Committee of the Communist Party of the Soviet Union is included because of its particular importance in the Soviet system.

(g) Japan:

	Prime Minister	Foreign Minister	Finance Minister
Nov. 1918	Hara Kei (Takashi)	Uchida Yasuya	Takahashi Korekiyo
Nov. 1921	Uchida Yasuya		
Nov. 1921	Takahashi Korekiyo		
Jan. 1922	Kato Tomosaburo		
June 1922			Ichiki Otohiko
Sep. 1923	Yamamoto Gombei	Yamamoto Gombei	Inoue Junnosuke
Sep. 1923		Ijuin Hikokichi	
Jan. 1924	Kiyoura Keigo	Matsui Keishiro	Shoda Kazue
June 1924	Kato Takaachi	Shidehara Kijuro	Hamaguchi Osachi
Jan. 1926	Wakatsuki Reijiro		
June 1926			Hayami Seiji
Sep. 1926			Kataoka Naoharu
Apr. 1927	Tanaka Gi'ichi	Tanaka Gi'ichi	Mitsuchi Chuzo
July 1929	Hamaguchi Osachi	Shidehara Kijuro	Inoue Junnosuke
Jan. 1931	Wakatsuki Reijiro		
Dec. 1931	Inukai Ki	Yoshizawa Kenkichi	Takahashi Korekiyo
May 1932	Takahashi Korekiyo	Saito Makoto	
May 1932	Saito Makoto		
June 1932		Uchida Yasuya	
Sep. 1933		Hirota Koki	
July 1934	Okada Keisuke		Fujii Sadanobu
Nov. 1934			Takahashi Korekiyo
Feb. 1936	Goto Fumio		Machida Chuji
Feb. 1936	Okada Keisuke		
Mar. 1936	Hirota Koki		Baba Eiichi
Apr. 1936		Arita Hachiro	
Feb. 1937	Hayashi Senjuro	Hayashi Senjuro	Yuki Toyotaro
Mar. 1937		Sato Naotake	
June 1937	Konoe Fumimaro	Hirota Koki	Kaya Okinori
May 1938		Ugaki Kazushige	Ikeda Shigeaki
Oct. 1938		Arita Hachiro	
Jan. 1939	Hiranuma Kiichiro		Ishiwata Sotaro
Aug. 1939	Abe Nobuyuki		Aoki Kazuo

cont.		Prime Minister	Foreign Minister	Finance Minister
Sep.	1939		Abe Nobuyuki	
Sep.	1939		Nomura Kichisaburo	
Jan.	1940	Yonai Mitsumasa	Arita Hachiro	Sakurauchi Yukio
July	1940	Konoe Fumimaro	Matsuoka Yosuke	Kawada Isao
July	1941		Toyoda Teijiro	Ogura Masatsune
Oct.	1941	Tojo Hideki	Togo Shigenori	Kaya Okinori

Source: B. Spuler, *Rulers and Governments of the World, Vol. 2, 1492–1929*, (Bowker: London, 1977 and B. Spuler, C. G. Allen and Neil Saunders, *Rulers and Governments of the World, Vol. 3, 1930–1970*, (Bowker: London, 1977). I also acknowledge the help of Mr. Manabu Morimoto, Financial Counsellor of the London Japanese Embassy, in compiling this list.

Appendix 2

Chronology of Events

Europe and the Atlantic	Far East and the Pacific

1918

11 Nov.   The Armistice.

1919

18 Jan.   Paris Peace Conference opens.

28 June   Signature of Treaty of Versailles. Signature of Anglo-French Pact of Guarantee, ultimately voided by failure of USA to ratify Versailles Treaty and a similar treaty.

10 Sept.   Signature of Treaty of St. Germain with Austria.

27 Nov.   Signature of Treaty of Neuilly with Bulgaria.

1920

10 Jan.   Entry into force of provisions of Treaty of Versailles.

6 Apr.   French occupation of Rhineland towns.

25 Apr.   Poland attacks Russia.

4 June   Signature of Treaty of Trianon with Hungary.

12 Oct.   Preliminary Agreement ending Polish–Soviet War.

1921

19 Feb.   Conclusion of Franco-Polish Alliance.

8 Mar.   Allied Occupation of Ruhrort, Duisberg etc.

cont.	Europe and the Atlantic	Far East and the Pacific
16 Mar.	Anglo–Soviet Trade Agreement.	
5 May	London Schedule of Reparations Payments.	
12 Nov.		Washington Conference opens.
Dec.		Termination of Anglo-Japanese Alliance.
		Conclusion of Pacific Four Power Pact.

1922

6 Jan.	Cannes Conference opens.	
6 Feb.		Conclusion of Washington Naval Treaty.
		Conclusion of Nine Power Treaty regarding China.
		Sino-Japanese Agreement.
		Japan agrees to evacuate Shantung.
15 Mar.	Soviet–German Military Agreement.	
10 Apr.–19 May	Genoa Conference.	
16 Apr.	Treaty of Rapallo.	
30 Oct.	Mussolini appointed Prime Minister of Italy.	
20 Nov.–17 July 1923	Lausanne Conference on Peace with Turkey.	
26 Dec.	Reparations Commission finds Germany in default by three votes to one.	

1923

11 Jan.	Franco–Belgian Occupation of the Ruhr.	
19 Jan.	Beginning of German Passive Resistance.	
26 Sep.	Ending of Passive Resistance.	
29 Sep.	Draft Treaty of Mutual Assistance adopted by League Assembly.	
30 Nov.	Reparations Commission creates Expert Committees.	

1924

25 Jan.	Conclusion of Franco–Czech Alliance.	
1 Feb.	British recognition of USSR.	
9 Apr.	Submission of Dawes Plan by Committee of Experts.	
16 Aug.	Adoption of Dawes Plan by London Conference.	
2 Oct.	League Assembly adopts Geneva Protocol for the Pacific Settlement of International Disputes.	

cont.	Europe and the Atlantic	Far East and the Pacific
28 Oct.	French recognition of USSR.	

1925

Jan.	German Note to British Government suggesting a Multilateral Rhineland Security Pact.	
9 Feb.	German Note to French Government suggesting a Multilateral Rhineland Security Pact.	
12 Mar.	Britain formally rejects the Geneva Protocol.	
16 Oct.	Locarno Pacts initialled.	
1 Dec.	Locarno Pacts signed.	

1926

31 Jan.	Evacuation of first Rhineland Zone.	
24 Apr.	German–Soviet Treaty of Berlin.	
July		Beginning of Kuomintang's Northern Expedition.
8 Sep.	Germany elected to League membership.	
17 Sep.	Stresemann–Briand Thoiry Talks.	

1927

6 Apr.	Briand proposes to USA bilateral treaty of non-aggression.	
27 May	Britain severs diplomatic relations with USSR.	
20 June–4 Aug.	Geneva Naval Conference.	

1928

June		Murder of Chang Tso-lin.
27 Aug.	Signature of Kellogg–Briand Pact.	
16 Sep.	Geneva Agreement opening the negotiations regarding reparations and evacuation of the Rhineland.	

1929

7 June	Young Plan submitted by Experts' Committee.	
6 Aug.–31 Aug.	First Hague Conference on Reparations.	
3 Oct.	Diplomatic relations restored between UK and USSR.	
30 Nov.	Evacuation of Second Rhineland Zone.	

1930

3 Jan.–20 Jan.	Second Hague Conference on Reparations and adoption of Young Plan.	

cont.	Europe and the Atlantic	Far East and the Pacific
21 Jan.– 22 Apr.		London Naval Conference.
22 Apr.		London Naval Treaty.
17 May	Briand Plan on European Union.	
30 June	Termination of Rhineland Occupation.	

1931

19 Mar.	Signature of Austro-German Customs Union Protocol.	
20 June	Hoover Moratorium.	
18 Sep.		Mukden Incident. Beginning of Sino-Japanese hostilities.

1932

7 Jan.		Stimson Note on Non-Recognition.
2 Feb.	Disarmament Conference opens.	
16 June–9 July	Reparations terminated at Lausanne Conference.	
14 Sep.	Germany withdraws from Disarmament Conference for first time.	
29 Nov.	Franco-Soviet Non-Aggression Pact.	
11 Dec.	Five-Power Declaration concedes to Germany equality of status and she returns to Disarmament Conference.	

1933

30 Jan.	Hitler becomes Reich Chancellor.	
16 Mar.	British Disarmament Plan.	
27 Mar.		Japan leaves League of Nations.
31 May		Tangku Truce between China and Japan.
7 June	Four Power Pact initialled in Rome.	
7 June–27 July	World Economic Conference.	
14 Oct.	Germany leaves Disarmament Conference and the League of Nations.	

1934

26 Jan.	German–Polish Non-Aggression Pact.	
17 Apr.	Frane rejects further Disarmament Negotiations with Germany.	
14 June–15 June	Hitler visits Mussolini in Venice.	
25 July	Abortive Nazi *Putsch* in Vienna.	

cont.	Europe and the Atlantic	Far East and the Pacific
18 Sep.	USSR enters League of Nations.	

1935

4 Jan.–7 Jan.	Laval–Mussolini Conversations in Rome.	
13 Jan.	Saar Plebiscite.	
4 March	British Defence White Paper.	
9 March	Germany announces existence of *Luftwaffe*.	
16 March	Germany announces introduction of conscription and denounces disarmament clauses of Versailles.	
14 Apr.	Declaration of Stresa Conference.	
2 May	Franco-Soviet Pact.	
16 May	Czechoslovak–Soviet Pact.	
18 June	Anglo-German Naval Agreement.	
3 Oct.	Italian invasion of Abyssinia.	
8 Dec.	Hoare–Laval Plan.	

1936

7 Mar.	Remilitarization of the Rhineland.	
1 Apr.	Britain reaffirms her Locarno obligations to France.	
9 May	Italy annexes Abyssinia.	
18 July	Spanish Civil War.	
2 Aug.	Appeal for Non-Intervention in Spain.	
20 Oct.–25 Oct.	Ciano visits Germany.	
25 Nov.	German–Japanese Anti-Comintern Pact.	

1937

2 Jan.	Anglo-Italian Mediterranean Agreement.	
28 May	Neville Chamberlain becomes Prime Minister.	
7 July		Marco Polo Bridge Incident and resumption of Sino-Japanese hostilities.
25 Sep.–29 Sep.	Mussolini visits Hitler in Germany.	
3 Nov.–24 Nov.		Brussels Conference on Far East.
5 Nov.	Hossbach Conference. Roosevelt's Quarantine Speech.	
6 Nov.	Italy adheres to Anti-Comintern Pact.	
17 Nov.	Lord Halifax visits Germany.	
11 Dec.	Italy withdraws from League of Nations.	

cont.	Europe and the Atlantic	Far East and the Pacific
14 Dec.		Fall of Nanking

1938

11 Jan.	Roosevelt proposes an International Conference.	
4 Feb.	Ribbentrop becomes German Foreign Minister.	
12 Feb.	Schuschnigg visits Hitler.	
20 Feb.	Eden resigns as UK Foreign Secretary.	
3 Mar.	British Colonial Offer to Germany.	
13 Mar.	*Anschluß* of Germany and Austria.	
16 Apr.	Anglo-Italian Agreement.	
28 Apr.–29 Apr.	Anglo-French Conversations.	
20 May–21 May	Crisis.	
11 July		Japanese–Soviet Battle of Chang-kufeng.
29 Sep.–30 Sep.	Munich Conference.	
Oct.		Chiang Kai-shek's government withdraws to Chungking.
21 Oct.		Fall of Canton.
25 Oct.		Fall of Hankow.
5 Nov.		Prince Konoe declares the New Order in Asia.
16 Nov.	Ratification of Anglo-Italian Agreement.	
6 Dec.	Franco-German Declaration.	

1939

11 Jan.	Chamberlain and Halifax visit Rome.	
14 Mar.	German occupation of Bohemia and Moravia.	
21 Mar.	Germany proposes to Poland a settlement of Danzig and Polish Corridor Questions.	
22 Mar.	Germany occupies Memel.	
28 Mar.	Franco's troops enter Madrid.	
31 Mar.	Franco-British Guarantee of Poland.	
7 Apr.	Italy occupies Albania.	
14 Apr.	Anglo-French Negotiations with USSR begin.	
17 Apr.	USSR proposes Three Power Alliance.	
26 Apr.	British Government proposes conscription.	

cont.	Europe and the Atlantic	Far East and the Pacific
28 Apr.	Hitler denounces Non-Aggression Pact with Poland and Anglo-German Naval Agreement.	
May–Sep.		Soviet–Japanese battle of Nomonhan.
3 May	Litvinov replaced by Molotov as Soviet Foreign Minister.	
22 May	Italo-German Pact of Steel.	
30 May	Soviet–German Negotiations begin.	
14 June		Beginning of Japanese blockade of British Concession at Tientsin.
July		United States government gives notice of abrogation of US–Japan Treaty of Commerce and Navigation.
11 Aug.	Ciano visits Hitler and Ribbentrop. Arrival of Franco-British Military Mission in Moscow.	
21 Aug.	Suspension of Anglo-Franco-Soviet Military Talks.	
23 Aug.	Conclusion of Nazi–Soviet Non-Aggression Pact.	
25 Aug.	Conclusion of Anglo-Polish Alliance.	
1 Sep.	Germany invades Poland. Unity of Danzig with the Reich proclaimed.	
3 Sep.	Britain and France declare war on Germany.	
17 Sep.	USSR invades Poland.	
30 Nov.	USSR invades Finland.	
1940		
12 Mar.	Finland capitulates to USSR.	
30 Mar.		Wang Ching-wei's puppet regime installed in Nanking.
9 Apr.	Germany invades Denmark and Norway.	
May	Britain occupies Iceland.	
10 May	Germany invades Low Countries and France. Winston Churchill becomes British Prime Minister.	
15 May	Surrender of Netherlands.	
27 May–4 June.	Dunkirk evacuation.	
28 May	Surrender of Belgium.	
10 June	Italy enters the war.	

cont.	Europe and the Atlantic	Far East and the Pacific
22 June	Capitulation of France.	
July–Oct.		Closure of Burma Road.
10 July–15 Sep.	Battle of Britain.	
3 Sep.	Anglo/US Bases-Destroyers Deal.	
14 Sep.	Italy invades Egypt.	
27 Sep.		Tripartite Pact between Japan, Germany and Italy.
28 Oct.	Italy invades Greece.	
Dec.		US embargo on scrap and war material sales to Japan.

1941

11 Mar.	Lend-Lease Act signed.	
Apr.	USA occupies Greenland.	
6 Apr.	Germany invades Yugoslavia and Greece.	
11 Apr.		Soviet–Japanese Non-Aggression Pact concluded.
22 June	Germany invades the USSR.	
July	USA joins in occupation of Iceland.	
2 July		Japan decides to move into Indo-China.
28 July–29 July		US, UK and Dutch East Indies impose oil and steel embargo on Japan.
14 August	Churchill–Roosevelt Meeting at Placentia Bay. Atlantic Charter.	
Sep.	US 'shoot on sight' order.	
17 Oct.		Tojo becomes Prime Minister of Japan.
26 Nov.		Cordell Hull informs Japan of American Peace Proposals.
7 Dec.		Japan sends declaration of war to USA. Japan attacks Pearl Harbor
8 Dec.		Japan attacks the Philippines, Hong Kong and Malaya.★
8 Dec.		USA and Britain declare war on Japan.
9 Dec.		China formally declares war on Germany and Japan.
11 Dec.		Germany and Italy declare war on USA.

★ The Japanese attack on Kota Bharu (Malaya) is dated 8 December because Kota Bharu lies west of the International Date Line. In terms of *real*, as opposed to local, time, it preceded the attack on Pearl Harbor by two hours.

Notes

Preface and Acknowledgements

1 Akira Iriye, *The Origins of the Second World War in Asia and the Pacific*, (Longman: London, 1987), p. 1.
2 Robert Holland, *The Pursuit of Greatness: Britain and the World Role, 1900–1970*, (Fontana: London, 1991), pp. 141–2 and David Dilks (ed.), *The Diaries of Sir Alexander Cadogan, 1938–1945*, (Cassell: London, 1971), pp. 189–90.
3 Stephen S. Large, *Emperor Hirohito and Showa Japan*, (Routledge: London, 1992), p. 103.

Introduction

1 See, for example, R.A.C. Parker, *Chamberlain and Appeasement: British Policy and the Coming of the Second World War*, (Macmillan: London, 1993), pp. 10 and 345.
2 See Ian Kershaw, *The Nazi Dictatorship: Problems and Perspectives of Interpretation*, (Arnold: London, Third Ed., 1993), pp. 108–30. See also below, pp. 227–32, for a discussion of the various interpretations that have been developed.
3 The war in Europe ended in May 1945; the war in East Asia and the Pacific the following August.
4 See John Whittam, 'The Origins of the Second World War,' in *Modern History Review*, 4, 1992–3, pp. 5–8.
5 Akira Iriye, 'The Asian Factor,' in G. Martel (ed.), *The Origins of the Second World War Reconsidered: The A.J.P. Taylor Debate after Twenty–Five Years*, (Allen & Unwin: Boston, 1986), p. 227.
6 ibid., pp. 227–8.
7 ibid., p. 228. Professor D. C. Watt takes the view that it was the Washington Conference of 1921–2 that made the linkage of a Pacific war with a European war likely. He also suggests that without the European war the military confrontation that took place between Japan and the United States might never have occurred. See D .C. Watt, 'The Relationship between the Far Eastern and European Wars, 1922–1941,' in Robert W. Love Jr., *Pearl Harbor Revisited*, (St. Martin's Press: New York, 1995), pp. 1–12.
8 Wolf D. Gruner, 'The Impact of the Reconstruction of Central Europe in 1814–15 on the System of Peace in the Nineteenth Century,' in Albert P. van Goudoever (ed.), *Great Peace Congresses in History 1648–1990*, (Universiteit Utrecht: Utrecht, 1993), p. 35.

9 ibid., pp. 26 and 37.
10 See V. R. Berghahn, *Germany and the Approach of War in 1914*, (Macmillan: Basingstoke, Second Ed., 1993), pp. 15–37. On the Anglo-German anatagonism that this resulted in see M. Fröhlich, *Imperialismus: Deutsche Kolonial– und Weltpolitik 1880–1914*, (Deutscher Taschenbuch Verlag: Munich, 1994), passim.
11 W. G. Beasley, *Select Documents on Japanese Foreign Policy 1853–1868*, (Oxford University Press: London, 1955), p. 117.
12 J. E. Hunter, *The Emergence of Modern Japan: An Introductory History Since 1853*, (Longman: London, 1989), pp. 17–8.
13 ibid., pp. 24–5.
14 ibid., pp. 26–7.
15 David Reynolds, *Britannia Overruled: British Policy and World Power in the Twentieth Century*, (Longman: London, 1991), pp. 11–25. For a fuller discussion of these issues see below pp. 18–21.
16 ibid., p. 9. See also John R. Ferris, ' "The Greatest Power on Earth"; Great Britain in the 1920s,' in *The International History Review*, 13, 1991, pp. 740–4.
17 P. R. Ghosh, 'Disraelian Conservatism: A Financial Approach,' in *English Historical Review*, 99, 1984, p. 289. See also Reynolds, p. 20. *Britannia Overruled*.
18 F. S. Northedge, *Descent from Power; British Foreign Policy, 1945–1973,* (Allen & Unwin: London, 1974), p. 18.
19 Joep Leersen, 'As Others See, Among Others, Us: The Anglo-German Relationship in Context,' in Harald Husemann (ed.), *As Others See Us: Anglo-German Perceptions*, (Peter Lang: Frankfurt am Main, 1994), p. 76. Leersen points out that England's former great rival, Spain, acquired in nineteenth-century English literature a picturesque image, while Germany's image became sinister (*unheimlich*).
20 David Head, ' "Made in Germany": the British Perspective as Revealed in Advertising,' in Husemann, p. 99, *As Others See Us*.
21 Harald Rosenbach,   *Das Deutsche Reich, Großbritannien und der Transvaal (1896–1902)*, (Vandenhoeck & Ruprecht: Göttingen, 1993), pp. 17–49.
22 Sir Eyre Crowe, senior Foreign Office official who later, during the 1920s, became the non-political head of the department, wrote this memorandum for Edward VII to explain why the British government's foreign policy was assuming an anti-German bias and the corresponding need to improve relations with Russia. See also Zara S. Steiner, *Britain and the Origins of the First World War*, (Macmillan: London, 1977), pp. 44–5. See P. Kennedy, *The Rise and Fall of British Naval Mastery*, (Macmillan: Basingstoke, 1983), pp. 216–20, regarding Fisher's naval reforms.
23 Keith Wilson, *The Policy of the Entente: Essays on the Determinants of British Foreign Policy, 1904–14*, (Cambridge University Press: Cambridge, 1985), p. 79.
24 Kennedy, *Naval Mastery*, p. 209.
25 The nature of the mandated territories is one of the most misunderstood issues in twentieth century history. They were not surrendered to and did not belong to the League of Nations. Under the terms of the Versailles Treaty sovereignty was transferred to the Principal Allied and Associated Powers. It was they who distributed them among themselves and, under Article 22 of the League Covenant, they agreed to administer them in accordance with certain conditions and rules which they themselves devised. Sovereignty continued to reside, however, with the Principal Allied and Associated Powers.
26 'So many Alexanders' was a reference to Alexander the Great, the Macedonian King of the fourth century B.C. who acquired an Empire stretching as far east as the Indus River in modern Pakistan.

27 Erik Goldstein, 'The Evolution of British Diplomatic Strategy for the Washington Conference,' in Erik Goldstein and John Maurer (ed.), *The Washington Conference, 1921–22: Naval Rivalry, East Asian Stability and the Road to Pearl Harbor,* (Cass: London, 1994) p. 6.

28 Below, pp. 18–21.

29 D. Cameron Watt, *Succeeding John Bull: America in Britain's Place 1900–1975,* (Cambridge University Press: Cambridge, 1984), p. 23. See also G. F. Kennan, *Russia and the West under Lenin and Stalin,* (Hutchinson: London, 1961), pp. 224–41.

30 Kathleen Burk, *Britain, America and the Sinews of War 1914–1918,* (Allen & Unwin: Boston, 1985), pp. 77–95.

31 See letter from Sir Mark Sykes to Georges Picot, March 1918, quoted in J. Nevakivi, *Britain, France and the Arab Middle-East, 1914–1920,* (Athlone Press: London, 1969), p. 50.

32 Robert Blake, *The Unknown Prime Minister: The Life and Times of Andrew Bonar Law, 1858–1923,* (Eyre and Spottiswoode: London, 1955), p. 448.

33 Anthony Adamthwaite, *Grandeur and Misery: France's Bid for Power in Europe 1914–1940,* (Arnold: London, 1995), p. 59.

34 ibid., p. 54.

35 On the differences between Britain and France, see A. Wolfers, *Britain and France between Two Wars: Conflicting Strategies of Peace from Versailles to World War II,* (Norton: New York, 1966).

36 See S. A. Shuker, *American "Reparations" to Germany,* (Princeton University Press: Princeton, 1986), passim. and S. A. Shuker, 'The End of Versailles,' in G. Martel (ed.), *The Origins of the Second World War Reconsidered: The A. J. P. Taylor Debate after Twenty-five Years,* (Allen & Unwin: Boston, 1986), pp. 55–6.

37 John Gillingham, *Coal, Steel, and the Rebirth of Europe, 1945–1955: The Germans and French from Ruhr Conflict to Economic Community,* (Cambridge University Press: Cambridge, 1991), pp. 11–2.

38 M. Lee and W. Michalka, *German Foreign Policy 1917–1933: Continuity or Break?,* (Berg: Leamington Spa, 1987), pp. 30–1.

39 Richard Bessel, 'Why did the Weimar Republic Collapse,' in Ian Kershaw (ed.), *Weimar: Why did Democracy Fail?,* (Weidenfeld and Nicolson: London, 1990), p. 148.

40 A. Hitler, *Hitler's Secret Book,* (Grove Press: New York, 1961).

41 A. Hitler, *Hitlers Politisches Testament: Die Bormann Diktate vom Februar und April 1945,* (Knaus: Hamburg, 1981), pp. 78–9.

42 K. Hildebrand, *The Foreign Policy of the Third Reich,* (Batsford: London, 1973), passim.

43 See, for example, T. Mason, *Social policy in the Third Reich: The Working Class and the 'National Community,'* (Berg: Oxford, 1993).

44 *Public Record Office,* FO 800/286, Sir John Simon Papers, R. Boothby to Sir J. Simon, 18.1.1932.

45 *Appeasement* now means 'concession' rather than 'pacification.'

46 Benny Morris, *The Roots of Appeasement* and Andrew J. Crozier, 'Chatham House and Appeasement,' in Andrea Bosco and Cornelia Navari (eds), *Chatham House and British Foreign Policy: The Royal Institute of International Affairs during the Inter-War Period,* (Lothian Foundation Press: London, 1994), pp. 205–60.

47 W. N. Medlicott, *British Foreign Policy Since Versailles 1919–1963,* (Methuen: London, 1968), p. xvi. See also *Documents on British Foreign Policy,* (HMSO: London, 1946–), Series IA, Vol. I, Appendix.

48 Ian Colvin, *The Chamberlain Cabinet*, (Victor Gollancz: London, 1971), pp. 63–4.
49 *House of Commons Debates*, V, vol. 333, cols. 1405–6.
50 A. J. Crozier, 'Prelude to Munich: British Foreign Policy and Germany, 1935–8,' in *European Studies Review*, 6, 1976, p. 376.

1 The Powers in 1919 and After

1 B. R. Mitchell with P. Deane, *Abstract of British Historical Statistics*, (Cambridge University Press: Cambridge, 1962), p. 403.
2 Gustav Schmidt, *The Politics and Economics of Appeasement: British Foreign Policy in the 1930s*, (Berg: Leamington Spa 1986), p. 228.
3 *House of Commons Debates*, V, vol. 309. col 1832.
4 Paul Kennedy, *The Realities behind Diplomacy: Background Influences on British External Policy, 1865–1980*, (Fontana: London, 1981), pp. 226–7.
5 Kathleen Burk, *Britain, America and the Sinews of War 1914–18*, (Allen & Unwin: Boston, 1985), p. 81.
6 S. Pollard, *The Development of the British Economy 1914–1990*, (Arnold: London, 1992), p. 90.
7 Mitchell with Deane, *Abstract of British Historical Statistics*, p. 66,
8 ibid., p. 188.
9 Pollard, *The Development of the British Economy*, p. 56. See also E. Hobsbawm, *Industry and Empire*, (Penguin, 1969), p. 207.
10 Mitchell with Deane, *Abstract of British Historical Statistics*, p. 119.
11 Pollard, *The Development of the British Economy*, p. 50.
12 Hobsbawm, *Industry and Empire*, (Penguin, 1969), p. 207.
13 Pollard, *The Development of the British Economy*, p. 53.
14 ibid., p. 90.
15 ibid., p. 43ff. There is a debate as to whether the improvement in British economic performance in the 1930s was due to the new industries, or due to improvement across the board. See B. W. E. Alford, 'New Industries for Old? British Industries between the Wars,' in R. Floud and D. McCloskey (eds), *The Economic History of Britain since 1700*, Vol. 2, (Cambridge University Press: Cambridge, 1981), pp. 316–7; N. K. Buxton, 'The Role of the New Industries in Britain during the 1930s: A Reinterpretation,' in *Business History Review*, 49 (1975), pp. 205–22; and J. A. Dowie, 'Growth in the Inter-War Period: Some More Arithmetic,' in *Economic History Review*, 21 (1968), p. 100.
16 See Corelli Barnett, *The Collapse of British Power*, (Eyre Methuen: London, 1972); Corelli Barnett, *The Audit of War: the Illusion and Reality of Britain as a Great Nation*, (Macmillan: London, 1986); and Paul Kennedy, *The Rise and Fall of the Great Powers: Economic Change and Military Conflict from 1500 to 2000*, (Unwin Hyman: London, 1989).
17 John K. Ferris, '"The Greatest Power on Earth"; Great Britain in the 1920s,' in *The International History Review*, 13, 1991, p. 731.
18 ibid., p. 743.
19 ibid., pp. 741–2. See also B. J. C. McKercher, '"Our Most Dangerous Enemy": Great Britain Pre-eminent in the 1930s,' in *The International History Review*, 13, 1991, pp. 751–83.
20 R. Girault and R. Frank, *Turbulente Europe et nouveaux mondes, 1914–1941*, (1988), p. 75, quoted in A. Adamthwaite, *Grandeur and Misery: France's Bid for Power in Europe 1914–1940*, (Arnold: London, 1995), p. 72.
21 D. H. Aldcroft, *From Versailles to Wall Street, 1919–1929*, (Penguin: London, 1977), p. 31.

22 A. Adamthwaite, *Grandeur*, pp. 65–70 and 73–6.

23 A. Wolfers, *Britain and France between the Wars*, (Norton: New York, 1966) p. 12.

24 G. Procacci, *History of the Italian People*, (Penguin: London, 1973) pp. 402–3.

25 Oil and natural gas were not discovered in Libya until 1959.

26 See William Appleman Williams, 'The Legend of Isolationism in the 1920s,' in *Science and Society*, 18, 1954, pp. 1–20 and D .C. Watt, 'U.S. Isolationism in the 1920s. Is it a Useful Concept?' in *Bulletin of the British Association of American Studies*, 6, 1962, pp. 4–19. See also M. J. Hogan, *Informal Entente: The Private Structure of Cooperation in Anglo-American Economic Diplomacy 1918–1928*, (University of Missouri Press: Columbia, 1977), p. 6.

27 Watt, *John Bull*, p. 44. The Anglo-Japanese alliance presented no threat to the United States. The text of the 1911 revision of the 1902 treaty made it clear that the alliance could not be operative against the United States. See D. C. Watt, 'The Relationship between the Far Eastern and European Wars, 1922-41,' in Robert W. Love Jnr., *Pearl Harbor Revisited*, (St. Martin's Press: New York, 1995), pp. 1–12.

28 Watt, *John Bull*, p. 41.

29 ibid., p. 42.

30 Akira Iriye, *The Globalizing of America, 1913–1945*, (Cambridge University Press: Cambridge, 1993), p. 92.

31 See above, pp. 8–9.

32 J. E. Hunter, *The Emergence of Modern Japan: An Introductory History Since 1853*, (Longman: London, 1989), pp. 26–7.

33 R. Storry, *Japan and the Decline of the West in Asia 1894–1943*, (Macmillan: London, 1979), p. 109.

34 ibid., p. 114.

35 See below, pp. 37–48.

36 See O. Busch and G. Feldman (eds.), *Historische Prosesse der deutschen Inflation 1914–1924*, (Colloquium Verlag: Berlin, 1978) and G. D. Feldman, C.-L. Holtfrerich, G. A. Ritter and C. Witt (eds.), *Die deutsche Inflation, eine Zwischenbilanz*, (De Gruyter: Berlin, 1982).

37 Eberhard Kolb, *The Weimar Republic*, (Unwin Hyman: London, 1988), p. 12.

38 ibid.

39 S. Haffner, *1918/1919: Eine deutsche Revolution*, (Rowohlt: Reinbek bei Hamburg, 1981), p. 10.

40 ibid., p. 39.

41 M. Lee and W. Michalka, *German Foreign Policy 1917–1933: Continuity or Break?*, (Berg: Leamington Spa, 1987). Quoted in preface with unnumbered pages.

42 The *Volksdeutsch*, the ethnic Germans, who had lived for centuries in various parts of Eastern Europe, such as Transylvania (the *Siebenbürgendeutsch*) did not share in this agitation. See Holm Sundhaussen, 'Deutsche in Rumänien,' in Klaus Bade (ed.), *Deutsche im Ausland – Fremde in Deutschland: Migration in Geschichte und Gegenwart*, (Verlag C. H. Beck: Munich, 1992), pp. 36–53.

43 C. J. Lowe and M. L. Dockrill, *The Mirage of Power: British Foreign Policy 1902–1922*, Vol. 3, (Routledge: London, 1972) p. 689.

44 G. Kennan, *Russia and the West under Lenin and Stalin*, (Hutchinson: London, 1961), pp. 45–7, 64–119. See also, M. Kettle, *Russia and the Allies 1917–20: The Road to Intervention, March–November 1918*, (Routledge: London, 1988).

45 M. L. Dockrill and J. Douglas Goold, *Peace Without Promise: Foreign Policy 1919–1923*, (Batsford: London, 1981) p. 124.

46 Marc Ferro, *The Great War 1914–1918*, (Routledge: London, 1973), pp. 212–3.

47 D. R. Watson, *Georges Clemenceau: A Political Biography*, (Eyre Methuen: London, 1974), pp. 372–9.

48 See Iriye, *Globalizing*, pp. 55–7 and M. A. Barnhart, *Japan and the World Since 1868*, (Arnold: London, 1995), pp. 57–71.

49 G. F. Kennan, *Soviet Foreign Policy 1917–1941*, (Van Nostrand: Princeton, 1960), pp. 30–1.

50 I. Maisky, *Who Helped Hitler?*, (Hutchinson: London, 1964), pp. 24–6.

51 Christopher Andrew, *Secret Service: The Making of the British Intelligence Community*, (Heineman: London, 1985), pp. 259–339.

52 G. Bonnet, *Quai d'Orsay*, (Times Press and Anthony Gibbs & Phillips: Douglas, IOM, 1965), p. 216.

53 T. H. von Laue, 'Soviet Diplomacy: G. V. Chicherin, Peoples Commissar for Foreign Affairs, 1918–1930,' in G. A. Craig and F. Gilbert (eds), *The Diplomats*, Vol. 1, (Atheneum: New York, 1965), p. 263.

54 S. J. Woolf (ed.), *The Nature of Fascism*, (Weidenfeld and Nicolson: London, 1968) p. 41.

2 The Making of the Inter-War World

1 A. J. Crozier, *Appeasement and Germany's last Bid for Colonies*, (Macmillan: London, 1988) p. 25.

2 It is interesting to note, however, that the best introduction recently to appear on the subject of peacemaking at the end of the First World War, A. Sharp, *The Versailles Settlement: Peacemaking Paris, 1919*, (Macmillan: London, 1991), does precisely this!

3 B. Kent, *The Spoils of War: The Politics, Economics, and Diplomacy of Reparations 1918–1932*, (Oxford University Press, 1989) pp. 265 and 236. See also below pp.44–5.

4 A. Sharp, *The Versailles Settlement*, pp. 61–2.

5 ibid., p. 122.

6 ibid., pp. 86–7.

7 See B. Kent, *The Spoils of War*, pp. 57–103.

8 See John W. Coogan, 'Wilsonian Diplomacy in War and Peace,' in G. Martel (ed.), *American Foreign Relations Reconsidered 1890–1993*, (Routledge, 1994), p. 84. 'Wilson acknowledged that there were flaws in the treaty. He regarded them as unfortunate but inevitable, given the bitterness the Allies felt after years of war. By creating the League and securing Allied participation in it, he believed he had created a mechanism to correct those flaws once the passions of war cooled. He could accept short-term compromises as the price to be paid for creating a viable League of Nations because he saw it as essential to a lasting peace.'

9 Akira Iriye, *The Globalizing of America, 1913–1945*, (Cambridge University Press: Cambridge, 1993), p. 69.

10 See William C. Widenor, *Henry Cabot Lodge and the Search for an American Foreign Policy*, (University of California Press: Berkeley, 1980).

11 Carl Parrini, *Heir to Empire: United States Economic Diplomacy 1916–1923*, (University of Pittsburgh Press: Pittsburgh, 1969), pp. 13–4.

12 Akira Iriye, *Globalizing*, p. 91.

13 Parrini, *Heir to Empire*, pp. 214–5.

14 M. J. Hogan, *Informal Entente: The Private Structure of Cooperation in Anglo-American Economic Diplomacy, 1918–1928*, (University of Missouri Press: Columbia, 1977), p. 218.

15 A. Sharp, *The Versailles Settlement*, p. 190.
16 Paul M. Kennedy, 'The Rise and Fall of British Naval Mastery,' (Macmillan: Basingstoke, 1983), p. 274. William R. Braisted, 'The Evolution of the United States Navy's Strategic Assessments in the Pacific, 1919–31,' in E. Goldstein and J. Maurer, *The Washington Conference, 1921–22: Naval Rivalry, East Asian Stability and the Road to Pearl Harbor*, (Cass: London, 1994), pp. 103–4.
17 Erik Goldstein, 'The Evolution of British Diplomatic Strategy for the Washington Conference', in Goldstein and Maurer, *The Washington Conference*, p. 16.
18 Iriye, *Globalizing*, p. 76.
19 Goldstein, 'Evolution of British Diplomatic Strategy,' p. 7.
20. R. Storry, *Japan and the Decline of the West in Asia 1894–1943*, (Macmillan: London, 1979), pp. 123–4.

3 The Failed Peace

1 G. Schulz, *Revolutions and Peace Treaties*, (London, 1972), pp. 194–207.
2 See below pp. 51–2.
3 Archives of the *Royal Institute of International Affairs*, 8/553, Lord Astor to A. J. Toynbee, 3.11.1938.
4 M. Beloff, *The Intellectual in Politics and other Essays*, (Weidenfeld and Nicolson: London, 1970), p. 197.
5 Sharp, *The Versailles Settlement*, pp. 78–9.
6 ibid., and Kent, 'The Spoils of War', pp. 33–4.
7 ibid., pp. 25–6 and Sharp, *The Versailles Settlement*, pp. 83–5.
8 ibid., p. 97.
9 W. Michalka and G. Niedhart (eds), *Die ungeliebte Republik*, (Deutscher Taschenbuch Verlag: Munich, 1980), pp. 124–32.
10 D. Lloyd George, *The Truth about the Peace Treaties*, (Victor Gollancz: London, 1938), pp. 404–20.
11 Sally Marks, 'Reparations Reconsidered: A Reminder,' in *Central European History*, 2, 1969, p. 361.
12 Stephen A. Schuker, 'The End of Versailles,' in G. Martel (ed.), *The Origins of the Second World War Reconsidered: The A. J. P. Taylor Debate after Twenty-Five Years*, (Allen & Unwin: Boston, 1986), p. 55.
13 Anne Orde, *British Policy and European Reconstruction After the First World War*, (Cambridge University Press: Cambridge, 1990), pp. 177–8.
14 ibid., pp. 177–9.
15 Michalka and Niedhart, *Die ungeliebte Republik*, pp. 141–2.
16 Carole Fink, 'Beyond Revisionism,' in Carole Fink, Axel Frohn and J. Heideking (ed.), *Genoa, Rapallo and European Reconstruction in 1922*, (Cambridge University Press: Cambridge, 1991), p. 15 and P. Krüger, 'A Rainy Day, April 16, 1922: The Rapallo Treaty and the Cloudy Perspective for German Foreign Policy,' in ibid., p. 63.
17 Orde, *British Policy and European Reconstruction*, p. 237.
18 A. Adamthwaite, *Grandeur and Misery: France's Bid for Power in Europe 1914–1940*, (Arnold: London, 1995), p. 101.
19 Schuker, 'The End of Versailles', p. 60 and S. A. Schuker, *The End of French Predominance in Europe: The Financial Crisis of 1924 and the Adoption of the Dawes Plan*, (University of North Carolina Press: Chapel Hill, 1976), passim.
20 Adamthwaite, *Grandeur and Misery*, pp. 117, 149–51.
21 See, for example, Mary Nolan, *Visions of Modernity: American Business and the Modernization of Germany*, (Oxford University Press: Oxford, 1994).

22 See, Ian Kershaw, 'Perspectives of Weimar's Failure,' in Ian Kershaw (ed.), *Weimar: Why Did Democracy Fail?*, (Weidenfeld and Nicolson: London, 1990), pp. 5–6. See also: K. Borchardt, *Wachstum, Krizen, Handlungsspielraüme der Wirtschaftspolitik*, (Vandenhoeck & Ruprecht: Göttingen, 1982) and *Perspectives on Modern German Economic History and Policy*, (Cambridge University Press: Cambridge, 1991).

23 E. Kolb, *The Weimar Republic*, (Unwin: London, 1988), p. 58.

24 E. Eyck, *A History of the Weimar Republic*, (University of Harvard Press: Cambridge, 1964), Vol. II, p. 43.

25 J. Jacobson, *Locarno Diplomacy: Germany and the West, 1925–1929*, (Princeton University Press: Princeton, 1972), pp. 372–3.

26 A. J. Crozier, 'The Colonial Question in Stresemann's Locarno Policy,' in *The International History Review*, IV, 1982, p. 39.

27 J. Wright, 'Stresemann and Weimar,' in *History Today*, (October, 1989), pp. 35–41.

28 For a full discussion of this issue see Marshall Lee and Wolfgang Michalka, *German Foreign Policy 1917–1933: Continuity or Break?* (Berg: Leamington Spa, 1987) and H. A. Turner, 'Continuity in German Foreign Policy? The Case of Stresemann,' in *The International History Review*, I, 1979, pp. 509–21.

29 F. G. Stambrook, 'Das Kind – Lord D'Abernon and the Locarno Pact,' in *Central European History*, 1, 1968, pp. 233–263 and Angela Kaiser, *Lord D'Abernon und die englische Deutschlandpolitik 1920–1926*, (P. Lang: Frankfurt am Main, 1989), pp. 306-407.

30 See above pp. 35–6.

31 G. F. Kennan, *Russia and the West Under Lenin and Stalin*, (Hutchinson: London, 1961), p. 224.

32 The *Zinoviev Letter* was in fact one of a number of letters allegedly sent by the President of the Communist International, Grigorii Zinoviev, to the British Communist Party during the life of the first Labour Government. This particular letter was dated 15 September 1924 and instructed the British Communist Party to exercise pressure on sympathizers in the Labour Party so that the recently concluded Anglo-Russian Commercial and General Treaties would more easily be ratified; to increase propaganda work amongst the British armed forces; and to continue generally preparations for the future British revolution. The *Letter* acquired considerable notoriety at the time because it was published, following its interception by British security services, in the *Daily Mail* on the the eve of the general election of 29 October 1924. Undoubtedly it had been leaked by the intelligence community to the Conservative press with the express purpose of discrediting Labour and at the time it was considered by both Labour and Conservative leaderships to have been instrumental in Labour's loss of office in 1924. It was subsequently denounced by Labour as a forgery and part of a dirty tricks campaign. The Soviet authorities always denied its authenticity. A British Cabinet Committee, however, was certain of its authenticity, see *Public Record Office* CAB 23/49/60th, Meeting. The most expert British authority on the subject also inclines to this view, see Christopher Andrew, *Secret Service: The Making of the British Intelligence Community*, (Heinemann: London, 1985), pp. 305–13. Whatever the authenticity of the *Zinoviev Letter*, it is doubtful whether it did more than marginally affect the election result. The Conservative leader, Baldwin, with his call for 'sane, commonsense Government', had already sensed the prevailing mood of the mid-1920s and that was probably most critical. In this context it was the Liberal decline and loss of one hundred seats, mainly to the Conservatives, that determined the outcome of the election and not the *Zinoviev Letter*.

Relations with the USSR were finally severed following a raid by British security services on the London premises of Arcos Ltd, a British Company organized to conduct trade with the USSR, which also contained the offices of the Soviet Trade Delegation. The object of the raid was to obtain evidence of Communist subversion. No such evidence was ever found and Anglo-Soviet relations were severed in the wake of the raid to conceal the government's incompetence.

33 G. F. Kennan, *Soviet Foreign Policy 1917–41*, (Van Nostrand: Princeton, 1960), pp. 60-2.

34 On the complexities of Germany's relationships with the West and the Soviet Union see L. Kochan, *The Struggle for Germany 1914–1945*, (University Press: Edinburgh, 1963).

35 W. L. Shirer, *The Collapse of the Third Republic*, (Pan Books: London, 1972), p. 132.

36 For a thorough survey of the background to the Briand Plan see C. H. Pegg, *Evolution of the European Idea*, (University of North Carolina Press: Chapel Hill, 1983). See also R. Boyce, 'Britain's First 'No' to Europe: Britain and the Briand Plan, 1929-1930,' in *European Studies Review*, 10, 1980, p. 39 and W. Lipgens, 'Europäische Einigungsidee 1923–1930 und Briand's Europaplan im Urteil der deutschen Akten,' in *Historische Zeitschrift*, 203, 1966, pp. 46–89 and 316–63. See also R. Lamb, *The Drift to War 1922–1939*, (St. Martin's Press: New York, 1989), pp. 43–6. In all essential points Lamb's views coincide with those of the author, although it should be stressed that the author's have been arrived at independently. See 'Britain, Germany and the Dishing of the Briand Plan,' in A. Bosco, *A Constitution for Europe: A Comparative Study of Federal Constitutions and Plans for the United States of Europe*, (Lothian Foundation Press: London 1991), pp. 213–30.

37 Sally Marks, *The Illusion of Peace: International Relations in Europe 1918–1933*, (Macmillan: London, 1976), pp. 108–136.

38 Adamthwaite, *Grandeur and Misery*, pp. 134–5, 137–8.

39 Akira Iriye, *After Imperialism: The Search for a New Order in the Far East, 1921-1931*, (Harvard University Press: Cambridge, Mass. 1968), pp. 86–7.

40 Christopher Thorne, *The Limits of Foreign Policy: The West, the League and the Far Eastern Crisis of 1931–1933*, (Macmillan: London, 1973), pp. 48–50. In 1931 British investments in China totalled £244 million. Of this £150 million was located in the Shanghai area.

41 For a fuller discussion of Far Eastern issues see below chapters VIII and X.

4 The Challenge of Fascism and the Democratic Response

1 G. Procacci, *History of the Italian People*, (Penguin: London, 1975), p. 373.

2 A. Cassels, *Fascist Italy*, (Routledge & Kegan Paul: London, 1969), p. 10.

3 ibid., p. 11 and D. Mack Smith, *Mussolini*, (Weidenfeld and Nicolson: London, 1981), p. 31.

4 G. Carocci, *Italian Fascism*, (Penguin: London, 1973), p. 12.

5 Cassels, *Fascist Italy*, pp. 27–35.

6 Mack Smith, *Mussolini*, p. 51.

7 B. Mussolini, *The Doctrine of Fascism*, (Valecchi: Firenze, 1938), pp. 24–5.

8 ibid., p. 51.

9 ibid., p. 28.

10 ibid., pp. 14–8.

11 Carocci, *Italian Fascism*, p. 71.

12 Philip Morgan, *Italian Fascism 1919–1945*, (Macmillan: Basingstoke, 1995) pp. 134–5.

13 K. Pinson, *Modern Germany*, (Macmillan: New York, 1966), p. 345.

14 There has been much debate on the impact of the Treaty of Versailles on the Weimar Republic. Early writers such as O. Braun, *Vom Weimar zu Hitler*, (Europa Verlag: New York, 1940) and L. Zimmermann, *Deutsche Aussenpolitik in der Ära der Weimarer Republik*, (Musterschmidt Verlag:Göttingen, 1958), tended to see the collapse of the Weimar Republic as the consequence of opposition to the Versailles System within Germany and of the failure to revise it in time. More recent writers, however, while accepting that Versailles contributed to the destabilization of the Weimar Republic in its early years, are inclined to attribute less significance to Versailles and foreign policy factors in its final disintegration. See, for example, A. Hillgruber, 'Unter den Schatten von Versailles,' in K. D. Erdmann and H. Schulz (ed.), *Weimar, Selbstpreisgabe einer Demokratie*, (Droste Verlag: Düsseldorf, 1980).

15 A. J. Nicholls, 'Germany,' in S. J. Woolf (ed.), *European Fascism*, (Weidenfeld and Nicolson: London, 1968), pp. 68–9.

16 J. Noakes and G. Pridham (ed.), *Nazism 1919–1945: The Rise to Power 1919 – 1934*, (University of Exeter: Exeter, 1983), p. 11.

17 ibid., p. 10.

18 A. J. Crozier, *Appeasement and Germany's Last Bid for Colonies*, (Macmillan: Basingstoke, 1988), pp. 34–5.

19 Noakes and Pridham, *Nazism 1919–1945*, p. 18.

20 A. Hitler, *Mein Kampf*, (Hutchinson: London, 1969), pp. 598–9.

21 A. Hitler, *Hitler's Secret Book*, (Grove Press: New York, 1961), p. 23 and A. Hitler, *Hitler's Table Talk*, (Weidenfeld and Nicolson: London, 1973), p. 619.

22 D. Cameron Watt, *How War Came*, (Heinemann: London, 1989), p. 623.

23 H. Tint, *France since 1918*, (Batsford: London, 1970), pp. 60 and 75.

24 James F. Macmillan, *Dreyfus to De Gaulle: Politics and Society in France 1898–1969*, (Arnold: London, 1985), pp. 102–5.

25 M. Vaisse, 'Against Appeasement: French Advocates of Firmness. 1933–8,' in W. J. Mommsen and L. Kettenacker, *The Fascist Challenge and the Policy of Appeasement*, (Allen & Unwin: London, 1983), p. 230.

26 ibid., pp. 230–1.

27 *Documents Diplomatiques Français, 1932–39*, (Imprimerie Nationale: Paris, 1964), Series 1, Vol. III, No. 378.

28 Vaisse, 'Against Appeasement', p. 231.

29 Kennan, *Foreign Policy*, pp. 85–6.

30 R. Girault, 'The Impact of the Economic Situation on the Foreign Policy of France, 1936–9,' in Mommsen and Kettenacker, *The Fascist Challenge and the Policy of Appeasement*, pp. 209–26.

31 W. H. Dawson, 'Can France and Germany br Reconciled?', *The Fortnightly Review*, September 1922, pp. 1–17.

32 J. L. Garvin, *The Economic Foundations of Peace*, (Macmillan: London, 1919), pp. 152–3, 257–9; N. Angell, *The Fruits of Victory*, (Collins: London, 1921), p. 54; and J. M. Keynes, *The Economic Consequences of the Peace*, (Macmillan: London, 1919), pp. 14 and 102.

33 S. King-Hall, *Chatham House*, (Oxford University Press: London, 1937), pp. 1–14; A. J. Toynbee, *Experiences*, (Oxford University Press: London, 1969), p. 61.

34 Toynbee, pp. 82–3.

35 M. Gilbert, *The Roots of Appeasement*, (Weidenfeld and Nicolson: London, 1966), pp. 130–2; Crozier, *Appeasement*, pp. 27–9.

36 See, for example, Wesley Wark, *The Ultimate Enemy: British Intelligence and Nazi Germany, 1933–1939*, (Tauris: London, 1985), passim.

37 Some British historians now argue that such a deal was attainable in 1939 and 1940 and that Britain should have accepted it. In this way, they argue, the British Empire would have been preserved and the Welfare State, introduced under Labour after 1945, avoided. These views, and the very considerable objections to them, are examined in more detail below, pp. 234–43.

38 D. C. Watt, *Succeeding John Bull: America in Britain's Place, 1900–1975*, (Cambridge University Press: Cambridge, 1984), p. 76.

39 See above, p. 2.

40 Thomas N. Guinsberg, 'The Triumph of Isolationism,' in G. Martel (ed.), *American Foreign Relations Reconsidered, 1890–1993*, (Routledge: London, 1994), p. 91.

41 Martin S. Alexander, 'The USA and the Coming of the Second World War,' in *Modern History Review*, 6, 1994, p. 28.

42 Iriye, *Globalizing*, pp. 140, 154, 162.

43 ibid., p. 143.

44 Alexander, 'The USA and the Coming of the Second World War', p. 29.

45 Iriye, *Globalizing*, p. 146.

46 Watt, *John Bull*, p. 76.

5 The International System Challenged

1 W. Lipgens (ed.), *Documents on the History of European Integration*, Vol. 1, (De Gruyter: Berlin, 1985), p. 11.

2 N. Frei, *National Socialist Rule in Germany: The Führer State 1933–1945*, (Blackwell: Oxford, 1993), p. 64.

3 ibid., p. 35 and Ian Kershaw, *Hitler*, (Longman: London, 1991), p. 66.

4 ibid., p. 102.

5 R. Gellately, *The Gestapo and German Society: Enforcing Racial Policy, 1933–1945*, (Oxford University Press: Oxford, 1991), passim.

6 Kershaw, *Hitler*, p. 68.

7 Frei, op.cit., p. 11.

8 J. Noakes and G. Pridham (ed.), *Nazism 1919–1945: Foreign Policy, War and Racial Extermination*, (Exeter University Press: Exeter, 1988), pp. 628–9.

9 *Documents on British Foreign Policy*, (HMSO: London, 1946 –), Second Series, Vol. V, No. 127.

10 E. M. Robertson, *Hitler's Pre-War Policy and Military Plans*, (Longman: London, 1963), p. 21.

11 Useful information on German rearmament is to be found in Matthew Cooper, *The German Army, 1933–1945: Its Political and Military Failure*, (MacDonald & Janes: London, 1978); Matthew Cooper, *The German Air Force, 1933–1945: An Anatomy of Failure*, (Janes: London, 1981); Wilhelm Diest, *The Wehrmacht and German Rearmament*, (Macmillan: London, 1981); and R. J. O'Neill, *The German Army and the Nazi Party*, (Corgi: London, 1968).

12 R. J. Overy, *The Nazi Economic Recovery 1932–1938*, (Macmillan: London, 1982), p. 29. There were, however, severe problems such as the raw materials and financial crises of 1936. See W. Carr, *Arms, Autarky and Aggression: A Study in German Foreign Policy, 1933–1939*, (Arnold: London, 1972), pp. 55–6.

13 ibid., p. 31.

14 T. Balogh, 'The National Economy of Germany,' in *Economic Journal*, 48 (1938), pp. 461–97; R. C. Erbe, *Die nationalsozialistische Wirtschaftspolitik 1933–1939 in Lichte der modernen Theorie*, (Zurich, 1958); and A. Milward, *The German Economy at War*, (Athlone Press: London, 1965), pp. 1–53. See also R. J. Overy, *War and Economy in the Third Reich*, (Oxford University Press: Oxford, 1994), pp. 177–204 and ibid., pp. 233–56 for a penetrating criticism of the *Blitzkrieg* theory.

15 Overy, *Economic Recovery*, pp. 47–8.

16 A. J. Toynbee (ed.), *Documents on International Affairs, 1933*, (Oxford University Press: London, 1934), pp. 196–208.

17 K. Hildebrand, *The Foreign Policy of the Third Reich*, (Batsford: London, 1973), pp. 38–46.

18 *Documents on German Foreign Policy*, (HMSO: London, 1951 –), Series C, Vol. II, No. 9.

19 R. Overy with A. Wheatcroft, *The Road to War*, (Macmillan: London, 1989), p. 159.

20 D. Schmitz, *The United States and Fascist Italy 1922–1940*, (University of North Carolina Press: Chapel Hill, 1988), p. 148.

21 E. Wiskemann, *The Rome–Berlin Axis*, (Fontana: London, 1966), p. 57).

22 A. J. Crozier, *Appeasement and Germany's Last Bid for Colonies*, (Basingstoke, 1988), p. 105 and *Documents on British Foreign Policy*, Second Series, Vol. VI, No. 472.

23 Christopher Thorne, *The Limits of Foreign Policy: The West, the League and the Far Eastern Crisis of 1931–1933*, (Macmillan: London, 1972), pp. 377–87. See also W. H. McNeill, *Arnold J. Toynbee: A Life*, (Oxford University Press: New York, 1989), pp. 152–3, 169–70.

24 A. J. Crozier, 'Philippe Berthelot and the Rome Agreements of January 1935,' *Historical Journal*, 26, 1983, pp. 413–22.

25 Hubert Lagardelle, *Mission à Rome*, (Paris, 1955), pp. 275–7.

26 Elizabeth Wiskemann, *The Rome–Berlin Axis*, (Fontana: London, 1966), p. 57 and A. J. Toynbee (ed.), *Documents on International Affairs*, (Oxford University Press: London, 1935), p. 293.

27 E. M. Robertson, *Mussolini as Empire-Builder*, (Macmillan: London, 1977), pp. 112–3 and 149–50. See also A. Adamthwaite, *The Making of the Second World War*, (Allen & Unwin: London, 1977), pp. 48–9 and 133–4.

28 Dame Adelaide Livingstone, *The Peace Ballot: The Official History*, (Victor Gollancz: London, 1935), pp. 49–51.

29 D. Mack Smith, *Mussolini*, (Weidenfeld and Nicolson: London, 1981), p. 194; Sir R. Vansittart, *The Mist Procession*, (Hutchinson: London, 1958), pp. 320–1; *Documents on British Foreign Policy*, Second Series, Vol. XIV, No. 301; Lord Avon, *Facing the Dictators*, (Cassell: London, 1962), pp. 220–9; and Robertson, op.cit., pp. 145–9.

30 M. Funke, *Sanktionen und Kanonen: Hitler, Mussolini und der internationale Abessinienkonflikt*, (Droste Verlag: Düsseldorf, 1970), passim. See also Crozier, *Appeasement*, pp. 111 and 134 and Robertson, *Mussolini as Empire-Builder*, pp. 138–41.

31 Philip Morgan, *Italian Fascism 1919–1945*, (Macmillan: London, 1995), p. 150.

32 Wiskemann, op.cit., pp. 73–83.

33 Crozier, *Appeasement*, pp. 21–2.

34 See above pp. 86–7.

35 A. J. Toynbee (ed.), *Documents on International Affairs 1933*, (Oxford University Press: London, 1934), pp. 381–3.

36 J. Degras, *Soviet Documents on Foreign Policy*, (Oxford University Press: London, 1953), Vol. III, pp. 89–90.

37 Dick Richardson and Carolyn Kitching, 'Britain and the World Disarmament Conference,' in P. Catterall and C. J. Morris (eds), *Britain and the Threat to Stability in Europe*, (Leicester University Press: London, 1993), p. 41 and D. Marquand, *Ramsay MacDonald*, (Cape: London, 1977), p. 754.

38 *Documents on British Foreign Policy*, Second Series, Vol. XII, No. 235.

39 D. Reynolds, *Britannia Overruled*, (Longman: London, 1991), pp. 122–8.

40 See below, pp. 196–7.

41 Crozier, *Appeasement*, p. 53.

42 ibid., pp. 130–1.

43 A. J. Crozier, 'Prelude to Munich: British Foreign Policy and Germany, 1935–8,' in *European Studies Review*, 6, 1976, 357–82.

44 *Documents Diplomatiques Français*, (Imprimerie Nationale: Paris, 1964) Series 2, Vol. 1, No. 283.

6 The Deepening Crisis

1 Elizabeth Wiskemann, *The Rome–Berlin Axis*, (Fontana: London, 1966), p. 92.

2 Malcolm Muggeridge (ed.), *Ciano's Diplomatic Papers*, (Heinemann: London, 1948), pp. 56–9.

3 J. T. Emmerson, *The Rhineland Crisis: 7 March 1936*, (Temple Smith: London, 1977), passim. and A. J. Crozier, *Appeasement and Germany's Last Bid for Colonies*, (Macmillan: Basingstoke, 1988), pp. 131–5.

4 ibid., pp. 169–70.

5 Paul Preston, *The Coming of the Spanish Civil War: Reform, Reaction and Revolution in the Second Republic*, (Methuen: London, 1978), p. 201.

6 On the origins of the Spanish Civil War see H. Thomas, *The Spanish Civil War*, (Penguin: London, 1965), pp. 21–165; P. Preston, op.cit., passim.; G. Brenan, *The Spanish Labyrinth*, (Cambridge University Press: 2nd. Ed., Cambridge, 1990), passim.; and R. Carr, *Modern Spain 1875–1980*, (Oxford University Press: Oxford, 1980), pp. 117–35.

7 Crozier, *Appeasement*, pp. 222–4. See also Enrique Moradiellos, 'British Political Strategy in the Face of the Rising of Spain in 1936,' in *Contemporary European History*, 1, 1992, pp. 123–37.

8 It is still only possible to speculate on the motivation of the Soviet leadership in respect of Spain. Clearly a Socialist victory in Spain would not have been unwelcome in Moscow, but it is probable that Spain was only of marginal interest to the Kremlin. It is interesting in this connection to note that the most recent treatment of Soviet foreign policy in the 1930s, G. Roberts, *The Soviet Union and the Origins of the Second World War: Russo-German Relations and the Road to War, 1933–1941*, (Macmillan: Basingstoke, 1995) completely ignores Spain and the Civil War.

9 Count Ciano, *Diary 1937–8*, (Methuen: London, 1952), Entries for 28.9.1937 and 6.11.1937; *Documents on German Foreign Policy*, (London, 1951–), Series D, Vol. I, No. 1; and Wiskemann, *The Rome–Berlin Axis*, pp. 95–108.

10 J. Noakes and G. Pridham (ed.), *Nazism 1919–1945: State, Economy and Society*, (University of Exeter: Exeter, 1984), pp. 281–7. See also *Documents on German Foreign Policy*, Series C, Vol. V, No. 490.

11 K. Hildebrand, *The Foreign Policy of the Third Reich*, (Batsford: London, 1973), pp. 38–50.

12 The Hossbach Memorandum has been subjected to a number of interpretations. See E. Robertson (ed.), *The Origins of the Second World War*, (Macmillan: London, 1970), pp. 93–6, 105–58.

13 Crozier, *Appeasement*, pp. 179–82. Schacht looked forward to a time, after Germany had completed her rearmament, when she could return to the world markets. W. Carr, *Arms, Autarky and Aggression: A Study in German Foreign Policy, 1933–1939*, (Arnold: London, 1972), pp. 52–3 and 62. See also G. Schmidt, *The Politics and Economics of Appeasement*, (Berg: Leamington Spa, 1986), p. 107.

14 Crozier, *Appeasment*, pp. 198–200.

15 A. J. Crozier, 'Prelude to Munich: British Foreign Policy and Germany, 1935–8,' *European Studies Review*, 6, 1976, pp. 357–382.

16 Wesley Wark, *The Ultimate Enemy: British Intelligence and Nazi Germany, 1933–1939*, (Tauris: London, 1985), pp. 23–35, 59–80 and 225–40.

17 D. Dilks (ed.), *The Diaries of Sir Alexander Cadogan*, (Cassell: London, 1971), p. 13.

18 J. Harvey (ed.), *The Diplomatic Diaries of Oliver Harvey*, (Collins: London, 1970), Entry for 26.3.1937.

19 Quoted in J. Joll, 'The Decline of Europe 1920–1970,' in *International Affairs*, November, 1970, pp. 1–18.

20 Crozier, 'Prelude to Munich'.

21 R. P. Shay Jnr., *British Rearmament in the Thirties: Politics and Profits*, (Princeton University Press: Princeton, 1977), pp. 68–9.

22 ibid., pp. 72–3.

23 ibid., p. 162.

24 Ian Colvin, *The Chamberlain Cabinet*, (Gollancz: London, 1971), p. 29. In a public speech Chamberlain pointed out that £1,500 million might not be sufficient to cover defence.

25 ibid., pp. 31–2.

26 Shay, *British Rearmament*, p. 159.

27 ibid., p. 162.

28 ibid., p. 167 and Colvin, *The Chamberlain Cabinet*, pp. 48–9.

29 PRO – CAB 24/273/CP(37)316. *Interim Inskip Report*, 15.12.1937.

30 ibid., 274/CP(38)24. *Final Report by Sir T. Inskip on Defence Expenditure in Future Years*, 8.2.1938. For a dicussion of the two-power navy standard, see N. Gibbs, *Grand Strategy*, Vol. 1, (HMSO: London, 1976), pp. 119, 259–60, 368 and 378.

31 ibid., CAB 23/92/5(38)9. Cabinet Meeting 16.2.1938.

32 ibid., T 172/1801, Memorandum by E. Hale, 10.8.1937, and Minute by Sir W. Fisher, 19.8.1937.

33 Shay, *British Rearmament*, p. 178.

34 Colvin, *The Chamberlain Cabinet*, pp. 63–4.

35 R. A. C. Parker, *Chamberlain and Appeasement: British Policy and the Coming of the Second World War*, (Macmillan: Basingstoke, 1993), p. 104.

36 ibid., p. 105.

37 PRO – FO 371/21015/F8143/6799/10, *Economic Pressure Against Japan*, 13.10.1937. Minute by Gladwyn Jebb, 15.10.1937.

38 Parker, *Chamberlain and Appeasement*, p. 106.

39 ibid., p. 107.

40 PRO – CAB 32/128/E(PD)37. Third Meeting, 21.5.1937.

41 G. Peden, 'The Burden of Imperial Defence and the Continental Commitment Reconsidered,' in *Historical Journal*, 27, 1984, pp. 405–23 and D. Reynolds, *Britannia Overruled*, (Longman: London, 1991), pp. 130–1. See also D. C. Watt, *Personalities and Policies: Studies in the Formulation of British Foreign Policy in the*

Twentieth Century, (Longman: London, 1965) and N. Mansergh, *The Commonwealth Experience*, (Praeger: New York, 1969).

42 Ritchie Ovendale, *'Appeasement' and the English Speaking World*, (University of Wales Press: Aberystwyth, 1975), p. 63.

43 John P. Fox, *Germany and the Far Eastern Crisis, 1931–1938*, (Oxford University Press: Oxford, 1982), pp. 292–3.

44 Crozier, *Appeasement*, pp. 236–7.

45 G. McDermott, *The Eden Legacy*, (Frewin: London, 1969), p. 52.

46 *Documents on German Foreign Policy*, Series D, Vol. I, No. 138.

47 On Austro-German Relations see J. Gehl, *Austria, Germany and the Anschluss, 1931-1938*, (Oxford University Press: London, 1963), passim.

48 Muggeridge, *Ciano's Diplomatic Papers*, pp. 161–2 and D. Mack Smith, *Mussolini*, (Weidenfeld and Nicolson: London, 1981), pp. 217–8. The reference to Canossa is an allusion to the homage paid to the Pope, Gregory VII (1073–1085) at Canossa by the German Emperor Henry IV in very humiliating circumstances during January 1077.

49 *Documents on British Foreign Policy*, (London, 1946–), Third Series, Vol. I, Nos. 46 and 54.

50 J. Noakes and G. Pridham (ed.), *Nazism 1919–1945: Foreign Policy, War and Racial Extermination*, (University of Exeter: Exeter, 1988), pp. 708–9.

51 Mack Smith, *Mussolini*, pp. 219–20.

52 E. Robertson, *Hitler's Pre-War Policy and Military Plans*, (Longmans: London, 1963), p. 109.

53 *Documents on German Foreign Policy*, Series D, Vol. II, No. 282.

54 Colvin, *The Chamberlain Cabinet*, pp. 103–12.

55 K. Robbins, *Munich 1938*, (Cassell: London, 1968), pp. 212–53 and A. Adamthwaite, *The Making of the Second World War*, (Allen & Unwin: London, 1977), pp. 188–9.

56 G. Roberts, *The Soviet Union and the Origins of the Second World War: Russo-German Relations and the Road to War, 1933–1941*, (Macmillan: Basingstoke, 1995), pp. 49–50.

57 PRO – CAB 24/273/CP(37)296, *A Comparison of the Strength of Great Britain with that of Certain Other Nations as at January 1938*.

58 A. Adamthwaite, *Grandeur and Misery: France's Bid for Power in Europe 1914–1940*, (Arnold: London, 1995), p. 208 and A. Adamthwaite, 'French Military Intelligence and the Coming of the War, 1935–1939,' in C. Andrew and J. Noakes (ed.), *Intelligence and International Relations 1900–1945*, (Exeter University Press: Exeter, 1987), pp. 197–8.

59 Richard Lamb, *The Drift to War 1922–39*, (St. Martin's Press: New York, 1989), p. 238.

60 Robbins, *Munich 1938*, pp. 254–36.

61 Colvin, *The Chamberlain Cabinet*, p. 192.

7 The Outbreak of War in Europe

1 D. Lammers, 'From Whitehall after Munich,' *The Historical Journal*, 16, 1973, pp. 831–56 and D. Morgan, *The Origins of British Aid Policy*, (Macmillan: London, 1980), pp. 19–22.

2 N. H. Baynes, *The Speeches of Adolf Hitler*, (Oxford University Press: London, 1942), Vol. II, pp. 1532–7.

3 Wesley Wark, *The Ultimate Enemy: British Intelligence and Nazi Germany 1933-1939*, (Tauris: London, 1985), pp. 212–5. See also Robert Young, 'La Guerre

de Longue Duree: Some Reflections on French Strategy and Diplomacy in the 1930s,' in A. Preston (ed.), *General Staffs and Diplomacy before the Second World War*, (Croom Helm: London, 1978), pp. 111–65.

4 D. Cameron Watt, *How War Came*, (Heinemann: London, 1989), pp. 99–107 and Michael Howard, *The Continental Commitment: The Dilemma of British Defence Policy in the Era of the Two World Wars*, (Penguin: London, 1974), pp. 129–30.

5 M. G. Gamelin, *Servir*, (Paris, 1946–7), Vol. I, pp. 124–30; A. Adamthwaite, *France and the Coming of the Second World War, 1936–1939*, (Cass: London, 1977), pp. 253, 296–7 and 313; and A. Adamthwaite, *The Making of the Second World War*, (Allen & Unwin: London, 1972), p. 84.

6 *Documents on German Foreign Policy*, (HMSO: London, 1951–), Series D, Vol IV, No. 68.

7 ibid., Nos. 202 and 209 and Watt, *How War Came*, pp. 148–54.

8 ibid., pp. 567–8.

9 Ian Colvin, *The Chamberlain Cabinet*, (Gollancz: London, 1971), p. 187.

10 ibid., pp. 188–90.

11 Waclaw Jedrzejewicz (ed.), *Diplomat in Berlin, 1933–1939: Papers and Memoirs of Jozef Lipski*, (Columbia University Press: New York, 1968), pp. 503–4.

12 Anita Prazmowska, *Britain, Poland and the Eastern Front*, (Cambridge University Press: Cambridge, 1987), pp. 52–6.

13 Elizabeth Wiskemann, *The Rome–Berlin Axis*, (Fontana: London, 1966), p. 180.

14 *Documents on German Foreign Policy*, Series D, Vol. VI, No. 334.

15 J. Noakes and G. Pridham (ed.), *Nazism 1919–1945: Foreign Policy, War and Racial Extermination*, (University of Exeter: Exeter, 1988), pp. 735–6.

16 Prazmowska, *Britain, Poland and the Eastern Front*, p. 56.

17 G. Bonnet, *Defense de la Paix*, (Geneva, 1951), Vol. I, p. 179.

18 Watt, *How War Came*, pp. 382–3 and G. Roberts, *The Unholy Alliance: Stalin's Pact with Hitler*, (Tauris: London, 1989), pp. 140–1.

19 I am most grateful to Mr. G. Roberts for this information.

20 Jane Degras (ed.), *Soviet Documents on Foreign Policy*, (Oxford University Press: London, 1953), Vol. III, pp. 315–22.

21 Watt, *How War Came*, p. 229.

22 ibid, pp. 462–73.

23 *Documents on British Foreign Policy*, (HMSO: London 1946–), Third Series, Vol. VI, No. 180.

24 R. A. C. Parker, *Chamberlain and Appeasement: British Policy and the Coming of the Second World War*, (Macmillan: Basingstoke, 1993), p. 253.

25 Watt, *How War Came*, p. 356.

26 ibid., pp. 356–7.

27 Parker, *Chamberlain and Appeasement*, p. 253.

28 *Documents on British Foreign Policy*, Third Series, Vol. IX, No. 244 and Parker, *Chamberlain and Appeasement*, pp. 259–60.

29 Noakes and Pridham, *Nazism*, pp. 736–43 and *Documents on British Foreign Policy*, Third Series, Vol. VII, No. 314.

30 Count Ciano, *Ciano's Diary, 1939–1943*, (Heinemann: London, 1947), Entries for 10-16.8.1939, 25–27.9.1939 and 1.9.1939. See also *Documents on German Foreign Policy*, Series D, Vol. VII, Nos. 43 and 47.

31 Ritchie Ovendale, *'Appeasement' and the English Speaking World: Britain, the United States, the Dominions and the Policy of Appeasement, 1937–1939*, (University of Wales Press: Cardiff, 1975), pp. 300–14.

32 On the Soviet war with Finland, see G. Roberts, *The Soviet Union and the Origins of the Second World War: Russo-German Relations and the Road to War, 1933–1941*,

(Macmillan: Basingstoke, 1995), p. 105 and P. Calvacoressi, G. Wint and J. Pritchard, *The Causes and Courses of the Second World War: The Western Hemisphere*, (Penguin: London, 1989), pp. 115–8 and H. Michel, *The Second World War*, (Deutsch: London, 1975), pp. 61–4.

33 Noakes and Pridham, *Nazism*, pp. 786–7.

34 D. Reynolds, *The Creation of the Anglo-American Alliance 1937–41: A Study in Competitive Co-operation*, (Europa: London, 1981), pp. 108–13.

35 See below pp. 202–3.

36 See below p. 208.

37 John A. Woods, *Roosevelt and Modern America*, (English Universities Press: London, 1959), p. 132.

38 Livingston Hartley, *Is America Afraid?: A New Foreign Policy for the United States*, (Prentice-Hall: New York, 1937).

39 A. Iriye, *The Globalizing of America*, (Cambridge University Press: Cambridge, 1993), pp. 168–9.

40 M. Leighton, *Mobilizing Consent: Public Opinion and American Foreign Policy 1937–1948*, (Greenwood Press: London, 1976), pp. 41–7.

41 See, for example, D. Prater, *Thomas Mann*, (Oxford University Press: Oxford 1995), pp. 239–40, 295, 319–20. Thomas Mann, the renowned German literary figure, who was in exile for most of the duration of the Third Reich, first in France (briefly) and Switzerland and then from 1938 onwards in the United States, was feted at the White House on a number of occasions.

42 S. I. Rosenman (ed.), *The Public Papers and Addresses of Franklin D. Roosevelt, 1928–1945*, Vol. 1940, (Random House: New York, 1938–50), p. 263.

43 A. Frye, *Nazi Germany and the American Hemisphere 1939–1941*, (Yale University Press: New Haven, 1967), pp. 131–6.

44 Rosenman, *The Public Papers*, p. 517.

45 J. M. Burns, *Roosevelt: The Soldier of Freedom, 1940–1945*, (Weidenfeld & Nicholson: London, 1971), p. 441.

46 Reynolds, *Creation*, pp. 121–32. Britain, though, was not a wholesale bankrupt. The problem was essentially one of lack of dollars and gold with which to fund purchases in the United States. Britain still had some £4,000 million in overseas assets and was able to fund a substantial part of her war effort by persuading creditors to run up large sterling balances.

47 ibid., pp. 98–9.

48 Woods, p. 138.

49 Reynolds, *Creation*, pp. 168–9, 251–82; Reynolds, *Britannia Overruled*, (Longman, London: 1991), p. 152; and Alan P. Dobson, *US Wartime Aid to Britain, 1940–1946*, (Croom Helm: London, 1986), passim.

50 E. Roosevelt (ed.), *The Roosevelt Letters*, Vol. 3, (Harrap: London, 1952), pp. 342–3.

51 Noakes and Pridham, *Nazism*, pp. 796–7.

52 ibid., pp. 802–9.

53 Hitler's Speech to the Generals 22.8.1939, Noakes and Pridham, *Nazism*.

54 W. L. Shirer, *The Rise and Fall of the Third Reich*, (Pan: London, 1969), p. 967.

55 Noakes and Pridham, *Nazism*, pp. 790–1.

56 ibid., p. 820.

57 Iriye, *Globalizing*, pp. 181–2.

58 William Carr, *Poland to Pearl Harbor: The Making of the Second World War*, (Arnold: London, 1985), p. 75.

59 ibid., p. 138.

60 Reynolds, *Creation*, p. 218.

8 Crisis in the Far East

1 Following the German attack on the Soviet Union, the United States government promised aid for the USSR, which ultimately was to be worth over $11 billion. But the American government's commitment was not immediate. Although the Soviet Union's assets were unfrozen fairly quickly, a formal commitment to aid the Soviets took some time, partly because of a belief that the USSR would soon succumb to the Third Reich and partly because of American hostility to Communism. Waldo Heinrichs, *Threshold of War: Franklin D. Roosevelt and American Entry into World War II*, (Oxford University Press: Oxford, 1989), pp. 103–4; P. Calvacoressi, G. Wint and J. Pritchard (ed.), *The Causes and Courses of the Second World War*, Vol. 1, (Penguin: London, 1989), p. 221; and R. A. Divine, *The Reluctant Belligerent: American Entry into World War II*, (Alfred A. Knopf: New York, 1979), pp. 129–35.

2 Antony Best, *Britain, Japan and Pearl Harbor: Avoiding War in East Asia, 1936–41*, (Routledge/LSE: London, 1995), p. 1.

3 Ian Nish, *Japanese Foreign Policy, 1869–1942*, (Routledge: London, 1977), p. 155.

4 Janet E. Hunter, *The Emergence of Modern Japan: An Introductory History Since 1853*, (Longman: London, 1989), p. 168.

5 ibid., p. 169.

6 David Anson Titus, *Palace and Politics in Prewar Japan*, (Columbia University Press: London, 1974), pp. 15–6.

7 Michael A. Barnhart, *Japan and the World Since 1868*, (Arnold: London, 1995), p. 21. See also, Titus, *Palace and Politics*, pp. 180–1. On the emergence of the *Genro*, see Lesley Connors, *The Emperor's Adviser: Saionji Kimmochi and Pre-War Japanese Politics*, (Croom Helm: London, 1987), pp. 43–77.

8 Connors, *The Emperor's Adviser*, pp. 211–24. After 1936 Saionji's influence waned dramatically. In 1937 the *Genro* lost the right to recommend the Prime Minister. Moreover, influence over foreign policy was virtually non-existent after this date.

9 Richard Storry, *The Double Patriots*, (Greenwood Press: Westport, 1973), p. 21.

10 ibid., Preface.

11 See above, pp. 47–8.

12 R. Storry, *Japan and the Decline of the West in Asia 1894–1943*, (Macmillan: London, 1979), p. 121.

13 W. R. Keylor, *The Twentieth Century World*, 2nd. Ed., (Oxford University Press: Oxford, 1992), pp. 233–4.

14 Storry, *Patriots*, pp. 32–3.

15 ibid., pp. 34–5.

16 Hugh Byas, *Government by Assassination*, (Allen & Unwin: London, 1943), p. 85.

17 Storry, *Patriots*, p. 38.

18 Hunter, *Emergence of Modern Japan*, pp. 174–5.

19 See above p. 4.

20 Storry, *Patriots*, p. 52.

21 See above p. 47.

22 Nish, *Japanese Foreign Policy*, pp. 162–3.

23 ibid.

24 Barnhart, *Japan and the World*, p. 86.

25 J. B. Crowley, *Japan's Quest for Autonomy: National Security and Foreign Policy 1930–1938*, (Princeton University Press: Princeton, 1966), pp. 25–6.

26 ibid., p. 46.

27 ibid., p. 51.

28 *Documents on British Foreign Policy*, (HMSO: London, 1946–), Second Series, Vol. VIII, No. 354.

29 Crowley, *Japan's Quest*, p. 102.

30 Storry, *Patriots*, pp. 56–64.

31 See R. Bassett, *Democracy and Foreign Policy: A Case History, The Sino-Japanese Dispute*, (Longmans: London, 1952, p. 65 and Eleanor Tupper and George Mac Reynolds, *Japan in American Public Opinion*, (Macmillan: New York, 1937).

32 Crowley, *Japan's Quest*, p. 158.

33 Sir John Pratt, *War and Politics in China*, (Jonathan Cape: London, 1943), p. 159. Sir John Pratt was the brother of the horror actor, Boris Karloff.

34 H. Stimson and MacGeorge Bundy, *On Active Service in Peace and War*, (Harper: New York, 1947), p. 236.

35 R. H. Ferrell, *American Diplomacy in the Great Depression*, (Yale University Press: New Haven, 1957), pp. 188–93.

36 W. Carr, *Poland to Pearl Harbor: The Making of the Second World War*, (Arnold: London, 1985), p. 11.

37 Dorothy Borg, *The United States and the Far Eastern Crisis of 1933–1938*, (Harvard University Press: Cambridge, Mass., 1964) p. 102.

38 *Documents on British Foreign Policy 1919–1939*, (HMSO: London, 1946–), Second Series, Vol. XIII, Appendix 1; A. Adamthwaite, *The Making of the Second World War*, (Allen & Unwin: London, 1977), p. 45.

39 Sir F. Leith-Ross, *Money Talks*, (Hutchinson: London, 1968), pp. 195–226.

40 Nish, *Japanese Foreign Policy*, pp. 204–8.

41 See above pp. 190–1.

42 Storry, *Decline of the West*, p. 146.

43 Storry, *Patriots*, p. 99.

44 H. Byas, *Government by Assassination*, (Allen & Unwin: London, 1943), pp. 22–31.

45 W. G. Beasley, *The Modern History of Japan*, (Weidenfeld & Nicolson: London, 1973), p. 249.

46 Storry, *Patriots*, p. 124.

47 Crowley, *Japan's Quest*, pp. 79–80. See also Stephen S. Large, *Emperor Hirohito and Showa Japan*, (Routledge: London, 1992), p. 50.

48 See Hunter, *Emergence of Modern Japan*, pp. 174–7 and Large, op.cit., pp. 60–5.

49 See above pp. 197–8.

50 Irie Sukemasa, 'My 50 Years with the Emperor,' in *Japan Quarterly*, 302, (1983), pp. 39–42.

51 E. Behr, *Hirohito: Behind the Myth*, (Penguin: London, 1990), p. 182. On German military aid to China, see above p.   .

52 Nish, *Japanese Foreign Policy*, pp. 215 and 229.

53 Connors, *The Emperor's Adviser*, pp. 182–3. Saionji's role in future would be carried out by the Lord Keeper of the Privy Seal, but he continued to be consulted by the latter.

54 Nish, *Japanese Foreign Policy*, pp. 216–7.

55 R. Storry, *A History of Modern Japan*, (Penguin: London, 1960), p. 202.

56 Behr, *Hirohito*, p. 185.

57 Richard Overy with Andrew Wheatcroft, *The Road to War*, (Macmillan: London, 1989), p. 241.

58 Crowley, *Japan's Quest*, p. 223. It is also doubtful whether pre-war Showa Japan can be considered a Fascist state.

59 Nish, *Japanese Foreign Policy*, p. 218.

60 ibid., p. 219.

61 Masao Maruyama, *Thought and Behaviour in Modern Japanese Politics*, (Oxford University Press: London, 1963), p. 97.

9 From War to World War

1 John P. Fox, *Germany and the Far Eastern Crisis 1931–1938*, (Oxford University Press: Oxford,1982), pp. 234–43.
2 S. I. Rosenman (ed.), *The Public Papers and Addresses of Franklin D. Roosevelt*, Vol. 1937, (Random House: New York, 1938–50), pp. 406–11.
3 D. Borg, *The United States and the Far Eastern Crisis of 1933–1936*, (Harvard University Press: Cambridge, Mass., 1964), p. 441.
4 See above pp. 135–6.
5 Antony Best, *Britain, Japan and Pearl Harbor: Avoiding War in East Asia, 1936–41*, (Routledge: London, 1995), pp. 44–5.
6 Stephen S. Large, *Emperor Hirohito and Showa Japan*, (Routledge: London, 1992), pp. 88–9.
7 J. Grew, *Ten Years in Japan*, (Simon & Schuster: New York, 1944), p. 236
8 Courtney Brown, *Tojo: the Last Banzai*, (Corgi: London, 1967), p. 81. See also Best, *Britain, Japan and Pearl Harbor*, p. 39. As Best points out, there was a view that the British themselves were not without blame for this incident. Knatchbull-Hugessen had undertaken this journey in a war zone without informing the Japanese authorities in advance.
9 See above p. 136. See also Borg, *The United States and the Far Eastern Crisis*, p. 502.
10 ibid., p. 500.
11 R. Storry, *Japan and the Decline of the West in Asia*, (Macmillan: London, 1979), p. 148.
12 See above p. 20. See also D. C. Watt, 'The Relationship between the Far Eastern and European Wars, 1922–41,' in Robert W. Love Jnr., *Pearl Harbor Revisited*, (St. Martin's Press: New York, 1995), pp. 1–12.
13 Large, *Emperor Hirohito*, p. 89.
14 J. B. Crowley, *Japan's Quest for Autonomy: National Security and Foreign Policy 1930–1938*, (Princeton University Press: Princeton, 1966), pp. 369–72.
15 ibid., p. 377.
16 Lesley Connors, *The Emperor's Adviser: Saionji Kimmochi and Pre-War Japanese Politics*, (Croom Helm: London, 1987), pp. 200–1.
17 Crowley, *Japan's Quest*, pp. 376–7.
18 R. J. C. Butow, *Tojo and the Coming of the War*, (Princeton University Press: Princeton, 1961), p. 113.
19 Sir Robert Craigie, *Behind the Japanese Mask*, (Hutchinson: London, 1945), p. 59.
20 I. Nish, *Japanese Foreign Policy, 1869–1942*, (Routledge: London, 1977), pp. 225–6.
21 Keith Scott Latourette, *A History of Modern China*, (Penguin: London, 1954), p. 171.
22 Butow, *Tojo and the Coming of War*, p. 120.
23 ibid.
24 See above pp. 137–8.
25 Cordell Hull, *The Memoirs of Cordell Hull*, Vol. 1, (Hodder & Stoughton: London,1948), pp. 596–70. See also Michael A. Barnhart, *Japan Prepares for Total War: the Search for Economic Security, 1919–1941*, (Cornell University Press: London, 1987), pp. 132–3.
26 Butow, *Tojo and the Coming of War*, p. 124 and J. Grew, *Turbulent Era: A*

Diplomatic Record of Forty Years, 1904–1945, Vol. 2, (Houghton Mifflin: Boston, 1952), pp. 1206–7.

27 Michael A. Barnhart, *Japan and the World since 1868,* (Arnold: London, 1995), p. 121.

28 Large, *Emperor Hirohito,* pp. 92–4.

29 Butow, *Tojo and the Coming of War,* p. 125.

30 Connors, *Emperor's Adviser,* p. 206.

31 Butow, *Tojo and the Coming of War,* p. 180.

32 Large, *Emperor Hirohito,* pp. 94–5.

33 ibid., p. 100.

34 Robert A. Divine, *The Reluctant Belligerent: American Entry into World War II,* 2nd Edition, (McGraw-Hill: New York, 1979), pp. 99–101.

35 See above pp. 168–9.

36 Waldo Heinrichs, *Threshold of War: Franklin D. Roosevelt & American Entry into World War II,* (Oxford University Press: Oxford, 1989), p. 38.

37 R. Storry, *Japan and the Decline of the West in Asia 1894–1943,* (London, 1979), p. 155.

38 Brown, *Tojo: The Last Bauzai,* p. 99.

39 Divine, *Reluctant Belligerent,* p. 124.

40 Brown, *Tojo: The Last Bauzai,* p. 125. See also Butow, *Tojo and the Coming of War,* pp. 224–5.

41 Significantly, though, the Japanese failed to destroy the four American aircraft carriers that were either at sea, or at base on the American Pacific coast during the attack. Furthermore the oil stocks and repair facilities remained undamaged.

42 Butow, *Tojo and the Coming of War,* pp. 402–3.

43 ibid.

44 Rosenman, *Public Papers,* Vol. 1940, pp. 514–30.

45 See W. Carr, *Poland to Pearl Harbor: The Making of the Second World War,* (Arnold: London, 1985), p. 169 and John Toland, *Adolf Hitler,* (Doubleday: New York, 1976), p. 952.

46 Rosenman, *Public Papers,* Vol. 1941, p. 557.

10 Interpretation and the Changing View

1 Sir Lewis Namier, *Diplomatic Prelude,*(Macmillan: London, 1948); *Europe in Decay,* (Macmillan: London,1949); *In the Nazi Era,* (Macmillan: London, 1952); and Sir John Wheeler-Bennett, *Munich, Prologue to Tragedy,* (Macmillan: London, 1948).

2 M. Cowling, *The Impact of Hitler,* (Cambridge University Press: Cambridge, 1975), p. 3.

3 H. Trevor-Roper, 'A. J. P. Taylor, Hitler and the War,' *Encounter,* 17, 1961, pp. 88–96.

4 A. J. P. Taylor, *The Course of German History,* (Hamilton: London, 1945).

5 A. J. P. Taylor, *The Origins of the Second World War,* (Penguin: London, 1964), p. 97.

6 ibid., p. 235.

7 Trevor-Roper, 'A. J. P. Taylor, Hitler and the War'.

8 A. Bullock, *Hitler: A Study in Tyranny,* (Penguin: London, 1962), pp. 285, 290–2.

9 Taylor, *Origins,* pp. 99–101, 170.

10 H. Trevor-Roper, 'Hitlers Kriegsziele,' *Vierteljahrshefte für Zeitgeschichte,* 8, 1960, pp. 121–33.

11 E. Jäckel, *Hitler's World View: A Blueprint for Power*, (Harvard University Press: Cambridge, Mass., 1981) and D. Aigner, *Das Ringen um England: Das deutsch-britische Verhältnis, die öffentliche Meinung, 1933–1939*, (Bechtle Verlag: Munich, 1969).

12 E. Jäckel, *Hitler in History*, (Brandeis University: Hanover, 1984), pp. 25–6.

13 See K. Hildebrand, *The Foreign Policy of the Third Reich*, (Batsford: London, 1973) and A. Hillgruber, 'England's Place in Hitler's Plans for World Dominion,' in *Journal of Contemporary History*, 9, 1974, pp. 5–22.

14 G. Stoakes, *Hitler and the Quest for World Dominion*, (Berg: Leamington Spa, 1986).

15 See I. Kershaw, *The Nazi Dictatorship: Problems and Perspectives of Interpretation*, (Arnold: London, 1989), pp. 61–81.

16 Hans Mommsen, 'National Socialism: Continuity and Change,' in W. Laqueur (ed.), *Fascism: A Reader's Guide*, (Penguin: London, 1979), pp. 179–210.

17 M. Broszat, 'Soziale Motivation und Führer Bindung des Nationalsozialismus,' in *Vierteljahrshefte für Zeitgeschichte*, 18, 1970, pp. 392–409. See also I. Kershaw, *The Nazi Dictatorship: Problems and Perspectives of Interpretation*, (Arnold, London, Third ed., 1993) , p. 111.

18 Tim Mason, 'Intention and Explanation: A Current Controversy about the Interpretation of National Socialism,' in G. Hirschfeld and L. Kettenacker (eds), *Der Führer Staat: Mythos und Realität*, (Klett Cotta: Stuttgart, 1981), pp. 38–9.

19 Timothy W. Mason, *Social Policy in the Third Reich: The Working Class and the 'National Community'*, (Berg: Oxford, 1993), pp. 24, 40.

20 ibid., pp. 296–7.

21 ibid.

22 ibid., pp. 262–3.

23 ibid., p. 297.

24 ibid., p. 265.

25 ibid., p. 260.

26 ibid., p. 262.

27 ibid., p. 297. For a penetrating critique of Mason's analysis, see R. J. Overy, *War and Economy in the Third Reich*, (Oxford University Press: Oxford, 1994), pp. 205–32.

28 Hugh Trevor-Roper, H. R. Trevor Roper, 'A. J. P. Taylor, Hitler and the War,' in *Encounter*, 17, 1961, pp. 88–96.

29 Translated into English as F. Fischer, *Germany's Aims in the First World War*, (Chatto & Windus: London, 1967).

30 Views similar to those of Fischer can be found in émigré literature, such as Arthur Rosenberg, *Entstehung der deutschen Republik, 1871–1918*, (Berlin, 1928). They are also stated in Hans Gatzke's *Germany's Drive to the West: A Study of Germany's Western War Aims during the First World War*, (John Hopkins Press: Baltimore, 1952).

31 Fischer, *Germany's Aims*, p. xxii.

32 See F. Fischer, *From Kaiserreich to Third Reich: Elements of Continuity in German History 1871–1945*, (Routledge: London, 1986).

33 Alan Cassels, 'A. J. P. Taylor and Italy,' in G. Martel (ed.), *The Origins of the Second World War Reconsidered: The A. J. P. Taylor Debate after Twenty-Five Years*, (Allen & Unwin: London, 1986), p. 76.

34 A. Cassels, *Mussolini's Early Diplomacy*, (Princeton University Press: Princeton, 1970), pp. 160–74.

35 E. Robertson, *Mussolini as Empire-Builder: Europe and Africa 1932–1936*, (Macmillan: London, 1977), pp. 99–102, 109–13.

36 D. Mack Smith, *Mussolini's Roman Empire*, (Longman: London, 1976), pp. 15–120.

37 C. J. Lowe and F. Marzari, *Italian Foreign Policy 1870–1940*, (Routledge: London, 1975), p. 366.

38 Count Ciano, *Diary 1939–1943*, (Heinemann: London, 1947), Entry for 3 September 1939.

39 M. Gilbert and R. Gott, *The Appeasers*, (Weidenfeld and Nicolson: London, 1964).

40 D. Cameron Watt, 'Appeasement: The Rise of a Revisionist School,' in *The Political Quarterly*, 35, 1965, pp. 191–213. Lord Beloff was later to claim to have intitiated the historical revision of appeasement, resulting in Sir Lewis Namier's refusal ever to speak to him again. See *Political Studies*, 26, 1978, p. 541.

41 M. Gilbert, *The Roots of Appeasement*, (Weidenfeld and Nicolson: London, 1966).

42 K. G. Robbins, *Munich 1938*, (Cassell: London, 1968), pp. 1–6 and K. G. Robbins, *Appeasement*, (Blackwell: Oxford, 1988), p. 7.

43 A. J. Crozier, 'Prelude to Munich: British Foreign Policy and Germany 1935–1938,' in *European Studies Review* (1976), pp. 357–82.

44 Neville Thompson, *The Anti-Appeasers*, (Oxford University Press: London, 1971).

45 A. J. Crozier, *Appeasement and Germany's Last Bid for Colonies*, (Macmillan: Basingstoke, 1988), pp. 99–206.

46 Cowling, *Impact*.

47 Corelli Barnett, *The Collapse of British Power*, (Eyre Methuen: London, 1972), pp. 8–15.

48 ibid., pp. 583–93. On British decline see also Barnett's, *The Audit of War: The Illusion and Reality of Britain as a Great Nation*, (Macmillan: Basingstoke, 1985) and *The Lost Peace, British Dreams, British Realities, 1945–1950*, (Macmillan: Basingstoke, 1995).

49 Cowling, *Impact*, p. 393.

50 ibid., p. 387.

51 ibid., p. 399.

52 ibid., p. 478, fn. 173. On this passage see also A. Adamthwaite, *The Making of the Second World War*, (Allen & Unwin: London, 1977), pp. 66–7.

53 D. Carlton, *Anthony Eden*, (Allen Lane: London, 1981), pp. 163–4.

54 D. Carlton, 'Were We Wrong in 1939?' in *National Review*, September 1989, pp. 44–7.

55 J. Charmley, *Chamberlain and the Lost Peace*, (Macmillan: Basingstoke, 1989), p. xiv.

56 Charmley, *Chamberlain*, p. 6.

57 ibid., pp. 8–9.

58 ibid., p. 212.

59 Michael Barber, Review, J. Charmley, *Chamberlain and the Lost Peace*, in *The Sunday Times*, 3.9.1989.

60 J. Charmley, *Churchill: The End of Glory*, (Hodder & Stoughton: London, 1993), p. 3.

61 ibid., p. 649.

62 ibid., p. 440. See also *The Times*, 2.1.1993 and J. Charmley, 'The Price of Victory,' *Times Literary Supplement*, 13.5.1994, p. 8.

63 Private information.

64 See Andrew Roberts, *Eminent Churchillians*, (Weidenfeld and Nicolson: London, 1994), for a discussion of Churchill's role in assisting in the creation of the post-

war British consensus from which Britain was 'rescued' by Mrs. Thatcher.

65 Michael Barber, *Review*.

66 Andreas Hillgruber, *Germany and the Two World Wars*, (Harvard University Press, Cambridge, Mass, 1981), p. 55.

67 On Ribbentrop's foreign policy concepts, see W. Michalka, *Ribbentrop und die deutsche Weltpolitik 1933–1940*, (Wilhelm Fink Verlag: Munich, 1980).

68 Andrew Roberts, *'The Holy Fox': A Life of Lord Halifax*, (Macmillan: Basingstoke, 1991), pp. 231–7.

69 Lloyd George considered Hitler to be the German equivalent of George Washington.

70 *Public Record Office*, CAB 23/98, Cabinet Meeting, 18 March 1939.

71 ibid., CAB 27/624, Cabinet Foreign Policy Committee, 27 March 1939.

72 The foregoing pages owe something, but not everything, to a lecture given by Professor Richard Overy on 25 February 1996 entitled 'Honour and Conscience – Winston Churchill in 1940: Was Peace with Hitler ever an Option?' It will be published in a forthcoming edition of *AJR Information*.

73 *Evening Standard*, 5.5.1996.

74 Crozier, *Appeasement*, passim.

75 Andrew Roberts, *The Holy Fox*, (London, 1991), pp. 132 and 145.

76 D. Cameron Watt, *How War Came: The Immediate Origins of the Second World War 1938–1939*, (Heinemann: London, 1989), p. 89.

77 Charmley, *Churchill*, pp. 156–9.

78 G. C. Peden, *British Rearmament and the Treasury 1932–1939*, (Scottish Academic Press: Edinburgh, 1979), pp. 60–1.

79 N. H. Gibbs, *Grand Strategy, Vol. I, Rearmament Policy*, (HMSO: London, 1976), pp. 283–4.

80 R. P. Shay, *British Rearmament in the Thirties: Politics and Profit*, (Princeton University Press: Princeton, 1977), pp. 92–128 and 289–91.

81 Gustav Schmidt, 'The Domestic Background to British Appeasement Policy,' in W. J. Mommsen and L. Kettenacker (eds), *The Fascist Challenge and the Policy of Appeasement*, (Allen & Unwin: London, 1983), p. 103. See also his *The Politics and Economics of Appeasement*, (Berg: Leamington Spa, 1986).

82 R. A. C. Parker, *Chamberlain and Appeasement: British Policy and the Coming of the Second World War*, (Macmillan: Basingstoke, 1990), pp. 324–5 and 342.

83 ibid., p. 1.

84 Wesley K. Wark, *The Ultimate Enemy – British Intelligence and Nazi Germany 1933-9*, (Tauris: London, 1985), passim.

85 James Margach, *The Abuse of Power: The War between Downing Street and the Media from Lloyd George to Callaghan*, (W. H. Allen: London, 1978), p. 50.

86 Richard Cockett, *Twilight of Truth: Chamberlain, Appeasement & the Manipulation of the British Press*, (Weidenfeld & Nicolson: London, 1989), p. 187.

87 Philip Taylor, *The Projection of Britain: British Overseas Publicity and Propaganda 1919–1939*, (Cambridge University Press: Cambridge, 1981), p. 28ff.

88 Cockett, *Twilight of Truth*, p. 19.

89 P. Taylor, *The Projection of Britain*, p. 297.

90 ibid., p. 36. On this entire issue, see also Anthony Adamthwaite's excellent article, 'The British Government and the Media, 1937–1938,' in *Journal of Contemporary History*, 18, 1983, pp. 281–97.

91 See, for example, W. R. Louis, *British Strategy in the Far East 1919–1939*, (Oxford University Press: Oxford, 1971); A. Trotter, *Britain and East Asia 1933–1937*, (Cambridge University Press: Cambridge, 1975); B. A. Lee, *Britain and the Sino-Japanese War, 1937–1939*, (Stanford University Press: Stanford,

1973); P. Lowe, *Great Britain and the Origins of the Pacific War, 1937–1941*, (Oxford University Press: Oxford, 1977).

92 A. Best, *Britain, Japan and Pearl Harbor: Avoiding War in East Asia, 1936–41*, (Routledge: London, 1995), pp. 193–4.

93 ibid., p. 195.

94 ibid., p. 158.

95 ibid., p. 199.

96 ibid., p. 201.

97 See H. Husemann (ed.), *As Others See Us: Anglo-German Perceptions*, (Peter Lang: Frankfurt am Main, 1994), pp. 81–148.

98 R. J. Young, 'La Guerre de Longue Durée,' in A. Preston (ed.), *General Staffs and Diplomacy before the Second World War*, (Croom Helm: London, 1978). See also R. J. Young, 'The Problem of France,' in Martel (ed.), *Origins*, pp. 106–7.

99 J. -B. Duroselle, *La Décadence, 1932–1939*, (Paris, 1979), pp. 11–27.

100 René Girault, 'Les décideurs français et la puissance française en 1938–1939,' in René Girault and Robert Frank (eds), *La Puissance en Europe, 1938–1940*, (Paris, 1948), p. 39.

101 Duroselle, *Le Décadence* chapters 12, 13, 14, 15.

102 Anthony Adamthwaite, *France and the Coming of War*, in Mommsen and Kettenacker (eds), *Fascist Challenge*, p. 251.

103 ibid., p. 255. See also Anthony Adamthwaite, *France and the Coming of the Second World War*, (Cass: London, 1977).

104 A. Adamthwaite, *Grandeur and Misery: France's Bid for Power in Europe 1914–1940*, (Arnold: London, 1995), pp. 224–8.

105 ibid., pp. 228–30.

106 See Arno J. Mayer, *Politics and Diplomacy of Peacemaking: Containment and Counterrevolution at Versailles*, (Alfred A. Knopf: New York, 1967) and John M. Thompson, *Russia, Bolshevism and the Versailles Peace*, (Princeton University Press: Princeton, 1966).

107 G. Niedhart, 'British Attitudes and Policies towards the Soviet Union and International Communism, 1933–9,' in Mommsen and Kettenacker (eds), *Fascist Challenge*, pp. 288–9.

108 Robert C. Tucker, 'The Emergence of Stalin's Foreign Policy,' in *Slavic Review*, 36, 1977, pp. 563–89 and Robert C. Tucker, 'Stalin, Bukharin and History as Conspiracy,' in Robert C. Tucker and Stephen F. Cohen Ed., *The Great Purge Trial*, (Grosset & Dunlap: New York, 1965).

109 G. L. Weinberg, *The Foreign Policy of Hitler's Germany*, Vol. 1, *Diplomatic Revolution in Europe 1933–36*, (Chicago University Press: Chicago, 1970), pp. 220–2, 310, and Vol. 2, *Starting World War II, 1937–39*, (Chicago University Press: Chicago, 1980), p. 214. See also Robert Conquest, *The Great Terror*, (Penguin: London, 1971), pp. 298–300.

110 Jiri Hochman, *The Soviet Union and the Failure of Collective Security, 1934–1938*, (Cornell University Press: Ithaca, 1984).

111 Teddy J. Uldricks, 'The Impact of the Great Purges on the People's Commissariat of Foreign Affairs,' in *Slavic Review*, 36, 1977, pp. 187–204 and Teddy J. Uldricks, 'Stalin and Nazi Germany,' in *Slavic Review*, 36, 1977, pp. 509–603.

112 Teddy J. Uldricks, 'A. J. P. Taylor and the Russians,' in Martel (ed.) *Origins*, pp. 176–9.

113 Geoffrey Roberts, *The Soviet Union and the Origins of the Second World War: Russo-German Relations and the Road to War, 1933–1941*, (Macmillan: Basingstoke, 1995), pp. 3–4.

114 Jonathan Haslam, *The Soviet Union and the Struggle for Collective Security in Europe, 1933–39*, (Macmillan: London, 1984), pp. 231–2. See also Geoffrey Roberts, *The Unholy Alliance: Stalin's Pact with Hitler*, (Tauris: London, 1989), Geoffrey Roberts, 'The Fall of Litvinov: A Revisionist View,' *Journal of Contemporary History*, 27, 1992, pp. 639–58 and 'The Soviet Decision for a Pact with Nazi Germany,' *Soviet Studies*, 41, 1992, pp. 57–78.

115 See, for example, James Rusbridger and Eric Nave, *Betrayal at Pearl Harbor*, (O'Mara: London, 1991).

116 D. Reynolds, *The Creation of the Anglo-American Alliance: A Study in Competitive Co-operation*, (Europa: London, 1981), p. 25.

117 W. Appleman Williams, *The Tragedy of American Diplomacy*, (World Publishing Co.: New York, 1972) and Lloyd G. Gardiner, *Economic Aspects of New Deal Diplomacy*, (Beacon Press: Boston, 1971).

118 Callum A. MacDonald, 'The United States, Appeasement and the Open Door,' in Mommsen and Kettenacker (eds), *Fascist Challenge*, p. 400.

119 ibid., p. 401.

120 Arnold A. Offner, 'The United States and National Socialist Germany,' in Mommsen and Kettenacker (eds), *Fascist Challenge*, p. 416.

121 ibid., p. 424. See also Arnold A. Offner, *American Appeasement: United States Foreign Policy and Germany 1933–1938*, (Harvard University Press: Cambridge, Mass., 1969) and 'Appeasement Revisited: The United States, Great Britain and Germany 1933–1940.' in *Journal of American History* 64, 1977, pp. 373–93.

122 R. Divine, *The Illusion of Neutrality*, (University of Chicago Press: Chicago, 1962).

123 Robert Dallek, *Franklin D. Roosevelt and American Foreign Policy, 1932–1945*, (Oxford University Press: New York, 1979). On the constraints on Roosevelt see James C. Schneider, *Should America go to War? The Debate over Foreign Policy in Chicago, 1939–1941*, (University of North Carolina Press: Chapel Hill, 1989). On Anglo-American relations see W. R. Rock, *Chamberlain & Roosevelt: British Foreign Policy and the United States, 1937–1940*, (Ohio State University Press: Ohio, 1988).

124 Reynolds, *Creation*, p. 288. Roosevelt's desire 'was that America's contribution to the war should be arms not armies – acting as the arsenal of democracy and the guardian of the oceans but not involved in another major land war in Europe.'

125 Charles A. Beard, *American Foreign Policy in the Making, 1932–1940*, (Yale University Press: New Haven, 1946 and *President Roosevelt and the Coming of War, 1941*, (Yale University Press: New Haven, 1948). See also Charles Tansill, *Back Door to War: the Roosevelt Foreign Policy, 1933–1941*, (Henry Regnery: Chicago, 1952) and W. H. Chamberlain, *America's Second Crusade*, (Henry Regnery: Chicago, 1950). For the response, Basil Rauch, *Roosevelt: From Munich to Pearl Harbor*, (Creative Age Press: New York, 1950).

126 Gordon W. Prange with Donald M. Goldstein and Katherine V. Dillon, *Pearl Harbor: the Verdict of History*, (Penguin: London, 1991), p. 35. This work was originally published by McGraw-Hill in 1986, six years after Prange's death. It was completed and prepared for publication by Goldstein and Dillon.

127 George Morgenstern, *Pearl Harbor: The Story of the Secret War*, (Devin Adair: New York, 1947) and Robert A. Theobald, *The Final Secret of Pearl Harbor*, (Devin Adair: New York, 1954).

128 Roberta Wohlstetter, *Pearl Harbor: Warning and Decision*, (Stanford University Press: Stanford, 1962).

129 Prange, *Pearl Harbor*, p. 42.

130 Rusbridger and Nave, *Betrayal*, pp. 151–4.

131 *Public Record Office*, HW 1/25, SIS to Winston Churchill, 15.8.1941.
132 Richard Overy with Andrew Wheatcroft, *The Road to War*, (Macmillan: London, 1989), p. 294.
133 *The Times*, 12.7.1993.
134 Prange, *Pearl Harbor*, p. 565. See also Stephen E. Ambrose, '"Just Dumb Luck": American Entry into World War II,' in Robert W. Love Jnr., *Pearl Harbor Revisited*, (St. Martin's Press: New York, 1995), pp. 93–103.
135 Akira Iriye, *The Origins of the Second World War in Asia and the Pacific*, (Longman: London, 1987), p. 1.
136 Herbert Feis, *The Road to Pearl Harbor: The Coming of the War between the United States and Japan*, (Princeton University Press: Princeton, 1950); W. L. Langer and S. E. Gleason, *The Challenge to Isolation*, (Harper: New York, 1952) and *The Undeclared War, 1940–1941*, (Harper: New York, 1953); F. C. Jones, *Japan's New Order in the Far East: Its Rise and Fall, 1937–1945*, (Oxford University Press: Oxford, 1954); J. B. Crowley, *Japan's Quest for Autonomy: National Security and Foreign Policy, 1930–1938*, (Princeton University Press: Princeton, 1966); and R. C. Butow, *Tojo and the Coming of the War*, (Princeton University Press: Princeton, 1961).
137 D. Bergamini, *Japan's Imperial Conspiracy*, (Heinemann: London, 1971). The defence of Hirohito has been based on Charles D. Sheldon, 'Japanese Aggression and the Emperor, 1931–1941, from Contemporary Diaries,' in *Modern Asian Studies*, 10, 1976, pp. 1–39. For a discussion of the Japanese system of government and the privatization of social conflict, see D. A. Titas, *Palace and Politics in Pre-War Japan*, (Columbia University Press: New York, 1974).
138 See Stephen S. Large, 'Imperial Princes and Court Politics in Early *Showa* Japan,' *Japan Forum*, 1, 1989, pp. 257–64. See also his *Emperor Hirohito and Showa Japan*, (Routledge: London, 1992). For a further favourable treatment of Hirohito, see Leonard Oswald Mosley, *Hirohito, Emperor of Japan*, (Weidenfeld & Nicolson: London, 1966).
139 E. Behr, *Hirohito: Behind the Myth*, (Penguin: London, 1989), pp. 15–8, 203–9. On Japanese biological and chemical warfare experiments on human beings see Sheldon H. Harris, *Factories of Death: Japanese Biological Warfare 1932–45 and the American Cover-Up*, (Routledge: London, 1994). Harris is of the opinion that it is unlikely that Hirohito knew of these experiments.
140 Saki Dockrill, 'Hirohito, the Emperor's Army amd Pearl Harbor.' *Review of International Studies*, 18, 1992, pp. 319–34.

Conclusion

1. John Whittam, 'The Origins of the Second World War,' *Modern History Review*, 4, 1992–3, pp. 5–8.
2. Lord Lothian, 'Issues in British Foreign Policy,' *International Affairs*, 17, 1938, pp. 360–77.
3. *Public Record Office*, FO 371/21723/C5425/1941/18. Lord Lothian to Lord Halifax, 31.5.1938 and Lord Halifax to Lord Lothian, 2.6.1938.

Bibliography

This is a selective and basic bibliography only. For a guide to more detailed works see Chapter 10.

1 General Studies

A. Adamthwaite, *The Making of the Second World War*, (Allen & Unwin:London, 1979).

P. M. H. Bell, *The Origins of the Second World War in Europe*, (Longman: London, 1986).

P. Calvocoressi, G. Wint and John Pritchard. *The Causes and Courses of the Second World War*, Vol. II, *The Greater East Asia and Pacific Conflict*, (Penguin: London, 1989).

W. Carr, *Poland to Pearl Harbor: The Making of the Second World War*, (Arnold: London, 1985).

A. Iriye, *The Origins of the Second World War in Asia and the Pacific*, (Longman: London, 1987).

Sally Marks, *The Illusion of Peace: International Relations in Europe 1918–1933*, (Macmillan: London, 1976).

R. J. Overy and A. Wheatcroft, *The Road to War*, (Macmillan: London, 1989).

A. Sharp, *The Versailles Settlement: Peacemaking in Paris, 1919*, (Macmillan: London, 1991).

D. Cameron Watt, *How War Came: The Immediate Origins of the Second World War*, (Heinemann: London, 1989).

2 British Policy

J. D. Charmley, *Neville Chamberlain and the Lost Peace*, (Macmillan: London, 1989).

A. J. Crozier, *Appeasement and Germany's Last Bid for Colonies*, (Macmillan: London, 1988).

R. A. C. Parker,
Chamberlain and Appeasement: British Policy and the Coming of the Second World War, (Macmillan: London, 1993).

K. G. Robbins, *Munich 1938*, (Cassell: London, 1968).

R. P. Shay, *British Rearmament in the Thirties, Politics and Profits*, (Princeton University Press: Princeton, 1977).
W. K. Wark, *The Ultimate Enemy: British Intelligence and Nazi Germany*, (Tauris: London, 1985).

3 German Policy

K. Hildebrand, *The Foreign Policy of the Third Reich*, (Batsford: London, 1973).
I. Kershaw, *The Nazi Dictatorship*, (Arnold: London, 1989).
I. Kershaw, *Hitler*, (Longman: London, 1991).
E. Jäckel, *Hitler's World View: A Blueprint for Power*, (Harvard University Press: Cambridge, Mass., 1981).
G. Stoakes, *Hitler and the Quest for World Dominion: Nazi Ideology and Foreign Policy in the 1920s*, (Berg: Leamington Spa, 1986).

4 French Policy

A. Adamthwaite, *France and the Coming of the Second World War*, (Cass: London, 1977).
A. Adamthwaite, *Grandeur and Misery: France's Bid for Power in Europe 1914–1940*, (Arnold: London, 1995).
R. J. Young, *In Command of France: French Foreign Policy and Military Planning, 1933–40*, (Harvard University Press: Cambridge, Mass., 1978).

5 Italian Policy

M. Knox, *Mussolini Unleashed 1939–41*, (Cambridge University Press: Cambridge, 1982).
E. M. Robertson, *Mussolini as Empire-Builder: Europe and Africa 1932–1936*, (Macmillan: London, 1977).
D. Mack Smith, *Mussolini's Roman Empire*, (Longman: London, 1976).
D. Mack Smith, *Mussolini*, (Weidenfeld & Nicolson, London, 1982).

6 Soviet Policy

J. Haslam, *The Soviet Union and the Struggle for Collective Security in Europe 1933–1939*, (Macmillan: London, 1984).
G. Roberts, *The Unholy Alliance: Stalin's Pact with Hitler*, (Tauris: London, 1989).
G. Roberts, *The Soviet Union and the Origins of the Second World War: Russo-German Relations and the Road to War, 1933–1941*, (Macmillan: Basingstoke, 1995).

7 American Policy

R. Dallek, *Franklin D. Roosevelt and American Foreign Policy 1932–1945*, (Oxford University Press: New York, 1979).
W. Heinrichs, *Threshold of War: Franklin D. Roosevelt & American Entry into World War II*, (Oxford University Press: Oxford, 1988).
C. A. MacDonald, *The United States, Britain and Appeasement 1936–39*, (Macmillan: London, 1981).

A. A. Offner, *American Appeasement 1933–38*, (Harvard University Press: Cambridge, Mass., 1969).

D. Reynolds, *The Creation of the Anglo-American Alliance 1937–41*, (Europa: London, 1981).

8 Japanese Policy

M. A. Barnhart, *Japan and the World since 1868*, (Arnold: London, 1995).

M. A. Barnhart, *Japan Prepares for Total War: The Search for Economic Security, 1919–1941*, (Cornell University Press: Ithaca, 1987).

R. C. Butow, *Tojo and the Coming of War*, (Princeton University Press: Princeton, 1961).

B. Crowley, *Japan's Quest for Autonomy: National Security and Foreign Policy, 1930–1938*, (Princeton University Press: Princeton, 1966).

F. C. Jones, *Japan's New Order in the Far East 1919–1939*, (Oxford University Press: Oxford, 1971).

I. Nish, *Japanese Foreign Policy, 1869–1942*, (Routledge: London, 1977).

R. Storry, *The Double Patriots: A Study of Japanese Militarism*, (Greenwood Press: Westport, 1973).

Index